Microeconomic Modeling in Urban Science

Microeconomic Modeling in Urban Science

Francisco Javier Martínez Concha

ELSEVIER

ACADEMIC PRESS
An imprint of Elsevier

Academic Press is an imprint of Elsevier
125 London Wall, London EC2Y 5AS, United Kingdom
525 B Street, Suite 1650, San Diego, CA 92101, United States
50 Hampshire Street, 5th Floor, Cambridge, MA 02139, United States
The Boulevard, Langford Lane, Kidlington, Oxford OX5 1GB, United Kingdom

Library of Congress Cataloging-in-Publication Data
A catalog record for this book is available from the Library of Congress

British Library Cataloguing-in-Publication Data
A catalogue record for this book is available from the British Library

ISBN: 978-0-12-815296-6

For information on all Academic Press publications visit our website at
https://www.elsevier.com/books-and-journals

Publisher: Candice Janco
Acquisition Editor: Scott J. Bentley
Editorial Project Manager: Billie Jean Fernandez
Production Project Manager: Swapna Srinivasan
Cover Designer: Christian J. Bilbow

Typeset by TNQ Technologies

To Sofía (for ever),
Camila, Nicolás, and Irune,
and our parents.

"Eppur si muove"
(And yet it moves),

Attributed to Galileo Galilei (1564–1642),
confronting the truth of the church and science.

Today, we may paraphrase him regarding our society as:
Eppur si muove, e più velocemente
(And yet it moves, and faster)

Contents

Foreword

Understanding the city is a little like peeling an onion. The more layers you take off, the more the subject of your inquiry seems to remain the same. In fact, you appear to be getting nowhere as you continue your peeling, except that like an onion, the frustration of not being able to make substantial advances on understanding its complexity brings tears (of frustration) to your eyes. The onion continues to look the same, almost impenetrable.

Cities are like this. Almost since the beginning of the industrial revolution in the West, more than 200 years ago, scholars have sought to understand how complex systems such as cities resolve the problem of remaining highly ordered in their form and function but without any top-down mechanisms that hold their structure together. This was Adam Smith's essential point in his ***Wealth of Nations*** published in 1776 where he posed the conundrum that there seemed to be an "invisible hand" guiding individual actions based on self-interest to generate structures such as markets that enabled society to get richer and trade to take place. In fact, economics has been spectacularly unsuccessful in deriving high theory to make sense of modern societies, particularly cities, although it is now widely recognized that the two different perspectives that evolved through the 19th and 20th centuries based on micro- and macroeconomics are different enough in kind not to be reconcilable other than in the most crudely fashioned ways. What is slowly taking its place is a deeper, more cognitive style of economics that draws from both the micro and the macro.

Our knowledge of cities manifests all the same problems and dilemmas that dominate economics. Moreover, it is clear that technology change is driving cities and societies to ever greater complexity, thus rendering our theories about how cities form and function increasingly obsolete, especially as new modes of human behavior come to dominate the way our cities are structured. Over the last 50 years, building on ideas first formalized by von Thunen in the early 19th century, an explanation for cities and much that pertains to their spatial organization across many scales has been forged from the perspective of microeconomics. In fact, what came to be called the New Urban Economics in the 1970s (Richardson, 1976) represented the most powerful approach there had ever been to explaining the way the city came to be spatially differentiated. This is built on the edifice of microeconomics and is constructed around the key idea that a typical "consumer" of the city optimizes the land and transportation they require to function at different housing and workplace locations. In essence, this theory of urban economics is based on the classical assumptions that an individual acts rationally in choosing their location by optimizing—maximizing—their utility. This is always subject to various constraints on their budget, typically their income, and some measure of the benefits received and costs incurred, such as transport and housing costs in the form of rent.

This model of utility maximizing lies at the basis of contemporary urban economics and is fundamental to the theories that Francisco Martinez develops here. In essence, his approach not only builds on microeconomic theory but also extends such theory to embrace various theories of spatial interaction and movement formalized over the last 50 years using approaches from statistical physics, discrete choice, and random utility theory. The great feat that Francisco Martinez accomplishes here is to extend urban economic models to demonstrate how such ideas can relate to agglomeration economies, in particular to scaling, which occurs as cities grow in size, and in this context, to systems of cities. He does this at the same time as demonstrating that the models he develops can be solved as equilibrium structures, thus balancing demand and supply. These he extends to the wider economy, thus providing a set of tools which are partial models that can be assembled by the astute reader to produce many different general model types. In this way, his is a unique approach to resolving the age-old aggregation problem in economics.

What is fascinating about the general theory that he seeks to promote is that when he unpeels the onion, layer by layer, he finds new ways of linking what appear to be quite different approaches together in formal ways. To an extent, the way he organizes the development of microeconomic modeling is by peeling the onion chapter by chapter. He gradually adds these layers together, establishing partial solutions which, in economic terms, are essentially partial equilibria, gradually moving toward more general equilibrium and thence aggregating his models to suggest ways in which they inform quantitative and qualitative changes as cities grow in size and organize themselves into more extensive systems. An important feature of the city system which he is at pains to emphasize is the fact that he treats location as a differentiated good with its own unique properties which makes comparability between places in spatially extensive systems very different from other kinds of economic market. It is into this nexus that he begins the development of a coherent economic theory of the world of cities, arguing that accessibility is one of the key determinants of how locations are differentiated. His initial focus on location gives strong credibility to the notion of a "general concept" of accessibility which he defines in two ways: as *physical accessibility*, which is the trade-off between the benefits that a person moving from one location to another receives and the transport costs incurred. In fact, this is a rather specific definition, and more generally, this kind of accessibility is the comparison or difference between benefits and costs of engaging in such interaction. In contrast but in a complementary way, he defines *attraction* as the benefits of locating in a place where many others are located, a kind of economy of scale, that takes account of the advantages to that individual in question of having other individuals located in the same place. After setting the context to his theory in Chapter 1, these ideas about accessibility and attraction are given formal substance in Chapter 2 where he relates them to spatial interaction, agglomeration, and random utility theory, key model tools that enable these concepts to be given true economic substance. It is worth noting that throughout the book at the end of most chapters, there are technical notes that take the formal mathematics of the various models he introduces further, thus enabling readers to probe these ideas in greater technical depth.

The major outline of his microeconomic theory begins in earnest in Chapter 3. The theory of the land market that lies at the basis of models treats individuals as agents and the market they engage in as an auction. In fact, this is simply a way of generalizing many agents acting to maximize their utility subject to their usual budget and external physical constraints to a system where prices are established when the market clears. The model is equally applicable to agents as households and agents as firms with the focus being respectively on utility and profit. These models of demand are set against the supply of land (or real estate) which introduces land owners and developers, and by the end of the introduction to these models, market clearing is demonstrated with respect to how an equilibrium—in traditional economic parlance a Walrasian equilibrium—is established. These models are all deterministic, but it is well known that the uncertainties of modern economic life are such that all decision-making takes place under uncertainty, and Francisco Martinez then follows this up with a chapter on what he refers to as the stochastic bid-auction model. One might think that adding a random element to the standard bid-rent models just introduced would be a straightforward matter, but in the process of doing this, many linear relations are transformed to nonlinear, and thus the overall models take on an aura of somewhat greater complexity.

All of this machinery sets up a more general discrete urban model of land use and transportation that contains all the rudiments for application. Building on the various equilibria that have been established in earlier layers of the theory, short- and long-term equilibria are established by bringing together the stochastic household and firm models, figuring out locational effects through accessibilities interpreted as consumer surplus measures, and introducing a series of external constraints such as overall demand and supply. This then evolves into a land use transportation structure in which traffic equilibrium models are embedded and which are akin to land use transportation integrated models (so-called *LUTI* models) which get closer to those in practice such as the *TRANUS* and *MEPLAN* models. So far, although firms have been modeled in the wider framework, the employment or economic sector has been avoided. But at this point, all the elements for modeling the firm, similar to input−output modeling but within the conditions of linearity and without their aggregate structure, have been assembled. Francisco Martinez then shows how this can be done. What is fascinating is that he is able to show that the model structure, which he calls *LUTE* (Land-Use-Transportation-Economy) that he evolves, is one with a unique, fixed-point solution. This is quite an achievement for in many instances such equilibria are neither established or if they are, it is never clear that such equilibrium points are unique. To my knowledge, this is the first time this has been done.

In the last elaboration of the *LUTE* model structure, the framework is extended to a system of cities, to *CLUTE* (Cities-Land-Use-Transportation-Economy). Migration is the force that binds cities in *LUTE* together, and the extended model *CLUTE* is able to show that economies of scale—agglomeration effects—are associated with even bigger cities in this framework. This is a nice tie-in to questions of scale and aggregation which have become popular, indeed iconic, in terms of our current interest in cities

(West, 2017). One of the features of economic theory with respect to cities is that much of it does not connect to either operational land use transport modeling or to the development of a science of cities that is based on social physics. This treatment and the models that are evolved is an exception, and although the formality and rigor of the presentation is not for the faint-hearted, what follows is a magnificent attempt at generalizing some very basic ideas that were developed many years ago and which continue to act as the only high theory we have when it comes to cities.

By the time these models are complete within the book, they can be used to consider much more empirical matters. Their applicability to testing scenarios, handling urban sprawl, addressing social exclusion, incorporating subsidies, and examining the impacts of regulations relating to the many elements that feature in the model both as inputs and outputs are all noted. The book is of course a theoretical treatment for the most part, but like all good theory, Francisco Martinez believes that this is good practice. By the end of the book, the reader is in a strong position to reflect and take forward these ideas to the many empirical questions and problems that must be urgently addressed in our contemporary cities.

Michael Batty
CASA, University College London

References

Richardson, H.W., 1976. The new urban economics: an evaluation. Socio-economic Planning Sciences 10 (4), 137–147.

Smith, A., 1776. An Inquiry into the Nature and Causes of the Wealth of Nations. W. Strahan and T. Cadell, The Strand, London.

West, G., 2017. Scale: The Universal Laws of Growth, Innovation, Sustainability, and the Pace of Life in Organisms, Cities, Economies, and Companies. Penguin Random House, New York.

Acknowledgments

My interest in cities started as a civil engineering student in transportation with Sergio Jara-Díaz's talks on how human behavior can be modeled in the space-time context, whom I thank for this first turn of my interest into the transportation economic field and for what I learned from him about research. The transportation field naturally expanded to urban problems in my PhD thesis, propelled by the question: why the first metro line in Santiago, Chile, brought significant development toward the west of the city center and none to the east, motivated by talks with Chris Nash and Peter Mackie at Leeds University, United Kingdom, in 1988, which opened a new area for me, rich of research questions and linking economics with sociospatial topics; thanks to them for this second turn into urban economics. This book contains most of my research, since then focused on urban systems.

The University of Chile, Faculty of Physical and Mathematical Sciences and its Civil Engineering department, is the home address of my research, where I found a motivating and intellectually rigorous environment of scientists and students, which pushed me hard to beat myself, reminding me that researchers in less developed countries have an unavoidable duty: pursue our dreams but also the dreams of our people, and do it with the highest excellence. In this environment, I particularly thank my transportation group for the collaborative spirit, kind atmosphere, and valuable friendship, which gave me the daily little push we all need to continue. In the last years, I also had the privilege of belonging to the Institute of Complex Engineering Systems, which provided a great support for my work and an exciting environment for transdisciplinary research. I have also been privileged by the research assistance of several enthusiastic, highly qualified, and hardworking students.

Over these decades of research, I benefit from the deep thinking of many colleagues, whom I am grateful for. I acknowledge the fruitful collaboration and discussions with: Sergio Jara-Díaz, Chris Nash, and Peter Mackie on transportation economics; Alex Anas on land-use equilibrium; John Roy on entropy modeling; Lars-Göran Mattsson on extreme value distributions; Roberto Cominetti, Cristián Cortés, and Alejandro Jofré on land-use and transportation equilibrium; Geoffrey West and Luis Bettencourt on scaling laws; and many others. My research stands on their shoulders.

I am especially grateful to my friend and partner Pedro Donoso for our join adventure of nearly 30 years building the land-use model and software MUSSA, now called CUBE-LAND, and other models. Our lively discussions were always beneficial to understand better our modeling approach and its implementation as an operational model.

His experience in real applications illuminated my persistent attempt to build a more consistent theory.

The preparation of the book manuscript was greatly benefitted from the valuable collaboration of my good friends and colleagues: Pedro Donoso on Chapters 2 and 9; Ricardo Hurtubia and Leonardo Basso on Chapter 3; Angelo Guevara on Chapter 4; Roberto Cominetti, Luis Briceño, and Mario Bravo on Chapters 5 and 6; Jorge Rivera on Chapter 7; Horacio Samaniego and Victor Rocco on Chapter 8; and Luis Briceño on Chapter 9. The book was significantly improved by their comments to the first draft. The book was also possible thanks to the collaboration of two dedicated research assistants, Marcelo León and Ariel Castillo, who did the hard work of revising the manuscript, and to other collaborators that improved the English language. Of course, all remaining mistakes are my responsibility alone.

I specifically thank the financial support to prepare the manuscript of this book provided by ISCI: CONICYT PIA FB0816.

Finally, I thank my great family for their unconditional love and support in this and other demanding adventures.

Francisco J. Martínez C.

Notation

The following notation is commonly used throughout the book; however, it is specifically defined when it is used in the text.

Indices

$n \in C$ Index for agent—households and firms—in the population set C.

$h \in H$ Index for household h in the households' set H; it may refer to an individual household or a socioeconomic cluster. This index also refers to a generic agent, i.e., a household or a firm, when it is indicated.

$f \in F$ Index for firm f in the firms' set F; it may refer to an individual firm or the firms in an industry. Note that $H \cup F = C$.

$r \in K$ Index for an industry in the set K.

$i, j, m \in I$ Index for locations in the set of discrete locations in set I. Locations are single properties in a disaggregated model or a zone in an aggregated one. In system of cities, the location set of a city indexed by c is denoted by I^c.

$v \in V$ Index for real estate type in the set V.

$vi \subset V \times I$ Index for real estate location $vi \in V \times I$; when it is convenient, this index is simplified, denoting $i \in VI$ with $VI = V \times I$.

$k \in K$ Index for goods and services industries in set K.

$i \in N$ Index for nodes in a network with a set of nodes N.

$d \in D$ Index for destinations nodes in the set D, with $D \subseteq N$.

$a \in A$ Index for arcs in the set of network arcs A.

$a \in A_i^+$ Index for arcs in the set of arcs whose tail (entry) is the *ith* node.

$i \in i^v$ Index for locations in the set of locations or zones defining the neighborhood of the *ith* location.

Variables

H_i Total number of members' agents in the city. In the context of a system of cities, H_i is the population of agents in the *ith* city.

H_h Number of members in cluster h.

$H_{hvi} \in M$ Number of members in cluster/agent h allocated in real estate vi; with M the allocation matrix.

S_{vi}, S_i Number of real estate units type v supplied at zone i, and the total at zone i, respectively.

$X_{r/vj}$ Production of industry r (measured in physical units per unit of time) conditional on the firm's location at vj.

$z_{vi} \in Z$ Vector of attributes of real estate type v in location i; it belongs to set Z.
c_{nij} Travel cost of individual n in a trip from origin i to destination j.
b_{nij} Net trip benefit of individual n in a trip between zones i to j.
q_{vj} Set of quality attributes at location vj.
p_{vi} Land price at location i.
c_{vi} Cost of building real state v at location i.
w_{hvi} Willingness to pay of agent h for real state v at location i.
x_k Amount of consumption of goods or services from industry k.
y_h Income of household h.
u_h Utility of household h.
λ_h Marginal utility of income of household h.
B_i Set of bidders at location i; note that $B_i \subseteq C$.
S_{vi} Number of real estate units type v supplied at zone i.
$P_{vi/h}$ Choice probability of agent h for location vi.
$Q_{h/vi}$ Bid-auction probability of agent h at location vi.
D_i Demand for locations at zone i.
x_a Total flow on arc a.
v_a^{dh} Flow of trips by agents of socioeconomic cluster h with destination node d traversing arc a.
t_a Travel time in arc a.
ω_{hij} Salary for household h with residence location i and job at location j.
ω_{fi} Salary at jobs type f located at location i.
N Size of urban population.
L Land size.
R Set of zoning regulations.
κ Cost of capital.
S Building's structural density.
$\Xi(\cdot)$ Equilibrium set.
$\phi(x)$ Cutoff factor
R_A Agricultural land rent.
E Per capita investment for population growth.

Abbreviations

CBD Central business district.
CLUTE Country land-use, transportation, and economic equilibrium.
LU Land-use system.
LUT Land-use and transportation subsystems.
LUTE Land-use, transportation, and the production economy or the general urban system.
T Transportation infrastructure or system.

Introduction

1

1.1 Initial Motivation

We now live in the urban era because more than 50% of the world's population lives in cities, and this number is expected to increase from 54.5% in 2016 to 60.0% in 2030 according to UN reports.[1] This fact has deep effects on human civilization, attracting global attention to understanding the city, its merits and difficulties, and its basic structures and their dynamics, which has been a difficult task to address in different disciplines.

The difficulties start with the definition of what we call a *city*, on which there is no consensus. For example, when defined via minimum population, we find the following levels: 100 inhabitants in Peru, 200 in Norway, 1000 in Canada and New Zealand, 2000 in Argentina, 2500 in Mexico and the United States, 5000 in Chile and India, and 10,000 in Senegal. However, we also find cities defined by density, as in China, with 1500 or more per square kilometer.[2] This variation shows that cities are human institutions, difficult to define and complex to describe.

Current cities have a large range of populations, as reported by the United Nations.[1] For the year 2016, the United Nations reports 551 cities in the range of 0.5−1 million population, 436 from 1 to 5 million, 45 from 5 to 10 million, and 34 cities over 10 million called *megacities*.

These statistics show the variety of city definitions and sizes, and announces the richness of their diversity, the comparability of their quality and functioning, and, perhaps more intriguing, what is common in their structures and dynamics. Moreover, they draw our attention because cities represent humanity's most complex social and economic organizations, perhaps the most complex constructs of our civilization and the results of the past few hundred thousands of years.

1.2 Toward an Urban Science

To think about the origin of cities and why they exist, we can look to what the anthropologist's story tells us (see for example, Diamond, 1999; Harari, 2013). The apparently more accepted theory is that *homo sapiens*, differentiated from other primates in prehistory, developed in Africa and emigrated to dominate the world. They substituted (and perhaps also mixed with) other archaic human species that

[1] See the World's Cities in 2016. http://www.un.org/en/development/desa/population/publications/pdf/urbanization/the_worlds_cities_in_2016_data_booklet.pdf.

[2] http://www.prb.org/Publications/Articles/2009/urbanization.aspx.

Microeconomic Modeling in Urban Science. https://doi.org/10.1016/B978-0-12-815296-6.00001-9

had previously dominated Europe, the Middle East, and Asia, which would have also emigrated from Africa some hundred thousand years earlier, although these original inhabitants had an even larger brain and a stronger body than the new wave of African primates.

What appears to have differentiated the sapiens was a cognition revolution; their organization capacity scaled from small groups or herds up to 150 members to a larger number of thousands of organized members. This singularity in human evolution was possible when sapiens imagined unreal situations and created myths, i.e., ideas of the unknown or unobservable, that large numbers of humans can believe in and obey, allowing them to set common organizing rules (Harari, 2013). To understand the power of this evolution, consider that today we cannot imagine life without myths, for example, without money, laws, companies, countries, or religions, that organize our complex society with rules that we all follow without thinking much about them until they require reform, a never-ending (re)evolution, which pushes us, the humans, to be in permanent alignment with evolving conditions, i.e., permanently increasing complexity.

This archeologist story is followed by the development of the more complex societies of prehistory, describing what appears to be a common process over thousands of years across very different, unconnected regions. A common thread appears to be that as the agricultural revolution developed, these societies became larger in number of members, the inhabited area was more densely populated by humans who developed tools and eventually guns, and the society became hierarchical, identifying not only the alpha person but also differentiating social levels of the population. This process not only allowed humans to develop more sophisticated tools (technology) and organizations (the archaic bureaucracy) but they also gathered in towns and primitive cities.

Jump some thousand years over the hunter–gatherer society and the agricultural society to find *homo economicus*, a term coined in the 19th century by the neoclassic school of economics to describe—or model—the individual behavior of modern sapiens living in complex societies, conceived to understand how they seek the production and consumption of goods and the generation of wealth. There is a corpus of rules that define the *homo economicus* system in the modern society, describing the vast network of economic interactions that spans the world.

Modern economics attempts to understand the already complex civilization or human organizations with its usual strategy—start from a simplified version. Its view considers egocentric individuals who maximize their own utility rather than addressing social ties or social well-being. The social institutions and common problems (e.g., security, environment, education, and health) are matters left to an upper-level institution, called The State. This simplistic view of *homo economicus* has been carefully extended to a more complex analysis of the social behavior of humans. In this process, the underlying idea is that a group of individuals might be represented by fictitious agents whose *utility* is affected not only by their consumption of goods and services but also by others or/and by the goals of the group. However, this framework remains too simplistic to understand cities.

The city is an organization that must be understood as an agglomeration of individuals who behave as *homo urbanus*, or the citizen. They are differentiated from their predecessors, *homo sapiens* and *homo economicus*, because they are predominantly a social species who, in addition to having survival rules to produce and consume efficiently, are conscious of the spatial context in which they apply these rules; i.e., the social context matters. The initial attempt to understand the city emphasized the role of the space in which interactions occur. The urban economic theory (Alonso, 1964) and the spatial interaction theory (Wilson, 1971) emphasized the role of the space in human interaction, highlighting the friction that distance imposes on these interactions, although these authors remain faithful to the *homo economicus* view of humans as workers. *Homo urbanus* is more complex; they regularly perform socioeconomic activities in a space that can be explored in the limited time of a day or a week, which is better described by the *activity-based* approach in transportation studies (Axhausen and Gärling, 1992). In this approach, the higher emphasis on integrating economic and social interactions is on the timescale, thus moving one step further from a static to a dynamic representation of individuals' behavior.

In addition to direct interactions involving traveling or communications, citizens are conscious of the physical and social environment in which they spend their life; they value and choose among optional locations to obtain the maximum benefit of belonging to a city. In other words, even when the individual is not explicitly interacting with their neighbor at the restaurant, in the bus, or at their residence, they perceive (dis)benefits from their neighbors only because they are inhabitants of a common space; some might consider that this benefit is associated with potential interactions, but this assumption limits the scope of the perceived environment to feasible interactions. This phenomenon has been identified as location externalities when it refers to the one-to-one effect on social and economic interactions or as agglomeration economies when it refers to a system effect such as the effect of densities in the location choice, although this concept is usually used only for economic interactions. This phenomenon is considered in the *new economic geography* (Fujita et al., 1999).

Therefore, *homo urbanus* pursues different types of interactions (explicit or implicit, social or economic) with other individuals and organizations, which contribute to their utility as a social being. This species inherits the rational behavior of its parents, that is, it is an efficient interaction maximizer; it must reduce its costs because time and wealth resources are limited. If many individuals seek this common objective, they will find it more efficient to gather together in towns and cities. If this behavior is universal among modern humans, then we can understand why the number of them who live in rural areas (with low interaction) has been recently overcome by citizens (with high interaction) and why in more developed societies, usually more than 80% live in cities. We can also understand the causality of the recently observed and apparently universal *scale law* of the relationship between cities' outputs (e.g., production, wealth, research, and crime) and the population (Bettencourt et al., 2007).

A realistic model that incorporates all of these factors describing the citizen's behavior requires sophisticated mathematical tools and rich data because it attempts to represent a *complex system*; both of these elements are becoming more available, particularly via access to telecommunication's big data. The contribution of urban economists, geographers, and transportation engineers from their different perspectives, coupled with advanced mathematical tools and massive data to analyze complex systems, has been proved difficult to merge into a unified framework, but the field appears now sufficiently mature to conceive a new *urban science* (Batty, 2013) by developing a theory of *homo urbanus*.

This book seeks to contribute to this emerging science by describing—and modeling with—a unified framework of the interaction-maximizer *homo urbanus*, who lives in a complex system of rules called the city. This model covers the microscopic decisions of each individual, passing by intermediate institutions, to a macroscopic universal rule of the cities' dynamics. It incorporates the abovementioned contributions in a coherent model of the urban system, built upon applying McFadden's *discrete choice–random utility* approach to describe all agents' behavior (Ben-Akiva and Lerman, 1985) integrated in the urban economic theory and fed by the experience of developing and applying predictive microeconomic models of cities in several metropolises.

1.3 About the Book

Book Content

This book is about cities—how to understand and model their complexity without becoming lost. It explains the mechanism of the intense interaction among citizens that makes cities efficient factories of social and economic outputs.

It is specifically designed for those who seek to understand and build predictive models of complex cities and systems of cities. They include students, teachers, and researchers from different disciplines such as geography, economics, engineering, computing, and urban planning, among others. Such diversity contributes with different perspectives to the same object, the city. These perspectives include, for example, the normative view, or how cities should be to fulfill a set of social goals usually defined after theoretical arguments, or the positive perspective of how the cities really perform, without any evaluation view. This book follows the positive perspective, seeking the ultimate goal of simulating the evolution of real cities; nevertheless, it also provides a normative modeling tool to plan cities and design policies that comply with a variety of social goals.

In this context, the book follows what economists call a microeconomic approach. In other words, we will imagine the city as an object that can be described by a set of agents interacting in the physical space; in the economic space, called the market; and in the social space, called the society. The agents include first, the social consumers, which are households and firms, that consume goods and services but also socialize; second, the producers of goods and services; and third, the suppliers of land and real estate units. The microeconomic approach describes their individual and differentiated behavior, assumed always rational, and their social and economic interactions that define the urban system.

This microeconomic perspective provides a simple process to model a city: define a model of the individual behavior of each agent and make them interact in the market to observe the resulting city. However, it is in the market that the model achieves its complexity. The model is specified with the market rules set by policymakers—or *regulations*—seeking societal goals by restricting agents' behavior. The model also represent the effects of distance, or transportation costs, and various forms of interaction between agents, e.g., social ties between residents, and economies of scale and agglomeration economies in the production of firms. Additionally, cities are open markets, with births and deaths and immigrant and emigrant flows. These factors make each city a member of a larger system of cities. Thus, complexity builds from both the agents' interactions occurring in different locations within the city and the interactions between cities. The model also comply with another requisite: cities are not built from scratch; they evolve as a long succession of infrastructure and planning decisions.

The microeconomic model is then analyzed at the aggregate level of the city to show how from the large number of microeconomic interactions a structural law emerges naturally, thus explaining the existence of scaling in cities based on economic principles and offering a deep understanding of the urban system and its mechanisms.

In simple words, this microeconomic and complex process is what is described in this book, with the aim of formulating a socioeconomic model of urban systems, i.e., the *urban socioeconomics*. The goal is a model of cities that extends urban economics to recognize the social–spatial–temporal dimensions of interactions, the diversity of agents, their complex behavior in the urban market, and the evolution of the city.

Book Structure

Two models will help to analyze each topic: the theoretical economic model, used here to explain general economic properties, and its stochastic version that allows the model to be based on more flexible assumptions but that also makes it possible to compute the system equilibrium and to develop operational models.

In its first seven chapters, the book is written following the idea that a system of cities can be described as an integration of subsystems: land use (LU), transportation (T), and the economy (E), i.e., the economic market for goods and services. These subsystems are consistently modeled with the same techniques that are usual in microeconomics; consumers and supplier agents follow behavioral rules: utility maximization and profit maximization, respectively. These techniques are applied to represent agent interactions in the geographical and time spaces subject to resource constraints. A special feature of this urban model is that space causes the economy to explode into many markets, one for each location, because goods, services, and dwellings become differentiated by their location, although they remain interconnected by transportation technology.

In this chapter, the book and the general context of the approach followed to model cities is introduced. In Chapter 2, the book describes the notion of accessibility, which is a synthetic index of the interaction between agents and is extensively used in transportation and geography. However, it is loosely related to consumer behavior; accessibility is dominated by the friction introduced by distance in potential interactions. Here, the attempt to link the classic approach with economic principles is pursued.

The following four chapters describe the microeconomic model of the urban system. We start with the LU model in Chapter 4, extending the urban economic theory, which is conceived for a continuous space in which real estate locations are differentiated only by distance. The model describes the equivalent theory in a discrete space, which allows modeling further differentiation between location options according their multiple attributes or dimensions and considers heterogeneous agents, incorporating the rich diversity of human systems. This theory is applied in Chapter 5 using the random utility framework, which is not only more realistic to represent agent behavior but also useful because it offers significant advantages in its mathematical properties to compute equilibrium in the urban complex system. In Chapter 6 we integrate LU and transportation systems in a model consistent with respect to economic assumptions and with a coherent modeling structure, which yields a land use and transportation (LUT) model. In Chapter 7 the model is completed with economy of the urban system, extending the LUT model to all economic interactions between consumers and producers agents, including the labor market, which link consumers and suppliers. This model yields the land use, transportation, and economic (LUTE) model, a microeconomic representation of all interactions in the urban system that explains and describes in rigorous economic terms the classic simplified notion of accessibility.

The urban microeconomic model is analyzed at an aggregate level in Chapter 8, which discusses two main topics. First, it extends the individual city model LUTE to a model of a system of cities (CLUTE), describing the population migration between cities and the mobility of households between socioeconomic groups. The second topic demonstrates that aggregating the socioeconomic indices of the LUTE model in the city totals generates scaling laws, i.e., superlinear production of wealth and goods, services, and labor. This result provides a microeconomic explanation of this surprising phenomenon, which has been empirically supported worldwide. Therefore, in this chapter, the essential characteristic of human beings, i.e., their rationality, is the plausible universally valid assumption in this model that explains the also universal empirical regularity of scaling in urban systems.

Urban planning for real cities, the classical topic in urbanism, is discussed later in the book in Chapter 9. The LU model is used as a tool to simulate different scenarios, describing urban policies and using two policy instruments, subsidies and regulations. Optimal policies are modeled contingent on specific social goals defined by the policy-maker; i.e., no normative a priori view is imposed by the model, not even the utilitarian goal of standard economics.

Finally, Chapter 10 uses frequently asked questions in urban planning and transportation concerning policies to explain how answers to difficult questions can be extracted from the model, i.e., what answers are supported by the theory. The chapter also examines how far we can go in modeling the complexity of urban systems and how close we are to merging several disciplines into a unified urban science.

This book does not attempt to offer a detailed review of previous contributions in the relevant fields of regional science, transportation or urban economics; interested readers are referred to previous studies for this purpose, e.g., Plane et al. (2007), Arnott and McMillen (2006), and Ortúzar and Willumsen (2002).

1.4 Issues in Urban Structures

The reader will find throughout this book several interesting and fundamental topics of theoretical and practical relevance concerning how urban centers emerge. These topics are summarized in this section as an introduction. The theoretical support for some comments and the explanation of how a model can be formulated are found in the pages of this book. Each of these topics is a difficult component contributing to define the complex system we want to understand.

Land Use Problem

All agents, households, and firms must reside somewhere in the city; otherwise, they are visitors. This rather obvious statement opens the discussion of several questions.

The city is a space in which people live and in which they perform social and economic activities. However, how can we define the limits of a city? Agreement is weaker on this matter. The simple answer is that they are defined by administrative decisions. Although this answer is normally useful, one can question whether it is an answer with scientific value, i.e., a generally useful definition for modeling, because someone must initially decide these administrative boundaries. A more general definition of city boundaries is that the city ends where the rural area begins, which can be identified by the imaginary line at which the building density decreases to a level common in rural areas. This definition, based on building densities, is consistent with the theory of urban economics and implies that the city border is not static but rather the endogenous outcome of the city's dynamic development.

The following questions are classical in LU studies: Why and how density is built up at each point in the city or how people and firms decide their preferred locations is called the *location problem*. The answer depends upon who is allocated at each location, called the *allocation problem*, which can be formulated as how the market sorts out the matching between the set of consumers and the set of locations at each point in time. A related question is how land values are determined and what is valued at each location. All of these questions are the matter of urban economics studies.

In general, we define the term location as points or sites in the space. In this book, however, the term represents an option to reside, described by multiple attributes, including its address, size of the land parcel, and dwelling characteristics, both for residents (houses and building apartments) and nonresidents (e.g., office space and industrial facilities). In fact, every spatial option to reside in the city or to establish a business is called a location.

The location and allocation problems are large in terms of modeling effort, because of the amount of information needed to describe the locations in which activities reside and in which the trades of land occur, but also due to the diversity of agents that reside in a city.

Land Auctions

An important feature of a city, worth mentioning from the beginning, is that the goods traded in this market are differentiated by their set of attributes, e.g., spatial location, land space, and dwelling characteristics. In other words, each location is different on some attributes from others in the same city. That is, it is theoretically defined as unique. Even in the extreme case of equal apartments on the same floor of a building, some characteristics such as orientation make them different.

This feature was recognized by Von Thünen in 1863 for rural areas and then by Alonso in 1964 for cities. Alonso identified transportation costs as a differentiating feature of each location that can explain in a simple model the emergence of different land values. Alonso also recognized that such differences naturally affect how that land is traded in auctions, i.e., is sold or rented to the highest bidder. Later, other differentiating features were analyzed, such as neighborhood quality and agglomeration economies, or natural amenities such as lakes, rivers, or mountains. All of these attributes make the city a collection of different locations rich in diversity.

Observe that modeling simultaneous auctions in space is a complex process because they occur by sharing information about agents' behavior and transactions in the market. Therefore, their outcomes influence each other.

Externalities

In the economic literature, externalities occur when a decision of one agent affects the decisions of other agents in the market, in way different than prices, called nonpecuniary effects. When a market is subject to externalities, some complex effects arise because they determine socioeconomic *pull* (centripetal) and *push* (centrifugal) forces between agents.

In the LU market, several forms of *location externalities* are usually present, produced by the fact that agents' valuation of a given location is determined by the built environment, i.e., human-made amenities, e.g., shopping and business. Such amenities include neighborhood attributes that define the quality of the area, i.e., who lives and what activities are performed in the neighborhood define some valuable attributes in every location.

Why do these attributes represent externalities? The decision of agents to locate themselves in a site inevitably contributes to define their neighbor's perception of the quality of the neighborhood. This contribution can be strong, such as a noisy family or a polluting industry, or marginal, and it can be negative or positive in eyes of the neighbors. However, it always defines what is perceived as the neighborhood quality. To reify this argument, the reader might consider what defines the quality of his or her neighborhood and what types of new residents and firms would improve or worsen its currently perceived quality.

Agglomeration economies refer to a special type of externality. It describes the *push* or *pull* power of the agglomeration of business activities in some areas, eventually causing the emergence of subcenters and transforming the initially monocentric city into a more complex polycentric urban system.

There are several attributes that induce externalities, some with physical effects (e.g., pollution) and others with socioeconomic effects (e.g., income or ethnic segregation), all simultaneously affecting agents' perceptions of the neighborhood quality and inducing the location patterns observed in cities. These diverse sets of externalities in the LU problem are the main cause of the complex processes that occur in urban systems because each agent's decision becomes dependent upon the location decision of all other agents, creating a circular interaction in the market.

Regulations

Despite the waves of deregulation in most economic markets worldwide in recent decades, the urban land market remains highly regulated. Why? A plausible answer is that because of the complexity of this market, policymakers prefer not to change the traditional plan-and-regulate scheme, which provides them a sense of predictability of the city. To some extent, this answer might be correct, at least initially, but predictability is usually much lower in complex systems in the medium- and long-term than is usually expected.

Regulations do not necessarily help to reduce the complexity of cities. The diversity of regulations and their projection over space makes each land point in the city subject to overlapping regulations, each of them restricting land parcel size, dwelling, and building type or LU. Moreover, a regulation in one zone has spillover effects that potentially affect all other zones of the city.

These regulations impose discontinuities in the city space that are difficult to handle with models and have a high effect on LU. The difficulties that their representation imposes on a complex process are not trivial.

Accessibility

Accessibility is a concept used generally by people; everyone understands it, and it is included in our common language. People refer to accessibility to identify the closeness of other people or activities to their own location. However, finding a theoretically sound and operational definition is not simple (e.g., see Koening, 1980; Geurs and Van Wee, 2004) because accessibility is a complex concept based on a rather intuitive notion.

In its simplest form, accessibility refers to a combination of two elements: the opportunities reached by a single trip and its cost (or effort), technically called *relative accessibility*. Researchers initially defined this accessibility as a physical entity, combining the travel distance of a trip from a given origin with some measure of the magnitude of the activity reached at the destination. Later, it was defined as an economic entity, using the individual's utility to combine the travel cost with the associated perceived benefit at the destination, i.e., following the individual traveler's value of money and opportunities. Although the physical measure is simple, it does not provide a theoretically sound means of combining travel cost with activity magnitude, which is given in the utility framework.

In LU studies, accessibility refers to the opportunities that a given location offers to the agent that has the right to locate there, i.e., instead of referring to a single trip, it is a permanent right to enjoy the benefits of the residence. It represents the aggregate of potential trips' relative accessibility across all of the activities the agent can perform, at any time, to every possible location in the city, at a transportation cost for each trip. This aggregation is called *integral accessibility* and is theoretically sound and operationally feasible to perform using the utility-based measure because the aggregation of benefits across potential trips is made by the same agent with common perceptions (Martínez, 1995).

Moreover, in LU, there is another form of accessibility associated with visits at a given location. This form represents the opportunities, usually for a business, that an agent might have at a given location because of all trips with a destination at that location. We will refer to this measure as integral *attractiveness*.

Thus, the location problem refers to how agents seek access. In particular, neighborhood quality is also a form of access to the nearest activities and is affected by transportation facilities such as walking paths. This definition reveals the complexity of the LU problem because one's perception of access at a location depends upon the location of all activities in the city and the perception of transportation costs; each person's perceptions are different. Hence, an agent valuing the accessibility of a given location implies that its preference depends upon others' preferences; thus, its own location affects the accessibility of all locations in the city. This arrangement describes a network of mutual influences among all agents in the city.

The Economy

Accessibility is a simplified concept that ignores the dynamics of the many goods and services markets and their effect on prices and quantities. Noting that these markets are spread out in a city, we first observe that the usual assumption in economics fails; i.e., the market cannot be represented as a spaceless entity. This observation has significant implications.

Because their access to goods and services depends upon the relative location between consumers and suppliers, the transportation cost differentiates the total price paid depending upon these locations. The theoretical consequence of this point is that goods and services are differentiated by location; thus, the number of markets in the model scales by the number of locations in the city. Additionally, the production of goods and services depends upon the technology and is simply differentiated by their economies of scale. Different technologies induce concentration of production in one or a few firms or its dispersion in many small firms that follow the location of consumers, which is another source of *pull* and *push* location forces. In this context, the simulation of prices, production, and delivery equilibrium of supply and demand is a challenging problem.

Urban System: Land Use and Transportation Interaction

There has been a long discussion about what are the main drivers of cities' development—investment in real estate or the development of the transportation system. Both actions directly affect the map of what we call accessibility because this geographically based concept depends upon the combination of transportation and the location of activities; hence, they have the potential to induce further opportunities and development. However, experience shows that none of them on their own are sufficient to ensure development of economic activity, nor are the two together sufficient for urban development; e.g., an economically declining city is unlikely to sustain development despite the impulse to invest in real estate and transportation.

If the city's economy is healthy, then better transportation is expected to make rural land more accessible to opportunities in the city. This accessibility potentially induces developers to invest beyond the city borders, i.e., ceteris paribus, the lower the transportation cost (including price and time), the larger we expect the city size to be. However, it is not necessarily true that an improvement of the transportation system in one direction of the city implies that the city development will concentrate toward that direction, simply because even when other directions might not have as good transportation facilities, they might, however, compete for development with better access to economic and social opportunities. For example, the first subway line in Santiago city, capital of Chile, crosses the city east-west through the city center. Although in the east section, where the wealthy population concentrates, development was quickly evident along the line, the west section showed almost no development over 30 years.

Thus, to predict whether a public investment in real estate or transportation is likely to produce development, a model is needed to simulate agents' preferences, real estate suppliers' behavior, and transportation performance, allowing the assessment of effects on the LU and transportation markets under changing conditions in the urban system. In other words, transportation and LU systems are mutually dependent; they have a circular cause—effect mechanism, very much like the chicken-and-egg dilemma in other complex systems.

1.5 Issues in Urban Modeling

The complexity of urban systems poses interesting and advanced challenges to modelers. These challenges range from the phycology problem of how to represent agent behavior in a large space of choices, to mathematical difficulties with estimating the emerging output of multiple, spatially disperse but mutually dependent markets.

Why Modeling?

There are theoretical and practical answers. Building a model is a methodology to test a theoretical hypothesis about cities' performance and dynamics. However, the limitations of available models also limit their use for this purpose. Conversely, model designers benefit from these tests and from the implementation of theoretical constructs. The use of models for practical purposes has increased in the last 50 years, despite initial skepticism. Policymakers find useful answers concerning the diversity of effects caused by different policy scenarios for a city's development, including LU regulations and developments, transportation investment, and pricing systems.

Nevertheless, modeling cities is also beneficial for pure science because doing so requires understanding the most complex social organization, a task that raises basic questions about human beings and challenges one's understanding of the fundamentals of a society.

Diversity of Choices and Their Perceptions

Individuals face the difficult task of making their location choice in a very large space of different options. Consider the number of optional locations, the attributes that describe each of them, plus the information required to assess accessibility at each location to understand that agents face a complex information problem: recollection, analysis, storing, and comparing in a large set.

Computers can perform this task better than individuals can, but models must reproduce human behavior, not their own calculation capacity. This requirement is an interesting challenge for LU models—how agents collect, synthesize, and compare information in big data problems. There is little scientific evidence to help modelers on this matter. The literature on consumer psychology shows evidence that the human capacity to process information in choice making is surprisingly small, falling in the range of 5−10 items of information, which motivated Miller's (1956) "magical number seven ± two." Beyond this threshold, consumers are overloaded, their analysis deteriorates and fail to choose the best options (see also Malhotra, 1982).

The city's population is also diverse in taste and objectives, which sets another challenge to modelers—how to model such a diverse space of agents' preferences. Choice models have improved in recent decades, introducing stochastic approaches in decision-making models, which consider this diversity and improve their capability to reproduce observed choices. However, the choice process in LU problems is far more complex than in most markets and so is the challenge of predicting human behavior. It is necessary to consider human limitations with respect to information and searching for best options, i.e., the intellectual and economic costs of such searches, which lead us to believe that we all search strategically to reduce our cognitive burden.

System Size

The dimensions of the LU problem are a source of computational complexity. The georeference of each microprocess increases the size of the problem with the city population. Moreover, the complex interaction between agents induced by externalities causes the computational burden of calculating the outcome of the LU problem to increase nonlinearly with the city size.

This matter is of technical concern in building operational models, which requires the use of best methodologies to minimize such computational cost and make the calculation feasible. Unless methods and model structures provide sufficient efficiency in calculations and provide guarantees that the computational processes converge, models will fail to be applicable or will be excessively simplified to obtain results. In the last decade, data collection became easier using advanced information technology, which made scientists more ambitious in building models of processes in greater detail, called microsimulation models, but these additional data increase the size and complexity of the LU problem. Therefore, having a tested theory of the urban system is fundamental to supporting the model.

Complex System

The topics listed above make the city a complex system, which is the natural outcome of the large diversity of interests of the population, all linked by their mutual interdependency and spatially and timely distributed. For the student and the researcher, it is a fascinating topic that remains open for research to be done.

Mathematically, complex systems can generate a given macroscale structure from different microscale processes, i.e., different microprocesses of agents' behavior can yield the same city, a many-to-one effect. Conversely, a given set of microscale processes does not ensure a unique outcome, a one-to-many effect. Hence, there is no unique path or cause—effect mapping between microscale processes and macrostructures in complex systems. However, a complex system might generate one or more expected macroscale outcomes, called attractors.

The good news in this book is that, with the help of modeling tools (e.g., the stochastic model), a relevant part of cities' complexity is treatable, allowing the calculation of expected outcomes addressing the many-to-one or one-to-many effects. The reader is invited to keep track of such tools because assumptions are necessary to make calculations feasible at some cost of losing generality, although not necessarily departing significantly from reality, as the experience in modeling shows. Theoretical support to consider the approximation of the model to reality good is given when observed macroscopic structures of the city emerge from microscopic simulations of individuals' interactions; the book proves this property for the modeling approach that it presents.

Bottom-Up Approach

The microscopic approach can also be called a bottom-up approach because the city macrostructure emerges from many microscale processes. The benefit of this approach is that it yields detailed explanations of each microscopic process, i.e., decisions of agents, which explains the emerging, observed structure of the city. This explanation allows researchers to test, for example, sociological changes such as the effect of future changes in social values at the city level or to assess economic effects such as the benefits of urban policies for each individual agent.

However, we recognize that the ambition embedded in the microscopic approach is currently distant from the modeling technology available. A testable model must have the capacity of testing each individual agent's behavior against a set of different contexts. This capability is, however, not available or is largely too costly in direct tests, but advances in information technology are generating new forms to "observe" individuals' behavior and thus build better models, which makes data science relevant for urban science.

The reader might foresee that the microeconomic perspective leads to an open space of diverse potential cities because all depends upon the individual's behavior. That expectation is partially true because although diversity does appear at a microscale, we will see in this book that such a space is closed or limited; that is, microeconomic forces do produce compact cities and, perhaps more surprising, follow similar evolutionary paths. Thus, the microscopic approach in a complex system is a feasible technique to represent the observed macroscopic features of cities.

A model is a representation of the complex reality of cities. The task of the modeler is to develop the best representation that is feasible with available resources and technology. Note that the best representation requires defining the purpose of the model. For example, the model might be used to analyze a theoretical hypothesis; then, many details can be simplified by specifying a stylized model able to represent rigorously and in detail only what matters to prove the hypothesis. Von Thünen's (1863) model is a good example, in which agricultural land was assumed flat and homogeneously productive to isolate other effects from what he wanted to understand—that is, why different crops are produced at different distances around the market, and why land values decay away from the central market place in which crops are sold by the peasants due to the transportation costs, up to a limit distance at which the peasant's profit vanishes due to transportation cost. More recently, Alonso (1964) analyzed the urban case, assuming a monocentric city in which all jobs are in the center, to propose that residents locate in rings around the center according to their willingness to pay, i.e., their preferences, and proved that land values decay outward from the center up to the city boundaries at which they match land values for agriculture.

These two models are considered the foundations of urban economics (see Arnott and McMillen, 2006), which have developed further from Alonso's model to consider complex issues in LU, for example, agents' interactions or agglomeration economies (Fujita and Thisse, 2002). The main task of urban economics is to understand, given the complexity of cities, how the different forces interplay in the market, what is called the *land-use market equilibrium*.

In simple terms, a model of the LU market comprises a demand submodel, i.e., of the behavior of land users for residential and nonresidential purposes; a supply submodel or land-dwelling options in which demand is satisfied; a submodel of the market that describes the protocols for buying–selling real estate properties and the renting protocol.

A simplified model will be used in this book to explain matters as simply as possible but not less than what is required to model the complexity of the LU model and to study the market equilibrium. References will help the reader to obtain further information on specific models.

Stochastic Approach

This book presents the basic models in two forms. The theoretical model is used to specify the theoretical relationships of the LU market, which is specified as a static and deterministic equilibrium. The stochastic model represents the LU market in which behavior of agents is assumed not deterministic but stochastic, which is then extended to model two complementary markets: the transportation and the economy. Because all of these subsystems are modeled using the same mathematical techniques and economic principles, the resulting integrated model is consistent.

The stochastic approach is more realistic because, first, agents make decisions using inaccurate information to assess the quality of each location option, which is described by a set of attributes also difficult to observe (e.g., accessibility), then evaluation of quality is made subject to the agents' information error. Second, the modeler has limited information about what values of the attributes the consumer observes, which induces the modeler's observation error. Nevertheless, once the stochastic model makes assumptions about the error distribution, it limits the model generality. Conversely, some error distributions help make the complexity of the equilibrium model more treatable for applied models; solutions exist and can be calculated.

Discrete Modeling

Discrete representation of space in the LU context is a necessary technique because, although space is continuous in nature, location quality is not; it is described as a vector of attributes discontinuous in space (e.g., buildings, land parcel size, natural amenities). Unless otherwise stated, this book considers the discrete representation of space to develop models applicable in real studies.

However, a discontinuous model of space has a very important effect in its mathematical construct, particularly concerning the complex market equilibrium problem, which becomes untreatable. To overcome this difficulty, one should realize that the discrete stochastic model can help to introduce convenient continuity in the model, which provides good properties in the mathematical problem of LU equilibrium.

Residential and Nonresidential Activities

The model of the demand side of the LU market must represent a set of different agents located or seeking location in the city. A taxonomy of these agents identifies households and firms (including different institutions), performing residential and nonresidential activities, respectively. The differences between these types of agents are studied in distinctive literature concerning their specific market conditions. For example, in the microeconomic literature, firms perform commercial or nonresidential activities modeled as profit maximizers, in which the issue is how their locations affect production costs and income. Conversely, households perform residential activities and are assumed to be utility maximizers, subject to their location being affected by their social ties and the location of service facilities.

From the modeler's point of view, however, all of them can be modeled as differentiated agents, each assumed to follow rational behavior described by a benefit maximization rule, be it a profit or a utility rule. In this book, the following approach is followed whenever possible: all agents are represented in the market by a *behavior rule* with an individual specification.

One technique to reduce the computation burden is to aggregate individual agents with similar behavior in the LU market into a *cluster* and define a representative agent of the cluster with a cluster behavioral rule. For example, households are normally clustered by income level and cultural background, and firms are clustered by industry (e.g., service, manufacturing, education, and health). Clustering reduces the calculation burden and the requirement of data at the cost of introducing an aggregation error in the model; the more similar the individuals' behavior rules are within a cluster of agents, the less is the approximation error of the cluster technique and vice versa.

Location Representation

Locations are real estate options in the city that represent the supply side of the LU market. They are diverse options based on the significant variety of attributes that suits the requirements and preferences of agents, which are different between household and firm clusters.

A property is described by a large vector of *location attributes*, including the location in the city and a description of the neighborhood quality and its accessibility; the land or the parcel size and other characteristics, such as street front, slope, and vegetation; and the building characteristics, such as number of rooms, build or floor space, and structure quality.

This variety of location options can be aggregated for computational purposes, again at the cost of introducing an aggregation error. The usual spatial aggregation for locations is to define *zones* with similar use and buildings. Building differences can also be clustered into similar real estate types, for example, detached, semidetached or back-to-back houses or apartments in high, medium, or low buildings. The term similar should reflect what agents perceive as similar when they seek locations in the city.

Location Prices

Does the model of the LU market represent the city's real estate trade market or the rental market?

This question arises because real estate consists of durable property bought as an investment—to generate profit from its rent or to be used as the residence of the owner. This dual use generates two interrelated markets: the property trade market and the real estate rental markets. The former yields *property prices* and the latter, *rent values*. These values are theoretically related because property prices represent the present value of expected land rents obtained over a long period. Additionally, the property price is the value of transferring the property rights for an unlimited period, whereas the rent is the value of transferring the right to use the real estate for a period defined in the contract.

An interesting question is how prices and rents are defined. Consider that a property consists of its land and its building. The cost of the building can be simply estimated by calculating the cost of inputs because the building construction market is competitive and input prices are known. Urban land, conversely, defines a very different market because there are no inputs; the value of a given location is precisely its location related to the location of all other activities, i.e., its accessibility to activities in the city. This feature makes each land parcel a differentiated good; i.e., it has different accessibility characteristics from other locations, and economic theory recognizes that this type of good is sold in *auctions*. Therefore, land prices and rents (not the building) reveal the value that the user—owner or renter—pays to enjoy its accessibility; conversely, it implies that accessibility renders benefits to the user equivalent to at least the rent value. Note that here and in this book, we use the concept of accessibility in the most general form; i.e., it refers to the benefit yielded by access—accessibility and attractiveness—to all activities available in the city, net of transportation costs.

In the land and real estate markets, one can observe what is called the asking price, which represents the owner's initial value to enter the auction. This price can change, occasionally significantly, during the auction bargain process to reach the selling price or rent value. Modeling this process has its own challenges because auctions are based on the strategic behavior of agents to address the ex ante limited information about the value of the property, which is only revealed ex post the auction.

The following question arises: why do prices and rents change? The rent or price of a location will change if some agents change their valuation of the location attributes, or they change their perception of the attributes, or if accessibility changes due to changes in transportation costs or due to changes in the location of residential and nonresidential activities. All of these changes in the city will affect land rents and prices; analogously to how our body's temperature reflects the status of our health, rents and prices reflect the economic energy of the city. One can think of this process as though cities provide opportunities to create economic activities and increase wealth. Because for a specific agent these opportunities and wealth depend upon its location, the landowner is able to capture a proportion of that wealth in the form of the rent or property price; i.e., wealth percolates into land values. This process encapsulates the capitalization of interaction opportunities of the city into its land values. Their differences reflect the differential opportunities within the city.

Static Versus Dynamic Approaches

The LU system, like any system, is composed of several interactions between its components presented above. Modelers use two ways to describe these interactions: the static and the dynamic approaches.

The static process describes a system subject to an external shock that changes the system from an initial state to the final one. The usual method considers that the original system state is in *equilibrium* and the model seeks the new equilibrium for the system after the shock. The equilibrium is attained when certain conditions hold, usually that demand and supply match at the equilibrium price. This state of the system is theoretical, useful to estimate the expected outcome of markets when the information about all agents in the market is shared and decisions are made in that context without interference from outside the system, i.e., under ceteris paribus conditions. The predictive power of static equilibrium models comes from the simulation of all market forces interacting in the LU system assuming only one rule for the market—the equilibrium condition.

Such an equilibrium state of the system might never actually occur in LU markets because too much time is required for all of the interaction to occur and the ceteris paribus condition does not hold for such a long period of time. Thus, the LU system is naturally dynamic, but we can add to it in slow motion. This slow motion of the city dynamic refers to the fact that real estate investment and relocation of households and firms take long periods of time, i.e., one or more years. Additionally, because the infrastructure is costly, only a very small fraction of the city buildings are renovated or developed in a period of few years. Thus, for an annual timescale, at any point in time, the system does not divert far from equilibrium conditions unless a large external shock occurs.

This book attempts to provide a coherent framework of how the equilibrium assumption can be reconciled with a dynamic view. The book posits the hypothesis that the dynamic system (closely) follows a sequence of short-term equilibrium states of the system, which means that the equilibrating forces are always active in the market and that the system is always moving toward equilibrium. Additionally, external conditions change over time, pushing the system from one state of equilibrium to another.

1.6 Remarks

The task of formulating a general theory of cities, developing applicable models, reproducing universal laws, and testing the validity of results against data is the attractive content of this book and the subject matter of the emerging *urban science*.

The task is challenging because it involves merging theoretical contributions from different disciplines, including economics, statistics, mathematics, sociology, geography, transportation, and urbanism. The new science needs a common language, a core of accepted principles, and sufficient testing to be convincing.

This book builds a model of cities that seeks to contribute to this task for the better understanding of our complex society.

References

Alonso, W., 1964. Location and Land-use, Towards a General Theory of Land Rent.

Arnott, R.J., McMillen, D.P., 2006. A Companion to Urban Economics. Blackwell Publishing, Malden, USA.

Axhausen, K.W., Gärling, T., 1992. Activity-based approaches to travel analysis: conceptual frameworks, models, and research problems. Transportation Reviews 12 (4), 323–341.

Batty, M., 2013. The New Science of Cities. MIT Press.

Ben-Akiva, M., Lerman, S.R., 1985. Discrete Choice Analysis: Theory and Application to Travel Demand. MIT Press.

Bettencourt, L.A., Lobo, J., Helbing, D., Kühnert, C., West, G.B., 2007. Growth, innovation, scaling and the pace of life in cities. Proceedings of the National Academy of Sciences of the United States of America 104 (17), 7301–7306.

Diamond, J., 1999. Guns, Germs and Steel: A Short History of Everybody for the Last 13,000 Years. WW Norton & Company.

Fujita, M., Krugman, P., Venables, A.J., 1999. The Spatial Economy. MIT Press.

Fujita, M., Thisse, J.F., 2002. Economics of Agglomeration: Cities, Industrial Location, and Regional Growth. Amsterdam, North-Holland.

Geurs, K.T., Van Wee, B., 2004. Accessibility evaluation of land-use and transportation strategies: review and research directions. Journal of Transport Geography 12, 127–140.

Harari, Y.H., 2013. From Animals to Gods: A Brief History of Human Kind. Random House Mondadori.

Koening, J.G., 1980. Indicators of urban accessibility: theory and application. Transportation 9, 145–172.

Malhotra, N.K., 1982. Information load and consumer decision making. Journal of Consumer Research 8 (4), 419–430.

Martínez, F.J., 1995. Access: the transport-land-use economic link. Transportation Research 29B (6), 457–470.

Miller, G.A., 1956. The magical number seven, plus or minus two: some limits on our capacity for processing information. Psychological Review 63, 81–97.

Ortúzar, J.D., Willumsen, L.G., 2002. Modelling Transport. Wiley & Sons, Chichester.

Plane, D.A., Mann, L.D., Button, K., Nijkamp, P., 2007. Regional Planning. Edward Edgar Publishing, Cheltenham, UK.

Von Thünen, J.H., 1863. In: Hall, P. (Ed.), See Von Thünen Isolated State. Pergamon Press, London (1966).

Wilson, A., 1971. A family of spatial interaction models, and associated developments. Environment and Planning 3, 1–32.

Accessibility*

2

2.1 The Concept

Interaction among humans has always been necessary to enable satisfying their needs in an efficient way. It can be said that *together, two people make more than just the sum of one plus one*. This applies to the vastly diverse variety of human activities, be they social, economic, or other. Being together in groups brings the extra benefits of a greater number of interaction opportunities that occur among those in the same area, or, conversely, we can say that spatial separation limits what a group of individuals can accomplish. Indeed, many social organizations have emerged from grouping people together to contribute to the following common goal: families to raise the new generations, firms to produce goods and services, and a variety of social groups for political, recreational, and other specific purposes. Here, we will call their functions generically *activities*, and we will focus on the interactions among the people in a city for productive and social purposes. Although communication technology—particularly mobile phones—provides efficient ways to interact without traveling, which has prompted ideas whereby travel demand may be reduced, the evidence shows that both travel and phone interactions have increased.

Accessibility is a term commonly used to measure the ease of individuals' interaction in a spatial context or, equivalently, the cost of covering the distance between the interaction activities. When this interaction is personal or face to face, it involves people's traveling costs, and when the interaction is a transaction of goods, it includes delivery costs. However, this view is clearly insufficient because the travel cost falls short of measuring the quality of the interaction, i.e., the perceived benefit that induces making the trips. Therefore, accessibility should always include this second factor that accounts for the effects—positive or negative—that the interaction induces to those participating in the activities. Thus, accessibility is a measure that should combine distance-related costs and the quality associated with the interactions.

An interesting characteristic of accessibility worth commenting on is that not only is it an intuitive concept, i.e., everyone seems to understand what it means, but it is also a polysemic and complex one, as we shall see in this chapter. We expect that the complexity lies in how to combine quality with costs in each interaction and how to combine or aggregate multiple and diverse activities in which individuals, households, and firms interact. Moreover, although accessibility is commonly associated with an interaction involving travel, the same trip involves another effect called attractiveness; these two concepts are linked in a way we shall clarify conceptually and regarding their measurement.

* This chapter is based on Martínez (1995) and Martínez and Araya (2000a, 2000b).

Microeconomic Modeling in Urban Science. https://doi.org/10.1016/B978-0-12-815296-6.00002-0

In this chapter, we analyze the concept of accessibility with special focus on its meaning from a microeconomic approach, i.e., what the rational reason for the interaction to occur is and how individuals choose among available feasible interactions. The rationality assumption implies that if an interaction occurs, a net positive benefit must be generated for the traveler or for the traveler's activity. Additionally, because interactions between individuals comprise the fundamental reason for building cities, we examine how microeconomically sound measures of accessibility identify the generation of agglomeration economies, which make cities, with their multiple interactions, the centers for development.

2.2 Alternative Measures

Intuition is naturally associated with which activities individuals perform and with whom and where they interact. This is a matter well known in transport studies as a choice of destination among the large set of destinations one can choose for a given activity. A physical explanation of how accessibility can be measured was given by Hansen (1959), who coined the definition of "the potential of opportunities for interaction," focusing not only on actual interactions but also on the opportunities to interact. He proposed the measure, $A_i = \sum_{j \in I} D_j d_{ij}^{-\alpha}$, to calculate the accessibility from location i to opportunities D_j located at a distance d_{ij}, with $i, j \in I$ and I a set of zones and α a parameter known as distance deterrence. Later, Wilson (1967) interpreted balancing factors of spatial interaction (entropy based) models as measures of accessibility, and then Neuburger (1971) and Williams (1976) gave them the interpretation of consumers' surplus. At that time, the random utility framework brought direct microeconomic support to the concept of accessibility, providing utility-based measures obtained from logit models (Domencic and McFadden, 1975; Williams, 1977; Ben-Akiva and Lerman, 1985). The gap between spatial interaction and multinomial logit (MNL) models was bridged by Anas (1983), who showed that these models are formally equivalent. For reviews see Morris et al. (1979) and Geurs and van Wee (2004).

In the rest of this chapter, we define the concept of accessibility as the individual's elemental interaction with distant activities. We focus on a microeconomic measure of such an interaction, and we also examine and define the related concept of attractiveness. After defining these concepts, we discuss how to measure them.

2.3 The Microeconomic Measure of Interactions

We assume that individuals are rational agents, i.e., they engage in interactions that are beneficial for them. Consider the interaction between an individual n located originally at a point denoted by i and another individual or activity located at point j (assuming that i and j belong to a given spatial partition denoted by I, e.g., a zone system).

Assume that the individual n faces a cost c_{nij} to visit location j, and the visit yields a benefit to individual n denoted by b_{nj}, and that benefits and costs are measured with the same units (utility or monetary units). This conventional view may be extended to include costs at the destination, e.g., the price of performing the activity and the benefits of traveling, e.g., enjoying the views or using the travel time to perform in-vehicle activities.

Thus, that interaction (n,i,j) is rational if, and only if, the net benefit b_{nij} is positive, i.e., if the following condition holds:

$$b_{nij} = b_{nj} - c_{nij} > 0 \tag{2.1}$$

which defines the microeconomic rule for elemental decisions.

Let us examine this rule in some detail. The net benefit b_{nij} may be positive or negative, and it should measure the (conditional indirect) utility of performing the activity at location j, discounting the cost that this activity may incur. b_{nij} is specific to the individual because it is essentially a benefit as perceived by n of the interaction with a distant activity and must be defined within a consistent timescale, for example, the whole duration of the interaction.

The amount of the benefit at the destination, b_{nj}, depends on the characteristics of the activity visited, which we describe by a set of quality attributes denoted by q_j, such that $b_{nij}(q_j)$. This benefit may be tangible, e.g., a salary when the activity is working, but it can also be intangible, such as emotional rewards, for example, visiting family. Thus, this benefit is necessarily specific to the individuals because it depends crucially on their preferences. The perceived utility that the activity yields to the individual is measured in monetary units. We assume that any cost (other than travel cost), e.g., the price of performing the activity, is included in b_{nj}. Additionally, the quality of these benefits may also depend on neighboring activities; e.g., the quality of the job location may be enhanced by other social activities occurring in that neighborhood.

The travel cost c_{nij} of the interaction accounts for every perceived cost associated with the distance between the spatial locations i and j. The travel cost is assumed to be different between individuals because it should include the monetary travel cost and the perceived time cost, which is usually called the composite travel cost.

The way we have defined benefits and costs makes it feasible to associate a net benefit with any type of interaction between individuals and or activities, including social, economic, and sentimental benefits. The readers are invited to think about their own experiences with daily interactions.

A provocative example, in the sense that it tenses the argument of the rational rule in Eq. (2.1), is visits of lovers to their loved ones. We can assume that the planned visits give large enough benefits to the visitors to make them willing to pay the travel cost. However, let us consider an increase of the distance between the loving couples up to the point where a travel cost equals the benefit. If that distance exists, i.e., is not infinite, then we would conclude that rational individuals would cease visiting their fiancé because the net benefit is null and thus, in a more controversial statement, we can say that the travel cost would become a measure of the couple's love. This example is striking because it suggests that love can be analyzed with a rational model, which is purposefully an extreme argument. The readers are invited to take a more parsimonious approach, replacing the visited lovers by other people, from the more to the less sentimental, and to see at what point the argument becomes—for the reader—unacceptable or unrealistic. Of course, virtual interactions are almost costless, so the couple may avoid or reduce the high travel cost by combining personal and virtual visits. In any case, this example helps us to understand that the definition of accessibility as a utility concept is not limited to the economic resources involved in interactions, but it encompasses a more holistic view of human perceptions.

2.4 Definition of Access

We define *accessibility* as the benefit yielded by visiting activities, and the net benefit b_{nij} as the microeconomic measure of *relative accessibility*, i.e., the accessibility of an elementary interaction between two agents.

An important merit of this relative measure as an economic benefit is that the aggregation of relative accessibility values across all interactions performed by the individual is straightforward. Indeed, adding benefits for the same individual is simply the direct sum of relative accessibility values, which represents the *integral accessibility* that measures the total benefit that the individual can obtain, per unit of time (say per day or week) at location i.

Let us now note that an interaction necessarily involves at least two agents, either individuals or activities. Indeed, in addition to the travelers, there are passive individuals or activities that do not travel but are affected by the visitors who introduce positive or negative benefits. Hence, we now define attractiveness as the benefit yielded by the interaction with the visited activity. This benefit is clearly different from accessibility because the individuals or activities that receive this benefit are different from the visitors and have an impact on their utility (or profit in the case of a firm visited). Note that, in contrast to the visitor, the passive activity makes no decision regarding the interaction, and hence, there is no decision rule to consider regarding the identification and measurement of the attractiveness benefit.

It is worth remarking that the number and type of travelers meeting at one destination affect both accessibility and attractiveness because they contribute to the intensity of potential interactions, i.e., the amount of benefit and therefore the perceived value of the associated activities available at the trip's destination. This is a phenomenon associated with agglomeration economies, i.e., the more participants at one activity or in its neighborhood, the larger the potential benefits.

The usual example of the importance of attractiveness is the location of retail establishments seeking locations that maximize their demand for goods, i.e., they locate at highly attractive sites where they will receive more visitors. The benefit in this case is economic and is measured by the profit of the activity. A less usual example of how attractiveness influences locations in social interactions is the case of elders who seek having visits from family members. They will have more visits, and hence higher benefits, by locating close to their family members or along their frequent routes; this strategy reduces the family visits' transportation costs, thus increasing the number of visits.

Therefore, every interaction yields (at least) the two interacting activities with different benefits, which we call accessibility (denoted as *acc*) and attractiveness (denoted as *att*). It follows that every location can be characterized by this pair of access measures and that they have different values for each individual or activity n, denoted as $(acc_{ni}, att_{ni})\ \forall\ n, i$.

2.5 Measuring Access

To measure access benefits, we have to observe the behavior of the interacting persons in their activities to be able to indirectly identify and measure the benefits from their decisions. The single decision that reflects the visitor's benefit is the trip to visit the activities because when the individual decides to take a trip, it reveals that the condition in Eq. (2.1) holds, i.e., the perceived benefit is at least higher than the transportation cost. Additionally, by observing the frequency—or travel demand—of such interactions and the amount of resources spent, the modeler can derive a measure of accessibility. Conversely, measuring the attractiveness of trips is not direct because the visited activity is passive, i.e., it makes no decision regarding the trip. In this case, the modeler can only observe the number and type of visitors and infer measures of benefits estimated indirectly; otherwise, complementary information of visited activities is needed to estimate benefits, for example, profits on sales.

Accessibility, defined as the benefit yield by a visit to a distant activity, is precisely what the transport modeler measures to derive the traveler's benefits associated with a change in the transportation system; therefore, we can use their techniques.

From microeconomics, a simple expression for calculating the benefit of a trip b_{ij} with the origin–destination (i, j) is obtained by integrating the *Marshallian* trip demand function $D_{ij} = D(q_j, c_{ij})$. Here, $(i, j) \in I \times I$ with I the set of alternative locations defined at any spatial aggregation, e.g., coordinates, property, block, or zone; q_j represents the quality of the activities at the destination, which depends on the attributes of the visited activity and the quality of the neighborhood, i.e., it depends on the LU and the location pattern, and c_{ij} is the transportation composite cost (including travel monetary cost and time), which depends on the infrastructure, transportation modes, and the system operation, particularly on the level of congestion in the transportation network. It is important to note that D_{ij} is the individual's demand for a trip, given the individual traveller n and the trip or interaction purpose $p \in \Gamma$, with Γ the set of activity purposes defined by the modeler, i.e., the extensive notation is D_{npij}. Thus, the trip benefit is

$$b_{npij} = \int_{x^0}^{x^1} D_{np}\left(q_j, c_{ij}\right) dx \tag{2.2}$$

where $x^k = \left(q_j^k, c_{ij}^k\right)$ with $k = (0,1)$ represents the scenario before and after the transportation changes in costs or quality.

Most transportation models are coarser in describing travel demand, as they aggregate individuals into clusters with similar socioeconomic characteristics; space is also aggregated in seemingly homogeneous zones and trip purposes. This aggregated model simplifies the calculus and reduces data requirements in real applications. Hereafter in this chapter, we shall denote by D_{npij} the aggregated demand per cluster, purpose, and origin–destination zone pair.

The resulting benefit measures depend on the model used to estimate travel demand. Here, we describe the benefits derived from the two most frequently applied travel demand models: the spatial interaction model based on entropy theory and the MNL model based on discrete choice theory.

Spatial Interaction Entropy Model

Technical Note 2.1 describes this trip demand model. The result of Eq. (2.2) using this model was calculated by Williams (1976) for a short-run case, in which the transportation cost c_{ij} changes but quality q_j remains unchanged, i.e., in Eq. (2.2) $x^1 = \left(q_j^0, c_{ij}^1\right)$. This result was then extended by Martínez and Araya (2000a, 2000b) to include changes in the LU that modify the quality; i.e., making $x^1 = \left(q_j^1, c_{ij}^1\right)$ in Eq. (2.2).

The trip demand model is

$$D_{npij} = A_{npi} O_{npi} B_{npj} E_{npj} e^{-\beta_{np} c_{pij}} \tag{2.3}$$

where A and B are known as the balancing factors respectively associated with the number of trips generated at zone i, denoted by O_{npi}, and the number of trips with destinations in zone j, E_{npj}, and β_{np} is called the deterrent cost parameter with inverse monetary units. The balancing factors are

$$A_{npi} = \left(\sum_{j \in I} B_{npj} E_{npj} e^{-\beta_{np} c_{pij}}\right)^{-1} \tag{2.4}$$

$$B_{npj} = \left(\sum_{i \in I} A_{npi} O_{npi} e^{-\beta_{np} c_{pij}}\right)^{-1} \tag{2.5}$$

The balancing factors A_i have been interpreted as measuring the potential accessibility of zone i and B_j as an attraction factor. The concept of potential accessibility refers to the fact that it aggregates benefits of potential trips across the entire city. Similar measures with economic interpretation in monetary units per trip are (see Martínez, 1995; Martínez and Araya, 2000a, 2000b)

$$acc_{npi} = \frac{-1}{\beta_{np}} \ln(A_{npi}) \tag{2.6}$$

$$att_{npj} = \frac{-1}{\beta_{np}} \ln(B_{npj}) \tag{2.7}$$

which, when added, account for the total user benefit associated with a single trip:

$$tub_{npij} = \frac{-1}{\beta_{np}} \ln(A_{npi} B_{npj}) \tag{2.8}$$

Therefore, the modeler can use balancing factors of the estimated spatial interaction travel demand model to calculate access measures, *acc*, *att*, and *tub*, per trip in the monetary units per time period used for transportation costs. We observe that the demand in Eq. (2.3) is unaffected by a constant scaling factor multiplying all A_i's and dividing all B_j's. Such a constant is unidentified in this model, which implies that *acc* and *att* are relative values with respect to some reference value, but *tub* is an absolute value because the constant cancels out.

We note that the information embedded in these measures of benefits is based on trip interactions only, ignoring other means of interactions such as communication. These measures are usually aggregated in space (a zoning system) and by socioeconomic clusters, although the level of disaggregation may be as fine as desired. Because the demand model is based on entropy theory, these measures represent the expected benefits associated with the most likely distribution of trips for a given number of trips produced O_{npi} and attracted E_{npj}.

Discrete Choice Random Utility Model

The most well-known application of the discrete random utility theory (Domencic and McFadden, 1975) is the MNL model presented in Technical Note 2.2. It calculates the probability of an individual n at location i, choosing the destination location option j for activity purpose p, $P_{j/npi}$, which results from the agent's optimization of utility from the set of optional destinations $C_{np} \subseteq I$. This model also yields the following expected maximum utility derived from the destination choice process:

$$V_{npi} = \frac{1}{\mu^{np}} \ln\left(\sum_{j \in I} e^{\mu^{np} V_{npij}}\right), \forall i \in I \tag{2.9}$$

where $V_{npij} = V_{np}(q_j, c_{ij})$ is the elemental utility yielded by a trip that combines interaction quality and travel costs, including the travel time. The variance of this choice process is specific to each trip purpose, which we represent by μ^{np}. This expression, known as the logsum function of utilities, is recognized (Ben-Akiva and Lerman, 1985) as measuring *accessibility* or the expected worth of a set of destination alternatives.

The logsum function can be derived from Eq. (2.2) defining $V_{npi} = \{V_{npij}(q,c), \forall j \in I\}$ and the elemental demand (only one trip) for destination j given by $D_{npij} = P_{j/npi}(V_{npi})$, with the logit conditional destination choice probability $P_{j/npi} = e^{\mu^{np}(V_{npij} - V_{npi})}$. Note that $P_{j/npi} = \frac{\partial V_{npi}}{\partial V_{npij}}$ defines V_{npi} as the generative function of the logit model. Observe that V_{npi} increases with the number of alternative destinations given by the size of set I; i.e., the number of options for interaction increases accessibility.

In the context of discrete choice models in transportation studies, modelers have naturally recognized that utilities are functions of quality, usually called the level of service, and travel costs, i.e., $D_{np}(q, c)$. The level of service includes travel time as a prominent variable that differentiates transportation modes and destinations. It also includes attributes of the activities at the destinations that correlate with the attraction of the trips.

The usual application of the logit model considers the aggregate version where n represents a cluster of individuals with similar behavior; there are O_{npi} trips generated at zone i and E_{npj} trips arriving at each zone j. Additionally, purposes do not represent a unitary interaction between two individuals but are more general, with several activities assumed to be similar for a given trip purpose. In this context, the trip origin constraint is $\sum_{j \in I} E_{npj} P_{j/npi} = O_{npi}, \forall i \in I$, and trip probabilities are $P_{j/npi} = e^{\mu^{np}(V_{npij} - \overline{V}_{npi})}$, with $\overline{V}_{npi}$ the aggregated accessibility given by

$$\overline{V}_{npi} = \frac{1}{\mu^{np}} \ln\left(\frac{1}{O_{npi}} \sum_{j \in I} E_{npj} e^{\mu^{np} V_{npij}}\right), \forall i \in I \tag{2.10}$$

Furthermore, the aggregated model can be restricted to also comply with an exogenous number of trips arriving at each destination called a doubly constrained logit model, i.e., $\sum_{i \in I} O_{npi} P_{i/npj} = E_j$, where $P_{i/npj} = e^{\mu^{np}(V_{npij} - \overline{V}_{npj})}$. For this condition to hold, we define $\overline{V}_{npj}$ as

$$\overline{V}_{npj} = \frac{1}{\mu^{np}} \ln\left(\frac{1}{E_{npj}} \sum_{i \in I} O_{npi} e^{\mu^{np}(V_{npij} - \overline{V}_{npi})}\right), \forall j \in I \tag{2.11}$$

where $\overline{V}_{npj}$ represents the attractiveness measure (*att*), i.e., the expected maximum benefits obtained by an np-type trip visiting zone j.

The similarity between the random utility and the entropy models has been observed by several authors (Anas, 1983; Williams, 1977), and Anas (1983) demonstrates that they are identical in that the MNL model can be derived by the maximum random utility with maximum likelihood (ML) estimates of parameters or by the maximum entropy (ME) approaches. However, this equivalence holds only for the linear utility parameters $\overline{\beta}$ in Technical Note 2.2 and Shannon's entropy parameters $\overline{\alpha}, \overline{\gamma}$, and $\overline{\theta}$ in Technical Note 2.1. In this case, the corresponding parameters are identical. Thus, the reader can observe that at least in the case of linear utility in the MNL model, access measures can be enriched by the respective interpretations of the estimated parameters: (1) from the ML model, the parameters of the MNL model represent the consumer's value of quality attributes and travel costs of any interaction, that is, the benefit of each attribute of interaction, and (2) from the ME model, they represent the Lagrange multipliers of an optimization function, for example, minimization of transportation costs.

2.6 Location Externalities and Agglomeration Economies

The significant property of location externalities and agglomeration economies is embedded in the access measures presented. We call the impact on residents and visitors that a resident in a neighborhood, either a household or a firm, induces on other agents in the same neighborhood, a *location externality*. This impact may be of different types, such as socioeconomic, religious or ethnic, attraction or exclusion, nuisance, or production opportunities, which could be induced by explicit (personal contacts) or implicit (attitudes) interactions. When such an effect is associated with the increment on density, this type of location externality is called an agglomeration economy.

To appreciate this property, consider the elemental interaction benefit given by Eq. (2.9) and its aggregation across interaction purposes given by

$$b_{ni} = \sum_{p \in \Gamma} V_{npi} = \sum_{p \in \Gamma} \frac{1}{\mu^{np}} \ln \left(\sum_{j \in I} e^{\mu^{np} V_{np}(q_j,\, c_{ij})} \right) \tag{2.12}$$

where we recall that the direct aggregation of benefits accrued by the same agent is legitimate if these benefits are measured in terms of utility.

Let us examine the impact of a new agent on the city by increasing the population from N to $N+1$. We identify the newcomer's activity and its location with a single index j_0 because each agent or activity has a unique location. Define $I' = I \cup \{j_0\}$, which considers that the newcomer adds a new location in the space by either expanding the city or by augmenting the density without changing the city limits. Then, the new benefit is

$$b'_{ni} = \sum_{p \in \Gamma} \frac{1}{\mu^{np}} \ln \left(\sum_{j \in I'} e^{\mu^{np} V_{np}\left(q'_j,\, c'_{ij}\right)} \right) \tag{2.13}$$

where μ^{np} recognizes that the variance of the destination choice behavior depends on the agent and the trip's interaction purpose. We observe that the new agent has two impacts on the interaction benefits of every agent in the city: (1) an additional positive term in the inner sum (it is positive because exponentials are strictly positive), which is a direct interaction effect, and (2) a change in the utility at each alternative destination $V_{np}\left(q_j', c_{ij}'\right)$ because of the change in quality due to agglomeration economies and in transport costs due to a change in congestion, from $V_{np}(q_j, c_{ij})$ to $V_{np}\left(q_j', c_{ij}'\right)$. The second impact represents the externality effect on the interactions.

To analyze these changes, we differentiate Eq. (2.13):

$$db'_{ni} = \sum_{p \in \Gamma} P_{npij_0} V_{npij_0} + \sum_{p \in \Gamma} \sum_{j \in I_{j_0}} P_{npij} \left(\frac{\partial V_{npij}}{\partial q_j} dq_j + \frac{\partial V_{npij}}{\partial c_{ij}} dc_{ij} \right) \tag{2.14}$$

where the utility $V_{npij} = V_{np}(q_j, c_{ij})$ is defined such that $\frac{\partial V_{npij}}{\partial q_j} \geq 0$ (quality attracts trips) and $\frac{\partial V_{npij}}{\partial c_{ij}} \leq 0$ (congestion cost deters trips). The first term is the direct benefit of the potential interaction with the new agent in the city, with $P_{j_0/npi} \frac{\partial V_{np}}{\partial N} = P_{npij_0} V_{npij_0}$ because the variation in utility is the final utility in this case where there is no previous interaction with the newcomer. The second term represents the induced change in utilities by agglomeration economies generated by the presence of j_0 in the neighborhood I_{j_0}, which represents a change in the interaction benefits between agent n and all other agents $j \in I_{j_0}$.

The induced effect on utilities represents *location externalities*, and it is the effect that a new agent introduces on the density and diversity of activities in the neighborhood, which is perceived by all citizens as a change in the potential interaction in that neighborhood. Observe that location externalities in Eq. (2.14) include a large number of potential direct and indirect impacts: (1) agents traveling and interacting directly with j_0, represented by the first term in the equation, (2) agents traveling and interacting with other agents in the neighborhood and benefiting indirectly via agglomeration economies induced by j_0, represented by the second term in the equation, and (3) residents in the neighborhood of j_0, represented in Eq. (2.14) when i is the neighbor of j_0, which is an indirect benefit induced by agglomeration economies that occurred without travel.

These impacts can be analyzed more closely according to the classical definition of agglomeration economies as a density effect. We have argued that the new agent increases the density in the neighborhood of location j_0, which has an impact on the perceived attraction utility of all the locations in this neighborhood, thus affecting the neighborhood quality. Here, we simply define neighborhood as the area affected by a new agent at j_0, but it is important to recognize that the size of this area and the magnitude and sign of the change in quality depend on who the new agent is and the magnitude of its activity at j_0, i.e., it matters if the newcomer activity is a retail or a manufactory firm and if it is a large or small activity. Additionally, the increase in density may also increase congestion in general, again depending on the type of the new agent. This can be represented denoting the density in the neighborhood I_{j_0} by ρ_{j_0} and rewriting the change in the traveler's utility as a result of the change in density:

$$db'_{ni} = \sum_{p \in \Gamma} P_{npij_0} V_{npij_0} + \sum_{j \in I_{j_0}} \sum_{p \in \Gamma} P_{npij} \left(\frac{\partial V_{npi}}{\partial q_j} \frac{\partial q_j}{\partial \rho_{j_0}} + \frac{\partial V_{npi}}{\partial c_{ij}} \frac{\partial c_{ij}}{\partial \rho_{j_0}} \right) d\rho_{j_0} \tag{2.15}$$

where $\frac{\partial q_j}{\partial \rho_{j_0}}$ is the positive or negative change in attraction, and $\frac{\partial c_{ij}}{\partial \rho_{j_0}} \geq 0$ is the change in the congestion cost.

The sign of the combined effect of density on attraction and congestion is ambiguous, but to understand the net impact, we must consider the significant role of the interaction probability in Eq. (2.15). Indeed, the probability P_{npij} weighs the term in brackets in a way that increases with utilities (when positive attraction outweighs congestion) and decreases with costs (when congestion costs outweigh attraction, or attraction change is negative). In fact, it is interesting to recognize that this adjustment on probabilities with externalities represents the agent's rational rule of choosing the interaction option that filters in favor of the highest benefit options for its benefit. Such a selection process induces that, on average, location externalities are positive, despite the increment in congestion, which is avoided as much as possible by travelers as the probabilities dictate. Additionally, this net positive effect increases with the size of the neighborhood I_{j_0} (number of terms of the outer sum of the externality), which depends on the type of the new agent (e.g., consider the size of the neighborhood impacted by a new shopping center vs. a new household residence) but also on the density in this neighborhood ρ_{j_0} because the greater the density, the larger the number of agents in the neighborhood impacted by the newcomer.

This analysis considers a simplified model of interactions because it does not recognize trip tours, i.e., chains of trips, but more complex transportation demand models could be considered to arrive at similar conclusions.

Therefore, noting that density on average increases with urban population N, we foresee that location externalities increase with the city's population size. Thus, on average, benefits of urban agents increase with the city size as

$$b_{ni} = a + g(N) \tag{2.16}$$

where a is the direct benefit, and $g(N)$ are the location externalities. This conclusion recognizes the existence of agglomeration economies associated with interactions in cities and explains its origins on a microscale. It is important to note that, as we have shown, these per capita economies are embedded in the economically sound definition of accessibility measures and emerge from the location externalities that new agents introduce on the travelers' utility. Additionally, we observe that the direct benefit in small cities, represented by the constant a in Eq. (2.16), is relatively larger than the externality compared with large cities.

Notice that the $g(N)$ factor may not be observed when comparing access measures of cities of different sizes in the same country if they have been derived from travel demand models developed independently for each city. This is because, as we noted, access values are relative measures affected by an unknown scale parameter, which is different for each demand model, i.e., different for each city. This difficulty is overcome, however, with a nation-wide travel demand model that combines inner and intercity trips in which access measures have a common scale parameter.

We have purposely introduced the effect of density on the notion of accessibility, which links the microscopic definition of accessibility as an individual's perception of interactions with a mesoscale variable of the system such as density. The purpose is to provide a clear interaction between two scales of the model and therefore model the aggregation process between these scales.

2.7 Summary

In this chapter, we have defined the concept of access as a vector with two components, *acc* and *att*, both associated with the potential benefit of a trip, which can be measured using the travel demand functions. They are specific for each traveler type (n) and trip interaction purpose (p) and can be defined for the individual trip or for an aggregate of trips between zones, travelers' clusters, and interaction purposes. The estimation of these benefits derives directly from a trip demand model, a methodology that applies for personal trips and the case of goods being delivered by using the corresponding trip demand function.

As we said at the beginning of this chapter, because the access measures presented represent net benefits associated with a trip, they depend on both the interaction quality and the transport cost (including travel time). We presented access measures for two travel demand functions, the spatial interaction or entropy demand model and the MNL model, and we have discussed the equivalence between them. This equivalence property reconciles these two approaches for travel demand modeling, originally considered as essentially different because the entropy model is a statistical concept applied to an aggregate of trips (or trip flows) between zones, while the logit is derived from microeconomic principles to model individuals' behavior. Hence, access can be estimated from an MNL derived from entropy or discrete choice approaches.

The fact that access is measured using the economic metric of benefit allows the simple addition of such benefits across the multiple agents' interactions with different purposes, which is feasible within a microeconomic approach, and makes these interaction benefits comparable with other benefits associated with the same agents' decisions, for example, the residential or firm location choice or investments. This added condition permits us their use in the microeconomic base model of agents' behavior in the urban system presented in this book.

Finally, we have shown that economies of agglomeration are embedded in the economic measure of accessibility and can be explained at the level of the microscopic interaction of each agent with others as the result of the intensified interaction occurring in larger cities with higher population density. Moreover, this analysis lets us conclude that benefits tend to be constant in small cities, whereas they increase with the city size as economies of agglomeration gradually emerge.

Technical Note 2.1: Spatial Interaction Entropy Model

The spatial interaction model (Wilson, 1970, 1971) estimates the number of trips between pairs of zones (i, j) in the space $I \times I$, denoted D_{ij}, for a known set of trip ends: $O_i = \sum_{j \in I} D_{ij}$ and $E_j = \sum_{i \in I} D_{ij}$, which comply with the total demand condition: $D = \sum_{ij \in I \times I} D_{ij}$. If the number of zones is n, this model estimates n^2 values based on $2n$ trip end values. The method to expand from $2n$ to n^2 values is the maximization of the entropy of the trips.

The entropy notion used in spatial interaction models is Shannon's definition, described for a discrete random vector $x = (x_i)$, $i \in I$ with probabilities $p(x_i)$ and defined by $Z = \sum_{i \in I} p(x_i) \ln p(x_i)$. Maximizing the value of Z yields the most likely value for the vector x following the Wilson (1970) criteria. Wilson shows that Shannon's entropy measures the number of possible microstates associated with the mesostate of the trip matrix, and if all microstates are assumed equally likely to occur, then the mesostate with the maximum number of microstates is the most likely to happen, i.e., the one associated with the ME. A microstate is a distribution of D trips, which complies with the macrostate constraints O_i and E_j, $\forall ij$; a mesostate is a matrix $[D_{ij}]$ that also complies with macrostate constraints. Spatial interaction models use this method to estimate the most likely matrix of trips $\left[D^*_{ij}\right]$, for a given set of trip origins O_i and destinations E_j, with $(i, j) \in I \times I$.

The entropy optimization problem, known as the doubly constrained model, is

$$Max_{D_{ij}} Z = -\sum_{ij \in I \times I} D_{ij}(\ln D_{ij} - 1) \quad \text{(T2.1)}$$

$$\text{s.t.} \quad \sum_{j \in I} D_{ij} = O_i \;\; \forall i \quad (\alpha_i)$$

$$\sum_{i \in I} D_{ij} = E_j \;\; \forall_j \quad (\gamma_j)$$

with $D = \sum_{i \in I} O_i = \sum_{j \in I} E_j$. According to information theory, Z measures the uncertainty of the trip matrix $[D_{ij}]$. To understand this, note that dividing D_{ij} by the total number of trips D, a constant in this problem, we obtain a new entropy term on $P_{ij} = D_{ij}/D$ variables. The entropy term $Z' = -\sum_{ij} P_{ij}(\ln P_{ij})$ represents the expected value of the uncertainty measure: $-\ln(P_{ij})$. This makes the entropy approach equivalent to finding a probability distribution $\{P_{ij}\}$ that complies with the constraints and maximizes uncertainty. The "maximum uncertainty" criteria implies that the resulting probability distribution itself induces the least bias into the solution, which is the uniform distribution, thus leaving the constraints as the only information that defines the trip matrix solution; i.e., in the absence of constraints, the matrix solution is uniform with $D_{ij} = \frac{D}{|I|^2}, \forall i,j \in I$. Additionally, transportation costs in each pair, c_{ij}'s, are introduced by a constraint on the total travel costs C:

$$\sum_{ij \in I\times I} D_{ij}c_{ij} = C \quad (\beta) \tag{T2.2}$$

The corresponding Lagrange multipliers of the optimization problem in Eqs (T2.1) and (T2.2) are in brackets. The model is presented in this Note, ignoring the subindices n and p used in the chapter text.

The constraint on total transport costs is introduced ad hoc, but the problem can be reformulated as

$$Max_{D_{ij},\theta}\, Z = -\sum_{ij} D_{ij}(\ln D_{ij} - 1) + \beta\left(C - \sum_{ij} D_{ij}c_{ij}\right) \tag{T2.3}$$

$$\text{s.t.} \quad \sum_{j\in I} D_{ij} = O_i, \quad \forall i \in I \quad (\alpha_i)$$

$$\sum_{i\in I} D_{ij} = E_j, \quad \forall j \in I \quad (\gamma_j)$$

With this form, we can interpret that the optimization problem yields the demand that minimizes travelers' costs, which implicitly assumes that travelers behave as cost minimizers rather than benefit maximizers. In this problem, β weighs the role of the uncertainty, such that only when $\beta \to \infty$ does the optimization problem become deterministic and based on transportation costs; otherwise, the system embeds uncertainty modeled by trips' probabilities, i.e., as expected, trips. Additionally, the Lagrange multipliers α and γ represent the increase in Z if the respective constraint is relaxed marginally, which are also called the shadow price of the constraint. Hence, given the stochastic context of this problem, α_i represents the expected benefit (or cost saving) for the last trip from zone i, whereas γ_j represents the expected benefit of the last trip arriving at zone j.

The optimization problem is solved using the Lagrange method, defining:

$$\begin{aligned}\mathcal{L}(Z') = &-\sum_{ij\in I\times I} D_{ij}(\ln D_{ij} - 1) + \beta\left(C - \sum_{ij\in I\times I} D_{ij}c_{ij}\right)\\ &+\sum_{i\in I}\alpha_i\left(O_i - \sum_{j\in I} D_{ij}\right) + \sum_{j\in I}\gamma_j\left(E_j - \sum_{i\in I} D_{ij}\right)\end{aligned} \tag{T2.4}$$

Calculating the first-order conditions $\frac{\partial \mathcal{L}}{\partial D_{ij}} = 0, \forall (i,j) \in I \times I$ yields the solution:

$$D_{ij}^* = e^{-\alpha_i - \gamma_j - \beta c_{ij}}, \quad \forall (i,j) \in I \times I. \tag{T2.5}$$

It is common practice to replace $e^{-\alpha_i} = A_i O_i$ and $e^{-\gamma_j} = B_j E_j$, so the solution is equivalently expressed in its usual form as

$$D_{ij}^* = A_i O_i B_j E_j e^{-\beta c_{ij}} \quad \forall (i,j) \in I \times I. \tag{T2.6}$$

Then, the solution depends on the unknown parameters α_i, γ_j or A_i, B_j, plus β. Imposing the trip end constraints for the solution, we obtain:

$$A_i^{-1} = \sum_{j \in I} B_j F_j e^{-\beta c_{ij}}, \quad \forall i \in I \tag{T2.7}$$

$$B_j^{-1} = \sum_{i \in I} A_i O_i e^{-\beta c_{ij}}, \quad \forall j \in I \tag{T2.8}$$

which are known as the balancing factors because they balance the values of D_{ij} to comply with the trip end conditions. The expressions for the balancing factors define a fixed point problem, for which it is well known that the iteration process starting with any set of initial values converges to the solution conditional on the parameter β (Macgill, 1977). There are several algorithms for the calibration of β (see Fang et al., 1997).

Notice that the travel demand model is invariant if the balancing factors are scaled as λA_i and $\lambda^{-1} B_j$. Although the solution for the matrix $\left[D_{ij}^*\right]$ is unique, the balancing factors are undefined by a single factor. Therefore, we can identify only relative values of each individual balancing factor and absolute values for $A_i B_j$, $\frac{A_j}{A_{j'}}$ and $\frac{B_j}{B_{j'}}$ because the scaling factor cancels out. This observation implies that accessibility and attractiveness measured by balancing factors can define relative values only.

An important merit of the entropy model is that it is a nonlinear optimization problem that can be solved efficiently for the unique solution of $\left[D_{ij}^*\right]$ and for relative values of the balancing factors, given trip ends $O = (O_i, i \in I)$, $E = (E_j, j \in I)$ and β.

Technical Note 2.2: Discrete Choice Random Utility Model

This note shows the derivation of the double-constraint MNL model from the maximum utility approach, following Anas (1983).

This MNL model can be applied to several spatial assignment problems for estimating the interaction between individuals or groups of individuals in the aggregate model. Such interaction may occur, for example, by means of trips and communication networks, and the model can also be applied for the allocation of individuals to spatial locations.

We consider the case of an agent choosing an origin–destination pair in the set of location options $I \times I$, with I the set of locations in the city; thus, this set includes all possible interactions in the city between agents. The agent maximizes the (indirect) utility $V\left(q_j, c_{ij}; \beta\right)$, where q_j is the quality of the interaction at location j, c_{ij} is the travel cost including time (also called the composite cost), and β is a vector of the perceived utility of quality and costs. Note that for simplicity, we ignore indices n and p used in the text, but what follows is valid for every np's trip. We consider the following random utility:

$$\overline{V}_{ij} = V_{ij} + V_i + V_j + \varepsilon_{ij}, \quad \forall i, j \in I \tag{T2.9}$$

The probability that a pair (i, j) yields the maximum utility is defined as

$$P_{ij} = \Pr ob\left(\overline{V}_{ij} \geq \overline{V}_{mn}, \forall m, n \in I\right), \quad \forall i, j \in I \tag{T2.10}$$

which, if ε_{ij} is an i.i.d. Gumbel variate yields the MNL model:

$$P_{ij} = \frac{e^{\mu(V_{ij}+V_i+V_j)}}{\sum\limits_{mn \in I \times I} e^{\mu(V_{mn}+V_m+V_n)}} \tag{T2.11}$$

To estimate the utility function of this model, let us assume that the modeler has a set of observed agents C, indexed by h and they have the same utility; i.e., the parameters of the utility function are the same because they belong to the same agent cluster. The criteria to estimate utilities, i.e., estimate $\beta' s$ parameters, are such that applied to the model $P_{ij}(\beta)$, the joint probability associated with observed choices is maximized; i.e., it is the set of parameter values that best replicate observed choices, which is evaluated in likelihood function $\mathcal{L} = \prod\limits_{h \in C} \prod\limits_{ij \in I \times I} \left(P_{ij}^h\left(\overline{\beta}\right)\right)^{\delta_{ij}^h}$. Using the logarithm of $\mathcal{L}$, the problem is to estimate the set of parameters $\overline{\beta}$ given by

$$Max_{\overline{\beta}} \log \mathcal{L} = \sum_{h \in C} \sum_{ij \in I \times I} \delta_{ij}^h \log P_{ij}^h\left(\overline{\beta}\right) \tag{T2.12}$$

where $\overline{\beta}$ is the estimate of the vector of parameters of the utility functions V_{ij}, V_i, and V_j. δ_{ij}^h is the indicator of the observed choices: $\delta_{ij}^h = 1$ if the observed agent $h \in C$ chooses pair (i, j), otherwise $\delta_{ij}^h = 0$. P_{ij}^h is the choice probability evaluated for the choice conditions of individual h.

For each elemental parameter $\beta_k \in \beta$, $k = 1,\ldots,K$, the first-order conditions for this problem are the following:

$$\frac{\partial \log \mathcal{L}}{\partial \overline{\beta}_k} = \sum_{h \in C} \sum_{ij \in I \times I} \frac{\delta^h_{ij}}{P^h_{ij}(\overline{\beta})} \frac{\partial P^h_{ij}(\overline{\beta})}{\partial \overline{\beta}_k} = 0 \tag{T2.13}$$

with

$$\frac{\partial P^h_{ij}}{\partial \overline{\beta}_k} = \frac{\partial P^h_{ij}}{\partial v_{ij}} \frac{\partial v_{ij}}{\partial \overline{\beta}_k} = P^h_{ij} \frac{\partial v_{ij}}{\partial \overline{\beta}_k} - P^h_{ij} \sum_{mn \in I \times I} P^h_{mn} \frac{\partial v_{mn}}{\partial \overline{\beta}_k} \tag{T2.14}$$

and $v_{ij} = V_{ij} + V_i + V_j$. Replacing Eq. (T2.14) into Eq. (T2.13) yields

$$\frac{\partial \log \mathcal{L}}{\partial \overline{\beta}_k} = \sum_{h \in C} \sum_{ij \in I \times I} \delta^h_{ij} \left(\frac{\partial v_{ij}}{\partial \overline{\beta}_k} - \sum_{mn \in I \times I} P^h_{mn} \frac{\partial v_{mn}}{\partial \overline{\beta}_k} \right) = 0, \quad \forall \overline{\beta}_k \in \overline{\beta} \tag{T2.15}$$

Let us now consider the simple case of the following linear in parameter utility, often used in applied choice models:

$$V_{ij}(\overline{\beta}) = \sum_{k \in K} \overline{\beta}_k x_{ijk}; \; V_i = \overline{\beta}_{0i}; \; V_j = \overline{\beta}_{0j}$$

where parameters $\overline{\beta}_0$ are called *alternative specific constants,* and x_{ijk} are trip attributes including travel time and cost. Note that parameter μ is not identifiable from choice data in the linear utility model, so we can only estimate the parameters scaled by μ, i.e., $\overline{\beta} = \mu\beta$.

This utility yields the following conditions for the ML estimate of parameters:

$$\sum_{h \in C} \sum_{ij \in I \times I} \delta^h_{ij} \left(x_{hijk} - \sum_{mn \in I \times I} P^h_{mn} x_{hmnk} \right) = 0, \quad \forall \overline{\beta}_k \neq \overline{\beta}_{0i}, \overline{\beta}_{0j} \tag{T2.16}$$

Organizing terms, we obtain:

$$\sum_{h \in C} \sum_{ij \in I \times I} P^h_{ij}(\overline{\beta}_k) x_{hijk} = \sum_{h \in C} \sum_{ij \in I \times I} \delta^h_{ij} x_{hijk} = X_k, \quad \forall \overline{\beta}_k \neq \overline{\beta}_{0i}, \overline{\beta}_{0j} \tag{T2.17}$$

where $\sum_{h \in C} \sum_{ij \in I \times I} \delta^h_{ij} x_{hijk} = X_k$ is the aggregate value of the kth attribute in the data set used for the estimation. This equation can be solved for $\overline{\beta}_k$ to obtain the estimates that guarantee that the model forecasts the observed total X_k for every attribute k in the utility function. In other words, the model fits the data at the aggregate level. Under weak conditions, the function $\mathcal{L}$ is globally concave, so if the solution for $\overline{\beta}_k$ in Eq. (T2.17) exists, it is unique (McFadden, 1974), and the ML estimator is consistent, asymptotically normal, and asymptotically efficient (Ben-Akiva and Lerman, 1985).

Similarly, for the specific constants $\overline{\beta}_{0i_0}$ and $\overline{\beta}_{0j_0}$, $x_{hijk} = 1$, so we write

$$\sum_{h \in C} \sum_{ij \in I \times I} P_{ij}^h(\overline{\beta}_{0i_0})\delta_{i_0j} = \sum_{h \in C} \sum_{j \in I} P_{i_0j}^h(\overline{\beta}_{0i_0}) = \sum_{h \in C} \sum_{j \in I} \delta_{i_0j}^h = O_{i_0}, \quad \forall \overline{\beta}_{0i_0} \tag{T2.18}$$

$$\sum_{h \in C} \sum_{ij \in I \times I} P_{ij}^h\left(\overline{\beta}_{0j_0}\right)\delta_{ij_0} = \sum_{h \in C} \sum_{i \in I} P_{ij_0}^h\left(\overline{\beta}_{0j_0}\right) = \sum_{h \in C} \sum_{i \in I} \delta_{ij_0}^h = E_{j_0}, \quad \forall \overline{\beta}_{0j_0} \tag{T2.19}$$

where $\sum_{h \in C} \sum_{j \in I} \delta_{ij}^h = O_i$ is the frequency observed in the data of agents choosing option i, and similarly for $\sum_{h \in C} \sum_{i \in I} \delta_{ij}^h = E_j$. This implies that solving Eqs (T2.18) and (T2.19) for specific constants $\overline{\beta}_{0i}$ and $\overline{\beta}_{0j}$, respectively, guarantees that the model forecasts the observed total number of choices with origin i and with destination j.

Note that the approach used here to derive the doubly constrained logit model assumes that the agent chooses a pair (i, j), which implies that it chooses the agent's residential location and the trip destination (e.g., job) simultaneously. This choice process may be plausible in the case of a new agent in the city who seeks residence and location simultaneously, but it is unlikely to represent other trips associated with interactions where residential location is fixed, such as shopping, entertainment, or even jobs in the case of old residents.

It is direct to define the conditional probabilities from the MNL marginal or joint choice probability (Eq. T2.11): the destination (job) choice model conditional on the origin (residence location) is:

$$P_{j/i} = \frac{e^{\mu(V_{ij}+V_j)}}{\sum_{n \in I} e^{\mu(V_{in}+V_n)}} \tag{T2.20}$$

and the origin (residence) choice model conditional on the destination (job):

$$P_{i/j} = \frac{e^{\mu(V_{ij}+V_i)}}{\sum_{m \in I} e^{\mu(V_{mj}+V_m)}} \tag{T2.21}$$

Exercise 2.1

Show that the doubly constrained logit probability may be written as $\left(\sum_{i\in I} \mathrm{O}_{npi}\right) P_{npij} = \left(\sum_{j\in I} \mathrm{E}_{npj}\right) P_{npij} = O_{npi} P_{j/npi} = E_{npj} P_{i/npj}$ and interpret the conditional probabilities $P_{j/npi}$ and $P_{j/npi}$. Additionally, consider Eqs (2.10) and (2.11) to prove that $\frac{\partial \overline{V}_{npi}}{\partial V_{npij}} = \frac{\partial \overline{V}_{npj}}{\partial V_{npij}} = P_{npij}$. Compare the logit and entropy double constraint models regarding accessibility and attractiveness and follow Anas (1983) to show the equivalence between these models.

References

Anas, A., 1983. Discrete choice theory, information theory and the multinomial logit and gravity models. Transportation Research B 17 (B), 13–23.

Ben-Akiva, M., Lerman, S.R., 1985. Discrete Choice Analysis: Application to Travel Demand. MIT Press, Cambridge.

Domencic, T., McFadden, D., 1975. Urban Travel Demand (North-Holland, Amsterdam).

Fang, S.C., Rajasekera, J.R., Tsao, H.S.J., 1997. Entropy Optimization and Mathematical Programming. Kluwer, Boston.

Geurs, K., van Wee, B., 2004. Accessibility evaluation of land-use and transport strategies: review and research directions. Journal of Transport Geography 12, 127–140.

Hansen, W.G., 1959. How accessibility shapes land use. Journal of the American Institute of Planners 25, 73–79.

Macgill, S.M., 1977. Theoretical properties of biproportional matrix adjustments. Environment and Planning A 9, 687–701.

Martínez, F., 1995. Access: the transport-land use economic link. Transportation Research B 29 (6), 457–470.

Martínez, F., Araya, C., 2000a. Transport and land use benefits under location externalities. Environment and Planning A 32, 1611–1624.

Martínez, F., Araya, C., 2000b. A note on trip benefits in spatial interaction models. Journal of Regional Science 40 (4), 789–796.

McFadden, D., 1974. Conditional logit analysis of qualitative choice behavior. In: Zarembka, P. (Ed.), Frontiers in Econometrics. Academic Press, New York, pp. 105–142.

Morris, J.M., Dumble, P.L., Wigan, M.R., 1979. Accessibility indicators for transportation planning. Transportation Research Part A 13, 91–109.

Neuburger, H., 1971. User benefit in the evaluation of transport and land use plans. Journal of Transport Economics and Policy 5, 52–75.

Williams, H.C.W.L., 1976. Travel demand models, duality relations and user benefit analysis. Journal of Regional Science 16 (2), 147–166.

Williams, H.C.W.L., 1977. On the formation of travel demand models and economic evaluation measures of user benefit. Environment and Planning A 9, 285–344.

Wilson, A.G., 1967. A statistical theory of spatial distribution models. Transportation Research 1, 253–269.
Wilson, A.G., 1970. Entropy in Urban and Regional Modeling. Pion, London.
Wilson, A.G., 1971. A family of spatial interaction models and associated developments. Environment and Planning 3 (1), 1–32.

Discrete Urban Economic Theory

3

3.1 Introduction

The land-use (LU) market is a system with multiple and heterogeneous agents interacting in processes that occur in the space, and the traded objects are real estate properties characterized as discrete, immobile and durable, requiring a time–path-dependent dynamic where the buildings stock lasts for a long time.

The analysis of this complex market requires a theoretical framework with the flexibility to realistically reproduce urban structures and processes. In this chapter, we discuss such a microeconomic framework in a static and discrete context, built upon the urban economic theory of urban land to develop a more realistic model. By assuming a discrete urban real estate market, we can consider the fact that a city's dynamic is dependent on its built stock and allocation of activities, i.e., path dependent.

Because the LU market is embedded in a larger urban system in which production and transportation markets interact with LU processes, this flexible framework allows us to extend this approach to the more complex model of the urban system developed in the rest of this book.

The Structure of a Land-Use System

The emergence of cities from agricultural land into complex systems of real estate units and population use can be represented by the multistage process shown in Fig. 3.1.

In the first stage, the *agricultural land owner* releases land at a price R_A per area unit to *land developers*, who partition the land optimally into land lots indexed by $i \in I$, with size q^l, urbanized at a cost of $c_i(q^l)$, and then sell them at price p_i. In the next stage, *real estate developers* build on the land lots, deciding on the optimal building type at each location, denoted by index $v \in V$ and characterized by the real estate (housing) size (q^f). The building cost of the units is c_{vi} and the units are sold at price p_{vi} as defined in the *real estate selling auction*, where potential owners bid according to their willingness to pay (w_{vi}). This process is identified as the *new stock market* in Fig. 3.1, where a different agent is defined for each stage, although real estate agencies may consolidate several steps in one business firm, e.g., a land lots and real estate developer.

The complete *real estate market* includes the supply of both the old and new stocks in a unified *real estate selling auction*, where property owners and developers offer real estate units. In this market, consumers are *owners* and *redevelopers* who invest in real estate property bidding according to their willingness to pay (w_{vi}) and also

Microeconomic Modeling in Urban Science. https://doi.org/10.1016/B978-0-12-815296-6.00003-2

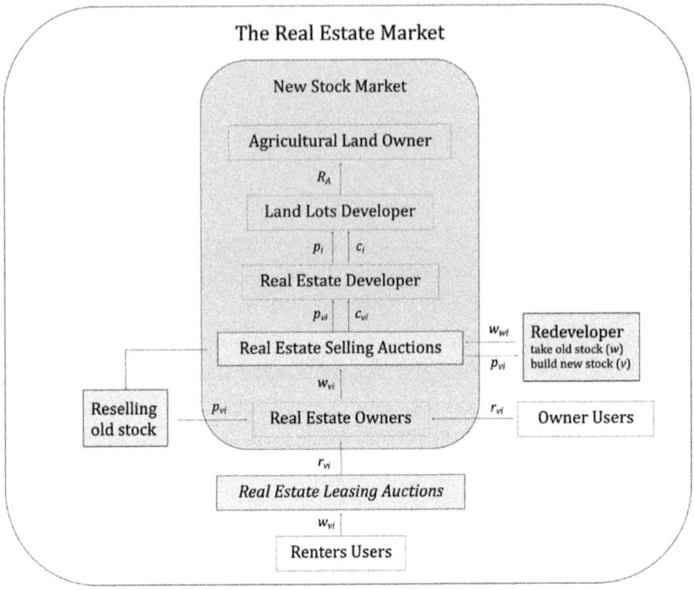

Figure 3.1 The land and real estate (re)development and use process.[1]
Inspired by Martínez, F., Roy, J., 2004. A model for residential supply. The Annals of Regional Science 38, 531–550.

supply old and redeveloped stock for reselling. The winners of real estate auctions are the new owners, who have the following three choices:

1. Lease their property for rent (r_{vi}) per time unit, e.g., per annum, in the *real estate leasing auction*;
2. Use the property for their own residential or nonresidential purposes (at the opportunity cost r_{vi}); or
3. Offer the property as old stock in the *real estate selling auction*, obtaining an auction price p_{vi}.

Redevelopers buy old stock (indexed by w) and recycle the land to produce new stock (indexed by v), at a demolition cost and a building cost, to offer the new stock back on the *real estate selling auction* market.

The problem of the *new real estate market* has been examined and reported in the classic urban economic literature, initiated by the seminal contributions of Alonso (1964), Mills (1972), and Muth (1969). The two developers stages collapse into one stage, i.e., real estate developers obtain the land input from empty agricultural and continuous land, i.e., the old stock is ignored. Therefore, the urban economic theory

[1] The price arrows point from the consumer to the supplier, i.e., the real estate developer pays a price p_i per unit of land to the land lots developer; in the inverse direction, cost arrows point from the supplier to the consumer, i.e., the real estate agent covers the land lot developer's cost. The net profit for the land lot developer is $p_i - c_i$ and for the real estate developer is $p_{vi} - c_{vi}$.

studies the emergence of a city from empty agricultural land into LU equilibrium. The theory benefits from the elegance of a continuous setting, i.e., land size and locations are continuous variables, and is able to reproduce certain general characteristics of real cities, including the stylized profiles of rents and densities and the theoretical city border. Nevertheless, it is difficult to represent other issues that add complexity, such as diversity of the population, agglomeration economies, neighborhood quality, detailed transportation networks, and interaction with other markets.

The *real estate market* involves the complex interaction of several agents: land lot developers, real estate developers, redevelopers, owners, and renters, and loops of reselling and redeveloping stock. Modelers have designed discrete choice models to simulate the market in the heterogeneous context of landscape, real estate, and population characteristics; see Pagliara et al. (2010). This approach also enables the representation of dynamic interactions among agents in this market in a simple way, fueled particularly by the city's population and economic change and delayed by the adjustment of the new stock supply.

The *real estate market* has been analyzed as a short-term agents' *allocation* equilibrium process, which includes an exogenous stock of buildings, and as a long-term *LU* process that allows for the adjustment of supply to demand, i.e., as an equilibrium where the market clears at any time or as a disequilibrium in which an excess of supply or demand may occur. This market can be studied as a closed system, without migration from other cities, or as an open system.

Characteristics of the Market

The analysis of urban land and real estate markets requires that we consider specific characteristics of this market: spatial context, real estate heterogeneity, consumer interactions, and inelastic demand; when combined, these characteristics yield a theory of the urban LU market.

The *spatial context* of this market, which was introduced in the previous chapter in the discussion of concepts associated with accessibility, is the first and most evident characteristic. Contrary to the classical notion of the market as the place where consumers and suppliers meet and trade, in this case, the spatial distribution of the land makes each location different or differentiable from all the others, i.e., each alternative location is different. Unlike products, the LU market has no factory that can produce as many equal copies as demanded at a price. This distinction was observed by classical economists, who interpreted the specific commodity of land to be a monopolistic market in which the owner holds the monopoly of the access, at a transportation cost, to the central business district (CBD). Alonso's seminal work (1964) proposed the bid-auction theory, interpreting this market as an auction of differentiated goods. From that point, the urban economic theory developed as a continuous space model.

The discrete modeling described in this book provides a more realistic approach by assuming a *heterogeneous space*, where buildings are developed from land previously used and partitioned into land lots in a continuous development process. Additionally, consumers are seen as heterogeneous and as valuing a variety of attributes of alternative locations. This setting provides the flexibility that explains why this approach is used in applied models of cities to analyze how the city is predicted to evolve from the current situation. Recognizing that land is already divided into land lots and built on, this approach provides the modeler with a highly diverse representation of real estate alternatives described by a large set of different attributes, including building characteristics, land size, neighborhood, and accessibility or transportation costs.

LU consumers are household and firm residents who value each location for the *interactions* that each one can perform with the rest. We discussed this concept in Chapter 2, observing the value that consumers assign to different locations according to their accessibility and location externalities. From the modeler's point of view, this calls for a theory of the impact of these interactions in the market that produces evident structures on a macroscale in the city, as for example, the social exclusion phenomena on household residents or the agglomeration of industries and commercial activities.

LU demand is highly *inelastic* because a population of consumers needs to be located somewhere in the city. More specifically, the total demand for real estate units is inelastic at any time, whereas building densities make demand for a specific land lot and floor space more elastic because the same number of agents may be accommodated with different floor space to land ratios.

In the first part of this chapter, we present a discrete theory of how consumers behave in this market. We then discuss how suppliers develop land into real estate options and how buildings are redeveloped. Finally, we propose a model of the market performance to show how prices are formed and how the auction process matches consumer and supplier behavior. In this chapter, the theory is presented for an ideal static equilibrium, which assumes that information is perfect for all agents and that all real estate units available in the market are sold simultaneously. This ideal scenario enables us to understand the fundamental forces and characteristics of this market. In the following chapters, we relax the perfect information assumption to develop more applicable models that remain consistent with the theory presented here.

3.2 The Consumer Location Problem

The consumer location problem studied in this section represents the *real estate selling and leasing auctions* shown in Fig. 3.1 for proprietors and renters, respectively. It describes the process through which agents decide on their preferred locations, which are allocated by an auction process to alternative location options at any point in time. This process considers that location options and all their characteristics are given, e.g., they are exogenous to the consumer. The problem involves the allocation of agents to available location options and the prices involved in these transactions. We examine a static model in which location decisions and interactions occur, reaching equilibrium conditions at each point in time.

The consumers are conceived as representative agents who seek residential locations to perform their social and economic activities in the city. We recognize that households are composed of members with different perceptions about location preferences, but it is also true that they must somehow decide on a common location after internal negotiations among the household members. For simplicity, we define a hypothetical representative consumer whose behavior is usually observed only as the outcome of the household negotiation; this consumer is called an agent. Although firms are also complex social organizations, we can similarly assume that their behavior in the land market can be described by that of a representative agent. This agent, however, may decide on locations for several establishments of the same firm. The assumption of a representative agent can, of course, be a topic of research for a more microscopic model of the internal decision process within households and firms.

The location problem has been formulated following two approaches. The utility approach applies the classical consumer problem of deciding what and how much to consume of each type of goods, with prices and income defined exogenously (see Anas, 1982). This framework considers location as one of these goods, the residence, although it is a good differentiated by the specific location. The second approach, called the bid auction, follows Alonso's seminal work (1964), in which he developed the argument that the market is an auction where agents participate, bidding for available locations. Because both approaches are founded on the same microeconomic principles, we will therefore observe their consistency and equivalence in a unified approach called the *bid-choice* model. We will present these approaches considering the case of households in the residential market and will then extend the framework to firms. In the next section, we discuss the location problem in a stylized form to explain the essentials of this interesting problem.

The Household Location Utility Approach

The main assumption in a microeconomic model is that each household, denoted by $h \in C$, *resides in only one location* and is rational, i.e., behaves in the land market to locate its residence in the location that, along with other consumption goods, yields the maximum utility. In this approach, the household is assumed to consider exogenous prices and its income in the location decision. Another assumption is that households have perfect information; that is, the household knows all the attributes of all the real estate alternatives, indexed by $i \in VI$, with $VI = V \times I$ the set combining locations $i \in I$ and real estate alternatives $v \in V$ available in the market. In the next chapter, we lift some of these assumptions.

Household h's behavior can be described by the following utility maximization problem:

$$\max_{x \in X, i \in VI} u_h(x, z_i) \tag{3.1}$$

where $x = (x_k \in \mathbb{R}^+)$ is the vector of consumption goods with $k \in K$, $z_i = (\{z_{mi}\} \in \mathbb{R})$ is the vector of discrete values describing the set of attributes of real estate $i \in VI$, and u_h is household h's utility function. In other words, the household searches simultaneously for an optimal pair (x, z_i), which combines continuous goods variables with discrete locations.

The utility function u_h is a quantitative latent (unobservable) measure of the agent's value of the pair (x, z_i). It only provides a preference order for different pairs, from high to low value, which is enough for the household to make a choice using the rational criteria: select the highest utility option, i.e., that utility quantities are nonobservable economic entities. This function may be different for each household but should comply with the usual requisites defined in microeconomic textbooks: that they be continuous, differentiable, and concave (see for example, Mas-Colell et al., 1995, pp. 46–50).

Note that the consumer's problem in Eq. (3.1) is set in a discrete space of location options described in set I, which is not only more realistic but also more mathematically treatable than a continuous model. The classical example of a continuous space model is the monocentric city proposed by Alonso (1964), which simplifies the set of location attributes to only two: the radial distance to the unique city center—the CBD that concentrates labor—and the size of the land lot; both are continuous variables.

The household's location choice is constrained by its income, i.e., the choice must be economically feasible. This can be stated by the following budget constraint expression:

$$p_x x + (1)p_i \leq y_h \tag{3.2}$$

with p_x the price of the set of goods, p_i the price of the property denoted by i, and y_h the household h's income; location prices, income, and consumption goods are per unit of time (e.g., per annum). Notably, in the discrete approach, the final consumer, i.e., the resident, is assumed to *demand just one location* in which to reside, not more and not less, making the expenditure on location dependent only on the price and not on the quantity consumed, that is to say, as it is made evident in Eq. (3.2), the residence quantity is inelastic and equal to one. This formulation departs from the classical urban economics approach in which land is empty and the consumer chooses not only any location in a continuous space but also the amount of land to occupy. In the discrete model, land consumption is an attribute of the real estate choice and is defined exogenously by the supplier.

The location problem is defined by Eq. (3.1), subject to the constraint Eq. (3.2). Despite the simplifications considered, this model contains the essentials of consumer behavior. To solve the problem, we proceed by solving for vector x first, using the budget constraint Eq. (3.2) to obtain consumer demand for each good in x, conditional on the residence location, denoted as x^*. This is a theoretical process that is not simple to perform due to the variety of goods in vector x; however, for our purpose it is enough to know that these demands are represented by $x^*(z_i, p_i; y_h)$, i.e., the optimal consumption of goods remains conditional on the location choice i, which explains why x^* is called the vector of conditional demands. The analysis, however, is usually presented in a simplified way by considering x to be a composite good, i.e., representing the bundle of goods, and p_x the bundle price. Additionally, it is assumed that all income is spent on goods and residence, i.e., Eq. (3.2) holds for equality, implying no intertemporal savings. In this context, it is convenient to divide Eq. (3.2) by p_x and assume $p_x = 1$ to be the *numeraire,* and redefine y and p_i as relative values with respect to price p_x. Finally, solving for x, we obtain $x^* = y_h - p_i$, a very specific form for the conditional demand function for goods because real estate demand is inelastic. We note that in land and real estate markets, location prices per unit of time p_i are also called rents.

Then, the conditional demands are replaced in the consumer's utility to obtain the *indirect utility conditional on the location choice*:

$$v_h(z_i) = u_h(x^*, z_i) = u_h(y_h - p_i, z_i) \tag{3.3}$$

which gives us the value of the utility achieved for each alternative location, depending on the location price, the set of attributes, the household's income, and the numeraire price.

Note that the utility in Eq. (3.3) should be an increasing function of $y_h - p_i$ because it represents the consumption of the bundle of goods x, assumed as normal goods, increasing x's consumption increases utility.

To solve the location problem, the household evaluates all available alternative locations using Eq. (3.3) and then chooses the one that yields the maximum value of v_h. That is:

$$i_h^* = \text{argmax}_{i \in VI}[v_h(z_i)] \tag{3.4}$$

where i_h^* denotes the optimal location choice conditional on household h.

Several important characteristics of this theoretical model are worth highlighting as follows:

1. The land lot size is a discrete variable, which differs from Alonso's monocentric model. His assumption of a continuous land size model implies the strong assumption that the consumer's optimal size choice is available on the market or that the model considers a city developing from empty land. Therefore, it is more realistic to assume that location options are discrete and heterogeneous, described by a set of attributes including the land size, and that the consumer should choose among available options. Nonetheless, the continuous model can be interpreted as the limited case of a discrete model following Anas' work (1990), in which a monocentric city was specified with continuous land lot sizes but with the innovation of considering discrete location options defined by small incremental distances to the CBD.
2. The household chooses only one location for residence. This assumption is explicit in the income constraint of Eq. (3.2) because the location price p_i is not multiplied by any quantity. In other words, although the consumer optimizes the quantities for the composite good x, the land and floor space quantities and all other characteristics are exogenous attributes of the discrete location choice i. This assumption is consistent with the consumer's residential location choice, as either a renter or owner-user, but does not represent the behavior followed by an investor choosing several locations to buy for renting, which is described not as a consumer but as a supplier of locations offered for a rent, as is shown in Fig. 3.1.
3. The set of location attributes is large and includes complex variables. It contains all the attributes of the property and of its location. Property attributes include, for example, land size and dwelling characteristics including floor space, number of rooms, etc. Location attributes are the neighborhood quality and accessibility to activities in the city relevant for

the household. Neighborhood attributes are important because they introduce location externalities, i.e., the location of one agent influences the neighborhood quality, hence affecting other consumers' utility, making the behavior of consumers interdependent and introducing complexity into the market process. Accessibility can be considered as the foremost important attribute in location problems, which also induces spatial interdependencies among all citizens. This large number of complex attributes confronts the household with a complex problem to solve because it requires a significant amount of information on attributes at each location and an assessment of how much the household values each of them.

4. The way in which this model represents transportation monetary costs and travel times in the location choice is worthy of comment. This important factor is implicit in the definition of the accessibility attribute in the household's utility. Specifying the model to represent the relevance of travel times and costs explicitly is not trivial in complex network structures because it requires an integration of all the choices of activities and transportation, including trip destinations, transportation modes, and route choices for all activities, including their duration and sequence, all of which leads to the accessibility measures considered in this model.

The Bid-Auction Approach

The Auction in the Real Estate Market

Economists identify certain goods as unique, such as art paintings and sculptures, although the clear majority of goods are "normal" in the sense that equal copies can be produced. Some goods can be defined as quasi-unique because they are similar but not equal, which is the case of urban properties. Unique characteristics define *differentiable* goods whose prices are related not only to their production costs, as is the case in normal goods, but also to consumers' valuations of their intrinsically different characteristics. To bring these values into the market, an auction process reveals consumers' values as willingness to pay.

The auction approach considers urban locations as differentiable. What makes urban properties intrinsically differentiable is their location, that is, their relative location with respect to all the city's activities, because it affects the opportunities for economic and social interactions, which we identify as accessibility. The location also provides access to natural amenities in the neighborhood, as well as to built environments, which differ at each location and which cannot be reproduced at will. More precisely, what is traded at an auction is the right to enjoy the benefits of the accessibility that the location offers, by either buying or renting the site. Once this right is traded, the access to these opportunities is transferred to the new owner or user. Of course, building characteristics also induce differences between properties, such as the number of rooms, lot size, etc., but they are not considered to be intrinsic because they can be produced and replicated at a cost.

A corollary, that what is traded in the LU market, is the value of the right to use the opportunities provided by a location, which is represented per time unit as the renting value or as the selling price of the property that grants the right to permanent use. In modeling the LU market, it is convenient to consider the rent value of a property rather than the selling price because it is consistent with the unit of the income constraint, i.e., per unit of time of income and consumption.

The behavior of a consumer in a market with several simultaneous location auctions must comply with one condition: bids for alternative locations should be defined in such a way that they ensure that the consumer attains the highest utility. To analyze this process, we must define how consumers build their willingness to pay.

The Willingness to Pay

We recall the indirect utility in Eq. (3.3). Following Solow (1973) and Rosen (1974), we define the willingness to pay as the solution of the following expression: $u_h = v_h(y_h - w_{hi}, z_i)$, where the location price is replaced by the willingness to pay w_{hi} in Eq. (3.3).

Here, we introduce a fundamental condition in LU: *we assume u_h to be equal for all locations*, i.e., consumers define the willingness to pay at each alternative location to be indifferent about locating at any of them. This assumption is fundamental because it assures that the consumer is indifferent to winning the auction of any location if the price is equal to the willingness to pay.

The indifference utility is called the *reservation utility*, representing the utility the consumer expects to attain ex ante entering the auction. Then, if the utility function is invertible in w, from Eq. (3.3) we obtain:

$$w_{hi}(z; u_h) = y_h - v_h^{-1}(z_i; u_h), \ \forall i \in VI \tag{3.5}$$

How can we interpret these functions?

The willingness-to-pay function of Eq. (3.5) represents a family of iso-utility willingness-to-pay functions. To illustrate this concept, in Fig. 3.2 we observe a family of willingness-to-pay functions in a monocentric city as a function of the distance to the CBD, $w(d,u)$, one for each utility reference: u_1, u_2, and u_3. In this idealized city,

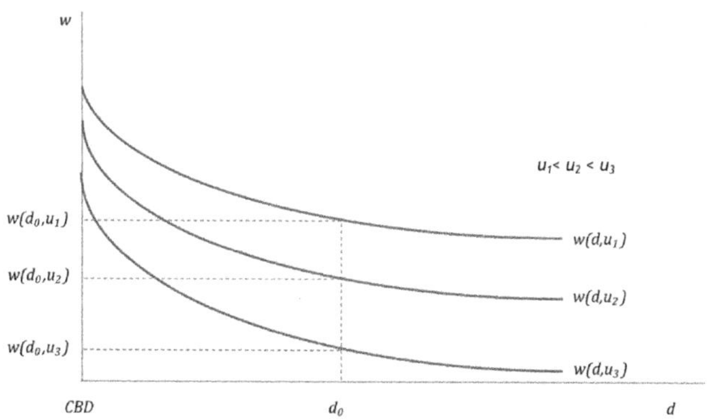

Figure 3.2 Willingness-to-pay curves in a monocentric city.

all location attributes are assumed to be homogeneous, except for the continuous locations defined by distance d to the CBD. At the CBD, the willingness to pay is at the maximum and decreases with distance because the travel costs to the jobs in the CBD increase with the sole attribute distance. In this figure, iso-utility willingness-to-pay curves are shown for utilities $u_1 < u_2 < u_3$. To determine which utility is the highest, observe that at distance d_0, the location yields a given utility that is complemented by the utility obtained from different amounts of the consumption of goods, given by $x = y - w(d_0, u)$, where $w(d_0, u)$ is shown on the vertical axis, which implies that $x(u_1) < x(u_2) < x(u_3)$. Then, if the location yields the same utility, and consumption is lower for u_1 than for u_3, this implies that $u_1 < u_2 < u_3$. Notably, consumers cannot identify their own willingness to pay without defining a reservation utility, and this reference value makes them indifferent to the set of location alternatives if they pay the value defined by the associated willingness to pay.

Observations include the following:

- To obtain the willingness to pay in Eq. (3.5), we have assumed that utilities are invertible in prices, that consumers demand only one residence, and that they have no intertemporal savings. Additionally, if utility is assumed to be quasi-linear, then willingness to pay is separable in the utility: $w_{hi}(z; u) = y_h - \lambda_h^{-1} u_h + f(z_i)$, with λ_h the consumer's marginal utility of income, which is a useful form for developing computable models.
- Considering the budget constraint in Eq. (3.2), then $w_{hi}(u) = y_h - p_x x$ must hold. Now we replace $w_{hi}(z; u)$ in Eq. (3.5) to conclude that $v_h^{-1}(z_i; u_h) = p_x x$ is the expenditure on all consumption goods conditional on the location option and the reservation utility level.
- Willingness to pay is a decreasing function on the reservation utility level u_h, as shown in Fig. 3.3, i.e., $\partial w / \partial u < 0$. This is because given the residential location (identified as d_0 in Fig. 3.3), a higher utility u_3 can be obtained only from a higher consumption of goods (x_3), at the cost of higher expenditure on goods and lesser expenditure on the residential location for the income constraint to hold, i.e., a lower willingness to pay.
- Although the household's income increases the willingness to pay, it is not true that the highest bidder will always be the wealthiest householder because the second term in Eq. (3.5) may strongly reduce the willingness to pay of the wealthiest bidder in locations with certain undesirable attributes, e.g., a neighborhood of poor quality or low accessibility.

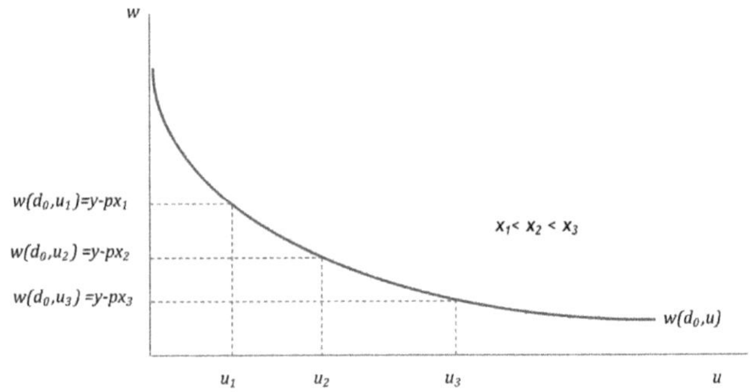

Figure 3.3 Willingness to pay decreasing with utility.

- Income is capitalized into land rents through willingness to pay in auctions, as defined in Eq. (3.5). This is calculated by $\frac{\partial w_{hi}}{\partial y} = 1 - \frac{\partial v_h^{-1}}{\partial u_h} \frac{\partial u_h}{\partial y_h}$, which combines a direct transfer minus an indirect utility effect through the impact of income on the expenditures on other goods. The direct effect (first term) transfers a change in income into willingness to pay, which is a consequence of the inelastic demand assumption of the static model Eq. (3.2), where there is no intertemporal savings; if such savings were incorporated, it would introduce a trade-off between saving resources for the future and expending income on goods and locations in the present; this effect is not included in Eq. (3.5). The indirect effect (second term) is positive because other goods are assumed to be normal, and therefore consumption increases with income. The combined effect is that the capitalization of income into land rents is only partial, splitting new income into location and consumption of other goods.

The Auction Allocation Process

Let us now briefly examine the auction, that is, the process that determines the "highest bidder" at a given location and defines prices. Attributed to Vickery (1961), the well-known "second-price" auction considers that bidders submit sealed bids for a single item which is sold to the highest bidder *but at the price of the second highest bid*; this auction protocol assures that at the chosen price, the item is demanded by only one consumer, which is the highest bidder, where the highest bidder only pays the minimum necessary to outbid others. The rationale of the second-price auction is to induce bidders to reveal their true value of the good because they are confident that they will pay a price that at least one other bidder is willing to pay, which eliminates the risk of excessive payment. For example, consider A submits a bid equal to 100 for a single item and B a bid equal to 90; the second-price protocol assigns the item to A at the price of 90 (or marginally higher, say 91) because B is outbid by A, who is the only consumer demanding the item at this price. This protocol yields approximately the same results as an auction without submitting bids: an auction initiates at a low price, say 50, increasing until there is only one bidder left; in the example, B will exit at the value of 90 and A wins the auction at any value slightly higher. These auction protocols are relevant for trading single items, i.e., for differentiated goods where only one consumer can buy the item; thus, bids increase up to the value where there is only one bidder. A property of the second-price auction is that it yields the smallest price equilibrium because for any lower price there is more than one bidder.

The generalization to multidifferentiated items is described by Demange et al. (1986), where each bidder is interested in acquiring at most one item, which is the case in residential real estate auctions. The auctioneer announces a price vector and each bidder calculates its surplus as the difference between its willingness to pay and the price; this assumes that consumers define ex ante arbitrary reservation utilities. The items with the highest surplus are included in the bidders' demand set, which is announced in the auction. A price vector yields equilibrium if *every bidder can be assigned an item in its demand set and no two bidders are assigned the same object.* Demange et al. note that the model always has an equilibrium and there is a unique price vector that is the smallest in the strong sense (is at least as small in every component as any other equilibrium price), i.e., is the best price vector from the bidders' point of view.

The authors also proposed a progressive auction mechanism that approximately yields the equilibrium allocation. In the case of multiple real estate auctions, the process is initiated at a set of low prices for units, e.g., prices equal to zero, and each bidder announces which locations are in its demand set, i.e., the set of items that yields the bidder the highest surplus. In the next step, the auctioneer increases the price of locations with excess demand and announces a new price vector. The procedure stops when each item has only one demanding bidder and each bidder is allocated to only one item.

If the number of items is larger or equal to the number of bidders, the mechanism has a solution which renders a minimum price equilibrium, i.e., the lowest equilibrium price or the best price for consumers. The progressive mechanism does not require that bidders announce their willingness to pay, i.e., their true value remains private. The mechanism is explained with an example in Technical Note 3.1, where it is easy to observe that the equilibrium prices $p^* = \left(\{p_i^*\}, \forall i \in VI\right)$ yielded by the solution of Demange et al.'s mechanism can be equivalently expressed by the vectors of ex post utilities $u^* = \left(\{u_h^*\}, \forall h \in C\right)$ because for the solution allocation the following holds: $p_i^* = w_{hi}\left(u_h^*\right)$ and $u_h^* = w_{hi}^{-1}\left(p_i^*\right)$.

Can we assume that the willingness to pay is the bid that the agent presents in the auction?

This question seems to imply that speculative behavior is ignored if the answer is yes because if consumers speculate, one could think that bidders will speculate presenting bids below the true willingness to pay. To analyze this issue, we assume that, ex ante entering the auction, bidders define their reservation utilities, evaluate the attributes of the specific real estate, and then define their willingness to pay for each available location Eq. (3.5). Additionally, we assume that bidders consider all the information available, such as the auction protocol and the number of bidders at the auction (the market thickness) (see McAfee and McMillan, 1987).

In this context, consider that an agent bids lower than the true willingness to pay that would yield u_h, which implies a speculative behavior to increase utility up to $u_h^{'} > u_h$, such that the speculative bid equals a lower willingness to pay $w_{hi}\left(z; u_h^{'}\right) < w_{hi}(z; u_h)$. This means that speculation behavior is equivalent to define a high reservation utility. Therefore, in our model, any speculative behavior is correctly represented by the reservation utility used to define willingness to pay and bids represent the consumer monetary value of the speculative reservation utility. Moreover, we can say that *speculation is a rational behavior in auctions* because it seeks to define the highest reservation utility.

How does a rational agent define the ex ante utility in multiple real estate auctions?

Assuming that these auctions are simultaneous and noting that ex ante the bidder ignores the price of the location and its value for other bidders, i.e., the bidder cannot compute ex ante the surplus of each alternative, the rational behavior is to pursue the following strategy: *define a common reservation utility across all auctions*, i.e., $u_{hi} = u_h, \ \forall i \in VI$. This strategy guarantees that despite the location won at the auctions, and despite the price paid, the consumer obtains the reservation utility. To observe the rationality of this strategy, consider the following cases: (1) if the bidder wins several auctions, then all belong to the demand set (maximum surplus) and any one can be chosen randomly because they are indifferent to the bidder or (2) if no auction is won, then it means that other agents had bid higher in all auctions and the auction price renders the agent a utility lower than the reservation utility; in this case, the bidder would have to reduce the reservation utility to win an auction.

How do households define reservation utility?

Because utility is theoretically unbounded, the rational agent would like to define a very high reservation utility, but this yields a very low willingness to pay that is unlikely to outbid other bidders. The solution in this case is that some bidders exit the market; indeed, losing all auctions is an acceptable outcome in the majority of cases.

However, if consumers are obliged to win an auction, then they will have to adjust their utility level downward to be able to win one auction. In this case, the ex ante utility does not affect the allocation solution because it is invariant to an additive constant of the consumer utility. Moreover, the equilibrium consumer's surplus may be positive or negative because it only represents the difference between the ex post utility and an arbitrary ex ante utility (see Technical Note 3.1).

Consider the set of household bidders at location i, denoted by B_i, to define the auction winner at location i, denoted by h_i^*, as follows:

$$h_i^* = \operatorname{argmax}_{h \in B_i}\{w_h(z_i; u_h)\} \tag{3.6}$$

The Hedonic Price

The auction defines not only which agent is the winner but also the location price (p_i) as the value of the highest bid:

$$p_i = \max_{h \in B_i}\{w_h(z_i; u_h)\} \tag{3.7}$$

This price reveals the opportunity value of the auction winner, who can obtain the highest economic benefit from the location; more precisely, this is the value of the right to use the location by purchasing or renting the real estate unit. Because the building costs of real estate do not vary significantly across the city, this price function embeds the consumers' value of land at different locations, i.e., the value of the right to benefit from the set of location amenities.

The price Eq. (3.7) represents a *hedonic price function* as defined by Rosen (1974) and Ellickson (1981) because prices are built from the consumers' valuation of the set of amenities z_i of the real estate. As noted by these authors, the hedonic price of attributes, given by $\frac{dp}{dz_k}$, reveals the intrinsic or hedonic value of the amenity z_k for the population, which is helpful and frequently used to estimate the value of intangibles such as air pollution, congestion, and neighborhood quality. Notably, Eq. (3.7) states that hedonic price functions are theoretically derived from the consumers' willingness-to-pay functions, and therefore from their utility functions. Hence, because utility functional forms are restricted, theoretically acceptable hedonic price functions are also restricted. Also note that a consistent hedonic price model should be dependent not only on attributes, as is usually the case, but also on the utility level attained at equilibrium, as was noted by Rosen (1974) and Wheaton (1977).

Firms' Location Problem

The behavior of firms in the land and property markets can be described as essentially similar to that of households, in that they enter the market with a willingness to pay with which they compete in land and real estate auctions, adjusting their bids to obtain a location in the city. However, there are very important differences in how the willingness to pay is built by the firm and in how their choices affect city structures, a phenomenon associated with agglomeration economies.

We define a firm as a complex organization with the common goal of seeking profit maximization. Regarding this goal, it is plausible to represent the firm's behavior by an agent, although recognizing that the organization follows a complex internal decision-making process. One difference between a firm and a residential location is that a firm may be distributed over several locations or establishments, which implies a multilocation decision problem. Such a problem can be considered in the static auction framework assuming the firm's profit as a multilocation profit problem, where the profit of one establishment depends on the location of the other firm's branches; this dependency is transferred to the corresponding willingness to pay. Here, however, we consider the case of a single location, which can represent the dynamic location of establishments, where the profit of adding a single new location is calculated given the establishments already owned and in operation.

The Firm Continuous Location Model

The single establishment location is analyzed in the urban economic literature where the impact of the firm's location choice in the urban structure, i.e., the formation of subcenters or hot spots, is emphasized because they determine the evolution from a monocentric to a polycentric city. This follows from the assumption that residents demand products from and provide labor to the most convenient firm regarding wages, prices, and travel cost differentials. Therefore, firms choose a location where such differentials yield the highest profit after discounting labor and land rent cost differentials.

In the study of Fujita and Ogawa (1982), the firms are homogeneous and their profit is defined by the "location potential" minus labor and land costs, where this potential describes the attraction of homogeneous consumers distributed in the city according to their travel costs. The authors establish certain conditions for the polycentric configuration, i.e., essentially when transportation costs become too large for commuting to the CBD. In this model, transportation costs ignore congestion because travel time increases only by the distance travelled by consumers. Similarly, Krugman (1996) defines the "market potential," including positive or negative effects due to business concentration, which decays with distance, and predicts a linear increase in subcenters within the city limits. Barthelemy (2016, p. 65) observes that these models do not predict the nonlinear scaling of subcenters with population observed in cities worldwide. He introduces congestion and simplifies the complex wages formation by assuming stochastic wages. He assumes that residents are labor providers who commute to locations where they maximize benefits defined as wage minus travel costs, and the firms emerge following the commuters' pattern.

These models provide interesting insights into understanding the basic elements of the location pattern of firms, but they simplify the complexity of a real urban system. They assume homogeneous agents, both firms and residents, simplistic and homogeneous transportation systems, and simplify or ignore agents' interactions other than labor. Although such extensions are difficult in a continuous space model, we observe that they can be integrated in the discrete framework.

The Firm Discrete Location Model

In this section, we consider the firms' location problem of a single establishment maximizing profit, with profit defined as income minus costs. Income depends on the firms' product prices and the demand for these products, which are both potentially dependent on the location, although in urban contexts the spatial price variability is limited. Demand varies in the spatial context according to consumers' attraction to each location and can be estimated from travel demand models, i.e., depending on consumers' benefit minus the travel costs. As we discussed in Chapter 2, this benefit not only considers the consumption of the firm's products and services but also includes the opportunities that the specific location provides to the visitors, what we termed location externalities at the destination, that depend on the density of the location.

The production cost depends on the transportation costs of input and output deliveries, which are variable depending on the location, wage profile, and the real estate or land price of the location.

We define the profit function of a firm indexed by f with input and output prices independent of the location, which is a plausible assumption in a competitive urban market. The demand for the firms' products and services depends on the relative accessibility of the firms' location to the consumers, represented as an attribute of the profit function. A firm's access to labor depends on the location of the residents and their transportation costs (including time and fare), which is also a measure of the accessibility of the firm's location to the residents. Additionally, economies of agglomeration are represented by the dependence of a firm's profit on the location of other firms, which can be a positive pull force (agglomeration economies) or a negative push force (spatial competition). In any case, economies of agglomeration are mathematically equivalent to the location externalities in the households' utility, although the functional dependency may be different and specific to the firm's industry. In this chapter, we synthesize push and pull forces as accessibility and attractiveness measures or attributes in the firms' profit function; in Chapter 7, we will discuss a more detailed model of the interaction among firms, consumers, and workers.

As urban economists have noted, an important feature of the firms' location process is the emergence of "hot spots," which are locations that emerge as subcenters in which firms agglomerate. A subcenter location emerges and is differentiated from previous production or service centers such as the CBD when the profit of a new location, built out of accessibility and attractiveness measures of benefits and costs, equals the profit attained at the previous center. That is, the new center location produces benefits from better accessibility that compensate for larger agglomeration benefits in previous center(s). Hence, "hot spots" are locations where accessibility and location externalities generate relatively higher profits. Nevertheless, when predicting the emergence of subcenters, it is crucial that accessibility functions are defined specifically for the firm's industry, so that the conditions for the emergence of "hot spots" in each industry can be captured.

We define the firm's profit as $\pi_{fi}(z_i, w_i, p_i)$, representing the monetary profit per unit of time; z_i is the set of attributes of the location relevant for the firm's profit, including accessibility, attractiveness, and agglomeration economies; w_i is the wage profile, with $\frac{\partial \pi}{\partial w_i} < 0$; and p_i is the real estate price per unit of time at location i, with $\frac{\partial \pi}{\partial p_i} < 0$. Note that this definition has complex interactions embedded in it: among firms as agglomeration (dis)economies; among household members and firms as consumers' potential demand, described by attractiveness measures by shopping transportation demand models; and among residents and firms as the attraction of commuters to work places. The discrete approach provides the flexibility of describing these attributes for each location differenced by the industry of the firms.

As in the residential case, by inverting the profit function in the location price, we obtain the firm's willingness to pay depending on the location and a nonnegative level of profit:

$$\begin{aligned} w_{fi} &= \pi^{-1}(z_i, \pi_f), \ \ \forall i \in I \\ &\text{s.t. } \pi_f \geq 0 \end{aligned} \tag{3.8}$$

where π_f is assumed to be the same for all the alternative locations because, similar to the reservation utility in the residential model, indifference bids are assured and $\frac{\partial w}{\partial \pi} < 0$. The firm's behavior is to maximize total profit in the auction, which implies that it follows the process of adjusting the π_f to locate in the city or exits the real estate market.

We can observe a general similarity between the behavior of households and firms in their willingness-to-pay functions depending on a utility (or profit) level and on a set of location attributes (plus a set of prices of goods not explicit in Eqs 3.5 and 3.8). The relevant differences occur when implementing the model: in the set of location attributes associated with each specific agent's utility/profit; the specific definition of access, both accessibility and attractiveness; the set of relevant prices of goods (if included); and, of course, the functional forms. These functions are likely to be nonlinear to make the prediction of spatial agglomeration and location externalities of activities feasible. In the case of firms, the behavior depends on the market structure of the specific firm's industry. In the simplest case, the market is fully competitive with numerous players, whereas in other cases, the industry may have more complex behavior, for example, in the case of an oligopoly (a small number of firms with a large majority of market share).

3.3 The Bid-Choice Equivalence

With the willingness-to-pay functions defined for households and firms, we then model a set C of generic agents, where specific willingness-to-pay functions differentiate between the behavior of different households and firms.

Although the utility—or choice—and the bid-auction approaches are both rooted in the same microeconomic framework, they have evident differences: in the choice approach, location prices are assumed to be defined exogenously by the market, and agents are considered as price takers with apparently no direct effect on land values. Conversely, in the bid-auction approach, they emerge from an auction in which agents' willingness to pay defines the price. Additionally, in the choice approach, agents search in the space of available location choices, whereas in the bid-auction approach, it is the supplier who searches the space of the set of bidders to select the highest bidder. These fundamental differences produce a dilemma concerning which approach to follow, raising the question of whether the results in terms of the allocation of agents and location prices are different (for a discussion of this issue, see Anas, 1982).

However, we observe that this dilemma vanishes and these approaches can be understood as a double-matching problem under the *bid-choice equivalence*. For a conceptual analysis, note that in the bid-auction approach, the reservation utilities of bids are all equal across alternative locations; thus, all auctions are linked at any point in time, i.e., adjustments to these utilities in one auction imply the same adjustment in all other auctions. In the choice approach, prices are adjusted, and then all simultaneous trades are linked by the perceived utility of agents who are sensitive to prices. If one price changes, the utility attained at that location decreases, and the demand is affected. Hence, prices in the choice approach and reservation utilities in the bid-auction approach represent dual variables that make market-clearing conditions hold.

To demonstrate that the two approaches are equivalent, Martínez (1992) redefined the utility maximization process into an equivalent consumer surplus maximization process, which allows us to compare these approaches based on the same monetary dimension for prices and willingness to pay.

To define consumer surplus at a given location, consider the level for the reservation utility $\overline{u}_h$, e.g., the utility obtained at the current residence location *ex ante* entering the LU market or any other theoretical value. The difference in the consumer surplus between the reservation utility $\overline{u}_h$ and the utility at any optional location choice u_{hi} can be measured by the *compensating variation*, i.e., the change in income that would be equivalent to a change in prices making the consumer indifferent to the price change (Mas-Colell et al., 1995). This measure of consumer surplus can be proven to be the difference between the willingness to pay and the price paid for a location (see Technical Note 3.2):

$$cs_{hi} = w_h(z_i; \overline{u}_h) - p_i \tag{3.9}$$

Thus, the consumer surplus is positive if the price paid is lower than the willingness to pay, i.e., the price paid yields a higher utility than the reservation value $\overline{u}_h$. Note that in Eq. (3.9), the consumer surplus is conditional on the reservation utility, i.e., if positive, it represents the monetary benefit measuring the location utility above the reservation utility.

Then, the maximum utility problem is equivalent to selecting the location that yields the maximum consumer surplus to the agent:

$$i_h^* = \text{argmax}_{i \in I}\{cs_{hi} = w_h(z_i; \bar{u}_h) - p_i\} \tag{3.10}$$

If we now assume that the location price emerges from the auction, with willingness to pay defined at the reservation utilities, then:

$$p_i = \max_{h \in B_i \subset C}\{w_h(z_i; \bar{u}_h)\} \tag{3.11}$$

Replace the price of Eq. (3.11) in Eq. (3.10) to obtain the *bid-choice equation*:

$$i_h^* = \text{argmax}_{i \in I}\{cs_{hi} = w_h(z_i; \bar{u}_h) - \max_{g \in B_i \subset C}\{w_g(z_i; \bar{u}_g)\}\}, \ \forall h \in C \tag{3.12}$$

where the set of bidders $B_i \subset C$ may be defined according to the type of location: residential, office, mixed, industrial, etc.

Let us examine this equation. The equation represents a double search process in different sets by different agents: the inner process is the bid auction, in which the auctioneer searches in the set of bidders $B_i \subset C$ for the highest bidder at a given location, which defines who obtains the location and the price paid by the winner of the auction. The outer process is the utility approach, in which the agents search in the set of available locations for their best option, conditional on the price emerging from the auctions.

The bid-choice equation implies that the maximum surplus is zero. To observe this, notice that agent h's willingness to pay is both in the outer and in the inner search processes because the consumer is a bidder, i.e., $h \in B_i$. We consider two possible outcomes of the auction. First, if consumer h is the highest bidder at a given location, then the two terms in the bid-choice equation are equal, the agent's surplus is zero, and the agent can locate at i. Conversely, in the second case, if the agent is outbid, then the price is higher than the agent's willingness to pay, the surplus is negative, and someone else is allocated the location. If the surplus is negative in all auctions, the agent exits the market.

However, notice also that reservation utilities ($\bar{u}_h$) do not comply with any requisite, i.e., the agent may take any value to enter the market. Then, the agent may set $\bar{u}_h$ too high (w_h too low) and fail in all auctions, exiting the market with no location; alternatively, the agent may reduce $\bar{u}_h$ (increase w_h) until it wins an auction. Conversely, $\bar{u}_h$ may be set too low (w_h too high) so the agent outbids other bidders in several locations, which induces it to increase $\bar{u}_h$ (reduce w_h) until it wins in one auction only. In the event, the agent wins in more than one option and cannot locate at a higher utility, then it randomly chooses among them because they are indifferent for that agent. Although the reservation utility is freely set by the consumer, there is an equilibrium utility level that is set by the market conditions that is exogenous for the consumer. We observe these equilibrium conditions in the following section.

The null surplus result applies under the assumption that the agent has no private information (not shared by other bidders) regarding any location or other bidders' preferences and bids. If the agent had private information about a location i_0, it would be equivalent to observing a positive or negative attribute not observed by others, which would make the agent adjust its reservation utilities everywhere, by $\overline{u}_h + \tau_{hi_0}$, with τ_{hi_0} the value of the private information, and adjust the bids correspondingly. Once this adjustment is made, the bid-auction model applies.

An important merit of the bid choice Eq. (3.12) is that it represents the double-matching process and the equivalence between the utility and the bid-auction approaches. Indeed, the result of the bid-auction based on the best bidder rule is precisely the same location where the consumer maximizes surplus, i.e., maximizes utility. The requisite for this equivalence to hold is that the trade process of the location market is the auction.

3.4 Suppliers' Behavior

The earlier sections assume that the real estate supply is exogenous. Although this assumption is helpful in analyzing the market in the short run, in the long run we must model the way in which suppliers generate real estate units, as shown in Fig. 3.1.

We first consider the simpler case of the *new stock market*, where the entire supply is developed from empty agricultural land by a single agent called a developer. This market setting is studied in the urban economic literature, which we first revise and then reformulate in a discrete setting. Then, we extend the model framework to an analysis of the *real estate market*, where we consider the redevelopment of old stock.

The Continuous Supply Model

The real estate supply problem, as formulated in urban economics, is described by Brueckner (1987). He considers the joint *real estate-land developer problem*, i.e., who buys empty and continuous (nonparceled) agricultural land, where homogeneous developers decide what type of real estate they should produce to maximize profit. He assumes that the supply market is competitive, achieving zero profit in the long run. In this context, building production is characterized by two inputs: capital (K) and land size (L), whose ratio K/L is the building's structural density (S) that defines the height of the building. Thus, the model has the merit of predicting the floor density at every location at equilibrium. Additionally, it shows that land rents and building heights decrease with distance from the city center when prices follow the Alonso–Muth–Mills' monocentric city model.

This model assumes a production function of floor space given by $H(K; L)$, with $\frac{\partial H}{\partial K} > 0$ and $\frac{\partial^2 H}{\partial K^2} < 0$. Then, the supplier's profit function at any location x is given by the income minus building and land costs:

$$\pi(x, K, L) = \overline{p}(x)H(K, L) - \kappa K - \overline{r}(x)L \tag{3.13}$$

with x the continuous spatial variable, e.g., defined as the distance to the CBD, $\overline{p}(x)$ the selling price per unit of floor space, and $\overline{r}(x)$ the rent per unit of land. The capital cost κ is assumed to be constant in the city. Considering constant building returns to scale, i.e., $H(\lambda K, \lambda L) = \lambda H(K, L)$, we can conveniently take $\lambda = 1/L$ to write $H\left(\frac{K}{L}, 1\right) = \frac{1}{L}H(K, L)$, which yields:

$$\pi(x, s) = L(\overline{p}(x)h(S) - \kappa S - \overline{r}(x)) \tag{3.14}$$

with $S = K/L$ and $h(S) = H(S,1)$ the floor space built per land unit. Observe that $\frac{\partial h}{\partial S} = H'(S, 1) > 0$ and $\frac{\partial^2 h}{\partial S^2} = H''(S, 1) < 0$.

The optimal conditions at every location are as follows:

1. Suppliers choose S to maximize profit:

$$\overline{p}h'(S) = \kappa \tag{3.15}$$

2. The profit is null:

$$\overline{p}h(S) - \kappa S = \overline{r}(x) \tag{3.16}$$

These two equations determine the optimal S and $\overline{r}$, conditional on the location x, on κ, and on the variables of the demand problem embedded in the price $\overline{p}$, i.e., on willingness-to-pay attributes.

Further insights are obtained by the author deriving these conditions with respect to the arguments of the price function, i.e., the arguments of the demand, e.g., from (1): $\overline{p}'h' + \overline{p}h''S' = 0$, yields:

$$S' = -\frac{h'}{h''\overline{p}}\overline{p}' \tag{3.17}$$

because $h'' < 0$, it follows that the $sign(S') = sign(p')$. From (2): $(\overline{p}'h' - \kappa)\cdot S' + \overline{p}' \cdot h = \overline{r}'$ and replacing Eq. (3.15) yields:

$$\overline{r}' = h\overline{p}' \tag{3.18}$$

Therefore, because $h > 0$, then $sign(\overline{r}') = sign(S') = sign(\overline{p})$. Moreover, in the case of the monocentric city where $\frac{\partial \overline{p}}{\partial x} < 0$, it follows that $\frac{\partial \overline{r}}{\partial x} < 0$ and $\frac{\partial S}{\partial x} < 0$. This is a fundamental result of this model because it explains the general real world observation that real estate prices, land prices, and building heights decrease with distance from the city center.

The last result (Eq. 3.18) is worth commenting on because it defines the suppliers' willingness to pay for the land input $(\overline{r})$ as a function of the floor space to be built (S)

and the real estate, or output price ($\overline{p}$), i.e., the land and the floor space markets are linked by the technical production function $h(S)$. As shown in Eqs (3.17) and (3.18), this link indicates that the shapes of land rents and building heights are caused by the decreasing slope of prices, i.e., by p' decreasing from the CBD, which is the fundamental result of the Alonso–Muth–Mills' model. Thus, consumers' willingness to pay for land and travel costs governs the city's landscape in this monocentric model.

The Discrete Model of Durable Stock

We now extend Brueckner's model to the *real estate market*, considering a discrete land context where land is partitioned. We also recognize that real estate is a durable good, in contrast to a consumption good, and that the land input may have been built previously and is taken for redevelopment. For this case, it is convenient to expand the notation indexing for supply units, making an explicit index for real estate type v and expanding index $i \in VI$ to vi ($i \in I$, $v \in V$).

Let us define building type v described by the triplet $\left(n_v, q_v^f, q_v^l\right)$, where n_v is the number of homogeneous housing units (house: $n_v = 1$; apartments: $n_v > 1$), q_v^f is the floor space of each unit in the building, and q_v^l is the land footprint of the building. In this case, developers of new buildings use developed land lots of different sizes indexed by $w \in W$, including empty land lots and old real estate stock, to build new real estate properties denoted by $v \in V$. Note that because the land lot is reused, then $q_v^l = q_w^l$. In this case, we define the capital as $K_v = \gamma_v n_v q_v^f$, with γ_v the capital input per unit of floor space, and $L = q_w^l$. The new building structural density conditional on the redeveloped land lot size is $S_{v/w} = \gamma_v n_v \frac{q_v^f}{q_w^l}$, which measures the number of floors of the building. Then, the constant returns production function implies that $H\left(\gamma_v n_v q_v^f, q_w^l\right) = H\left(\frac{\gamma_v n_v q_v^f}{q_w^l}, 1\right) = q_w^l h\left(S_{v/w}\right)$. Additionally, consider the capital cost of demolition given by $\kappa d n_w q_w^f = \kappa d S_w q_w^l$, with d the demolition cost per floor space unit.

The supplier's profit on a building project, conditional on converting building w into v, is

$$\pi_{vi/w} = \overline{p}_{vi} q_w^l h\left(S_{v/w}\right) - \kappa K_v - \overline{r}_{wi} q_w^l - \kappa d S_w q_w^l$$

or

$$\pi_{vi/w} = q_w^l \left(\overline{p}_{vi} h\left(S_{v/w}\right) - \kappa\left(S_{v/w} + dS_w\right) - \overline{r}_{wi}\right) \tag{3.19}$$

Development from empty land lots is represented by assuming a specific old stock characterized by $\left(n_w, q_w^f, q_w^l\right) = \left(0, 0, q_w^l\right)$, i.e., the input is empty land previously divided into land lots.

Observe that Eq. (3.19) introduces a dynamic process of the building stock of cities. Conditional on the land lot size and location, the supplier will maximize profit by choosing land with the least demolition cost, i.e., houses and small buildings are likely to be preferred for redevelopment.

The optimal condition Eq. (3.15) holds for discrete values, i.e., $\overline{p}_{vi}h'_{vw} = \kappa$ applies for each $w \rightarrow v$ redevelopment, which enables the optimal building type conditional on the old-stock land input (w) to be identified at each location: $S^*_{v/wi} = \frac{\left(n_v q^f_v\right)^*}{q^l_w}$. Note that the optimal structural density leaves the supplier with one degree of freedom to decide between the number of dwellings (n_v) and the size of them $\left(q^f_v\right)$, which is a consequence of the constant return assumption per floor space unit; the profit is invariant to changes in the number and size of dwellings if the total floor space remains unchanged. Moreover, Eq. (3.17) also holds.

The null profit condition yields the maximum rent value per land unit that the supplier is willing to bid for real estate indexed as wi, denoted by $\overline{w}_{wi}$, given by:

$$\overline{w}_{wi} \equiv \overline{r}_{wi} = \overline{p}_{vi}h\left(S^*_{v/w}\right) - \kappa\left(S^*_{v/w} - dS_w\right) \tag{3.20}$$

Additionally, totally differentiating the willingness to pay with respect to the arguments of $\overline{p}_{vi}$ and using $\overline{p}_{vi}h'_{vw} - \kappa = 0$, yields:

$$\overline{w}'_{wi} = \overline{p}'_{vi}h_{vw}\left(S^*_{v/w}\right) \tag{3.21}$$

This result reproduces Eq. (3.18) for a discrete set of values of the h-function and links the willingness to pay for land with real estate prices through a factor $h_{vw}\left(S^*_{v/w}\right)$, indicating the most profitable use of the land. Note that this function is applied to the feasible set $w \in W$ to build a building of type v, including new developed land into empty land lots and redeveloped land from old stock. The case of undeveloped agricultural land at the city's edge where the city sprawls requires a model of the *land lots developer* stage as proposed by Martínez and Roy (2004) and represented by the continuous land model.

The Unified Land–Real Estate Market

Notably, old stock unifies land and real estate markets because the set of prices is the same, despite the final use of the property for leasing or for redevelopment, i.e., $\overline{r}_{wi}q^l_w = p_{wi}$. Moreover, regarding the owners' three options, including resale, lease, or personal use, as shown in Fig. 3.1, their optimal choice is to allocate the property to the highest bidder (including the owner-user's value). Therefore, renting (r_{wi}) and property prices differ only in the annualizing factor, i.e., prices reflect the present value of the property rent (DiPasquale and Wheathon, 1996), and in the annual maintenance cost denoted m_v. Therefore, we conclude that the three prices are related by $p_{vi} = \overline{r}_{vi}q^l_v = (r_{vi} + m_v)\kappa^{-1}$, with κ the cost of capital or its interest rate. Because land, property, and leasing prices are all correlated, a fundamental conclusion follows: price differences for land are explained by the final users' willingness to pay for locations, and in addition to this price pattern, building and maintenance costs affect prices.

The Generalized Model

The supply model can be generalized to consider a less competitive and regulated market. Here, the supplier is assumed to be willing to sell or rent for a nonnegative profit, i.e., the limit is zero profit in a fully competitive real estate market. In a dynamic context, negative profit implies that the supplier exits the market and holds the real estate in stock for future auctions.

Additionally, planners establish regulations that limit the options of the supplier for developing new real estate stock. Regulations may be of very different types. Usually, they are specifically defined for each zone; they may regulate building types, e.g., floor space density per land unit, or at a more aggregate level, they may restrain the zone density.

Thus, consider the following problem:

$$\begin{aligned} &Max_{vi\in VI}\,\pi\,(p_{vi}-c_{vi}) \\ &\text{Subject to: } \pi(p_{vi}-c_{vi})\geq 0 \\ &\qquad vi\in R \end{aligned} \tag{3.22}$$

where nonnegative profit extends the competitive model and supply is restricted to comply with zoning regulations, denoted by the set R.

The optimization problem in Eq. (3.22) leads to different supply models depending on the cost function and the set of regulations. Building costs may exhibit economies of scale, i.e., $c_{vi}=c(S_v)\leq \kappa S_v$, with $\frac{dc}{dS}<0$. Another phenomenon concerns economies of scope, when cost decreases with the number of projects in a portfolio with different locations and building types, for example, because of shared costs of marketing.

Economies of scale in real estate developments would induce denser floor space per land unit compared with the constant returns assumption made earlier, and economies of scope would make the real estate industry concentrate on fewer firms, i.e., an oligopoly. However, these potential tendencies are mediated by other factors. The fact that locations and building options are differentiated dictates that suppliers have different specialized submarkets to operate: by zone, building type, or use type, which induce more firms to enter the market. Second, large-scale production implies an extensive amount of capital in stock, which is costly because production plus selling delays increase and are less predictable with the size of the stock. The literature reports evidence of significant economies of scale in the real estate investment market (Ambrose et al., 2005; Bers and Springer, 1997) and economies of scope in the brokerage service market (Zumpano and Elder, 1994). However, the influence of these types of economies is not directly observed in the building process of real estate but rather in the investment in real estate assets, which are likely to be dominated by the land capitalization of rents rather than scale economies associated with the cost function.

Zoning regulations are used by policy makers as a common tool in urban land markets, despite the extent to which the rest of the economy is deregulated. Regulations imply that policy makers foresee that making this market completely free does not guarantee a social optimum somehow defined. Issues such as access to land by all citizens, location externalities, and access to several public goods and services, such as transportation and parks, environmental issues, and congestion, are all common concerns of urban planners. These regulations are represented as constraints on the feasible supply $vi \in R$, with R the set of regulations. The impact of regulations on the allocation of agents and prices can be estimated with applied models, although one can predict that the more binding the regulation is, the higher its impact on land prices.

In summary, the cost function is dependent on land values and it is likely to be nonlinear with production size, with some level of economies of scale but also diseconomies of capital risk on long-term larger stocks. Profits are uncertain because they are subject to the *ex ante* forecasts of land prices.

3.5 Market Clearing[2]

The model of consumer behavior discussed earlier represents the process of how a set of agents assess location options and define their choices by evaluating their utility, which they compare with the location price to assess the surplus at each supplied location. They then choose maximizing surplus, i.e., maximizing utility. For this process to occur, agents are assumed to be perfectly informed about location prices and the attributes describing the quality of alternative locations.

The classical market-process-clearing condition of products is to adjust prices to clear the market, i.e., to match demand and supply; that is to say, equal items can be produced and supplied in any quantity for a price, and then the market adjusts the prices and the quantities consumed. This process is called Walras's equilibrium, and the essential role of the market is to distribute the information to all agents regarding the prices that clear the market. However, we have observed that real estate units are not such products in the sense that they are differentiated by their location; thus, they are sold in auctions to the highest bidder where the price is the result of the auction.

We described the auction process assuming that the consumer enters the auctions with an *ex ante* reservation utility equal for all auctions, setting bids for this utility by evaluating the willingness to pay at each location, and participates in all auctions simultaneously. The assumption of simultaneous participation defines a *static*

[2] The LU equilibrium problem is discussed in Chapter 5 for the stochastic LU model and extended to transportation and production markets in Chapters 6 and 7. In this section, we anticipate the more classical market-clearing problem of the LU market in the deterministic case.

equilibrium that assumes rational behavior under perfect information, i.e., the consumer gathers all information to compare options accurately and to select the best option.

We will now formalize the *static short-term equilibrium* for a given set of real estate auctions; the supply is exogenous. Consider the bid-auction process and define $\delta_{ih}^{*}=1$ if $i_h^{*}=\text{argmax}_{i\in I}\{cs_h^{*}=w_h(z_i;u_h^{*})-p_i^{*}\}$ and $\delta_{ih}^{*}=0$ otherwise, with $p_i^{*}=\max_{g\in B_i\subset C}\left\{w_g\left(z_i;u_g^{*}\right)\right\}$, $\forall i\in I$. Then, consider the following conditions:

1. The number of agents ($|C|$) demanding locations equals the number of locations supplied $|I|$:

$$\sum_{h\in C}1=\sum_{i\in I}1 \tag{3.23}$$

This condition is necessary for the existence of a static equilibrium and is independent of the allocation process.

2. Every bidder is allocated to one, and only one, location:

$$\sum_{i\in I}\delta_{ih}^{*}=1 \quad \forall h\in C \tag{3.24}$$

3. Every location is sold to one, and only one, bidder:

$$\sum_{h\in B_i}\delta_{ih}^{*}=1 \quad \forall i\in I \tag{3.25}$$

Note that one of the above conditions is redundant: if every location is sold (condition 3) and there are as many locations as bidders (condition 1), it is obvious that every bidder is allocated and condition 2 holds. Similarly, if every bidder is allocated to one, and only one, location (condition 2) and condition 1 holds, then all locations are sold and condition 3 holds.

The second condition implies that during the bargaining process, each agent should adjust its *ex ante* reservation utility to an ex post equilibrium utility $u^{*}=\left(u_h^{*},h\in C\right)$, such that at equilibrium only one agent is the maximum bidder and the price is the maximum bid. The adjustment mechanism yields equilibrium utilities that can be obtained by solving the equations' system in Eq. (3.24) for the set of agents' utilities. Eq. (3.24) has as many equations as bidders and the same number of unknown utilities. The solution may yield ambiguous (nonunique) solutions that should be solved by an absentee auctioneer, e.g., by random assignment: (1) multiple auctions won by one bidder; (2) multiple winners with the same bid at one location, which again is solved by the auctioneer by random assignment. The auctioneer assignment is indifferent for the agents: in case (1) because consumers are indifferent to any allocation, i.e., they yield the same equilibrium utility u^{*}; in case (2), suppliers are also indifferent because the price is the maximum bid which is equal among winners. Once u^{*} is calculated, despite the auctioneer assignment, real estate prices can be directly calculated as the highest bid at each location evaluated at the equilibrium utilities.

Notably, a specific set of bidders B_i is defined at each location; thus, auctions may be differentiated by the set of bidders, creating a potential segmentation of the LU market. Moreover, if regulations prevent certain bidders from occupying a specific real estate property, then they can be eliminated from set B_i; e.g., certain industries are forbidden in designated zones, which also segment the LU market. Second, observe that in Eq. (3.24), the equilibrium utilities are interdependent among all the bidders in the static equilibrium, i.e., all bidders participating in the set of auctions being held simultaneously. Additionally, because prices depend on the equilibrium utility through successful bids, equilibrium prices are also mutually dependent, as they should be in a market-clearing process.

The short-term static equilibrium considers that supply is developed in a dynamic process, i.e., prices are anticipated and residential units developed for future periods of time; hence, supply is exogenous at any point in time. In this case, however, condition 1 (Eq. 3.23) is less realistic because it requires that suppliers perfectly foresee the total number of agents demanding real estate units and the auction prices to produce the total supply distributed according to a maximum profit rule.

The static short-term equilibrium may also be defined in the case where condition 1 does not hold, i.e., total demand does not match total supply. This leads to two cases: excessive supply or excessive demand. In the case of excessive supply, suppliers exit the market following a rule such as nonnegative profit. In this case, agents may increase equilibrium utilities, inducing reduced prices and profits. The least profitable real estate units exit the market and the equilibrium is set when the number of remaining units equals the total demand. At the margin, the least profitable unit sold attains zero profit. In the case of excessive demand, consumers decrease their utilities seeking a scarce location, thus increasing the auction prices and the suppliers' profit, with some agents exiting the market because of binding income constraints; those who exit the market remain without a residence and their number equals the excessive demand. At the margin, the last bidder is the poorest among those winning an auction. Therefore, under excessive supply, prices are lower and bounded by a rule such as nonnegative profit, whereas under excessive demand, prices are upper bounded by residents' income.

It is convenient to discuss the effects of location externalities and agglomeration economies on urban locations at equilibrium. This phenomenon is represented by including an attribute of neighborhood quality depending on the neighbors, i.e., if neighbors are of certain ethnic or socioeconomic groups, or if there are nuisance commercial activities, etc. This implies that bidders will adjust their bids on a given location according to others being allocated to the neighborhood, which implies that one's bids depend on the bids of others, i.e., we should write $w_h(z_i(w); u_h)$, with $w = (w_{gi}, g \in C)$. The consequence of this mutual dependence on agents' behavior is that equilibrium is a highly complex process and the calculation of equilibrium utilities and prices requires sophisticated mathematical techniques. Conversely, the merit of this more complex model is that equilibrium can predict more interesting city structures, such as subcenters, socioeconomic segmentation of residents, and spatial clustering of industries.

Auctions are organized by an auctioneer (who may be absent), who establishes the auction rules. Once bidders are informed of these rules, the auction occurs with bargaining between consumers who seek a minimum price (maximum utility) and suppliers who seek the opposite, a maximum price. Different auction rules are suited to specific markets; in the land market, one rule is top-down, in which the auctioneer sets a high initial price and decreases it until a first bidder is willing to accept the price. Another rule is bottom-up, in which bidders offer bids until no one bids higher. The theoretical framework presented here applies for different auction rules that may be used in different countries because it affects the bidder set and information differentials between bidders, which are both exogenous in the model described.

3.6 Summary

In this chapter, the theoretical process of the allocation of agents to location options, i.e., real estate units or land lots, is described as the interaction of the agents of suppliers and consumers in an auction process. The process itself is performed by an (absent) auctioneer who follows a set of prescribed rules defined to maximize the price. Although this process ensures that suppliers obtain the highest price for each unit sold or rented, we have also shown that this process yields the maximum utility attainable in the market for the set of location options available to consumers.

Additionally, we have shown that the classical Walrasian equilibrium that sets prices to clear the market of differentiated goods, called the choice approach, is equivalent to the bid-auction equilibrium wherein consumers define bids (conditional on utilities), and the auction process establishes equilibrium utilities. This is called the bid-choice equivalence.

This chapter describes a static equilibrium model in a discrete spatial setting, which of course requires strong assumptions about the process, including the simultaneous auctions of available locations and full information on the attributes of alternative real estate units and on the bargaining process for the bidders. These ideal assumptions are necessary for equilibrium conditions to hold, which helps us to understand how the market yields prices and allocates consumers to locations in the city. More realistic models about the information and simultaneity of the auctions can be considered to define more applicable models, introducing, for example, random behavior of agents to model the lack of perfect information or defining a dynamic setting.

We have shown in this chapter that all agents behave in a similar way once their specific willingness to pay has been identified. This similarity is also reflected in the agents' willingness to pay, whether they are households or firms, because they depend on similar attributes: accessibility and attractiveness, location externalities, agglomeration economies, and land or real estate prices. Moreover, access measures essentially define special benefit differentials, either households' utilities or firms' profits. This allows us to conceive a generic consumer agent, carrying a profile of willingness-to-pay rules differentiated by their specific attributes and bid functions, and a real estate supplier agent carrying a profile of profit rules, which is enough to predict the distribution of equilibrium prices, utilities and profits, agglomeration clusters, and urban limits.

The theoretical model presented has been used to develop operational models that will be described in the following chapters, which requires an identification of more specific details of the agents' behavior and the auction process. These models extend the theory presented here, which holds for a utility concept limited to perfect information of the agents and the modeler regarding the agent's preferences and the quality of the alternative consumption sets. Additionally, for simplicity, the individual's behavior represented in this theory faces only one constraint: income for households and profit for firms.

To overcome certain limitations, the basic discrete and deterministic bid-auction model is extended in the following chapters assuming the random behavior of agents leading to probabilistic models. This approach generates continuous demand models that are more treatable for studying market equilibrium and its dynamics, policy analysis, and the replication of city dynamics.

Technical Note 3.1: The Auction Mechanism

The following Fig. T3.1 depicts an example of Demange et al. (1986) progressive mechanism. In this example, bidders, denoted by index $h = (A,B,C)$, define their values for locations, denoted as $i = (1,2,3)$, as shown in Fig. T3.1A and B. We denote such willingness-to-pay values as w_{hi}, which are kept private, i.e., unknown by the auctioneer and by other bidders.

Step 1: The auctioneer announces an initial price vector, in this case $p^1 = (0,0,0)$, and consumers calculate their surplus at each location for that vector, as shown in Fig. T3.1C. Then, consumers identify their demand, i.e., the location with the highest surplus, which is $d_h^1 = (3,1,3)$ and defines the demand for each location $d_i^1 = (1,0,2)$, indicating an excessive demand for location 3.

(A)

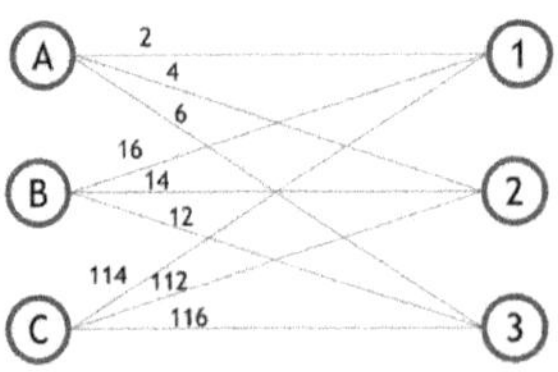

(B)

Bidder	Locations		
	1	2	3
A	2	4	6
B	16	14	12
C	114	112	116

(C)

Bidder	Locations			Demand by consumer
	1	2	3	
A	2	4	6	3
B	16	14	12	1
C	114	112	116	3
Price	0	0	0	
Demand by location	1	0	1	

(D)

Bidder	Locations			Demand by consumer	
	1	2	3		
A	2	4	4	2	3
B	16	14	10	1	
C	114	112	114	1	3
Price	0	0	2		
Demand by location	2	1	2		

Figure T3.1 Example of a real estate auction. (A) Consumers' bids. (B) Consumers' bids matrix. (C) First step: initial prices are announced. (D) Second step: price of location 3 is increased.

Step 2: The auctioneer increases the price of the overdemanded location 3, announcing $p^2 = (0,0,2)$, which produces the surpluses shown in Fig. T3.1D and the demands $d_h^2 = (\{2,3\},\ 1,\ \{1,3\})$. In this case, there is a feasible allocation assigning (2,1,3) because consumers with two items in their demand set are indifferent at prices p^2. Therefore, the auction finishes because consumers are allocated to only one unit in their demand set and no location has been assigned to more than one consumer.

This example is useful for making remarks regarding this auction procedure:

1. The highest bidder in all locations is *C*, and *A* is the lowest; in this auction, the price equilibrium is the lowest, even lower that consumer A's willingness to pay. Thus, prices are the best for consumers and the worst for sellers.
2. The auction proceeds through interdependent steps. Indeed, note that A demands location 3 in step 1 but demands locations 2 and 3 in step 2; the reader can observe that location 1 would enter in A's demand set at the price vector (0,2,4) and would include all units, i.e., (1,2,3). Then, as prices increase, bidders' demand sets change. Therefore, the assignment occurs simultaneously at the end of the auction.
3. The reader may apply the auction procedure for different vectors of initial prices, which represent the set of a seller's reservation prices.

We can use the example for a general observation.

1. Each consumer defines the willingness-to-pay values shown in Fig. T3.1B using its ex ante utility u_h^0, i.e., $w_{hi}(u_h^0)$, and the solution yields the set of consumer surplus $cs_{hi} = w_{hi}(u_h^0) - p_i,\ \forall i \in I$, as shown in Fig. T3.1D.
2. The equilibrium allocation maximizes consumer surpluses, with optimum values $cs_h^* = (4,\ 16,\ 114)$, and yields ex post utilities (u_h^*) attained given by solution prices $p_i^* = w_{hi}(u_h^*)$.
3. The solution, in prices, allocations, and surpluses, is invariant to a change in k_h in the consumer's ex ante utility, i.e., invariant to $u_h^0 + k_h$, if k_h is constant for all locations although different for consumers $(k_h \neq k_{h'})$.
4. A basic assumption of this auction procedure is that all consumers are obliged to be allocated at one, and only one, location, and there are equal numbers of consumers and locations. Therefore, consumer surpluses may be negative. This means that their ex ante utility is too high to comply with the obliged location condition.

An important note is that the vectors of ex post utilities $u^* = (\{u_h^*\}, \forall h \in C)$ and prices $p^* = (\{p_i^*\}, \forall i \in I)$ are alternative ways to express the same solution because for the solution allocation the following holds: $p_i^* = w_{hi}(u_h^*)$ and $u_h^* = w_{hi}^{-1}(p_i)$.

Technical Note 3.2: Consumers' Surplus

Recall that the price paid for a location is constrained to income by $p_i = y_h - p_x x$. Consider Eq. (3.5) where the willingness-to-pay function at any location *i* is

$$w_{hi}(z; u) = y_h - v_h^{-1}(z_i; u_h),\ \forall i \in I \tag{T3.1}$$

and bids are constrained by $w_{hi} = y_h - p_x x$. It follows that expenditure on other goods is $p_x x = v_h^{-1}(z_i; u_h) = y_h - w_{hi}(z_i; u_h)$.

Let us define the total expenditure function as $e(p, u) = p_i + p_x x$, i.e., the sum of the price paid for the location, equal to the willingness to pay at utility u, plus the expenditure on other goods. Then, the expenditure conditional on location i is

$$e(z_i, p, u_h) = p_i + y_h - (w_{hi}(z_i; u_h)) = y_h - (w_{hi}(z_i; u_h) - p_i) \quad \text{(T3.2)}$$

The consumer surplus between two locations, denoted as 0 and 1, can be measured rigorously by the compensating variation, denoted as CV, which measures the amount of income that would exactly match the change in utility when moving from locations 0 to 1. The CV is defined as the following variation in expenditure:

$$\begin{aligned} CV &= e(z^1, p^1, u^1) - e(z^1, p^1, u^0) \\ &= y - (w(z^1; u^1) - p^1) - (y - (w(z^1; u^0) - p^1)) \end{aligned} \quad \text{(T3.3)}$$

If this variation is measured at the auction equilibrium of allocations and prices, then bids equal price paid, i.e., $w(z^1; u^1) = p^1$. Therefore, we obtain

$$CV = w(z^1; u^0) - p^1 \quad \text{(T3.4)}$$

This result can be applied to evaluate consumer h's surplus at location i paying a price p_i to attain a reservation utility u_h^0 as:

$$cs_{hi} = w_h(z_i; u_h) - p_i \quad \text{(T3.5)}$$

Exercise 3.1

Consider Anas' (1990) setup of a monocentric city with homogeneous population N with utility function $u = (1 - \beta)\ \ln(x) + \beta\ \ln(q)$, with $x \in \mathbb{R}^+$ the consumption of goods and $q \in \mathbb{R}^+$ the land size, both continuous variables, and $\beta \in [0,1]$ a parameter describing the household's preferences. The budget constraint is $x + rq + kt = y$, with $r \in \mathbb{R}^+$ the land value and $t \in \mathbb{R}^+$ the distance to the city center (or CBD) that concentrates jobs where the population travels to work daily. For every location t, find the demands for goods and land, the indirect utility, and the willingness to pay. Plot these functions against distance t to CBD.

Answer 3.1: From the income constraint $x(q, t) = y - kt - rq$, replace it in $u(x, q)$ to obtain $u(q, t)$ and derive it on q to obtain $q^* = \beta(y - kt)r^{-1}$.

Then, $x^* = (1 - \beta)(y - kt)$ and $v(t,r) = \ln(y - kt) - \beta\ \ln(r) + a$; invert on r to obtain $w(t, u) = b(y - kt)^{\frac{1}{\beta}} e^{-\frac{u}{\beta}}$; replace r by $w(t, u)$ in $q^*(t)$ to obtain $q^*(t) = c(y - kt)^{\frac{\beta - 1}{\beta}} e^{\frac{u}{\beta}}$; with $a = \beta\ \ln\beta - (\beta - 1)\ \ln(1 - \beta)$, $b = \beta(1 - \beta)^{\frac{1-\beta}{\beta}}$, and $c = (1 - \beta)^{\frac{\beta - 1}{\beta}}$.

References

Alonso, W., 1964. Location and Land Use. Harvard University Press, Cambridge.

Ambrose, B.W., Highfield, J., Linneman, P.D., 2005. Real estate and economies of scale: the case of REITs. Real Estate Economics 33 (2), 323–350.

Anas, A., 1982. Residential Location Markets and Urban Transportation. Academic Press, London.

Anas, A., 1990. Taste heterogeneity and urban spatial structure: the logit model and monocentric city reconciled. Journal of Urban Economics 28, 318–335.

Barthelemy, M., 2016. The Structure and Dynamics of Cities. Cambridge University Press.

Bers, M., Springer, T., 1997. Economies of scale for real estate investment trusts. Journal of Real Estate Research 14 (3), 275–290.

Brueckner, J.K., 1987. The structure of urban equilibria: a unified treatment of the Muth-Mills model. In: Handbook of Regional Science and Urban Economics, vol. II. Elsevier Science Pub., pp. 821–845

Demange, G., Gale, D., Sotomayor, M., 1986. Multi-item auctions. Journal of Political Economy 94 (4), 863–872.

DiPasquale, D., Wheathon, W., 1996. Urban Economics and Real Estate Markets. Prentice-Hall, New Jersey.

Ellickson, B., 1981. An alternative test of the hedonic theory of housing markets. Journal of Urban Economics 9, 56–79.

Fujita, M., Ogawa, H., 1982. Multiple equilibria and structural transition on non-monocentric urban configurations. Regional Science and Urban Economics 12 (2), 161–196.

Krugman, P.R., 1996. The Self-organizing Economy. Blackwell Publishers, Cambridge.

Mas-Colell, A., Whinston, M.D., Green, J.R., 1995. Microeconomic Theory. Oxford University Press, New York.

Martínez, F., 1992. The bid-choice land use model: an integrated economic framework. Environment and Planning A 24, 871–885.

Martínez, F., Roy, J., 2004. A model for residential supply. The Annals of Regional Science 38, 531–550.

McAfee, P., McMillan, J., 1987. Auctions and bidding. Journal of Economic Literature 25, 699–738.

Mills, E.S., 1972. Studies in the Structure of the Urban Economy. John Hopkins Press, Baltimore.

Muth, R.F., 1969. Cities and Housing. University of Chicago Press, Chicago.

Pagliara, F., Preston, J., Simmonds, D. (Eds.), 2010. Residential Location Choice: Models and Applications. Springer, Berlin-Heidelberg.

Rosen, S., 1974. Hedonic prices and implicit markets: product differentiation in pure competition. Journal of Political Economy 62, 34–55.

Solow, R.M., 1973. On equilibrium models of urban location. In: Parkin, M. (Ed.), Essays in Modern Economics. Longman, London, pp. 2–16.

Vickery, W., 1961. Counterspeculation, auctions and competitive sealed tenders. The Journal of Finance 16, 8–37.

Wheaton, W.C., 1977. A bid-rent approach to housing demand. Journal of Urban Economics 4 (2), 200–217.

Zumpano, L.V., Elder, H.W., 1994. Economies of scope and density in the market for real estate brokerage service. Real Estate Economics 22 (3), 497–513.

The Stochastic Bid-Auction Land-Use Model

4

4.1 Introduction

The theoretical model of the bid-auction market in land use (LU) was presented in Chapter 3, assuming deterministic and discrete real estate housing units and nonresidential location alternatives. In this chapter, we formulate and analyze this theoretical approach in the context of the random behavior of agents.

The Stochastic Approach

Modeling cities essentially means modeling individual agents' behavior in a complex system of interactions and is subject to constraints imposed by limited resources and regulations. This implies that the modeler faces the challenge of defining a suitable modeling approach. The first choice to make is the theoretical support, which in this book was described in Chapter 3 based on microeconomics, discrete choice, and bid-auction theories. The second basic choice is how to model agents' behavior. In this chapter, we assume that heterogeneous consumers are grouped into socioeconomic clusters, each one with different utilities and income, and that cluster members have idiosyncratic differences represented by random utilities.

The random utility model was justified theoretically by Manski (1977) as follows: although agents are assumed to know their utilities, the analyst cannot observe the agents' utilities with certainty because of unobserved attributes, taste variations, measurement errors, and instrumental variables (proxies to the actual attributes of choices). Therefore, by assuming random utilities, unobserved behavior is included.

Under this assumption, the random utility as a model of individual decision-making was pioneered by Daniel McFadden and has evolved into a dominant model since then, with the contribution of many researchers in transportation and marketing studies (e.g., Ben-Akiva and Lerman, 1985). This approach considers discrete choices instead of the consumption of continuous goods, which suits a basic requirement for the urban application. Although space is continuous, developed land is not; land lots, modes of transportation, activities, real estate options, etc. are all discrete in developed cities. Moreover, real estate options are represented by a set of discrete attributes, including the land lot size in the case of developed land.

The stochastic model can be formulated for continuous and discrete variables. Anas (1990) used Alonso–Mills–Muth's monocentric city and continuous land lot size (undeveloped land), which is the standard urban economics model that assumes consumers to be identical in incomes and tastes; however, he introduced stochastic utilities representing random taste, thus representing idiosyncratic heterogeneity.

Microeconomic Modeling in Urban Science. https://doi.org/10.1016/B978-0-12-815296-6.00004-4

He found that most results are similar and that the deterministic model yields an upper limit for the rent gradient and a lower bound for the city size compared with the stochastic model.

The random utility discrete model leads to a probabilistic choice and consumers' allocation model. The result does not provide a definitive answer regarding who is allocated at each location, but it determines the probability of each consumer to be allocated there. Therefore, the resulting LU pattern is not a map of a single consumer cluster populating each location but rather a mixture of heterogeneous consumers with different concentrations of each socioeconomic type at each location area.

Although the space is assumed discrete, usually partitioned as land lots and homogeneous zones, the probabilistic approach yields continuous demands and supply models for each location, allowing analysts to study economic and mathematical conditions equivalent to those of the continuous model and to perform efficient calculations.

In this chapter, we revise stochastic models formulated from assuming random − extreme value−indirect utilities, and this assumption is justified theoretically. We consider *choice* models in which consumers are assumed to be price takers and *bid-auction* models in which consumers bid for differentiated location options and prices emerge from the auction process. These models are specified assuming the Gumbel and the Fréchet distributions for basic behavior variates: consumers' surplus and willingness to pay.

The Aggregation

The aggregate model considers the aggregation of elemental units of three dimensions of the urban system: consumers, buildings, and land. This method reduces the computational burden in the calculation of the model outputs, at the cost of a reduction in the diversity of consumers' behavior and alternatives. The stochastic model represents this diversity in a simplified way.

Consumers, both households and firms, are grouped according to their similar behavior, and the behavior of individuals in each cluster is described by a representative agent. In the case of households, clusters are defined by income and a set of other socioeconomic attributes, whereas clusters of firms are defined by the type of economic activity (e.g., commercial, service, and industrial).

Supply is grouped into building types and location zones. Building types are defined by a set of characteristics in the same range, e.g., land lot size, building height, dwelling type (detached, semidetached, back to back). Space is aggregated into zones whose attributes, e.g., density, quality, accessibility, and attractiveness, are assumed to be homogeneous, normally following administrative borders.

We shall use the following notation for the aggregate model: the agent cluster is denoted by $h \in C$, with H_h members and C the set of clusters; the building type by $v \in V$, with V the set of dwelling types; and the zones by $i \in I$, with I the set of zones. The number of units in the building type v at zone i is denoted by S_{vi}. This notation is also valid for the disaggregate model, making $H_h = S_{vi} = 1 \ \forall \ h \in C, v \in V, i \in I$. Thus, the dimension of the model is $|C| \cdot |V| \cdot |I|$ ($|X|$ denotes the cardinal of the set X).

Therefore, a tuple (h,v,i), indexed as hvi, defines agents of cluster h, assigned to building type v in location zone i. Whenever it is convenient, the tuple notation hvi may be simplified as a duple (h,i), where a single index i denotes the combined building-location option, with $i \in VI$ and $|VI| = |V| \cdot |I|$.

4.2 The Random Utilities

The deterministic indirect utility yielded by the duple (h,i), defined in Chapter 3, is redefined in the stochastic approach as a stochastic variate thus defining the origin of a family of discrete stochastic models of consumers' behavior.

Consider the following stochastic indirect utility:

$$U_{hi} = u_{hi} + \varepsilon_{hi} \tag{4.1}$$

which is represented by two additive components, the deterministic or systematic utility u_{hi}, and the stochastic term ε_{hi}; additivity is the usual simplifiying assumption.

The Interpretation of the Stochastic Term

There are two potential sources that generate stochastic utilities: the agents' own variability of information about the quality and location attributes of goods, called here endogenous randomness, and the measurement error from the perspective of the analyst, as proposed by Manski (1977), which we call the analyst's error.

The most common assumption is that the stochastic term reflects the analyst's measurement error in observing the consumers' behavior while agents know their utility deterministically, i.e., random utility does not affect the rational assumption of utility maximization. In addition to this theoretical argument, the choice of a Gumbel distribution function (d.f.) for the indirect utility has been justified frequently based on utilitarian arguments, such as the convenience of a closed form of the probability model and the similar bell shape of the normal distribution, which assumes this one to be the natural d.f. associated with the analyst's measurement errors (see Ben-Akiva and Lerman, 1985)[1].

Although the measurement error argument is fine for theoretically justifying the estimation of demand models, there is another more fundamental justification for choosing an extreme value d.f. provided by the extreme value theorem and mentioned by Domencich and McFadden (1975, pg. 61): *Extreme value distributions are asymptotically stable distributions under the maximization operator*. The argument is stated as follows: the indirect utility conditional on the location choice represents the result of a maximization of a direct utility under income constraint. Then, if we assume that the underpinning direct utilities as random variates with any d.f., this theorem states that the asymptotic distribution of maximized utilities, i.e., the conditional indirect utilities, is one of the three types of extreme value distributions: Type I or

[1] In page 70 of the sixth printing, 1994.

Gumbel, Type II or Fréchet, or Type III or reversed Weibull. In the case of utilities, with unbounded domain and support set $\mathbb{R}$, *the Gumbel distribution is the natural* d.f. because the domain of the Fréchet d.f. has a lower bound and the reversed Weibull has an upper bound. An evident source of randomness in direct utilities is the information variability on the quality of the large set of consumption goods that consumers demand in the market.

This view is fundamentally different from that of the measurement error because it is inherent to the consumers and independent of the measurement tools of the analyst. However, the measurement error approach has a merit that is clearly consistent with the rational assumption, i.e., consumers know their utility fully, with no error, and behave deterministically, but the modeler lacks information and can only estimate utilities with an error.

A theoretical question arises regarding whether the inherent randomness of the consumer utility is consistent with rational behavior. To address this issue, let us first recognize that it is easy to criticize the assumption that the consumer knows the utility ex ante consumption, i.e., there is no perception or information error compared with the consumer utility evaluated ex post. If a more plausible assumption is that such error exists, then we may assume that the consumer is conscious about the mismatch between the ex ante and ex post utilities, and that, in fact, the consumer observes a random utility: the information is uncertain and the perception is variable. Then, we conclude that consumer utility can be assumed to be inherently random because consumers draw information from random quality information and define a deterministic value of the utility for that draw.

In practice, this theoretical discussion does not affect the model formulation. In fact, despite the views on this theoretical issue, the stochastic discrete choice approach has been implemented in applied models assuming two basic distributions for the stochastic term. The normal distribution is natural to the measurement error and yields a family of models called *probit*, and the Gumbel distribution generates *logit* models. The latter is the more commonly used because under some assumptions, its closed form simplifies the mathematical analysis in complex processes such as market equilibrium.

4.3 The Random Willingness to Pay

In Chapter 3 we defined the willingness to pay as derived from utilities, i.e., as the inverse of the utility function in prices or $w_{hi}(z;u) = y_h - v_h^{-1}(z_i;u_h)$. Assuming that utility is invertible, we shall now invert the random utility to obtain the stochastic willingness to pay.

The random indirect utility in Eq. (4.1) is $v_{hi} = u_{hi}(z_i, y_h - p_i) + \varepsilon_{hi}$ and is dependent on the available income, which inverted in the rents p_i, yields the willingness to pay conditional on the reservation utility u_h: $w_{hi} = y_h - v_h^{-1}(z_i, \varepsilon_{hi}; u_h)$. Observe that the distribution of the stochastic willingness to pay is clearly dependent on the inverse function v_h^{-1}. Then, we consider two interesting cases derived from the functional form of the indirect utility: linear and nonlinear utilities in prices (rents). For the following, see Technical Note 4.1.

Linear Utilities

In this case, consider the indirect utility as:

$$v_{hi} = \lambda_h(y_h - p_i) + f_h(z_i) + \varepsilon_{hi} \tag{4.2}$$

with ε_{hi} Gumbel (0, μ_h) and λ_h the marginal utility of income ($\lambda_h > 0$). Inverting utility in rents yields the following willingness to pay:

$$\theta_{hi} = w_{hi} + \varepsilon'_{hi} = y_h + \frac{f_h(z_i) - u_h}{\lambda_h} + \frac{\varepsilon_{hi}}{\lambda_h} \tag{4.3}$$

where $\varepsilon'_{hi} = \frac{\varepsilon_{hi}}{\lambda_h}$ is distributed Gumbel with parameters (0, β_h), $\beta_h = \lambda_h\mu_h$ and u_h is the reservation utility. This implies that the shape parameter of the willingness to pay is larger than the parameter of the utility ($\beta_h > \mu_h$) and the variance is smaller and decreases with the marginal utility of the income. Because it is expected that λ_h decreases with income, the variance of the willingness to pay increases with income $\left(\frac{\partial\sigma_\theta}{\partial y} = \frac{\partial\sigma_\theta}{\partial\lambda}\cdot\frac{\partial\lambda}{\partial y} > 0\right)$, reflecting the larger variability of high-income groups' willingness to pay regarding their less constrained income.

Because the willingness to pay preserves the Gumbel distribution, it preserves the properties of a closed form for the associated probabilities and the *logsum* function to measure the maximum expected value. The drawback, however, is that this distribution yields negative values for the willingness to pay, i.e., $w \in [-\infty, +\infty]$, which has no simple interpretation in real markets. This inconsistency follows from the linear assumption of the indirect utility because it is unable to impose income constraints. Despite this drawback, the Gumbel distribution under the assumption of independent and identical distribution (i.i.d.) generates the family of *logit* models, with the multinomial logit (MNL) model the most widely used in applications.

Nonlinear Utilities

In this case, the indirect utility is nonlinear in prices, for example:

$$v_{hi} = \lambda_h \ln\left(\frac{y_h}{p_i}\right) + f_h(z_i) + \varepsilon_{hi} \tag{4.4}$$

This formulation is more consistent economically with the income constraint because utility tends to $-\infty$ when the price p_i exceeds the consumer's income y_h and becomes unfeasible; thus, option i is unlikely to be chosen.

Inverting Eq. (4.4) in rents yields:

$$\theta_{hi} = w_{hi}\cdot\xi_{hi} = y_h e^{\lambda_h^{-1}(-u_h + f_h(z_i))}\cdot e^{\left(\lambda_h^{-1}\varepsilon_{hi}\right)} \tag{4.5}$$

where the willingness to pay variates $\theta = (\theta_{hi};\ \forall\ h \in C,\ i \in VI)$ distribute Fréchet (w_{hi}, β_{hi}) with $w_{hi} = e^{\lambda_h^{-1}(\ln y_h - u_h + f_h(z_i))}$ and the stochastic term $\xi_{hi} = e^{\left(\lambda_h^{-1}\varepsilon_{hi}\right)}$, with shape parameter $\beta_h = \lambda_h \mu_h > 0$. In this case, the willingness to pay is positive, i.e., $\theta \in (0,\infty)$, and the variance is also inversely proportional to the shape parameter and increases with income. This distribution also yields a closed form for probabilities and expected maximum values.

The Fréchet distribution generates a lesser-known family of models, named here as *frechit* models, with the multinomial model denoted as MNF. For a study on the relationship between the *logit* and the *frechit* models see Mattsson et al. (2014).

The multiplicative model in Eq. (4.5) has been studied previously in the context of a cost-minimization choice process. Gálvez (2002) proposed the multiplicative form in a cost-minimizing model. Castillo et al. (2008) and Fosgerau and Bierlaire (2009) derived this model from the Weibull distribution (Type III extreme value). The latter found empirically that for transportation demand choices, whether the *logit* or *frechit* model best fits data depends on the utility specification, leaving the question of the best model inconclusive and to be defined as an empirical issue.

It is worth remarking how the *logit* and *frechit* models of willingness to pay has been introduced, because they where formulated based on two theoretical arguments, instead of on their mathematical nice properties: 1) the indirect utility emerges naturally —although asymptotically— as an *extreme value function*, despite the assumptions made on the distribution of the underpinning direct utilities; 2) the choice of the Gumbel or the Frèchet distributions is based on whether the *indirect utility is linear or nonlinear in land prices.*

4.4 The Stochastic Demand Model

The demand for a location is calculated by the choice model, as was presented in Chapter 3, assuming deterministic utilities and consumers as price takers. In this section, this approach is applied for i.i.d. Gumbel utilities to generate the stochastic demand model. If consumer h's choice probability for a given location i is $P_{i/h}$, then the demand for this location option is $D_i = \sum_{h \in C} P_{i/h}$. In this section, we analyze models to calculate the choice probability.

The stochastic demand model calculates the probability $P_{i/h}$ of demanding a given discrete alternative from a set of alternative locations $i \in VI$. This probability represents the choice frequency generated by the realizations of Gumbel indirect utilities. Such realizations of the ε_{hi} term in Eq. (4.1) represent the random information of a single consumer h's utility with expected value given by u_{hi}, which we call the disaggregated model, or may represent the idiosyncratic variability of utilities associated with different individuals of the cluster with the same expected value u_{hi}, i.e., who belong to the same socioeconomic cluster, which we call the aggregate model.

The Assumptions of the Multinomial Logit Model

The assumption that the stochastic utility is represented by the Gumbel distribution generates a family of models called *logit*, in which each model is differentiated by the structure of the utility variance, e.g., the multinomial, hierarchical, and mixed *logit*. For a good reference on the MNL model see Ben-Akiva and Lerman (1985) and see Technical Note 4.1. on extreme value distributions.

The MNL model assumes the utility's stochastic term as *identically and independently distributed* (called i.i.d.) Gumbel. The i.i.d. assumption means they have the same variance and null covariance, i.e., the variance matrix of utilities is $\sigma_u^2 = \sigma^2 I_m$, with σ^2 the constant variance and I_m the identity matrix, with dimension m equal to the number of elements in the set of alternatives VI. Then, the variance matrix is

$$\sigma^2 = \begin{bmatrix} \sigma^2 & 0 & \cdots & 0 \\ 0 & \sigma^2 & \cdots & 0 \\ \cdots & \cdots & \cdots & \cdots \\ 0 & 0 & \cdots & \sigma^2 \end{bmatrix}$$

Notably, this is a strong assumption that induces forecasting limitations but that also provides the useful simplicity of the MNL model.

In this case, the Gumbel distribution of the stochastic terms has parameters $(0, \mu_h)$, where the *shape parameter* μ_h is inversely related to the constant variance, i.e., $\sigma^2 = \frac{\pi^2}{6\mu^2}$. Then, the MNL model assumes utilities as random variables and distributed i.i.d. Gumbel with parameters (u_{hi}, μ_h), $\forall h \in C, i \in VI$.

The Multinomial Logit Choice Probability: Utility Approach

The multinomial choice probability of a duple (h,i) is defined as:

$$P_{i/h} = Prob(v_{hi} \geq v_{hj}, \forall i, j \in VI) \tag{4.6}$$

This expression states that the choice probability of the MNL model is the result of the utility maximization process. In other words, the resulting probabilities encapsulate the theoretical assumption that individuals are rational beings. For convenience, hereafter we use the conditional probability notation $P_{i/h}$, i.e., the probability that the location alternative is chosen conditionally on consumer h.

The probability can be computed to obtain the useful closed form of the MNL model:

$$P_{i/h} = \frac{e^{\mu_h u_{hi}}}{\sum_{j \in VI} e^{\mu_h u_{hj}}} \tag{4.7}$$

This choice probability represents the odds that the agents of cluster h will choose a building-location option i.

In the aggregate model, each location i represents a zone and building type with a number of elemental locations described by vector $(S_j; j \in VI)$. We write the aggregate probability, i.e., the probability that an agent of cluster h will choose one of the elemental building-zone locations of the group indexed by i, as follows:

$$P_{i/h} = S_i \frac{e^{\mu_h u_{hi}}}{\sum_{j \in VI} S_j e^{\mu_h u_{hj}}} \tag{4.8}$$

This result was obtained by McFadden (1978), assuming a random sample is taken from the cluster. Eq. (4.8) is the simplest aggregate model, including a cluster *size factor* which is intuitive and easy to explain.[2] S_j in the denominator is the number of elemental alternatives with equal exponential terms: $e^{\mu_h u_{hj}}$, so the sum is simplified by grouping terms and multiplying by S_j; additionally, $\frac{e^{\mu_h u_{hi}}}{\sum_{j \in VI} S_j e^{\mu_h u_{hj}}}$ is the probability of choosing an elemental alternative. Thus, the aggregate probability calculates the odds that any one of the cluster's elemental alternatives is chosen, which is the sum of S_i equal elemental probabilities.

An important feature of the MNL probability is the closed form formula of the probability, which allows the analyst to perform analytical studies and efficient evaluation. This feature has enabled this model to be used more than others; for example, more than the *probit* model based on the normal distribution of the stochastic term. In addition to this closed form, it is important to emphasize that the *logit* model is natural to the maximization of utilities. This last feature, less recognized in the literature, provides the MNL with theoretical elegance and consistency.

Observe that the sum of the choice probabilities across alternatives is equal to one, and that the probability increases with the choice utility u_{hi}, whereas it decreases with both the utility of the alternative competing options $u_{hj}, j \neq i$ and with the number of alternative options. It is known that if the variance decreases (i.e., μ increases), then the choice probability tends to yield all-or-nothing extreme values: equal to one for the alternative with the highest utility and zero for the rest. Conversely, as the variance increases, location choices become less dependent on the deterministic values of utilities (u) and more dependent on the stochastic term, up to the other extreme where deterministic utilities are irrelevant compared with the error terms and all choice probabilities become equal to the inverse of the number of alternatives.

It is also useful to write the choice probability as:

$$P_{i/h} = \frac{1}{\sum_{j \in VI} e^{\mu_h (u_{hj} - u_{hi})}} \tag{4.9}$$

to show that choice probabilities depend on the utility differences, not on their absolute values. This is consistent with the definition of utility as an ordinal, i.e., the absolute

[2] Different factors are derived from other assumptions of the sampling protocol of elemental alternatives in the cluster. Another correction factor measures the variability of the elemental alternatives in the cluster. For more details, the reader is referred to Ben-Akiva and Lerman (1985), pg. 258.

values of utilities are meaningless for choice making; what is relevant is the difference in preferences expressed here by the difference in utilities. This implies that probabilities are invariant to an additive constant utility: $P(u) = P(u + c)$, with $c \in \mathbb{R}$ any constant value.

The i.i.d. assumption implies that the choice probability exhibits the property of *irrelevance of alternative options*, which can be explained by writing:

$$\frac{P_{i/h}}{P_{j/h}} = e^{\mu_h(u_{hi} - u_{hj})} \tag{4.10}$$

showing that the probability ratio between two alternative locations is independent of the utility yield by other alternatives. This property is commonly criticized as a limitation of the MNL model, particularly because neighbor zones are expected to share common unobserved attributes. Therefore, some correlation is expected between their stochastic terms, a topic studied in more detail as spatial econometrics (Anselin, 1988).

Another useful feature of the MNL model is that the expected maximum utility that a consumer can attain from a set of location options can be easily computed. Here, we use the property that the Gumbel distribution is preserved under the maximization operator, i.e., that the maximum value of a Gumbel variate is also a stochastic variate with the same distribution. It follows that the maximum utility also distributes Gumbel with parameters (η_h, μ_h), where $\eta_h = \frac{1}{\mu_h}\ln\left(\sum_{i \in VI} S_i e^{\mu_h u_{hi}}\right)$ is the mode of the distribution known as the *logsum* function, and the mean is $\eta_h + \frac{\gamma}{\mu_h}$. Thus, the expected value of the maximum utility is given by:

$$v_h^* = \frac{1}{\mu_h}\ln\left(\sum_{i \in VI} S_i e^{\mu_h u_{hi}}\right) + \frac{\gamma}{\mu_h} \tag{4.11}$$

where $\gamma \sim 0.577$ is Euler's constant. Observe that the maximum utility increases with the number of options, i.e., with the city size $S = \sum_{i \in VI} S_i$ and with the variance of the stochastic distribution. Note that the maximum utility is also a dimensionless ordinal value, so the constant $\frac{\gamma}{\mu_h}$ has a statistical interpretation as the difference between the mode and the expected values but has no economic significance because it modifies only a meaningless utility level.

The Multinomial Logit Choice Model: Consumer Surplus Approach

The choice model can also be derived by maximizing the consumer surplus. Under the assumption of the i.i.d. Gumbel willingness to pay, the consumer surplus is defined by:

$$cs_{hi} = w_{hi} - p_i \tag{4.12}$$

Because the consumer is assumed to be a price taker, i.e., the asking price p_i is exogenous and known to the consumer, the consumer's surplus preserves the i.i.d. Gumbel distribution of the willingness to pay with shape parameter $\beta_h = \lambda_h \mu_h$, although the location parameter is displaced to the left in p_i.

In this context, the maximum consumer surplus or choice model is represented by the following MNL probability:

$$P_{i/h} = \frac{e^{\beta_h (w_{hi} - p_i)}}{\sum_{j \in VI} e^{\beta_h (w_{hj} - p_j)}} \tag{4.13}$$

which also admits an aggregated version such as Eq. (4.8). As expected, the choice probability increases with the willingness to pay and decreases with prices.

To understand why this choice process yields maximum utility, it is worth recalling that willingness-to-pay values across the set of alternative locations are set such that they yield the same reservation utility, i.e., $w_{hi}(u_h)$, $\forall\ i \in VI$, and therefore, the consumer is indifferent to choosing any location if the price equals the willingness-to-pay value. It follows that at the location where the willingness to pay is below the asking price, there is a gain in utility with respect to its reservation value and where the price is higher, there is a loss. Then, maximizing gains implies maximizing utility and the consumer surplus.

The expected maximum consumer surplus of a set of options VI with i.i.d. Gumbel distributed variates is calculated as:

$$cs_h^* = \frac{1}{\beta_h} \ln \left[\sum_{i \in VI} e^{\beta_h (w_{hi} - p_i)} \right] + \frac{\gamma}{\beta_h} \tag{4.14}$$

and the maximum consumer surplus is also a Gumbel variate with parameters (η_h, β_h) and mode $\eta_h = \frac{1}{\beta_h} \ln \left[\sum_{i \in VI} e^{\beta_h (w_{hi} - p_i)} \right]$. In this case, because the consumer surplus has the dimension of income, then $\frac{\gamma}{\beta_h}$ is meaningful not only statistically but also economically.

The Multinomial Frechit Choice Model: Consumer Surplus

As a reminder, the multinomial *frechit* (MNF) model is derived from nonlinear in price indirect utilities and i.i.d. Gumbel and that bids are stochastic variates $\theta_{hi} = w_{hi} \cdot \xi_{hi}$, asymptotically distributed Fréchet with parameters (w_{hi}, β_h), mode $w_{hi} = y_h e^{\lambda_h^{-1}(-u_h + f_h(z_i))}$, and shape parameter $\beta_h = \lambda_h \mu_h > 0$; μ_h is the shape parameter of the Gumbel utilities. This assumption ensures that bids are positive, which is consistent with the income constraint that imposes a nonlinear in price (rents) utility function.

In the MNF model, the consumer surplus is defined in a multiplicative form, as the ratio between the willingness to pay and the price instead of the difference between them. Under the assumption that the consumer is a price taker, with prices assumed to be deterministic and exogenous values, the consumer's surplus preserves the identical and independent Fréchet distribution of the willingness to pay, although the location parameter is different. Then:

$$cs_{hi} = \frac{\theta_{hi}}{p_i} = \frac{w_{hi}}{p_i} \cdot \xi_{hi} \tag{4.15}$$

which is also a Fréchet variate with parameters $\left(\frac{w_{hi}}{p_i}, \beta_h\right)$.

The maximum consumer surplus or choice model is represented by the following MNF choice probability:

$$P_{i/h} = \frac{\left(w_{hi}/p_i\right)^{\beta_h}}{\sum_{j \in VI} \left(w_{hj}/p_j\right)^{\beta_h}} \tag{4.16}$$

which also admits an aggregated version. As in the *logit* model, the *frechit* choice probability has a close form, increases with the willingness to pay and decreases with prices. In this case the probability is invariant to a multiplicative constant $c \in \mathbb{R}$, i.e: $P_{i/h}(w) = P_{i/h}(w \cdot c)$.

The expected maximum consumer surplus of a set of options *VI*, with i.i.d. Fréchet distributed variates, is calculated as:

$$cs_h^* = K \left[\sum_{j \in VI} \left(w_{hj}/p_j\right)^{\beta_h} \right]^{\frac{1}{\beta_h}} \tag{4.17}$$

and the maximum consumer surplus is also a Fréchet variate with parameters (η_h, β_h), mode $\eta_h = \left[\sum_{j \in VI} \left(w_{hj}/p_j\right)^{\beta_h} \right]^{\frac{1}{\beta_h}}$, and media $\eta_h K$.

4.5 Substitution Property of Stochastic Demand

The demand for a location in the stochastic choice models described above, given by $D_i = \sum_{h \in C} P_{i/h}$, satisfies the strict gross substitution conditions: $\frac{\partial D_i}{\partial p_i} < 0$ and $\frac{\partial D_i}{\partial p_j} > 0$, with $\frac{\partial D_i}{\partial p_i} = \sum_{h \in C} H_h \frac{\partial P_{i/h}}{\partial p_i}$.

In the case of the *logit* demand model, consider Eq. (4.7) with $\frac{\partial u_{hi}}{\partial p_i} < 0$. It follows that:

$$\frac{\partial P_{i/h}}{\partial p_i} = \mu_h P_{i/h}\left(1 - P_{i/h}\right)\frac{\partial u_{hi}}{\partial p_i} < 0 \tag{4.18}$$

$$\frac{\partial P_{i/h}}{\partial p_j} = -\mu_h P_{i/h} P_{j/h} \frac{\partial u_{hj}}{\partial p_j} > 0 \tag{4.19}$$

The same holds for the consumer surplus MNL (Eq. 4.13):

$$\frac{\partial P_{i/h}}{\partial p_i} = -\beta_h P_{i/h}\left(1 - P_{i/h}\right)\frac{\partial cs_{hi}}{\partial p_i} < 0 \tag{4.20}$$

$$= \beta_h P_{i/h} P_{j/h} > 0 \tag{4.21}$$

because $\frac{\partial w_{hi}}{\partial p_i} = 0$.

In the case of the *frechit* demand model, using Eq. (4.16) we obtain:

$$\frac{\partial P_{i/h}}{\partial p_i} = -\frac{\beta_h}{p_i} P_{i/h}\left(1 - P_{i/h}\right) < 0 \tag{4.22}$$

$$\frac{\partial P_{i/h}}{\partial p_j} = \frac{\beta_h}{p_i} P_{i/h} P_{j/h} > 0 \tag{4.23}$$

4.6 The Stochastic Bid-Auction Approach

Let us now consider the bid-auction approach. In contrast to the demand model, which assumes that prices (rents) are exogenous, the bid-auction assumes that location options are *differentiable*, and, thus, the market represents an auction, as proposed by Alonso (1964). In this section, we discuss the stochastic approach of the bid-auction model. This approach assumes that consumers bid for each available location according to their willingness to pay, which is conditional on a reservation utility.

The first bid-auction model was proposed by Ellickson (1981). He considered a set of bidders, B_i, each one represented by a stochastic bid function, and defined the following auction outcome probability conditional on the location:

$$Q_{h/i} = Prob(w_{hi} \geq w_{gi}, \forall g \in B_i) \tag{4.24}$$

which defines the probability of consumer h being the highest bidder at the auction of real estate i.

This expression and the assumptions regarding the distribution of bids lead to a stochastic bid-auction model that represents the result of the maximization of bids across the set of bidders $B_i \subset C$ for an auction at location i. In other words, the resulting probabilities encapsulate the maximization process that defines the outcome of the auction.

Ellickson's (1981) argument for bids to be extreme value variables is worth mentioning. He indicates that those bids that are presented in auctions are expected to show an extreme value distribution because he asserts that only the maximum bid of a socioeconomic cluster is relevant for the auction. Hence, no matter what the distribution of elementary bids is within the cluster, the maximum bid relevant to the auction is an extreme variable. He used this argument to justify a Gumbel distribution of bids, ignoring other extreme value distributions; in fact, he seems to have not recognized that Gumbel bids have positive and negative values. He also asserts that bids are independent because they emerge from groups of different bidders with independent utilities but provides no justification for assuming that bids are identical.

Although Ellickson used these arguments to assume a Gumbel distribution of bids, they can be generalized to all extreme value d.f. We add to his argument that the extreme value distribution is the natural distribution for bids because they result from the individual's indirect utility, which we have argued is naturally asymptotically Gumbel. From this, we showed that the distribution of bids is Gumbel or Fréchet depending on whether the indirect utility is linear or nonlinear.

Nevertheless, the argument for assuming identical distribution remains useful because it is convenient to obtain closed simple multinomial models, although it is an important assumption because it imposes an identical variance of bids across different consumers.

The Multinomial Logit Bid-Auction Probability

The MNL bid-auction assumes bids that are i.i.d. and Gumbel distributed with shape parameter β_i; $\forall i \in I$ to obtain the following probability:

$$Q_{h/i} = \frac{e^{\beta_i w_{hi}}}{\sum_{g \in B_i} e^{\beta_i w_{gi}}} \tag{4.25}$$

which represents the odds that consumer h will be the highest bidder in the auction of the building-location option i.

Notably, Eq. (4.25) is different from the usual choice models in which an individual chooses among a set of alternatives; thus, the choice probability is conditional on the individual. Conversely, Eq. (4.25) represents an auction, a process in which an auctioneer chooses a bidder from among a set of bidders, making the probability, in this case, conditional on the location rather than on consumers, whom represent the choice set for the auctioneer. Then, the auction is a process that chooses in the space of consumers, whereas the usual choice process chooses in the space of supply alternatives. It is worth noting this difference to avoid confusion.

In the aggregate model, bidders represent clusters denoted by $h \in B_i$, each one with a number of agents described by vector $(H_h; h \in C)$. In this case, we write the aggregate probability, i.e., the probability that an agent of cluster h will be the highest bidder in a building-zone location indexed by i, as:

$$Q_{h/i} = H_h \frac{e^{\beta_i w_{hi}}}{\sum_{g \in B_i} H_g e^{\beta_i w_{gi}}} \tag{4.26}$$

Note that the bid-auction probability is invariant to an additive constant $c \in \mathbb{R}$ on bid values, $Q_{h/i}(w) = Q_{hi}(w + c)$, and the auction outcome depends on the difference between bids rather that its absolute values.

The Logit Hedonic Price

The term "hedonic" refers to the implicit value of an amenity, which is not revealed in the market (Rosen, 1974). Consider, for example, the consumer value of a free-entry park. Because this amenity has no price, one method to identify the consumers' value is by observing the change in real estate or land prices in the presence of a park in the neighborhood, i.e., if the amenity is valued, it should have a differential impact on real estate and land prices. In the stochastic model, the auction yields hedonic prices and provides a specific functional form.

The maximum bid in the auction represents the transaction price of the auctioned location. If bids are Gumbel variates, the price preserves this d.f. with parameters (p_i, β_i), and the *expected value* p_i^* is given by:

$$p_i^* = p_i + \frac{\gamma}{\beta_i} = \frac{1}{\beta_i} \ln \left[\sum_{h \in B_i} H_h e^{\beta_i w_{hi}} \right] + \frac{\gamma}{\beta_i} \tag{4.27}$$

This equation represents a *logit hedonic price* function because it is the result of the consumers' value of the set of amenities of the auctioned location. More rigorously, this is the value of the right of use of the location. It represents the expected transaction price in the real estate market or the expected land price for empty land lots.

From this price function, the hedonic value of an amenity z_k is:

$$h_{z_k} = \sum_{h \in B_i} Q_{h/i} \frac{dw_{hi}}{dz_k} \tag{4.28}$$

which states that the expected hedonic value of the amenity is the average value across the set B_i of consumers who participate in the auction.

Note that the hedonic price in Eq. (4.27) increases with the number of bidders, because the larger the number of bidders, the larger the possibility of receiving higher bids. To observe this, consider N_i equals bidders that bid w_i to obtain that $p_i^* = w_i + \frac{1}{\beta_i} \ln(N_i) + \frac{\gamma}{\beta_i}$, showing that prices increase with the logarithm of the number of bidders and decrease with β_i (i.e., increase with the bid's variance); this also shows that for the extreme case of $N_i = 1$ we find that $p_i^* = w_i + \frac{\gamma}{\beta_i} > w_i$.

It is also worth noting that using Eq. (4.27), the probability in Eq. (4.25) may be rewritten as:

$$Q_{h/i} = e^{\beta_i (w_{hi} - p_i)} \tag{4.29}$$

This expression shows a direct relationship between the consumer surplus and the bid-auction probability; i.e., the bid-auction probability is the logistic function of the consumer surplus. Observe that $w_{hi} - p_i^* < 0$ because the price is the expected maximum bid, as shown in Eq. (4.27). It is then easy to conclude that the highest bidder attains the highest location probability, which tends to one when consumer $h's$ bid tends to match the auction price.

Additionally, Lerman and Kern (1983), extending Ellickson's (1981) previous work, proposed a model in which hedonic prices and bid-auction location models are estimated simultaneously, correctly recognizing that they depend on the same set of bid functions. As noticed by McMillen (1997), this approach introduces a correction to the selection endogeneity problem of the isolated hedonic price model.

The Multinomial Frechit Bid-Auction Probability

In this model, bids are assumed to be i.i.d. and Fréchet, with shape parameter β, which yields the following multinomial *frechit* bid-auction probability:

$$Q_{h/i} = \frac{(w_{hi})^{\beta_i}}{\sum_{g \in B_i} (w_{gi})^{\beta_i}} \tag{4.30}$$

and represents the odds that consumer h will be the highest bidder in the auction of building-location option i.

In the aggregate model, the aggregate probability, i.e., the probability that an agent of cluster h will be the highest bidder in a building-zone location indexed by i, is

$$Q_{h/i} = H_h \frac{(w_{hi})^{\beta_i}}{\sum_{g \in B_i} H_g (w_{gi})^{\beta_i}} \tag{4.31}$$

Note that in this case, the bid-auction probability is invariant to a multiplicative constant bid, $Q_{hi}(w) = Q_{hi}(w \cdot c)$, with $c \in \mathbb{R}$ a constant; i.e., the auction outcome depends on the ratio between bids rather than on its absolute values, which is evident when writing:

$$Q_{h/i} = H_h \frac{1}{\sum_{g \in B_i} H_h \left(\frac{w_{gi}}{w_{hi}} \right)^{\beta_i}} \tag{4.32}$$

The Frechit Hedonic Price

In the case of Fréchet bids, the price which is also a Fréchet distributed variate with parameters (p_i, β_i), with an expected value p_i^*, is defined when $\beta_i > 1$ as:

$$p_i^* = Kp_i = K\left[\sum_{g \in B_i} (w_{gi})^{\beta_i}\right]^{\frac{1}{\beta_i}} \tag{4.33}$$

where $K = \Gamma\left(1 - \frac{1}{\beta_i}\right) > 0$ is constant for β_i and Γ is the gamma function.

This equation represents the *frechit hedonic price* function, and the hedonic value of an amenity z_k is

$$h_{z_k} = p_i^*\left[\sum_{g \in B_i} Q_{g/i}\frac{1}{w_{gi}}\frac{\partial w_{gi}}{\partial z_k}\right] \tag{4.34}$$

Note that the *frechit* hedonic price also increases with the number of bidders. To observe this, consider N_i equal bidders that bid w_i to obtain that $p_i^* = Kw_iN_i^{1/\beta_i}$, showing that prices increase exponentially with the number of bidders and decrease with β_i (increase with the bid variance): at the limit case where $N_i = 1, p_i^* = Kw_i$. Note also that the bid-auction probability in Eq. (4.30) can be written as: $Q_{h/i} = K^{\beta_i}\left(\frac{w_{hi}}{p_i}\right)^{\beta_i}$ with $\frac{w_{hi}}{p_i}$ the consumer surplus ratio.

Estimation of Willingness to Pay

Observe that both choice probabilities $P_{i/h}$ and bid-auction probabilities $Q_{h/i}$ are functions of a set of willingness-to-pay functions. Let us now remark on the differences when the willingness-to-pay functions are estimated using these models.

Recall that the willingness-to-pay functions are $w_{hi} = y_h + \frac{f_h(z_i) - u_h}{\lambda_h} + \frac{\varepsilon_{hi}}{\lambda_h}$ in the *logit* model (Eq. 4.3) and $w_{hi} = y_h e^{\lambda_h^{-1}(-u_h + f_h(z_i))}$ in the *frechit* model (Eq. 4.5). The *logit* choice probability is

$$P_{i/h} = \frac{e^{\beta_h(w_{hi} - p_i)}}{\sum_{j \in VI} e^{\beta_h(w_{hj} - p_j)}} = \frac{e^{\beta_h\left(\lambda_h^{-1} f_h(z_i) - p_i\right)}}{\sum_{j \in VI} e^{\beta_h\left(\lambda_h^{-1} f_g(z_i) - p_j\right)}} \tag{4.35}$$

and the *frechit* probability is

$$P_{i/h} = \frac{(w_{hi}/p_i)^{\beta_h}}{\sum_{j \in VI}(w_{hj}/p_j)^{\beta_h}} = \frac{\left(e^{\lambda_h^{-1}(f_h(z_i))}\Big/p_i\right)^{\beta_h}}{\sum_{j \in VI}\left(e^{\lambda_h^{-1}(f_h(z_j))}\Big/p_j\right)^{\beta_h}} \tag{4.36}$$

These equations show that the choice probabilities are invariant with consumers' income and in utility if the utility function is quasi-linear. Therefore, the estimation can only obtain parameters for the truncated willingness-to-pay function: $\lambda_h^{-1}(f_h(z_i))$. This truncation does not occur when the willingness-to-pay functions are estimated using bid-auction probabilities.

Nevertheless, the estimation of the willingness-to-pay functions can be performed using the system of equations: $P_{i/h}(w, \beta)$, $Q_{h/i}(w, \beta)$ and $p_i(w, \beta)$, $\forall h \in B_i, i \in VI$. For this process, the modeler requires observations of the allocation of agents H_{hi} and prices (rents) p_i. An estimation method integrating probabilities and rents was developed by Lerman and Kern (1983). Note that unlike the usual discrete choice models in which the shape parameter is unidentifiable, in the LU model price Eqs (4.27) and (4.33) let us identify the bid-auction shape parameter.

4.7 The Stochastic Bid-Choice Equivalence

In the context of deterministic behavior, in Chapter 3 we showed that both of the demand models—based on maximum utility or maximum consumer surplus—are equivalent to the bid-auction model if prices emerge from the auction process, i.e., assuming an auction market. Here, we analyze this equivalence for the stochastic behavior in the *logit* and *frechit* models.

Equivalence in the Logit Model

The assumption required to define equivalence is that the shape parameters of the choice and bid-auction probabilities are identical, i.e., $\beta = \beta_h = \beta_i$, $\forall h \in B_i, i \in VI$. Then, consider the MNL consumer surplus choice probability (Eq. 4.13) and the bid-auction probability, $Q_{h/i} = e^{\beta\left(w_{hi} - p_i^*\right)}$, to write:

$$P_{i/h} = \frac{Q_{h/i}}{\sum_{j \in VI} Q_{h/j}} \tag{4.37}$$

In Eq. (4.37), the denominator $\sum_{j \in VI} Q_{h/j} = Q_h$ is the aggregate probability that the consumer is the highest bidder in the set of available location auctions. Then, the equality $P_{i/h} = Q_{h/i}$ holds if $Q_h = 1$, i.e., under the condition that the consumer is expected to be allocated somewhere in the city; the condition $Q_h < 1$ means that there is a probability that the consumer is without a home, in which case the equality does not hold.

Conversely, consider $Q_{h/i}$ in Eq. (4.25) and multiply each term by $e^{-\beta p_i}$ to obtain $Q_{h/i} = \frac{e^{\beta\left(w_{hi} - p_i\right)}}{\sum_{g \in B_i} e^{\beta\left(w_{gi} - p_i\right)}} = \frac{P_{i/h}}{\sum_{g \in B_i} P_{i/h}}$. Therefore, when $P_i = \sum_{g \in B_i} P_{i/h} = 1$, then the equivalence holds, i.e., when the location is auctioned to some consumer.

Notably, the double condition $P_i = Q_h = 1$ holds if total demand equals total supply, a condition usually considered for the LU equilibrium between demand and supply that sets the utility levels and prices to clear the market. Hence, we conclude that, under this equilibrium condition, the bid-choice equivalence holds for the *logit* model. For this equivalence to hold, however, we impose the following: the consumer surplus and the bid-auction shape parameters for all bidders are identical, i.e., $\beta = \beta_h = \beta_i$, $\forall h \in C$, $i \in VI$; the underpinning indirect utility is linear in price; and prices emerge from auctions.

Equivalence in Frechit *Model*

Under the assumption of equal shape parameters, i.e., $\beta = \beta_h = \beta_i, \forall h \in B_i, i \in I$, we consider the MNF choice probability in Eq. (4.16) and the bid-auction probability, $Q_{h/i} = K^{\beta}\left(\frac{w_{hi}}{p_i}\right)^{\beta}$, to write:

$$P_{i/h} = \frac{Q_{h/i}}{\sum_{j \in VI} Q_{h/j}} \tag{4.38}$$

Again, imposing the equilibrium condition $Q_h = 1$, the equivalence holds. Conversely, consider the bid-auction probability in Eq. (4.30) and divide each term by p_i to obtain $Q_{h/i} = \frac{\left(\frac{w_{hi}}{p_i}\right)^{\beta}}{\sum_{g \in B_i}\left(w_{gi}/p_i\right)^{\beta}} = \frac{P_{i/h}}{\sum_{g \in B_i} P_{i/g}}$. If $\sum_{g \in B_i} P_{i/g} = 1$, the equivalence holds.

Therefore, we conclude that the bid-choice equivalence also holds in the *frechit* model at market equilibrium. For this equivalence to hold, we impose the following: the consumer surplus and the bid-auction shape parameters are identical and prices emerge from an auction process. However, we lift the condition that the indirect utility be linear in price.

Additionally, the equivalence for aggregate *logit* and *frechit* models holds under the same equilibrium conditions, as shown for the *logit* model by Martínez (1992). The bid-choice equivalence replicates the similar property of the deterministic model shown in Chapter 3.

It is worth commenting on the assumption of equal shape parameters, $\beta = \beta_h = \beta_i$, $\forall h \in B_i$, $i \in VI$, because this is a strong assumption for real studies. It means that the bell shape of the willingness-to-pay function is identical, i.e., the distributions have the same variance. In the absence of this condition, the choice approach models the demand for locations at exogenous prices, whereas the bid-auction approach models the allocation with endogenous prices, i.e., these models are different. It is only when the condition holds that we obtain the equivalence property: the expected auction prices ensure that the expected demand clears the market.

4.8 The Stochastic Supply Model

The total number of location options available in the LU market is denoted by $S = \sum_{i \in VI} S_i$, where S_i is the market share of the location type indexed by i, including the type of building and location. For a better understanding, in this section we use the expanded notation for indexing supply units, making the real estate type index v explicit, then $i \in VI \rightarrow vi$, $i \in I$, $v \in V$; therefore, $S = \sum_{vi \in VI} S_{vi}$. We now consider the suppliers' behavior in Chapter 3 as profit maximizers for different market assumptions.

The Stochastic Profit

Supplier profit is a stochastic variable if auction prices are stochastic. Indeed, if profit is defined as the real estate price minus the supply cost, then stochastic prices are enough for profit to be stochastic, independent of the assumption of cost.

The justification of a specific distribution of profit requires certain assumptions. In the above sections, we justified real estate prices as Gumbel and Fréchet variables. Then, if costs are assumed to be deterministic, the random profit follows the same corresponding distribution of prices. However, under the assumption that profits are nonnegative variates, the Fréchet distribution is more appropriate because it complies naturally with this condition. Nevertheless, the multinomial *logit* model has been widely used as an applied model, whereas the *frechit* model hasn't been applied in the context of LU.

The Competitive Supply Market

To introduce the random profit, consider a simple model at the aggregate level of the supplier industry in a competitive market. In this context, the auction takes place ex post and real estate suppliers make the optimal partition of the market into real estate units facing incomplete information of prices; hence, we assume that selling prices (or rents) are random variables. Additionally, building and capital costs may be associated with competitive markets with known prices and hence are deterministic, but the land input is highly correlated with real estate values, which also makes costs random. With selling prices and production costs assumed to be random, profits are also random variables. However, the supplier can observe the distribution of prices from historical auctions to estimate an expected value.

We define the probability that the industry will provide a supply unit vi as:

$$P_{vi} = Prob(\pi_{vi} > \pi_{v'i'};\ \forall i' \in I; v' \in V) \tag{4.39}$$

where π_{vi} is a random variable.

In Chapter 3, real estate development costs are defined as $c_{vi} = c_v(p_{\cdot i}, S_{vi})$, and they depend on the vector of real estate prices at the development location $(p_{\cdot i})$, including both empty and developed land. Additionally, development costs depend on the project itself because economies of scale make costs nonlinearly dependent on the number of real estate units (S_{vi}) and the characteristics of the building given by index v, which include floor space density.

The optimum number of real estate units is obtained as a partition of the exogenous total number of supply units (S) multiplied by the supply probability Denoting $\pi_{vi} = \pi(p_{\cdot i}, S_{vi})$ and the multinomial *logit s*upply by P^S_{vi}, the supply model is

$$S_{vi}(p, S) = SP^S_{vi} = S\frac{e^{\theta\pi_{vi}}}{\sum_{wj\in VI} e^{\theta\pi_{wj}}} \tag{4.40}$$

with θ the shape parameter of the i.i.d. Gumbel distribution of profits, and the expected maximum profit is

$$\pi = \frac{1}{\theta} ln\left[\sum_{wj\in VI} e^{\theta\pi_{wj}}\right] + \frac{\gamma}{\theta} \tag{4.41}$$

with $\gamma \approx 0.577$ the Euler's constant.

The multinomial *frechit supply* model is

$$S_{vi}(p, S) = SP^S_{vi} = S\frac{\pi^{\theta}_{vi}}{\sum_{wj\in VI} \pi^{\theta}_{wj}} \tag{4.42}$$

with the θ shape parameter of the i.i.d. Fréchet distribution of profits, and the expected maximum profit is

$$\pi = K\left[\sum_{wj\in VI} \pi^{\theta}_{wj}\right]^{\frac{1}{\theta}} \tag{4.43}$$

where $K = \Gamma\left(1 - \frac{1}{\theta}\right) > 0$ and Γ is the gamma function.

4.9 Summary

In this chapter, we have described stochastic discrete models for the urban real estate market. From the basic assumption that direct utilities (of goods and location) are random variates with any distribution, it follows that the corresponding indirect utilities and willingness-to-pay random variates are naturally extreme values distributions.

Two different models were obtained based on whether the indirect utilities/profits are assumed to be linear or nonlinear in prices. The linear case justifies the Gumbel distribution for willingness-to-pay variates, which yields the most commonly used *logit* model (MNL). The nonlinear case justifies the Fréchet distribution for these variables, which yields the *frechit* model (MNF). We have noticed that the MNF bid-auction model has the advantage of imposing agents' income and profit constraints consistently, minimizing the probability of choosing a location that is not affordable to the consumer, and yields positive willingness-to-pay values. Similarly, *logit* and *frechit* supply models were developed with the same advantage of the MNF regarding positive profit constraints.

We used these models to develop the demand model for locations at different prices and the bid-auction model with the respective probabilities for building-location options. We proved that these approaches are equivalent under certain equilibrium conditions, i.e., yield the same pattern of consumer allocation, subject to the assumption of identical distributions of bids and prices emerging from auctions. A more thorough analysis of equilibrium with stochastic models is provided in the next chapter.

Therefore, the MNL and MNF stochastic models provide alternative frameworks consistent with the standard microeconomics of consumer and supplier behavior but with different assumptions regarding the underpinning utility. Each one provides modelers with the flexibility to represent the agents' behavior in making optimal choices in the vast heterogeneity of urban space and real estate options and allows the representation of significant heterogeneity in population preferences.

It is worth recalling that the discrete representation of building-location units allows us to define specific attributes for each unit, including the complex measures of accessibility and attractiveness discussed previously. This means that transportation systems, with their transport technology, network, and travel patterns, are represented in these models. Hence, the mutual interaction between transportation and LU is fully considered. The implication of this point is that consumers are assumed to make location and travel choices within a unified framework that is consistent with microeconomics, such that preferences and constraints can be considered consistently.

In the stochastic *logit* and (the newly baptized) *frechit* models, the discrete representation yields continuous and differentiable closed form demand and supply models. This flexibility, largely provided by the independent and identical assumption (i.i.d.), is accompanied by an efficient calculation of probabilities and prices; moreover, we shall see that they provide an even more powerful computing capacity for solving the complex equilibrium of the urban system to be discussed in the following chapters.

In practice, modelers may adopt the choice approach or the bid-auction approach because they are theoretically equivalent under certain assumptions.

Technical Note 4.1: Extreme Value Distributions

This note revises the relevant role of the extreme value distributions for the consumer's behavior theory. The fundamental argument for using extreme value distributions emerges from the extremal types theorem (Fisher and Trippett, 1928), generalized by Gnedenko (1943). For a set of independent stochastic variates, they proved that the asymptotic (nondegenerative) distribution functions of the maximum of a set belongs to a set of three types of extreme value distribution functions (d.f.), regardless of the d.f. of the maximized variates. See also Leadbetter et al. (1983), Galambos (1987), and Mattsson et al. (2014) for references. Hence, the extreme value distribution is—by the extremal types theorem—to the maximum operator equivalent to what the normal distribution is—by the central limit theorem—to the addition operator.

Logit Model

The Type-I, Gumbel or double exponential distribution function is $F(x) = e^{-e^{-\mu(x-\nu)}}$, with $\mu > 0$. The expected value is $E[x] = \nu + \gamma/\mu$, where Euler's constant is approximately 0.577; the variance is $Var[\omega] = \pi^2/(6\mu^2)$; and the mode is ν. This distribution function is particularly relevant in utility-maximizing models because out of the three extreme value distributions; this one is the attractor of a larger number of maximized functions, and the support set is $\mathbb{R}$. For a set of identical and independent Gumbel variates with parameters (ν_i, μ), the probability of choosing alternative $i \in C$, with C the set of available alternatives, is given by the now popular closed-form multinomial *logit* model (called MNL):

$$P_i = \frac{e^{\mu v_i}}{\sum_{j \in C} e^{\mu v_j}}, \forall i \in C \tag{T4.1}$$

and the expected value of the maximum utility, given by the known *logsum function*, is

$$\nu = \frac{1}{\mu} \ln \sum_{i \in C} e^{\mu v_i} + \frac{\gamma}{\mu} \tag{T4.2}$$

The Gumbel distribution function became popular with the individual discrete choice theory with random utilities proposed by Domencic and McFadden (1975).

Another well-known Gumbel-based model is the nested *logit* model (with a similar closed-form probability function), which is of interest in spatial contexts because of its hierarchical choice, where space is analyzed at an scale appropriate to the scale of the choice process.

The Frechit Model

The Fréchet distribution, also called the Type-II extreme value distribution, is the domain of attraction or the limiting nondegenerative distribution of the maximum operator of a set of independent Fréchet variables, among other distributions; i.e., this distribution function is closed with respect to maximization. The Fréchet c.d.f. is $F(x) = e^{\left(-\left(\frac{\nu}{x}\right)^{\beta}\right)}$, defined for $\beta > 0$, but the expected value is only defined for $\beta > 1$, with $E[\theta] = \nu\Gamma\left(1 - \frac{1}{\beta}\right)$ and Γ the gamma function; for $\beta > 2$, the variance is $Var[\theta] = (\nu)^2\left[\Gamma\left(1 - \frac{2}{\beta}\right) - \left(\Gamma\left(1 - \frac{1}{\beta}\right)\right)^2\right]$, inversely related to β. For a set of identical and independent Gumbel variates with parameters (ν_i, μ), the probability of choosing $i \in C$ is given by the following closed-form multinomial model (called MNF):

$$P_i = \frac{\nu_i^\beta}{\sum_{j \in C}\nu_j^\beta} \tag{T4.3}$$

and the expected maximum is

$$\nu = K\left(\sum_{j \in C}\nu_j^\beta\right)^{\frac{1}{\beta}} \tag{T4.4}$$

with $K = \Gamma\left(1 - \frac{1}{\beta}\right)$. Recall that $\Gamma \in \mathbb{R}_{++}$, $\Gamma(z) = \int_0^\infty t^{z-1}e^{-z}dz$, and for any positive integer n, $\Gamma(n) = (n-1)!$.

References

Alonso, W., 1964. Location and Land Use. Harvard Univ. Press, Cambridge, MA.

Anas, A., 1990. Taste heterogeneity and urban spatial structure: the logit and monocentric city reconciled. Journal of Urban Economics 28, 318–335.

Anselin, L., 1988. Spatial Econometrics: Methods and Models. Studies in Operational Regional Science. Springer, New York, NY.

Ben-Akiva, M., Lerman, S.R., 1985. Discrete Choice Analysis: Theory and Application to Travel Demand. MIT Press.

Castillo, E., Menéndez, J.M., Jiménez, P., Rivas, A., 2008. Closed form expressions for choice probabilities in the Weibull case. Transportation Research Part B 42 (4), 373–380.

Domencic, T., McFadden, D., 1975. Urban Travel Demand. North-Holland, Amsterdam.

Ellickson, B., 1981. An alternative test of the hedonic theory of housing markets. Journal of Urban Economics 9, 56–79.

Fisher, R.A., Trippett, L.H.C., 1928. Limiting forms for the frequency distribution of the largest or smallest member of the sample. Proceedings of the Cambridge Philosophical Society 24, 180–190.

Fosgerau, M., Bierlaire, M., 2009. Discrete choice models with multiplicative error terms. Transportation Research Part B 43, 494–505.

Galambos, J., 1987. The Asymptotic Theory of Extreme Order Statistics. John Wiley, New York.

Gálvez, T., 2002. El Modelo Powit (The Powit Model). Urbana, 30, 61–67 (in Spanish).

Gnedenko, B.V., 1943. Sur la distribution limite du terme maximum d'une série aleatórie. Annals of Mathematics 44, 423–453.

Leadbetter, M.R., Lindgren, G., Rootzén, H., 1983. Extreme and Related Properties of Random Sequences and Processes. Springer, New York.

Lerman, S.R., Kern, C.R., 1983. Hedonic theory, bid rents, and willingness-to-pay: some extensions of Ellickson's results. Journal of Urban Economics 13 (3), 358–363.

Manski, C., 1977. The structure of random utility models. Theory and Decisions 8, 229–254.

Martínez, F., 1992. The bid-choice land-use model: an integrated economic framework. Environment and Planning A 24, 871–885.

Mattsson, L.G., Weibull, J., Lindberg, P.O., 2014. Extreme values, invariances and choice probabilities. Transportation Research Part B 59, 81–95.

McFadden, D., 1978. Modelling the choice of Residential location. In: Karlquist, A., et al. (Eds.), Spatial Interaction Theory and Residential Location. North Holland, Amsterdam, pp. 75–96.

McMillen, D.P., 1997. Multiple regime bid-rent function estimation. Journal of Urban Economics 41 (2), 301–319.

Rosen, S., 1974. Hedonic prices and implicit markets: product differentiation in pure competition. Journal of Political Economy 82 (1), 34–55.

Land-Use Stochastic Equilibrium

5

5.1 Introduction

In the land-use system (LU), equilibrium refers to a situation in the system where different push and pull economic and social forces are balanced, leaving the system in a steady state in which agents choosing property in a different location would leave them no better off than before.

This situation includes complying with classical market-clearing conditions, attained by setting equilibrium prices in the choice approach or utilities in the bid-auction approach. However, it also requires other forces to be equilibrated, including those generically called location externalities and agglomeration economies.

The relevance of these "other forces" will be made clear in this chapter with regard to their economic implications, their role in building city structures, and the mathematical complexity that they introduce into the equilibrium problem.

The extension of random LU equilibrium to include location externalities and agglomeration economies is the subject matter of this chapter. Here, we assume that the transportation system (travel and cargo time and costs) and the economic system (goods prices and salaries) are exogenous. These assumptions are relaxed in the next two chapters.

City Structures

The structures that emerge in a city define its macro footprints, i.e., those features that typify the city and differentiate it from others. In addition to natural landmarks, such as rivers, mountains, lakes, and sea frontage, macrofeatures are also created by the built environment. These features include the socioeconomic distribution of the population in the city and the concentration of activity in subcenters and along the main corridors of the transportation system.

Given the natural landmarks, the built structures emerge from two major forces: agent behavior and urban policies (e.g., transportation infrastructure, zoning regulations), which define scenarios in which the urban LU market operates following particular rules. The market rules are fundamental in determining which structures emerge and how the city evolves. In this chapter, we examine marrket equilibrium as a rule that helps to describe market performance.

A set of stylized city structures is sketched in Fig. 5.1, which helps us to visualize certain basic ideas. For simplicity, we use the classical urban economics model in this figure, with land as a continuous space and agents having deterministic behavior. Each figure provides a bird's-eye view on the left side, showing concentrations as seen on maps; on the right side is a radial vertical axel diagram, in which densities and rents are collapsed in a single line because their general shape is similar. Fig. 5.1A (left) shows

Microeconomic Modeling in Urban Science. https://doi.org/10.1016/B978-0-12-815296-6.00005-6

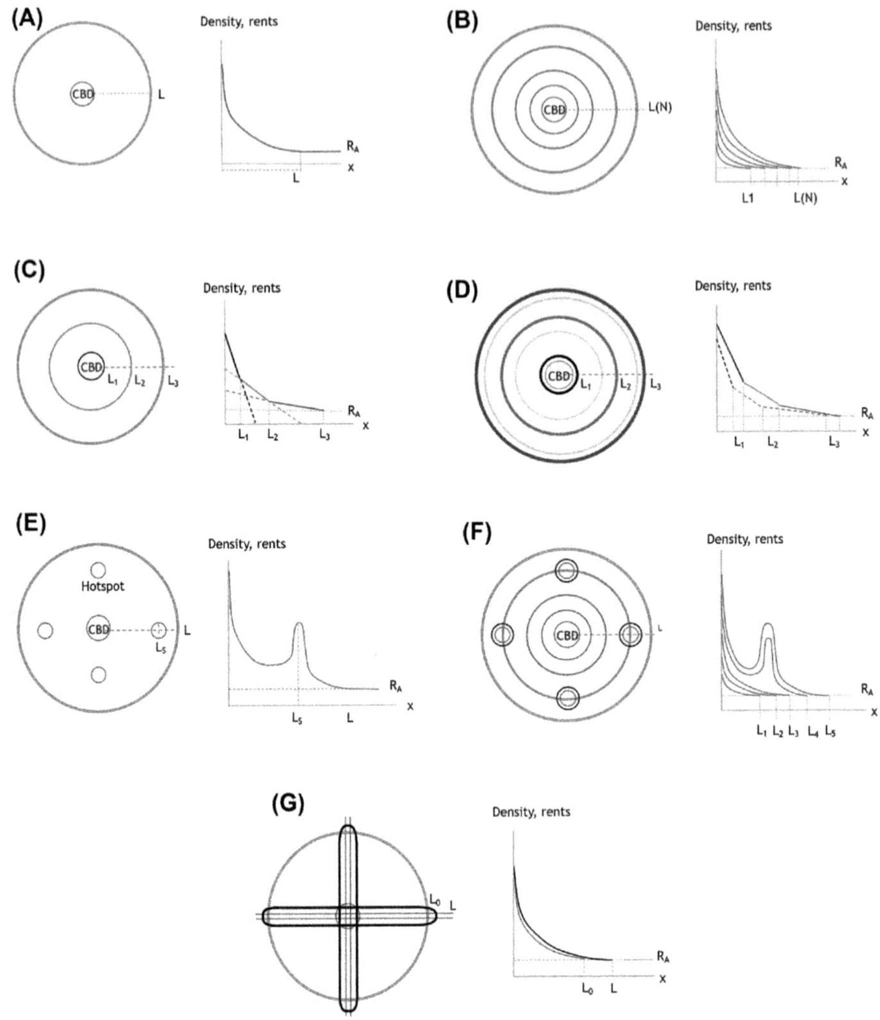

Figure 5.1 Urban structures. (A) Static monocentric city. (B) Dynamic monocentric city population increase. (C) Static monocentric city with heterogeneous population. (D) Dynamic monocentric city with heterogeneous population. (E) Static multicentric city. (F) Dynamic multicentric city. (G) Static transport network city. *CBD*, central business district.

the classical monocentric city with an inner ring called the central business district (CBD) concentering all jobs and an outer ring of residents that expands out to the city limit (L). On the right, land rents decrease with distance (x) from the CBD, with rents meeting an agricultural land rent (R_A) where agricultural activities outbid residents. Additionally, land consumption per resident increases with distance, inducing a decrease in density. This figure shows the first feature: for a given population, the city limit depends on agricultural land rents. The evolution of the city as population (N) increases is shown in Fig. 5.1B, depicting urban sprawl by the expanding city limit $L(N)$ and increasing densities and rents at every location. This figure demonstrates that the city limit depends on total population and agricultural land rents in a way that we will discuss in this chapter.

Figure 5.1 introduces the formation of a city's structures. Fig. 5.1C depicts the socioeconomic segregation between heterogeneous residents, forming rings with limits (L_1,L_2,L_3) that differentiate residents according to their trade-offs between a more central area with high density, high land rents, and low transportation costs, and outer rings with low density, low rent, and high transportation costs. In Fig. 5.1D, these rings expand with population growth (from dotted to solid lines) at different speeds depending on how the population's socioeconomic profile evolves over time.

In Fig. 5.1E, subcenters (or hot spots) break the smooth downward slopes of densities and rents with the emergence of nonresidential subcenters at distance L_s from the CBD where transportation costs offset the benefits of scale economies of the CBD. At the subcenter, densities and rents increase as a result of a peak in demand for nonresidential land. Fig. 5.1F shows that the subcenter emerges at a critical population level and expands thereafter with increased population. Finally, Fig. 5.1G shows how the transportation network disrupts the notion of accessibility, decreasing monotonically with distance to CBD, introducing improved access in nearby corridors, which leads to higher densities and rents and expands the city limit along these corridors (from L_0 to L). Thus, the city's dynamics follow the development of the transportation network (not shown in Fig. 5.1).

Real cities combine these elemental structures in a dynamic process, generating diverse and complex structures because of the underpinnings of the diverse behaviors of agents. The challenge of modeling is to reproduce this complexity, the resulting structure, and its evolution as a market process, which is the topic of this chapter.

The Concept of Equilibrium

Although LU market equilibrium is defined by the classical clear market condition existing between supply and demand, it also includes a state wherein the agents' complex interactions, e.g., location externalities and agglomeration economies, are resolved to a steady state situation in which urban structures emerge. The equilibrium condition guarantees that no agent, for either households or firms or real estate suppliers, can improve their own utility or profit by making a different choice.

In urban land modeling, the concept of equilibrium is sometimes disputed by questioning whether this market ever attains equilibrium. This dispute is worthy of comment because market equilibrium yields the prices in the system, i.e., land and real estate rents. Moreover, because real estate units are differentiated goods, rents are a large set of values with the dimension of real estate types times the optional locations. Thus, equilibrium is a highly valuable mechanism that provides a rule for calculating these values consistently with economic principles, establishing the ways in which they are related across the city.

In the absence of market equilibrium, the modeler must use an alternative rule for calculating prices. For this purpose, modelers often use the *hedonic price* rule, which is an econometric model of prices as a function of real estate attributes. As was shown in Chapter 4, hedonic price models are theoretically consistent with urban economic theory. Lancaster (1966) first proposed that utility is derived from the attributes of the goods, and Rosen (1974) applied this concept in the urban land market. However, the important issue to mention here is that hedonic prices are point values of the theoretical equilibrium prices, i.e., they describe how cross-section values of rents can be explained by the differentials of attributes among real estate units. Therefore, they are very helpful in identifying the value of unpriced goods, such as access to parks or public transportation, which are implicitly valued by residents and revealed in real estate prices (Rosen, 1974). The difficulty arises when they are used to estimate future rents but ignore the nonlinear mechanism that yields these prices, which depends on the complex dynamics of location externalities and agglomeration economies. Hence, using this rule to extrapolate prices in the future may be deemed valid for only a very short time from the observation of prices; its use is unable to predict equilibrium prices in the medium or long run (Hurtubia et al., 2010). Hence, the use of the hedonic price technique is limited.

The critical view, that static equilibrium is a theoretical construct that never occurs, is realistic but does not invalidate the cautious use of the concept to obtain an approximation of reality. Indeed, every market is in constant change, i.e., a dynamic process of interactions among agents sharing information about their values for different goods in the market. In this dynamic process of information exchange, market forces operate by pushing prices toward the equilibrium prices, which are the signals that all agents perceive at any point in time. Therefore, we consider here that equilibrium prices are the most informed values that the modeler can calculate given the diversity of agents and real estate options.

Furthermore, LU equilibrium is a dynamic concept because land prices always depend on the economy in which the urban land market is embedded, which undergoes constant change. In the case of the urban land market, this dynamic is also influenced by demographics, in addition to urban policies. Therefore, by *static equilibrium* we refer to a point in time at which the clear market condition holds in the urban LU market for a given set of external conditions, i.e., it is a static picture of a dynamic system.

Finally, the LU and rents equilibrium involves the transference of different and complex pieces of information through the market, with different speeds of reactions. For example, buildings take significant time to be built, whereas auctions of old stock are quicker. Thus, the modeler can represent the dynamic system with delays in the acquisition of information and in the auctions, differentiating between *short-term and long-term equilibrium* states. In this context, rents and location equilibrium conditions may be conceived and modeled to account for the delays. Hence, the static equilibrium without delays defines an idealistic situation in the long term when all relevant delays have been accounted for, whereas the short-term equilibrium represents a market-clearing condition with delayed information and actions.

Notably, the discussion above is valid for every market and is a common issue in microeconomics. What is specific to the LU market is that real estate units are *differentiable goods*, and therefore the load of information required in the assumption of perfect information in the static equilibrium is more demanding. Second, goods are *durables* in this market; thus, certain consumers are proprietors of an investment that is used but not consumed. In this case, the information required to model the demand process involves the future evolution of the market. This requires the modeler's decision on how agents, both consumers and suppliers, foresee the future, with two extreme points: agents with perfect foresight or agents who are short-sighted. We suggest that the myopic assumption is more consistent with the static equilibrium model because agents are assumed to be reacting to current information, whereas perfect foresight assumes that agents know the future dynamic of the system. Because the myopic perception is based on historical information, regardless of its quality, it is realistic, whereas perfect foresight can only be taken as a theoretical assumption.

Levels of Analysis

The urban system may be studied at the different levels depicted in Fig. 5.2. The LU partial equilibrium shown in Fig. 5.2A focuses on the distribution of agents in the

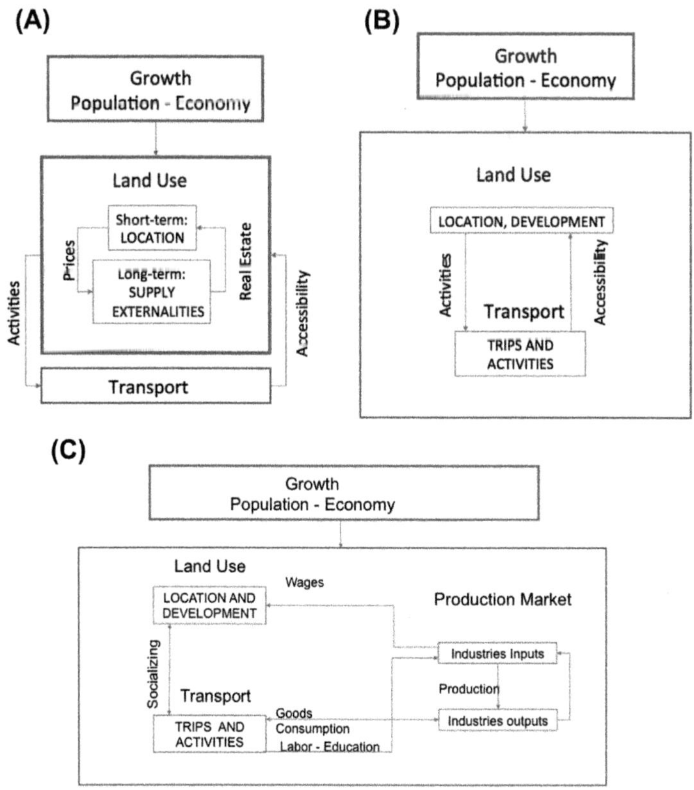

Figure 5.2 Levels of urban equilibrium. (A) Land-use equilibrium with transport interaction. (B) Land-use and transport equilibrium. (C) General land-use, transport, and production markets equilibrium.

space and the emergence of city structures, conditional on transportation and other system conditions. These systems can be represented by accessibility and attractiveness indices, generated from specific interacting models but without attaining equilibrium. The next level integrates the land-use and transportation (LUT) subsystems at equilibrium, with the economic system (prices of goods, jobs, and salaries) assumed to be exogenous (Fig. 5.2B). This level is followed by the general urban equilibrium, in which the model integrates land-use, transportation, and the production economy (LUTE), i.e., production and labor relations (Fig. 5.2C). The system of cities is the largest model, in which cities are objects that compete for population and economic development. In this chapter, we discuss LU market equilibrium, leaving the integration of transportation and economic markets for the next chapters.

These market levels are combined with specific resolution levels, i.e., with aggregation levels of the heterogeneity of the population and the firms, real estate diversity, spatial resolution (from real estate units to blocks and to zones), and the transportation system description. The spatial resolution defines different model types: macro (few zones and homogeneous agents), meso (usually zones and groups of agents), and micro (individual and real estate unit resolution) models. For each of these levels, the corresponding market equilibrium can be defined depending on the exogenous system, whose variability can be represented by scenarios.

External Scenarios

Market equilibrium always depends on the set of external or exogenous scenarios. These scenarios include the economy of the country where the city is located, which defines the income of its residents, the demand for its firms' exports, and the prices of imported commodities based on transport costs and import taxes.

Another external force is demographics, the human birth and death dynamics which define the population's age profile and their life cycles. Modelers are usually comfortable with predictions of demographic dynamics because they are not significantly susceptible to unexpected shocks. This is important for modelers because population is an essential fuel of the city's dynamic, i.e., even if hypothetically the economy remains static, the urban system continues to change.

Nonetheless, the external conditions (or parameters) in the urban system are largely a definition of the modeler, who decides what is included in the model and what is assumed to be exogenous. Theoretically, this limit between external conditions and internal processes does not exist because the entire world's socioeconomic system can be considered as a complex set of interdependent mechanisms. Therefore, this boundary is only a utilitarian definition necessary for developing models.

Behavior of Agents

Described by the set of utilities and profit functions, the behavior of agents, including resident households, firms, and real estate developers, defines the internal or endogenous dynamics of the urban market and drives the formation of macroscale structures in the city. Indeed, given the external conditions, the allocation of agents in the space, the use of land, the development of real estate units, the spatial profiles of the population, the floor-space densities, and the land and real estate rents are the result of the signals defined by agents' behavior.

The macrostructures of the city, i.e., the concentration of activities in special clusters of socioeconomic groups, or the emergence of productive subcenters, etc., depend on how agents behave in their location process, specifically with regard to the interactions among agents. Therefore, the specification of these behavioral functions determines the emergence of the city structures.

At a general level, agents' behavior can be considered to be dependent on the following characteristics: their value of the interaction with other agents, i.e., some form of accessibility or attractiveness; their sensitivity to prices; and their perceptions of local conditions, i.e., location externalities and agglomeration economies. Agents are also subject to feasibility conditions that limit their actions, such as income constraints and nonnegative profits. Thus, a simplified way of understanding the LU model is to consider a model of generic agents, each one governed by a behavioral rule (called utility or profit) but differentiated by the specific rule attached to each one. Agents use the rule to evaluate the attributes of the system (i.e., to assess utility or profit) and make optimal choices. This simplifies the modeling to the specification of each agent's behavioral function and the definition of the market equilibrium rules that combine the behavior of all the individual agents.

In the case of households, the specification of rules considering location externalities, such as neighborhood quality indices, creates segregation structures among resident groups, whether socioeconomic, ethnic, religious, or other. These structures emerge even without the influence of pecuniary effects (without the effect of land prices), e.g., when the location pattern is the result of only the value of locating a residence close to peers. The segregation of households by group type emerges even in the theoretical case in which land prices are flat, i.e., land prices are equal everywhere (Shelling, 1978). In the case of firms, agglomeration economies define the emergence of clusters of firms and subcenters.

Additionally, for all agents, transportation costs mediate their location choices. Thus, the extent to which agents value transportation costs (mainly travel time) and quality is another force in the emergence of the structures of cities. Urban locations are the result of multiple forces, in addition to land rents.

The Role of Constraints

Regulations in the urban system are usually more relevant and numerous than in other competitive markets because planners seek social objectives that the unregulated market may not provide. The presence of social externalities that are not internalized in agents' perceptions but that emerge as unwanted features of the market process, e.g., socioeconomic segregation, high congestion, and environmental impacts, explains why cities continue to be regulated, whereas other markets have been largely deregulated.

Subsidies and taxes represent another policy considered as a vehicle for socially and environmentally sustainable cities. This policy has been applied to internalize congestion costs in the transportation system, following the social objective of minimizing total transportation costs. In the LU system, subsidies have usually been applied as a social policy to provide residential solutions for people who cannot afford it.

The impact of regulations and economic incentives on the equilibrium outcome should not be ignored by modelers. They have a strong potential to shape cities away from what a purely competitive market would dictate. Even if the impacts of regulations may eventually be overcome by market forces, they still have strong long-term effects because the evolution of the city is guided by regulations and incentives, i.e., they create the prevailing city structures that create the future city.

This Chapter

In our discussion on the LU bid-auction equilibrium, we first address the short term when supply is exogenous and then the long term, both without location externalities and agglomeration economies. Next, we extend the model to the situation with externalities in the LU market and explain how to model constraints.

We examine the LU of a closed city, i.e., assuming that the population is exogenous and inelastic, and where transportation and the production markets (goods and labor) are considered to be exogenous to the equilibrium. These topics will be examined in the next chapters, where these conditions are relaxed.

Because equilibrium is a feature at the market level, it is more intuitive to discuss this topic considering the aggregated model, i.e., where bidders are categorized into socioeconomic clusters denoted by $h \in B$, with H_h the number of members in each cluster, and totaling a population of H agents in the city. Moreover, we assume that the set of bidders at each auction is the population, i.e., $B = C$, and in the cases where certain bidders are forbidden in an auction, e.g., if regulations apply, this is modeled using constraints as shown later. Real estate units are aggregated into zones and real estate types, with S_i units in each type of zone group $i \in VI$. Nevertheless, the disaggregated equilibrium is obtained by setting $H_h = S_i = 1,\ \forall h \in C,\ i \in VI$ in the following equations.

5.2 Short-Term Land-Use Equilibrium

Short-term LU partial equilibrium is characterized by exogenous demand by cluster, and supply by real estate type and zone, i.e., H_h and S_i are given as the modeling scenario. Additionally, transportation and production markets are also exogenous and defined as a scenario for this equilibrium. In this context, the LU market equilibrium considers the situation in which the total number of real estate supply units equals the number of consumers (H), i.e., $|VI| = |B| = H$, with the set of bidders $B = \bigcup_{i \in VI} B_i$. Note that because the set of supply units VI is exogenous, building densities at each location and the urban bounds are given.

This represents a situation where prices and location decisions are adjusted for an exogenous supply. The assumption of exogenous supply is realistic in the short term because new stock involves a construction period; thus, the location and building characteristics of a real estate unit are decided some time before it is available on the market, which is when the auctions take place.

The *short-term equilibrium conditions* (STEqC):

1. Total supply equals total demand.
2. All agents are allocated.
3. Demand matches supply at each location.
4. Prices at the edge of the city match agriculture land rents.

We shall see that conditions 1 to 3 are mutually dependent. If demand matches supply at each location (condition 3), and all agents are allocated (condition 2), it follows that total demand equals total supply because condition 1 is an aggregation of the other two conditions. Hence, one of these conditions is redundant.

Total Demand Equals Supply

The bid-auction equilibrium yields the solution matrix $M_H = \{H_{hi},\ h \in C,\ i \in VI\}$, which describes the allocation of consumers to available real estate units, subject to: $\sum_{\substack{h \in C \\ i \in VI}} H_{hi} = H = \sum_{h \in C} H_h = \sum_{i \in VI} S_i$.

Consumers' Equilibrium

The second equilibrium condition is that the population of agents is allocated to the available supply, what we call the *consumers' equilibrium*.

Considering the bid-auction model discussed in Chapter 4, this equilibrium condition holds if:

$$H_h = \sum_{i \in VI} H_{hi} = \sum_{i \in VI} S_i Q_{h/i}(u^*),\ \forall h \in C \tag{5.1}$$

where $Q_{h/i}$ is the auction probability.

This equation guarantees that every consumer agent h is located somewhere, i.e., the consumer is the highest bidder at some of the available locations. For this condition to hold, consumers' relative utilities are adjusted to equilibrium values (u^*), while the solution depends on the probability model $Q_{h/i}$—*logit or frechit*—defined in Chapter 4.

Demand Equals Supply at Each Location

This condition assures that demand and supply match at each submarket, i.e., in each zone and real estate type. This is expressed by:

$$S_i = \sum_{h \in C} H_{hi} = \sum_{h \in C} H_h P_{i/h}(p^*),\ \forall i \in VI \tag{5.2}$$

where $P_{i/h}$ is the consumer choice probability. For this equation to hold, *relative prices* are adjusted in the equilibrium of the auction process (p^*).

The City Boundary

Additionally, Alonso (1964) states that equilibrium land prices at the city limit should match agricultural land rents. In the real estate model, however, the equivalent condition is that profit at the city limit should match the profit of renting the land for agriculture. For this condition to hold, relative prices should be adjusted to absolute values; thus, utilities are also simultaneously adjusted. These adjustments must retain the relative values of the prices and utilities of the previous conditions.

Equilibrium of Utilities and Prices

The Logit Model

For Eq. (5.1) to hold, it is necessary that all consumers in the market (households and firms) adjust their reservation utilities and profits simultaneously up to the level where the equilibrium condition is satisfied assuming the *logit* bid-choice model. The outcome of the auctions can be estimated by solving Eq. (5.1) for the equilibrium utilities (or profits in the case of firms), denoted u^*, such that:

$$\sum_{i \in VI} S_i Q_{h/i}(u^*) = \sum_{i \in VI} S_i \frac{H_h e^{\beta w_{hi}\left(u_h^*\right)}}{\sum\limits_{g \in C} H_g e^{\beta w_{gi}\left(u_g^*\right)}} = H_h, \forall h \in C \tag{5.3}$$

This equation defines a fixed-point problem on the set of equilibrium utilities, such that $u_h^* = F^u(u^*), \forall h \in C$. The solution of this fixed-point problem depends on the specification of bid functions.

For the case of utilities linear in price, i.e., bids linear in utility, $w_{hi}\left(u_h^*\right) = y_h - \frac{u_h^*}{\lambda_h} + \frac{f_h(z_i)}{\lambda_h}$, the fixed-point equation is treatable. In this case, the equilibrium problem can be written more conveniently using $\overline{u}_h^* = \frac{u_h^*}{\lambda_h}$, and solving for $\overline{u}_h^*$ in the numerator yields:

$$\overline{u}_h^* = \frac{1}{\beta} \ln\left(\sum_{i \in VI} S_i \frac{e^{\beta\left(y_h + \frac{f_h(z_i)}{\lambda_h}\right)}}{\sum\limits_{g \in C} H_g e^{\beta w_{gi}\left(\overline{u}^*\right)}} \right), \forall h \in C \tag{5.4}$$

This equation can be written as: $F^{\overline{u}}(\overline{u}^*) = \frac{1}{\beta} \ln\left(\sum_{i \in VI} S_i \frac{e^{\beta z_{hi}}}{\sum_{g \in C} e^{\beta\left(z_{gi} - \overline{u}_g\right)}} \right)$, with β, S_i and $z_{hi} = H_h e^{\beta\left(y_h + \frac{f_h(z_i)}{\lambda_h}\right)}$ constants in this problem.

In Technical Note 5.1 we prove that Eq. (5.3) is the solution of a convex optimization problem. The solution is unique in terms of normalized utilities because Eq. (5.4) is invariant to an additive constant of utilities; i.e., if $\overline{u}^*$ is the solution, then $(\overline{u}^* + c) = F^{\overline{u}}(\overline{u}^* + c)$.

Let us now consider the equilibrium condition in Eq. (5.2):

$$S_i = \sum_{h \in C} H_h \frac{S_i e^{\beta(w_{hi} - p_i)}}{\sum_{j \in VI} S_j e^{\beta(w_{hj} - p_j)}}, \ \forall i \in VI \tag{5.5}$$

Solving for price p_i in the numerator, we obtain the prices at equilibrium given by:

$$p_i^* = \frac{1}{\beta} \ln \left(\sum_{h \in C} H_h \frac{e^{\beta(w_{hi})}}{\sum_{j \in VI} S_j e^{\beta\left(w_{hj} - p_j^*\right)}} \right), \ \forall i \in VI \tag{5.6}$$

We now examine equilibrium Eqs (5.4) and (5.6) because utilities and prices are mutually dependent. Let us define the location price as: $p_i^* := \frac{1}{\beta} \ln \left(\sum_{g \in C} H_g e^{\beta(w_{gi})} \right)$, $\forall i \in VI$, which, in Eq. (5.6), holds if $H_h = \sum_{j \in VI} S_j e^{\beta\left(w_{hj} - p_j^*\right)}$. Using this condition in Eq. (5.4) yields $\sum_{i \in VI} S_i e^{\beta\left(w_{hi}\left(u_h^*\right) - p_i^*\right)} = 1$ for equilibrium utilities. Then, Eq. (5.5) imposes that $\sum_{h \in C} H_h e^{\beta\left(w_{hi}\left(u_h^*\right) - p_i^*\right)} = 1, \forall i \in VI$, which holds by the definition of bid probabilities.

We conclude that the solution of the equilibrium conditions in Eqs (5.3) and (5.5) hold if:

$$\overline{u}_h^* = \frac{1}{\beta} \ln \left(\sum_{i \in VI} S_i e^{\beta\left(y_h + \frac{f_h(z_i)}{\lambda_h} - p_i^*\right)} \right), \ \forall h \in C \tag{5.7}$$

$$p_i^*(\overline{u}^*) = \frac{1}{\beta} \ln \left(\sum_{g \in C} H_g e^{\beta w_{gi}\left(\overline{u}_g^*\right)} \right), \ \forall i \in VI \tag{5.8}$$

Note that the solution of equilibrium utilities in Eq. (5.4) is sufficient to calculate equilibrium prices in Eq. (5.8). This is consistent with our conclusion in previous chapters that in the bid-auction model, the equilibrium utilities define equilibrium prices or that STEqC 3 presented earlier is redundant if STEqC 1 and 2 hold. To calculate the solution on relative values of utilities, normalize utilities setting one element of the vector at any constant (e.g. zero), and iterate Eq. (5.4) until convergence is attained; then, use the result in Eq. (5.8) to obtain expected prices.

The economic interpretation of Eq. (5.7) is that because utilities are random variables, the equilibrium solution u^* is the set of maximum expected utility that agents can obtain on the market to outbid others somewhere and be allocated, with the corresponding location probability given by $Q_{h/i}(u^*)$. Additionally, note that because consumers bid with the same expected utility level u_h^* in all auctions, this implies that the indifference condition holds.

As expected, equilibrium utilities increase and prices decrease, with the supply size given by $|VI|$, called the market supply thickness, due to the larger variety of options. Conversely, prices increase with market demand thickness $|C|$, while utilities decrease.

From Relative to Absolute Prices

Mathematically, the fixed-point problem $\overline{u} = F^u(\overline{u})$, with $\overline{u} = \left(\overline{u}_h^*, \forall h \in C\right)$ in Eq. (5.4), is invariant for an additive constant $k \in \mathbb{R}$, i.e., it admits multiple solutions because if $\overline{u}^*$ is a solution, then $\overline{u}^* + k$ is also a solution because the constant cancels out. Additionally, real estate prices comply with $p(\overline{u}^* + k) = p - k$. These multiple solutions are reduced to a unique solution imposing the fourth equilibrium condition, originally proposed by Alonso (1964), for the continuous monocentric city: land prices at the edge of the city must equal agricultural land rents (denoted R_A). The underlying concept is that the land owner at the city limit must be indifferent to the use for selling it. In the discrete model, this means holding no preference between selling the land for agricultural use or for real estate development as long as the profits are equal.

The implementation of this condition implies the identification of the real estate unit in the city that yields the minimum profit at the relative prices obtained from Eq. (5.8), which we identify by $i_0 \in VI$ with q_{i_0} its land size, i.e., we define $i_0 = \text{argmin}_{i \in VI}\{p_i(\overline{u}^*) - c_i\}$, with c_i the building cost. Then, constant k is adjusted appropriately to match its profit with the profit of renting this land for agriculture for a value of $q_{i_0}R_A$ (ignoring any agricultural costs of LU). Thus, equalizing the expected profits, we write: $p_{i_0}(\overline{u}^*) - k - c_{i_0} = q_{i_0}R_A$. Replacing Eq. (5.8) and solving for the constant yields:

$$k(R_A) = \frac{1}{\beta}\ln\left[\sum_{g \in C} e^{\beta w_{gi_0}(\overline{u}_g^*)}\right] - c_{i_0} - q_{i_0}R_A \tag{5.9}$$

where development costs c_i are known because the real estate supply is exogenous. Because $k(R_A)$ is constant for all locations, $\overline{u}^* + k(R_A)$ identifies a unique solution for the fixed point in Eq. (5.4) and absolute prices for Eq. (5.8).

Nevertheless, this analysis is overly simplistic. Indeed, it is worth considering that Alonso's condition is restrictive for our more complex context because it assumes a monocentric city with a circular border where agricultural rents are constant along this border. It is more realistic to implement this basic idea but for heterogeneous agricultural rents, given by a vector $R_A = \{R_{Ak}, k \in I_b \subset I\}$, where I_b is the set of locations at the city border. In this case, we redefine $K_0 = \text{argmin}_{k \in K_b}\{p_k(\overline{u}^*) - c_k - R_{Ak}\}$ and apply the corresponding correction $k(R_{Ai_0})$ to all prices and utilities. Because $k(R_A)$ is a scalar, i.e., a constant adjustment of all prices in the city locations, it follows that the profit at locations other than i_0 is expected to exceed the agricultural land rents at the city borders, (except at i_0), generating a mismatch in the price profile at these borders, i.e., a singularity in the form of a step on the land price profile from rural to urban land. This mismatch in prices at certain borders is expected to induce urban sprawl in a dynamic process not captured in the static model. Although this method for adjusting prices to heterogeneous agricultural land values is more realistic, it is also more difficult to implement because it requires collecting not one value but a vector of values $\{R_{Ak}\}$.

The underlying intuition of the constant adjustment is as follows. Consider the case in which bidders' reservation utilities and profits are high; thus, expected bid-auction prices are low, such that the minimum profit at the "city border" (i.e., minimum profit location) is less than the profit yield if land is rented for agriculture. The constant will be negative, and the adjustment reduces all the agents' reservation utilities and increases land prices at the border and everywhere in the city, up to a match with agricultural land profits. Note that because real estate supply is exogenous in this case, this adjustment only affects the profile of utilities, prices, profits, densities, and the allocation of consumers but does not influence supply, city structures, or city size.

An important observation is that Eq. (5.9) assures the suppliers a positive expected profit on all real estate units because the expected profit at the city limit is $q_{i_0}R_A > 0$. Notably, the price adjustment assumes that the suppliers have no reservation prices, i.e., that they are willing to sell or rent at any price above the threshold R_A per land unit.

The Frechit Model

In this case, bids are nonlinear at the utility level with a multiplicative form: $w_{hi}(u_h) = y_h e^{\lambda^{-1}(-u_h + f_h(z_i))}$; additionally, $Q_{h/i} = \frac{H_h w_{hi}^{\beta}}{\sum_{g\in C} H_g w_{gi}^{\beta}}$ and $p_{i/h} = \frac{S_i \left(w_{hi}/p_i \right)^{\beta}}{\sum_{j\in VI} S_j \left(w_{hj}/p_j \right)^{\beta}}$.

Then, the equilibrium utilities' fixed-point problem derived from Eq. (5.1) is

$$\overline{u}_h^* = \frac{1}{\beta} \ln \left(\sum_{i\in VI} S_i \left[\frac{y_h \bullet e^{\lambda^{-1} f_h(z_i)}}{p_i(\overline{u}^*)} \right]^{\beta} \right), \forall h \in C \quad (5.10)$$

with

$$p_i(\overline{u}^*) = \left[\sum_{g\in C} H_g w_{gi}(\overline{u}^*)^{\beta} \right]^{\frac{1}{\beta}} \quad (5.11)$$

In this case, $\sum_{g\in C} H_g \left(w_{gi}/p_i \right)^{\beta} = 1$ holds for $p_i = p_i(u^*)$.

Note that Eq. (5.10) is also invariant for an additive constant, although this is not the case for prices because $p_i(\overline{u}^* + k) = p_i(\overline{u}^*)e^{-k}$ for any constant $k \in \mathbb{R}$. Additionally, the solution of equilibrium utilities is unique (see Technical Note 5.1); optimal utility and real estate prices are calculated simultaneously and iteratively using Eqs (5.10) and (5.11); Alternatively, utilities can be calculated directly solving by iterations the fixed-point Eq. (5.10) after replacing prices by Eq. (5.11).

Here, the price adjustment to agricultural land values yields:

$$k(R_A) = \frac{1}{\beta} \ln \left[\sum_{g \in C} w_{gi_0} \left(\overline{u}_g^* \right)^{\beta} \right] - \ln\left(c_{i_0} + q_{i_0} R_A \right) \tag{5.12}$$

with i_0 defined above.

Comments on Short-Term Equilibrium

Technically, there is a unique solution for short-run equilibrium, defined in Eq. (5.1), given for utilities normalized by an additive constant. This holds only if the total supply equals the total demand, i.e., $S = H$. In this case, the iterative algorithm $u^t = F^u(u^{t-1})$ converges for any initial value $u^{t=0}$; (see the proof in Technical Note 5.1). The solution does not exist if $\sum_{i \in VI} S_i < H$ because total demand is inelastic; equilibrium conditions are not unique if $\sum_{i \in VI} S_i > H$ because there are multiple sets of unsold (unused) real estate units with one equilibrium solution for each set.

The algorithm for calculating equilibrium has two general steps: first, solve the fixed-point equations on relative utilities to obtain $\overline{u}^* + k$ and calculate relative equilibrium prices $p(\overline{u}^* + k)$ and second, find the minimum profit real estate unit i_0, calculate $k(R_A)$ for the corresponding model (*logit* or *frechit*), and adjust equilibrium utilities and prices to obtain absolute values.

Denote by $\varphi^{ST} = (\{H_h\}, \{S_i\}, Z(T), R_A, E)$ the set of parameters defining the short-term exogenous scenario: $\{H_h\}$ is the population by cluster; $\{S_i\}$ the supply by real estate type and location; $Z(T)$ the location attributes (including accessibility measures that are dependent on the transportation system denoted as T); R_A the agricultural land rents; and E the set of parameters defining the economy, i.e., the prices of goods and salaries. Then, the short-term equilibrium is denoted by:

$$\Xi(u; \varphi^{st}) = \left(\{u_h^*\} = F^u \right) \tag{5.13}$$

The economic mechanism of the short-term LU equilibrium has several topics to revise regarding the dynamics of the cities; in this analysis, other variables are considered *ceteris paribus*. An increase in agricultural land rents is an external shock that causes a reduction in the constant $k(R_A)$ and thus an equal reduction in utilities for all agents and an increase in prices everywhere. In the short run, however, the *logit* and *frechit* models presented earlier predict that agents' allocations are unaffected because bid-auction probabilities are insensitive to constant change in utilities across individuals for quasi-linear utilities, even though the induced change in prices has a different impact on the income constraint across consumers. This counterintuitive feature is a shortcoming of these models, not of these random models per se, but caused by the simplistic formulation of utilities, i.e., the model does not eliminate consumers from the market when prices exceed their income constraints. Instead, every consumer is allocated at equilibrium. To address this topic properly, we extend the model below, explicitly modeling the constraints regarding the behavior of the agents.

The impact of an increase in the population's incomes induces an increase in utilities and prices, impelling urban sprawl because residents outbid agricultural activity in a wider area. An important observation is that the *increase in land prices represents the capitalization of the wealth of the population into land values*, captured in the model through the change in willingness to pay.

Notably, in a scenario with higher prices induced by exogenous forces such as agricultural land rents, consumers would tend to compensate utility in their willingness to pay with lower land inputs and transportation costs, thus increasing the demand for real estate units with a smaller size (higher density) at locations closer to the center of the city. However, because equilibrium supply is exogenous in the short term, such compensation is not realized, and in a short period of time, available suppliers capitalize on the shock in prices until the supply is adjusted.

5.3 Long-Term Land-Use Equilibrium

Long-term equilibrium considers the short-term equilibrium conditions but with an endogenous supply. That is, total demand is exogenous and satisfied by the supply at any point in time, i.e., $H = \sum_{i \in VI} S_i(p)$. The demand for real estate units at any location is also satisfied because the amount of supply of each real estate type is elastic with regard to prices. These conditions are assumed to hold in the long term, depending on the exogenous scenario $\varphi^{LT} = (\{H_h\}, Z(T), R_A, E)$ defining the demography, accessibility, and the economy, respectively.

The long-term equilibrium condition defines the supply of real estate units at each location, the city's boundaries, the building density profile, and the city's structures. In this case, the auction process leads to a situation in which consumers attain maximum utility and suppliers simultaneously attain maximum profit, a process known as a *double matching* mechanism.

The supplier's stochastic profit model is

$$S_i(p) = HP_i^s(p), \forall i \in VI^* \tag{5.14}$$

with $P_i^s(p) \leq 1$ the probability that the real estate type i is supplied according to the maximum profit rule. Notably, Eq. (5.14) applies for a set of real estate options that is also endogenously defined at equilibrium, denoted by the optimum set VI^*. This means that the city border is endogenous. This topic will be discussed later.

The supply probability model was discussed in Chapter 4.

1. The *logit* maximum profit model is the MNL model:

$$S_i(p^*) = H \frac{e^{\theta\pi(p_i^* - c_i)}}{\sum_{j \in VI^*} e^{\theta\pi(p_j^* - c_j)}}, \forall i \in VI^* \tag{5.15}$$

where *logit* equilibrium prices are given by Eq. (5.8). Notice that $p_i^* = p_i^*(\overline{u}^*)$ with $\overline{u}_h^* = \overline{u}_h^*(S(p^*))$. Then, we conclude that in the absence of scale economies (discussed below), the solution of the long-term *logit* equilibrium is given by the set of fixed point equations $\overline{u} = F^u(\overline{u}, S(\overline{u}))$.

2. The *frechit* maximum profit model is the MNF model:

$$S_i(p) = H\frac{\pi\left(p_i^*/c_i\right)^{\theta}}{\sum\limits_{j\in VI^*}\pi\left(p_j^*\Big/c_j\right)^{\theta}}, \forall i \in VI^* \tag{5.16}$$

with *frechit* equilibrium prices given in Eq. (5.11). As before, this yields the fixed point problem $\overline{u} = F^u(\overline{u}, S(\overline{u}))$.

Scale Economies and Land Price Dependency in Supply Costs

In the previous analysis, we assumed exogenous production costs in the real estate supply industry. However, in Chapter 3 we discussed production costs of real estate units theoretically, indicating that they depend on real estate prices and on the scale of the development project, which can be expressed as $c_i = c(p_i, S_i)$. The price in the cost function represents the vector $p_{i\in VI} = \{p_{vi}, v \in V, i \in I\}$ and is the cost of the land input taken from the redevelopment of land at the same location. Under scale economies, the cost also depends on the number of units produced.

Recognizing the more complex and realistic costs, the supply model (SM) is

$$S_i(p, S) = HP_i^s(p, S) \tag{5.17}$$

where $\{S_i(p, S)\}$ and the supply probability $P_i^s(p, S)$ are specific to the *logit* and *frechit* models. Solving this equation, we obtain the number of equal real estate units at each location of the city. This expression represents a supply fixed-point problem, denoted as $S_i = F^s(p, S)$, which is conditional on the equilibrium prices.

Notice that Eq. (5.17) has the same mathematical form as the *logit* or *frechit* fixed-point problems of the location model with externalities that are analyzed in Technical Note 5.2. Therefore, if the variance of the SM complies with the bounds for the parameter of the probability $P_i^s(p, S)$, as discussed in Technical Note 5.2, then it is guaranteed that F^s has a unique solution, and the succession converges to the solution.

Economically, this model represents a complex decision-making process for suppliers because identifying their optimal supply choice implies the ability to evaluate all alternative real estate choices and to identify and exploit production scale economies. This complexity creates an information barrier that justifies market segmentation in production at least partially, for example, by housing type, size of projects, and areas of the city. Such specialization of the market can be modeled assuming heterogeneous producers facing different production costs.

The Optimal Supply Choice Set

The supply given by Eq. (5.17) is conditional on the real estate and location options denoted by set *VI**. We shall now analyze the optimal choice set of real estate units on which both the *logit* and *frechit* equilibrium models depend. Indeed, in contrast to the short-term case, here the choice set *VI** is endogenous. This issue arises when using the discrete choice theory, in which the choice set is considered to be exogenous. However, this assumption is inconsistent with the long-term LU problem, in which the choice set and the city's limit are endogenously defined by optional locations.

The problem that we must address is that for any set *VI* that is arbitrarily large, the *logit* and *frechit* probabilistic models yield a positive supply to all alternatives in that set, i.e., $S_i(p) > 0,\ \forall i \in VI$. This causes a problem in the discrete model because the numbers of units supplied at each location depend on the size of this choice set assumed to be exogenous by the modeler. In other words, unless there is a model of the optimal choice set, the modeler is compelled to define ex ante the borders of the city.

To identify the optimal choice set of real estate alternatives within the urban border $\{i \in VI^* \subseteq VI\}$, the market must follow the rational rule of choosing the choice set *VI** that yields the maximum profit. To implement this rule, we consider an arbitrarily large set *VI*, calculate equilibrium, and reindex real estate units in descending expected profit order, that is, $\pi_{m=1} \geq \pi_{m=2} \cdots \geq \pi_{m=H} \geq \pi_{m=H+1} \cdots \geq \pi_{m=|VI|}$. Then, we identify the critical location m^* that complies with the following condition: $\pi_{m=m^*} \geq \pi_A > \pi_{m=m^*+1}$, with π_A the profit of renting land for agriculture. The solution set is $VI^* = \{m = 1,\ldots,m^*\}$. With *VI**, we can apply the price adjustment procedure $k(R_A)$ discussed above, with $i_0 = m^*$.

However, a difficulty arises here because the order of the profits is not indifferent to the equilibrium and to the adjustment of prices, as seen in Eqs (5.8) and (5.11) with $k(R_A)$. This induces an iterative procedure where, at iteration *n*, we calculate equilibrium for the set of alternatives VI^n $(n = 1,2,\ldots)$, adjust the constant $k^n(R_A)$, and update prices. We then reindex profits in descending order to find VI^{n+1}, continue incrementing *n*, and proceed iteratively until VI^n stabilizes. However, this iterative procedure may be highly demanding on computing resources.

A convenient and more efficient alternative algorithm is as follows. Define the probability that a candidate real estate unit *i* from the set *VI* belongs to the optimal set *VI**, called P_i^{VI}. This represents the probability that the profit of the candidate exceeds the profit yield of agricultural use of the land:

$$P_i^{VI} = Prob(\pi_i \geq q_i R_{Ai}),\ \forall i \in VI \tag{5.18}$$

This probability is calculated for an exogenous and large set *VI*.

In this case, the profit-ordering procedure is unnecessary. However, we note that the profit is calculated for the equilibrium, conditional on set *VI*. The iterative procedure is avoided if this probability is calculated endogenously and simultaneously with the equilibrium. The implementation of this method requires defining constrained probabilities to comply with Eq. (5.18), a topic we shall discuss later in this chapter.

Comments on Long-Term Equilibrium

To summarize, the long-term equilibrium, denoted by $\Xi(x;\varphi)$ with $x=(u, p,\{S_i\},VI)$ the set of endogenous variables, is described by the tuple of fixed points:

$$\Xi\left(x;\varphi^{LT}\right)=\left(\left\{u_h^*\right\}=F^u,\left\{p_i^*\right\}=F^p,\left\{S_i^*\right\}=F^s,VI^*\right) \tag{5.19}$$

which is conditional on the scenario given by the set $\varphi^{LT}=(\{H_h\}, Z(T), R_A, E)$: the city's population vector (by cluster), transportation accessibility, the agricultural land rent, and economic conditions. The size of this system of equations is given by the number of consumer clusters $|C|$ and real estate types $|VI|$, as: $|C|$ for F^p plus $|VI|$ for F^p and for F^s; i.e., $|C|+2|VI|$ equations, which equals the number of variables $(\{u_h\},\{p_i\},\{S_i\})$.

The dynamics of this long-term equilibrium represent a complex system. For example, an external demographic shock induces higher building densities as the reaction of suppliers to higher demand and expected prices at every location, which leads to higher land values and thus higher profit by creating real estate options with less intensive land input. A shock increasing agricultural land rents induces higher prices and thus a shrinking city with higher densities and lower utilities, leading to consumers' losses and producers' surpluses.

5.4 Long-Term Equilibrium With Externalities

In the previous sections, externalities were ignored. For example, in the *logit* model, households are assumed to bid according to $w_{hi}(u_h)=y_h-\frac{u_h}{\lambda_h}+f_h(z_i)$ and firms to bid according to $w_{hi}(\pi_h)=y_h-\frac{\pi_h}{\lambda_h}+f_h(z_i)$, with all attributes described in z_i assumed to be exogenous. The implicit assumption is that the relocation of agents does not affect consumer bids. This can represent a short-term situation where only a small fraction of the city's total stock, including old and new, is offered on the market, such that the impact of the (re)location of residents and activities, i.e., households and firms, is negligible in the calculation of bids.

Now we consider the case where the number of relocations and new agents is high enough to affect residents' perceptions, that is, the long run. It also represents the situation of agents with *perfect foresight*, where consumers can forecast the relocation process occurring in the market and are thus able to anticipate the change in LU when they evaluate their bids.

We consider two types of externalities. In the case of households, changes in LU affect the quality of the neighbors, a phenomenon known as *location externality*. In the case of firms, such changes affect *agglomeration economies*. Mathematically, both externalities are similar and induce a complex system. The actual form of the externality in the bids function was discussed previously in Chapter 3; therefore, we will focus here on the calculation of equilibrium.

Both location externalities and agglomeration economies induce push (repulsion) and pull (attraction) forces in different agents at the individual agent level. They may combine both forces, for example, when the households value the neighbor quality because of the level and quality of services and labor opportunities (a push force) but may assess the high density of these types of locations negatively. These microinteractions at the agent level give rise to one of the most relevant structures at the city level: the spatial segregation of the population, differentiating areas according to socioeconomic, ethnic, religious, and other such factors, and the spatial allocation of economic activity. These interactions explain the majority of the urban structures shown in Fig. 5.1.

Location externalities and agglomeration economies are represented in the willingness-to-pay function by the agents' evaluations of the LU pattern. The push and pull attributes are included in vector z_i. The important feature for equilibrium analysis is that these attributes evolve with the allocation of agents as endogenous attributes denoted as $z_i = g(H_{\cdot i^v})$, where $H_{\cdot i^v} = (H_{hi}, \forall h \in C, i \in i^v)$ is the vector of the allocation of activities (residential and nonresidential), with i^v denoting the set of locations or zones defining the neighbor of location i. The most common attributes mentioned in the literature are the population and buildings density in the neighborhood, where the definition of neighbors in applied studies is usually the administrative zoning.

These endogenous attributes define the interactions among all the residents' decisions, induce the agents' location decisions and LU change, and are modeled by bid-auction probabilities, with $H_{hi} = S_i Q_{h/i}(H_{hi^v})$ and $H_{\cdot i^v} = g\left(Q_{\cdot/v}\right)$. Thus, these externalities induce another fixed-point problem in the location model.

In the case of the multinomial *logit* (MNL) bid-auction model, the location fixed point is

$$H_{h/i} = S_i \frac{e^{\beta w_{hi}(H_{\cdot i^v})}}{\sum_{g \in C} e^{\beta w_{gi}(H_{\cdot i^v})}}, \forall h \in C, i \in VI \tag{5.20}$$

In the case of the multinomial *frechit* bid-auction model, the fixed point is

$$H_{h/i} = \frac{w_{hi}(H_{\cdot i^v})^{\beta}}{\sum_{g \in C} w_{gi}(H_{\cdot i^v})^{\beta}}, \forall h \in C, i \in VI \tag{5.21}$$

The mathematical properties of *logit* and *frechit* multinomial models with externalities guarantee that a unique solution exists and that the succession converges to the solution. However, as proved in Technical Note 5.2, this conclusion holds only if the shape parameter β is below a maximum, i.e., for a minimum variance in the stochastic bids. This result means that the variability in the location choice process softens the reaction of agents after a relocation of neighboring agents, thus reducing the strength of the cascade changes induced by location externalities.

This result deserves special attention because it is very powerful to calculate the location equilibrium in the complex context with push and pull externalities. Indeed, this is exceptional because most other models yield multiple equilibria and convergence is not guaranteed. This valuable property of *logit* and *frechit* models is usually not emphasized sufficiently, although it provides a tool for studying complex urban systems with heterogeneous agents and microinteractions on a detailed spatial scale. Moreover, this property applies to a wide variety of problems in the social sciences that can be characterized as complex interactions among individuals.

Thus, the long-term equilibrium with externalities is

$$\Xi\left(x;\varphi^{LT}\right) = \left(\left\{u_h^*\right\} = F^u, \left\{p_i^*\right\} = F^p, \left\{S_i^*\right\} = F^s, VI^*, Q = F^Q\right) \tag{5.22}$$

with F^Q the fixed point Eqs (5.20) and (5.21). The number of equations defining this equilibrium increases significantly to $|C| + 2|VI| + (|C| \cdot |VI|)$ compared with the same case without externalities. The basic ideas of the long-term equilibrium $\Xi(x;\phi^{LT})$ of Eq. (5.22) with several fixed-point problems were first formulated for the *logit* model in Martínez and Henríquez (2007) and called the random bidding and supply model (RB&SM).

Location externalities generate nontrivial city structures. For example, as population and city size increase, higher transportation costs are mitigated by the emergence of subcenters, which are created because the firms profits increase by reducing the labor travel cost. This also makes jobs and services more accessible from outer residential locations (a pull force), leading to urban sprawl. These dynamics of the location patterns of firms and residences are fueled by the evolution of demographics and consumers income (i.e., by economics). Another classic example of location externalities is the emergence of segregated cities based on socioeconomic, ethnic, religious, and other differences. In this case, as the majority group moves to areas where peers live (pull force among peers) or where land is rural, the prices of these areas increase because of the increased demand, shown by higher willingness to pay, making this area less affordable for the poor or less attractive for nonpeers (a push force), which leads to patterns of sociospatial segregation.

5.5 Maximization of Total Surplus

We have obtained the LU equilibrium solution by solving the following set of constraints:

$$\sum_{i \in VI} H_{hi} = H_h, \forall h \in C \tag{5.23}$$

$$\sum_{h \in C} H_{hi} = S_i, \forall i \in VI \tag{5.24}$$

where S_i is exogenous in the short-term model and endogenous in the long-term model. If we assume the *logit* bid-auction probability, such that:

$$H_{hi} = S_i Q_{h/i} = S_i H_h e^{\beta\left(z_{hi} - \overline{u}_h^* - p_i^*\right)}, \forall h \in C, i \in VI \tag{5.25}$$

with $z_{hi} = y_h + \frac{f_h(z_i)}{\lambda_h}$, the solution yields Eqs (5.7) and (5.8):

$$\overline{u}_h^* = \frac{1}{\beta} \ln\left(\sum_{i \in VI} S_i e^{\beta\left(z_{hi} - p_i^*\right)}\right), \forall h \in C \tag{5.26}$$

$$p_i^* = \frac{1}{\beta} \ln\left(\sum_{g \in C} H_g e^{\beta\left(z_{gi} - \overline{u}_g^*\right)}\right), \forall i \in VI \tag{5.27}$$

To analyze the socioeconomic impact of the *logit* LU equilibrium allocation, it is convenient to consider the following equivalent optimization problem (Bravo et al., 2010):

$$(P) \max_{H_{hi}} \Psi(\{H_{hi}\}) = \sum_{\substack{h \in C \\ i \in VI}} H_{hi} z_{hi} - \frac{1}{\beta} \sum_{\substack{h \in C \\ i \in VI}} H_{hi}[\ln(H_{hi}) - 1] \tag{5.28}$$

subject to:

$$\sum_{i \in I} H_{hi} = H_h \quad (1)$$

$$\sum_{h \in C} H_{hi} = S_i \quad (2)$$

which represents the doubly constrained entropy model of the LU problem. The long-term model can be represented by the elastic supply $S_i = S(p_i)$.

The primal entropy problem (P) reproduces the auction LU short-term *logit* equilibrium discussed in the previous chapter. In this formulation, the optimization function $\Psi(\{H_{hi}\})$ is interpreted directly as the *maximization of total benefit* obtained from location accessibility and other attributes (z_{hi}), given by the sum of elementary benefits $H_{hi}\, z_{hi}$. The maximization occurs in the stochastic process modeled by the entropy term, given by the second term.

The standard solution of problem (P) is

$$H_{hi} = S_i H_h e^{\beta\left(z_{hi} - \overline{u}_h^* - p_i^*\right)}, \forall h \in C, i \in VI \tag{5.29}$$

with $\overline{u}_h^*$ and p_i^* known as balancing factors in entropy literature. These factors replicate Eqs (5.7) and (5.8). The solution is unique and can be obtained using the biproportional matrix method of Macgill (1977).

Additionally, the entropy optimization problem (P) provides a standard interpretation of the Lagrange multipliers. These factors represent the marginal increment of the objective function, i.e., the *marginal increment in benefits*. Then, in Eq. (5.28) constraint (1) yields the optimal utilities, $\overline{u}^*$, representing the consumers' marginal benefit, and (2) yields the optimal prices, p^*, representing the marginal suppliers' profit.

The total benefit at equilibrium is calculated by evaluating $\Psi(\{H_{hi}\})$ at the solution $H_{hi}^* = S_i H_h e^{\beta\left(z_{hi}-\overline{u}_h^*-p_i^*\right)}$, which yields

$$\Psi\left(\{H_{hi}^*\}\right) = \sum_{h\in C} H_h\left(\overline{u}_h^* - \frac{1}{\beta}\ln(H_h)\right) + \sum_{i\in VI} S_i\left(p_i^* - \frac{1}{\beta}\ln(S_i)\right) + \frac{H}{\beta} \tag{5.30}$$

For details, see Technical Note 5.3.

The primal LU optimization problem (P) yields a socioeconomic surplus (Eq. 5.30) equal to the sum of the consumers' utilities and suppliers' profits, with both reduced by the logarithm of the respective constraints, plus a positive system constant $\beta^{-1}H$. This last constant term is a social benefit that increases with the population size of the city, which emerges from the entropy model. (This result is shown, for example, in the trip distribution model in Martínez and Araya, 2000.) We therefore further conclude that the MNL model of the LU equilibrium problem can be formulated as the entropy doubly constrained model, which is in line with Anas' (1983) conclusions on the entropy-logit equivalency.

This formulation provides the interpretation that the solution of the LUT model maximizes total social economic surplus, also called the utilitarian or Benthamite (in honor to Jeremy Bentham) welfare function (W), i.e., social welfare is measured as the sum of individuals' utilities: $W = \sum_{n=1}^{N} w_i$, with N the population of the society considered (e.g., the nation). However, other measures for social welfare are associated with different views and measurement techniques; for example, for a concern about living in an equalitarian society, John Rawls proposed the minimum utility $W = \max\left(\min_{n=1,\ldots,N} w_i\right)$, which emphasizes the social value of the poorest, and Amartya Sen proposed $W = \frac{1}{N}\left(\sum_{n=1}^{N} w_i\right)(1 - G)$, with G the Gini index; for these other social objectives, the market equilibrium is not optimum in the general case.

5.6 Modeling Constrained Choices

The behavior of consumers and suppliers in the LU system is subject to numerous constraints that should be modeled to properly represent the agents' reactions to such constraints. Constraints induce a highly influential nonlinear utility with high impact in the choice process; in fact, in many cases, constraints may be dominant in the choice process. Although implementing constraints makes the model much more realistic, they also make the calculation of equilibrium in the model more complex.

This complexity is such that the majority of applied models avoid the explicit representation of constraints. For example, a MNL model may not represent income constraints in the utility function explicitly; i.e., the price of a choice may increase above the income level, but the corresponding bid-auction probability is not null, which is to say the agents cannot afford a location that the model still assigns a nonnull probability of being the best bidder. Another example is a supply probability model that develops profitable locations although land is constrained by planning regulations.

The origin of all these problems is the misspecification of behavior rules, which consider unbounded utilities and profits that theoretically can be circumvented if indirect utilities and profits properly represent these constraints. However, implementing bounded behavioral rules requires complex nonlinear utility and profit functions, which are usually noncontinuous, thereby leading to unstable models and making the equilibrium calculation highly demanding with regard to computer power and requiring sophisticated algorithms.

Therefore, in this section we address methods to represent constraints in the *logit* and *frechit* models that are able to reduce the computational and algorithmic burden in calculating equilibrium, and perhaps more importantly, preserve the mathematical properties of the equilibrium. These methods address two cases: first, when agents' behavior is constrained by thresholds affecting utility or profit functions, such as consumers' income constraints, and second, when the choice set is constrained by external conditions that eliminate certain alternatives, as was discussed for the long-term equilibrium.

Mathematically, consider the behavioral rule $\max \tau_h(z_i)$, with the vector of K attributes $z_i = \{z_{ki}, k = 1,\ldots, K; i \in I\}$ and τ_h an unbounded rule that represents a utility or a profit function. The problem is

$$\begin{aligned} &\max_{i \in I} \tau_h(z_i) \\ &\text{subject to:} \quad \tau_h \le \Gamma_h \\ &\qquad\qquad\quad z_{ki} \le Z_k \\ &\qquad\qquad\quad i \in I_h^* \subset I \end{aligned} \tag{5.31}$$

with the constraints here assumed as upper bounds (lower bounds are similarly modeled), representing the different cases: agents' bounds on utilities or profits (Γ_h), on attributes (Z_k), and on the feasible choice set for agent h, I_h^*. Thus, this problem generalizes the constrained choice processes of any consumer or supplier agent.

We now consider a method that introduces explicit constraints in a choice process modeled by MNL or MNF models. Specifically, this method can be applied for the bid auction ($Q_{h/i}(w)$), consumers' choice ($P_{i/h}(w - p)$) and supplier' choice $\left(P_i^S(\pi)\right)$ probabilities, with τ-functions representing bids w, surplus $w - p$, and profit π respectively.

Research on the constrained choice problems in random utility modeling offers several methods. Manski's (1977) work models the choice set generation explicitly, reducing the options to the feasible set. This approach faces the difficulty of a combinatorial search problem; for each subset of alternatives, the method calculates the choice probability multiplied by the probability of being a feasible set, for example, in the case of spatial sets and the combinatory of subsets of locations that would be analyzed with this method. Regarding this approach, see also Swait and Ben-Akiva (1987) and Ben-Akiva and Boccara (1995).

An alternative approach assumes that all potential alternatives are feasible but penalizes those that are not available with a negative factor in the behavior rule. The penalties, instead of eliminating infeasible alternatives, strongly repel their choice, drastically reducing the choice probability to very low values. This approach was implemented by Cascetta and Papola (2001), Swait (2001), and Martínez et al. (2009) with different implementation techniques. To explain this approach, we consider the first two sets of constraints in Eq. (5.31) and write them more simply as $x_k - \overline{x}_k \leq 0$, with k the index for the set of constraints, and $\overline{x}_k$ the upper constraint for x_k. Then, the constrained choice problem is modeled as the following unconstrained problem: $\max_{i \in I} \tau_h(z_i, h(x))$, with $h(x)$ the penalty factor. The third constraint simply defines the set of alternatives available in the market.

The Constrained Choice Models

The constrained multinomial logit model (CMNL) proposed by Martínez et al. (2009) assumes that x is a random variable and defines the binomial probability of these variables as belonging to the feasible set, denoted by $\phi(x)$ and called the cutoff factor. Then, the CMNL choice probability of problem in Eq. (5.31) is

$$P_i = \frac{\phi(x_i) e^{\mu \tau(x_i)}}{\sum\limits_{j \in VI} \phi(x_j) e^{\mu \tau(x_j)}} \tag{5.32}$$

where x_i is the vector of attributes of the ith alternative and μ is a shape parameter of the choice model. In the general case, ϕ may represent several constraints, not a single constraint, associated with each alternative in the choice set. In this case, we can define a vector of cutoffs $\{\phi(x_{ki}),\ k \in K\}$ and the joint cutoff $\phi(x_i) = \prod\limits_{k \in K} \phi(x_{ki})$, which defines the joint probability of the alternative of belonging to the feasible space defined by the set of independent constraints.

The *logit* binomial cutoff is

$$\phi^U(x_{ki}) = \frac{1}{1 + e^{\eta(x_{ki} - \overline{x}_k + \rho_k)}},\ \phi^L(x_{ki}) = \frac{1}{1 + e^{\eta(\overline{x}_k - x_{ki} + \rho_k)}} \tag{5.33}$$

where $\phi^U(x_{ki})$ models an upper bound and $\phi^L(x_{ki})$ a lower bound of x_{ki}. Fig. 5.3 depicts the binomial lower and upper cutoff functions. Notice that at the boundary φ is

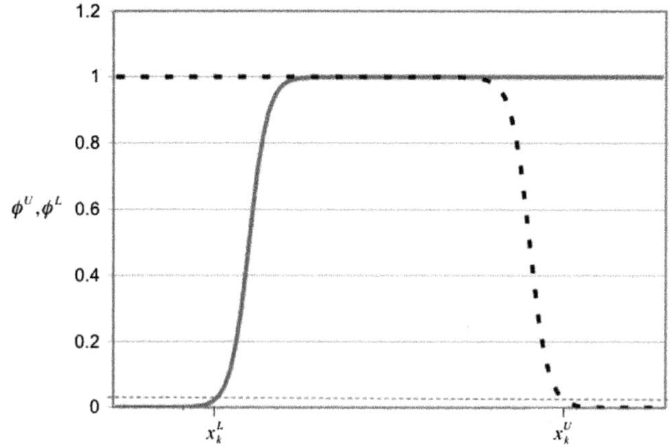

Figure 5.3 The upper and lower binomial cutoffs.

not null, with the position parameter ρ_k defining the choice probability at the boundary, i.e., $\phi(\overline{x}_k) = \frac{1}{1+e^{\eta\rho_k}}$. We interpret this probability as the model *tolerance of violating the constraint*. Defining the constraint tolerance parameter ρ_k such that the tolerance is as low as desired, is recommended. Hence, in the CMNL model, there is a nonnull probability that a choice violating the constraint is considered as feasible and as being chosen.

The shape parameter η of the binomial logit defines the steepness of the probability function in the neighbor of the constraints, that is, where $x_{ki} - \overline{x}_k \approx 0$. As shown in Fig. 5.4, if η increases, the implicit variance of the cutoff decreases, and the cutoff has a faster effect as $x_{ki} \rightarrow \overline{x}_k$.

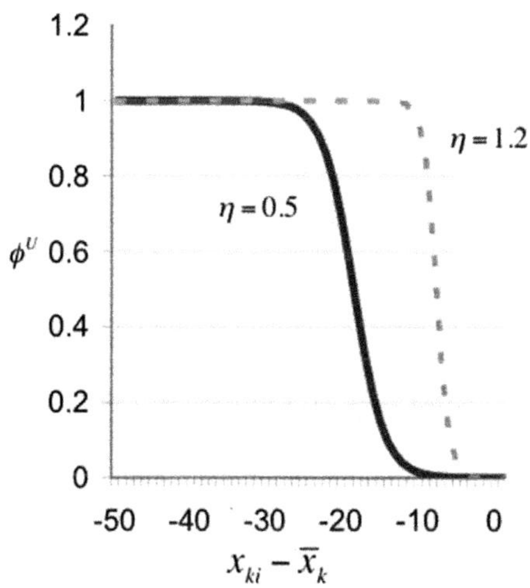

Figure 5.4 The steepness of the binomial cutoff.

The method can be extended to consider a *frechit* binomial cutoff, such that:

$$P_i = \frac{\phi(x_i)\tau(x_i)^{\mu}}{\sum\limits_{j \in VI} \phi(x_j)\tau(x_j)^{\mu}} \tag{5.34}$$

with

$$\begin{aligned} \phi^U(x_{ki}) &= \frac{1}{1 - \left(\dfrac{x_{ki}+\rho}{\overline{x}_k+\rho}\right)^{\eta}} \\ \phi^L(x_{ki}) &= \frac{1}{1 - \left(\dfrac{\overline{x}_k+\rho}{x_{ki}+\rho}\right)^{\eta}} \end{aligned} \tag{5.35}$$

The parameter η is proportional to the inverse of the binomial probability model and controls the tolerance in violating the constraint, i.e., it controls the probability of violating each constraint. When $\eta > 0$ increases (variance decreases), the probability is reduced up to the limit $\eta \rightarrow \infty$ where the violation tends to zero. Thus, in the constrained choice model, bounds are made to comply with a probability.

To interpret the cutoff as a penalty, it is useful to rewrite Eqs (5.32) and (5.34), embedding the cutoff factor in the behavior rule by adding $^1/_{\mu}\ln(\phi)$ in the *logit* model and by multiplying the behavior rule by $\phi^{1/\mu}$ in the *frechit* case. In this formulation, these terms are interpreted as the respective penalty factors of the behavior rule, adjusting utilities and profits to minimum values when a constraint is violated, thus reducing the choice probability, not to zero, but to a minimum. In other words, these penalties are innocuous in the interior of the feasible set but activate a push back effect once the alternative violates any constraint.

The CMNL and the extension to the *frechit* constrained choice models represent a heuristic approach because they only approximate Manski's (1977) original model. Nevertheless, they have the merit of a minimum computational additional cost in calculating equilibrium compared with the corresponding choice model without constraints. The simplicity can be seen in Eqs (5.32) and (5.34) because the model remains as with *logit* and *frechit* probability functions and the corresponding properties prevail.

In the LU equilibrium, the application of cutoffs for modeling the optimal real estate set, where the bid-auction probabilities are modified with cutoffs, is interpreted as the following joint choice model: the choice of a specific real estate alternative in the universe of real estate alternatives (*VI*) depends on that alternative being feasible, i.e., belonging to *VI**. In the case of supply subject to regulations, the supply probability is conditional on the real estate unit(s) fulfilling the regulation conditions.

We interpret the CMNL model as accepting a controlled degree of tolerance (externally defined by parameters ρ and η), which is justified conceptually by considering that the constraint is perceived by the agent, but there is a degree of uncertainty in the perception. Thus, for example, income is a constraint, but how much this constraint is violated in the neighborhood of the agent's income is difficult to assess with high precision given the large and variable set of goods on which the total income is spent. Then, in this context, the perception of a constraint being violated is evaluated with errors.

The Constrained Entropy

An alternative approach to incorporating constraints in a random choice process is proposed in Martínez and Henríquez (2007). This approach was inspired by the entropy model (see Technical Notes in Chapter 2) and has proven to be useful in contexts where aggregated choices are bounded to external totals, such as when total population, supply, or costs are known. Therefore, predicted choices must comply with them. For example, consider the following entropy problem:

$$\begin{aligned} x_{hi} &= \max_{i\in VI}(\tau_h(z_i) - \beta(\ln(\tau) - 1)) \\ \text{subject to :} \quad & \sum_{i\in VI} x_{ki} \le X_k \quad \forall k \in K(\alpha_k) \\ & \sum_{i\in VI} b_k x_{ki} \le B_k \quad \forall k \in K(\gamma_k) \end{aligned} \tag{5.36}$$

where α_k and γ_k are the Lagrangian multipliers of the respective constraints. This optimization problem leads to an unconstrained optimization problem whose solution is equivalent to the *logit* model with penalizing factors α_k's and γ_k's. These multipliers may be calculated in the equilibrium model using the well-known method explained in Technical Note 2.1 for balancing factors, which yields a fixed-point problem of a coercive function that converges very efficiently to the solution. The difference between this approach and the binomial cutoffs is that in this case, the penalizing factors are not probabilities but rather positive multipliers such that $\alpha_k > 0$ if $\sum_{i\in VI} x_{ki} - X_k \le 0$ and $\alpha_k = 0$ otherwise; similarly with γ_k's. This implies that if the choice is not feasible, it is not chosen at all.

A difficulty with this approach, however, is that it requires solving the fixed-point problem. In addition, the model is discontinuous at $\alpha_k = 0$ and $\gamma_k = 0$. This is addressed in Martínez and Henríquez (2007) with a heuristic algorithm. Additionally, it is not useful to model constraints on the agent's behavior rule (e.g., income constraint) because it only applies to bounds on the aggregates of model outputs or choices. However, one advantage is that bounds are modeled as hard constraints, i.e., constraints are deterministically complied, not only up to a probability.

Thus, bounds can be represented in the LU equilibrium model in two ways: as soft cutoff constraints by a binomial choice formulation or as hard constraints by classic balancing (entropy) factors. Because both methods represent a Lagrange method, these penalizing factors have an economic interpretation: they represent the shadow price of the constraint, i.e., they are interpreted as the increase of the objective function under a marginal relaxation of the constraint. For example, a penalizing factor in the SM associated with a planning regulation represents the expected extra profit that the supplier can obtain if the regulation is relaxed marginally. Another example is if the constraint is the household's income, these factors represent the impact on the consumers' welfare (or utility) caused by a marginal increase in the households' income. These factors provide valuable information regarding the impact on the system induced by the city conditions, called the scenario. Therefore, the planner can design policies oriented by this information. For more details, see Martínez et al. (2009) and Castro et al. (2013).

The Impact on Land-Use Equilibrium

The relevance of constraints on the LU model can be assessed by analyzing their impact on the market equilibrium. There are two cases: constraints on consumers and constraints on real estate supply.

In the first case, the penalizing factor, either CMNL, CMNF or entropy factor, modifies the consumers' willingness to pay, directly affecting equilibrium utilities (Eqs 5.7 and 5.10), which affects real estate prices (Eqs 5.8 and 5.11) and adjustments of prices (Eqs 5.9 and 5.12). A simple way to understand the impact of these penalizing factors is to consider them as nonlinear attributes in the willingness-to-pay function. For example, the income constraint imposes upper bounds on bids, prices and utilities. In the case of constraints representing the thresholds of attributes, such as maximum density, they introduce an endogenous variable if the threshold depends on the location pattern (e.g., densities). Mathematically, neither the parameters nor the endogenous penalties affect the uniqueness of an equilibrium solution or the solution algorithm because they represent either constants in the equilibrium fixed-point problems in Eqs (5.7) and (5.10) or an externality in Eqs (5.20) and (5.21).

Economically, constraints on agents' behavior alter the equilibrium solution. For example, consider a reduction in certain household clusters' incomes to observe that the model predicts an equilibrium where bids are reduced, inducing lower prices and higher densities everywhere and a smaller city.

In the case of constraints on real estate supply, the most common constraints are planning regulations, usually defined by a zoning system. The associated penalizing factors affect the suppliers' profit in the equilibrium, which can be analyzed by interpreting them as supply costs, represented as parameters or endogenous variables. Endogenous penalties are mathematically equivalent to the case of scale economies represented in Eq. (5.17). Thus, the properties of a unique solution and the convergence of the solution algorithm prevail for exogenous and endogenous penalizing factors.

Economically, constraints in the supply of real estate have an impact on real estate development costs differentiated by real building types, inducing a specific profile of development and densities in the city. For example, a regulation on maximum densities differentiated by zones is represented by zone-specific penalizing factors or costs, affecting profits and urban development. Furthermore, the impact on supply percolates into equilibrium utilities to satisfy equilibrium conditions and then into real estate prices.

In summary, constraints are modeled in the LU model by altering the behavior of consumers and producers, such that their decisions comply with the agent and the system constraints. A relevant and practical conclusion for modelers is that the modified behavior can be applied in the modeling equilibrium equations without altering the mathematical properties of equilibrium while capturing the economic impacts.

5.7 Remarks and Comments

In this chapter, the *logit* and *frechit* partial LU equilibrium models were analyzed for different scenarios with incremental complexity, from the most simple and restricted short-term to the more complex long-term scenario with externalities.

The short-term LU equilibrium, denoted by $\Xi(x;\varphi^{ST}) = \left(\{u_h^*\} = F^u\right)$, imposes the consumer equilibrium condition with the scenario defined by $\varphi^{ST} = (\{H_h\},\{S_i\}, Z(T), R_A, E)$. The long-term LU equilibrium considers supply vector $\{S_i\}$ endogenous, introducing two fixed points on prices F^p and on supply scale economies F^S, denoted by $\Xi(x;\varphi^{LT}) = \left(\{u_h^*\} = F^u, \{p_i^*\} = F^p, \{S_i^*\} = F^s, VI^*\right)$, with $\varphi^{LT} = (\{H_h\}, Z(T), R_A, E)$. The third level of complexity considers the equilibrium with externalities, denoted by $\Xi(x;\varphi^{LT}) = \left(\{u_h^*\} = F^u, \{p_i^*\} = F^p, \{S_i^*\} = F^s, VI^*, Q = F^Q\right)$.

The *logit* model of short-term equilibrium is formalized as an equivalent optimization model, with primal and dual problems (not available for the *frechit* model), that characterize the solution economically and mathematically. The primal yields an economic interpretation for the bid-auction market equilibrium. It yields the maximum social benefit, aggregating consumer and supplier surpluses plus a system entropy constant benefit depending on the city's population. The dual has the mathematical properties that guarantee the uniqueness of the solution and the convergence of the succession to the solution.

Furthermore, applying fixed-point analysis in the case with externalities, we extended the mathematical properties to be applied for the *logit* and *frechit* LU models if, and only if, $H = S$ and if utilities and prices are adjusted to absolute levels, e.g., using the agricultural rent at the city's border $k(R_A)$. In this case, these mathematical properties hold for a minimum variance characterized by upper bounds in the shape parameters of the bid auction and the supply probabilities.

The long-term case motivated the introduction of techniques for modeling constraints on the agents' choices, thus improving the model's flexibility to represent complex nonlinear processes. These are handy techniques in the SM because the feasible set of real estate types is bounded by numerous planning regulations. Additionally, constrained choices are naturally useful to assist in modeling the nonlinear inflections of agents' bids and profit functions when the choice process reaches the feasible set's bounds, e.g., income or attribute thresholds.

Notably, the existence and uniqueness of the LU equilibrium is not a property in the classical urban economic model; in fact, these properties only hold in the discrete model under the assumption of stochastic equilibrium. Indeed, in a similar context, but under the deterministic behavior of the agents, multiple equilibrium solutions are expected because there are different combinations of attributes that compensate accessibility and amenities, which generate a set of equilibria that yields the same maximum utilities and profit levels. The merit of the stochastic model formulated wit extreme value distributions, is that it yields a unique solution representing the expected equilibrium under the stochastic behavior of agents.

Technically, the stochastic model maps the discrete and deterministic set of all or nothing location alternatives into a continuous set of choice probabilities, which causes our discrete choice to be represented in a continuous probabilistic model. In this continuous space, our model uses the extreme value distributions—the *logit* and *frechit* models—to represent stochastic behavior, which discriminates larger values of behavior rules positively, e.g., utilities and profits, against lower values. This leads us to interpret this biased process in a continuous setting as a "selection" of the equilibrium that yields the maximum expected utilities and profits among the feasible equilibria sets. This interpretation is reinforced in the next chapter, where the stochastic LU equilibrium is presented with an equivalent optimization problem.

Finally, the LU model is defined as a partial equilibrium because it models a LU market embedded in a larger urban system characterized by the long-term scenario $\varphi^{LT} = (\{H_h\}, Z(T), R_A, E)$. In the following chapters, we will extend the LU equilibrium model to the larger context of the urban system equilibrium, where the exogenous scenario is eventually reduced to $\varphi = (\{H_h\}, R_A)$, with endogenous transportation-related attributes $Z(T)$ and production/labor markets E.

Technical Note 5.1: Uniqueness of Equilibrium Utilities

In this note we prove that the short-run equilibrium without externalities given by Eq. (5.1) has a unique utilities solution for the *logit* and *frechit* LU models.

The Logit Model

Here, we prove the existence and uniqueness of utilities $\overline{u}_h^* = \frac{u_h^*}{\lambda_h}, \forall h \in C$, for the consumer equilibrium condition Eq. (5.3):

$$\sum_{i \in VI} S_i Q_{h/i}(\overline{u}^*) = \sum_{i \in VI} S_i \frac{H_h e^{\beta w_{hi}(u_h^*)}}{\sum_{g \in C} H_g e^{\beta w_{gi}(u_g^*)}} = H_h, \forall h \in C \tag{T5.1}$$

with $w_{hi} = y_h + \frac{1}{\lambda_h} f_h(z_i) - \overline{u}_h$.

The proof of existence and uniqueness, presented in Bravo et al. (2010), uses the following convex optimization problem, whose solution yields the equilibrium equation (T5.1)[1]:

$$\min_{\overline{u}} \varphi(\overline{u}) = \sum_{h \in C} H_h \overline{u}_h + \frac{1}{\beta} \sum_{i \in VI} S_i \ln\left[\sum_{g \in C} H_g e^{\beta w_{gi}(\overline{u}_g)}\right] \tag{T5.2}$$

[1] Eqs (T5.1) and (T5.2) are slightly different from Bravo et al.'s original formula because here the exponentials are multiplied by H_h to be consistent with aggregate bid-auction probabilities.

This problem yields multiple solutions because utilities are relative magnitudes, then $\varphi(\overline{u}) = \varphi(\overline{u} + c)$. For any normalizing constant $c \in \mathbb{R}$ (for convenience we consider setting $\overline{u}_{h=1} = 0$), we now prove that the problem is strictly convex and coercive, recovering a unique solution.

To prove convexity, it is enough that function $f(\overline{u}) = \frac{1}{\beta}\ln\left(\sum_{g\in C} e^{\beta\overline{u}_g + \ln(H_g)}\right) = \frac{1}{\beta}\ln\left(\sum_{\substack{g\in C\\ g\neq 1}} e^{\beta\overline{u}_g + \ln(H_g)} + 1\right)$ is strictly convex. Define $x_g = e^{\beta\overline{u}_g + \ln(H_g)}$ with $x \in \mathbb{R}^{|C|-1}$ and $v \neq 0 \in \mathbb{R}^{|C|-1}$. Then, $\frac{\partial f(\overline{u})}{\partial \overline{u}_h} = \frac{x_h}{\sum_{\substack{g\in C\\ g\neq 1}} x_g + 1}$ and

$$v^t H^f v = \frac{\left(\sum_{h\in C} x_h v_h^2\right)\left(\sum_{h\in C} x_h + 1\right) - \left(\sum_{h\in C} x_h v_h\right)^2}{\left(\sum_{h\in C} x_h + 1\right)^2} > \frac{\left(\sum_{h\in C} x_h v_h^2\right)\left(\sum_{h} x_h\right) - \left(\sum_{h\in C} x_h v_h\right)^2}{\left(\sum_{h\in C} x_h + 1\right)^2} \geq 0 \tag{T5.3}$$

where the last inequality is the Cauchy–Schwartz inequality with vectors $\left(v_h\sqrt{x_h}\right)_h$ and $\left(\sqrt{x_h}\right)_h$.

To prove the coercivity of $\varphi(\overline{u})$, we write the associated recession function. Noting that the recession function of $\frac{1}{\beta}\ln\left(\sum_{g\in C} H_g e^{\beta w_{gi}}\right)$ and of $g(\overline{u}_h) = \frac{1}{\beta}\ln\left(\sum_{g\in C} H_g e^{-\beta\overline{u}_g}\right)$ are the same, and $y_g + \frac{1}{\lambda_g} f_g(z_i) = z_{gi}$ is constant in this problem, we write:

$$g^{\infty}(\overline{u}_g) = \lim_{\lambda\to\infty} \frac{1}{\lambda\beta}\ln\left(\sum_{g\in C} H_g e^{-\lambda\beta\overline{u}_g}\right) = -\min_h \overline{u}_h = -\overline{u}^{\min} \tag{T5.4}$$

with $\overline{u}^{\min} \leq 0$ because $\overline{u}_{h=1} = 0$. Then,

$$\varphi^{\infty}(\overline{u}) = \sum_{h\in C} H_h \overline{u}_h - \overline{u}^{\min} \sum_{i\in VI} S_i \geq 0 \tag{T5.5}$$

where $\varphi^{\infty}(\overline{u}) = 0$ if, and only if, $\overline{u}^{\min} = \overline{u}_h = 0, \forall h \in C$.

The Frechit *Model*

The consumer's equilibrium condition is

$$\sum_{i \in VI} S_i Q_{h/i}(\overline{u}^*) = \sum_{i \in VI} S_i \frac{H_h w_{hi}\left(\overline{u}_h^*\right)^{\beta}}{\sum\limits_{g \in C} H_g w_{gi}\left(\overline{u}_g^*\right)^{\beta}} = H_h, \forall h \in C \tag{T5.6}$$

Consider the solution of the following optimization problem:

$$\min_{\overline{u}} \varphi(\overline{u}) = \sum_{g \in C} H_g \overline{u}_g + \frac{1}{\beta} \sum_{i \in VI} S_i \ln \left[\sum_{g \in C} H_g w_{gi} \left(\overline{u}_g\right)^{\beta} \right] \tag{T5.7}$$

which has no direct economic interpretation. We first prove that this problem yields the equilibrium LU conditions. The Lagrange optimal conditions yield:

$$\frac{\partial \varphi}{\partial \overline{u}_h} = 0 \Rightarrow H_h = \sum_{i \in VI} S_i \frac{H_h w_{hi}(\overline{u}_h)^{\beta}}{\sum\limits_{g \in C} H_g w_{gi}\left(\overline{u}_g\right)^{\beta}} = \sum_{i \in VI} S_i Q_{h/i}$$

with $Q_{h/i}$ the *frechit* bid-auction probability. Therefore, we conclude that the optimization problem in Eq. (T5.7) is equivalent to the *frechit* LU equilibrium problem.

We assume that $\overline{u}_{h=1} = 0$ and recall that $w_{hi} = y_h e^{\lambda_h^{-1}(-u_h + f_h(z_i))}$. We define $w_{gi}\left(\overline{u}_g\right) = e^{\left(z_{gi} - \overline{u}_g\right)}$, where $z_{gi} = \ln y_g + \lambda_g^{-1} f_g(z_i)$. Then, we write

$$\min_{\overline{u}} \varphi(\overline{u}) = \sum_{h \in C} H_h \overline{u}_h + \frac{1}{\beta} \sum_{i \in VI} S_i \ln \left[\sum_{g \in C} H_g e^{\beta\left(z_{gi} - \overline{u}_g\right)} \right] \tag{T5.8}$$

Observe that Eqs (T5.2) and (T5.8) are mathematically identical; thus, the proofs of convexity and coercivity are the same as those in the *logit* model.

Technical Note 5.2: Fixed-Point Externalities

In this note we follow Bravo et al.'s (2010) approach to prove the contractiveness of the fixed-point externalities problems in the *logit* and *frechit* models, valid for location externalities, agglomeration economies, and supply economies of scale.

The Logit Model

The MNL bid-auction fixed-point problem is

$$f_h = f\left(Q_{h/i}\right) = \frac{H_h e^{\beta w_{hi}(Q_{\cdot i})}}{\sum\limits_{g \in C} H_g e^{\beta w_{gi}(Q_{\cdot i})}} \tag{T5.9}$$

We shall prove the existence of a unique solution under certain conditions of β. Consider the Lagrange conditions:

$$\frac{\partial f_h}{\partial Q_{k/i}} = \beta Q_{h/i}\left(\frac{\partial w_{hi}(Q_{\cdot i})}{\partial Q_{k/i}} - \sum_{g \in C} Q_{g/i}\frac{\partial w_{gi}(Q_{\cdot i})}{\partial Q_{k/i}}\right), \forall h \in C \tag{T5.10}$$

and

$$\|J\|_\infty = \max_h \sum_{k \subset C}\left|\frac{\partial f_h}{\partial Q_{k/i}}\right|$$

$$= \max_h \sum_{k \in C}\left|\beta Q_{h/i}\left(\left(\frac{\partial w_{hi}(Q_{\cdot i})}{\partial Q_{k/i}} - \sum_{g \in C} Q_{g/i}\frac{\partial w_{gi}(Q_{\cdot i})}{\partial Q_{k/i}}\right)\right)\right|$$

$$= \max_h \sum_{k \in C}\left|\beta Q_{h/i}\left(1 - Q_{h/i}\right)\left(\frac{\partial w_{hi}(Q_{\cdot i})}{\partial Q_{k/i}} \quad \sum_{\substack{g \in C \\ g \neq h}} \frac{Q_{g/i}}{\left(1 - Q_{h/i}\right)}\frac{\partial w_{gi}(Q_{\cdot i})}{\partial Q_{k/i}}\right)\right|$$

(T5.11)

Because $\beta > 0$, $Q_{h/i} > 0$, $1 - Q_{h/i} > 0$, then $\beta Q_{h/i}(1 - Q_{h/i}) > 0$, we can write:

$$\|J\|_\infty = \beta Q_{h/i}\left(1 - Q_{h/i}\right)\max_{h \in C}\left(\sum_{k \in C}\left(\left|\frac{\partial w_{hi}(Q_{\cdot i})}{\partial Q_{k/i}}\right| + \sum_{\substack{g \in C \\ g \neq h}}\left|\frac{Q_{g/i}}{\left(1 - Q_{h/i}\right)}\frac{\partial w_{gi}(Q_{\cdot i})}{\partial Q_{k/i}}\right|\right)\right) \tag{T5.12}$$

Then, define a uniform bound $M \geq \left|\frac{\partial w_{hi}(Q_{\cdot i})}{\partial Q_{k/i}}\right|; \forall h, k \in C$, and note that $\sum_{g \neq h} \frac{Q_{g/i}}{(1-Q_{h/i})} = 1$ and $\sum_h Q_{h/i} = 1$ to obtain:

$$\|J\|_\infty \leq \beta Q_{h/i}\left(1 - Q_{h/i}\right)\max_{h \in C}\left(\sum_{k \in C} M\left(1 + \sum_{\substack{g \in C \\ g \neq h}} \frac{Q_{g/i}}{\left(1 - Q_{h/i}\right)}\right)\right)$$

$$\|J\|_\infty \leq 2M\beta Q_{h/i}\left(1 - Q_{h/i}\right) \tag{T5.13}$$

Because $\max_{x \in [0,1]} x(1 - x) = 1/4$, then we conclude that $\|J\|_\infty \leq \frac{1}{2}\beta M$. It follows the condition $\|J\|_\infty \leq \frac{1}{2}\beta M < 1$ and holds for $\beta < 2/M$.

This result states that if the shape parameter complies with the upper bound, i.e., the variance of the stochastic bids is high enough, then the fixed point is contractive, the solution is unique, and the succession converges.

The Frechit *Model*

The MNL bid-auction fixed-point problem is

$$f_h = f\left(Q_{h/i}\right) = \frac{H_h w_{hi}(Q_{\cdot i})^\beta}{\sum_{g \in C} H_g w_{gi}(Q_{\cdot i})^\beta} \tag{T5.14}$$

with $w_{hi}(Q_{\cdot i}) = y_h e^{\lambda_h^{-1}(-u_h + f_h(z_i(Q)))}$; we shall prove the existence of a unique solution under certain conditions of β.

Observe that because:

$$\frac{\partial f_h}{\partial Q_{k/i}} = \beta Q_{h/i}\left(\frac{\partial w_{hi}(Q_{\cdot i})}{\partial\left(Q_{k/i}\right)} - \sum_{g \in C} Q_{g/i}\frac{\partial w_{gi}(Q_{\cdot i})}{\partial\left(Q_{k/i}\right)}\right), \forall h, k \in C \tag{T5.15}$$

is identical to the *logit* case, the proof is the same and $\beta < 2/M$.

Technical Note 5.3: The Social Benefit of the Land-Use Market

To obtain the social benefit at equilibrium LU, we evaluate the objective of the primal problem (P) in Eq. (5.28) at the solution, as:

$$\Psi\left(\left\{H_{hi}^*\right\}\right) = \sum_{\substack{i \in VI \\ h \in C}} H_{hi}^* z_{hi} - \frac{1}{\beta}\sum_{\substack{i \in VI \\ h \in C}} H_{hi}^*\left[\ln\left(H_{hi}^*\right) - 1\right] \tag{T5.16}$$

Consider the solution $H_{hi}^{*} = S_i H_h e^{\beta\left(z_{hi} - \overline{u}_h^{*} - p_i^{*}\right)}$, $\forall h \in C, i \in VI$ and replace it in $\Psi\left(\left\{H_{hi}^{*}\right\}\right)$ to obtain the following:

$$\Psi\left(\left\{H_{hi}^{*}\right\}\right) = \sum_{\substack{i \in VI \\ h \in C}} H_{hi}^{*} z_{hi} - \frac{1}{\beta} \sum_{\substack{i \in VI \\ h \in C}} H_{hi}^{*} \ln\left(H_{hi}^{*}\right) + \frac{H}{\beta} \tag{T5.17}$$

Let us analyze the term

$$\begin{aligned} \Psi\left(\left\{H_{hi}^{*}\right\}\right) &= \sum_{\substack{i \in VI \\ h \in C}} H_{hi}^{*} z_{hi} - \frac{1}{\beta} \sum_{\substack{i \in VI \\ h \in C}} H_{hi}^{*} \ln\left(H_{hi}^{*}\right) \\ &= \sum_{\substack{i \in VI \\ h \in C}} H_{hi}^{*} z_{hi} - \frac{1}{\beta} \sum_{\substack{i \in VI \\ h \in C}} H_{hi}^{*} \ln\left(S_i H_h e^{\beta\left(z_{hi} - \overline{u}_h^{*} - p_i^{*}\right)}\right) \end{aligned} \tag{T5.18}$$

Where we use cancel the terms $\sum_{\substack{i \in I \\ h \in C}} H_{hi}^{*} z_{hi}$ to write:

$$H_{hi}^{*} = S_i H_h e^{\beta\left(z_{hi} - \overline{u}_h^{*} - p_i^{*}\right)} = S_i Q_{h/i} = H_h P_{i/h}$$

$$\begin{aligned} \Psi\left(\left\{H_{hi}^{*}\right\}\right) &= \sum_{\substack{i \in VI \\ h \in C}} H_h P_{i/h} \overline{u}_h^{*} + \sum_{\substack{i \in VI \\ h \in C}} S_i Q_{h/i} p_i^{*} - \frac{1}{\beta} \sum_{\substack{i \in VI \\ h \in C}} H_h P_{i/h} \ln(H_h) + \sum_{\substack{i \in VI \\ h \in C}} S_i Q_{h/i} \ln(S_i) \\ &= \sum_{h \in C} H_h \overline{u}_h^{*} \sum_{i \in VI} P_{i/h} + \sum_{i \in VI} H_h p_i^{*} \sum_{h \in C} Q_{h/i} - \frac{1}{\beta} \sum_{h \in C} H_h \ln(H_h) \sum_{i \in VI} P_{i/h} + \sum_{i \in VI} S_i \ln(S_i) \sum_{h \in C} Q_{h/i} \end{aligned} \tag{T5.19}$$

Because $\sum_{i \in VI} P_{i/h} = \sum_{h \in C} Q_{h/i} = 1$, rearranging the terms, we obtain the result:

$$\Psi\left(\left\{H_{hi}^{*}\right\}\right) = \sum_{h \in C} H_{hi}^{*} \left(\overline{u}_h^{*} - \frac{1}{\beta} \ln H_h\right) + \sum_{\substack{i \in VI \\ h \in C}} H_{hi}^{*} \left(p_i^{*} - \frac{1}{\beta} \ln S_i\right) \tag{T5.20}$$

References

Alonso, W., 1964. Location and Land-Use. Harvard University Press, Cambridge, MA.

Anas, A., 1983. Discrete choice theory, information theory and the multinomial logit and gravity models. Transportation Research Part B 17, 13–23.

Ben-Akiva, M.E., Boccara, B., 1995. Discrete choice models with latent choice sets. International Journal of Research in Marketing 12 (1), 9–24.

Bravo, M., Briceño, L., Cominetti, R., Cortés, C., Martínez, F., 2010. An integrated behavioral model of the land-use and transportation systems with network congestion and location externalities. Transportation Research Part B 44, 584–596.

Cascetta, E., Papola, A., 2001. Random utility models with implicit availability/perception of choice alternatives for the simulation of travel demand. Transportation Research Part C 9 (4), 249–263.

Castro, M., Martínez, F., Munizaga, M., 2013. Estimation of a constrained multinomial logit model. Transportation 40, 563–581.

Hurtubia, R., Martínez, F., Flötteröd, G., Bierlaire, M., 2010. Comparative analysis of hedonic rents and maximum bids in a land-use simulation context. In: Proceedings Swiss Transport Research Conference.

Lancaster, K., 1966. A new approach to consumer theory. Journal of Political Economy 74 (2), 132–157.

Macgill, S.M., 1977. Theoretical properties of biproportional matrix adjustments. Environment and Planning A 9, 687–701.

Manski, C.F., 1977. The structure of random utility models. Theory and Decision 8, 229–254.

Martínez, F.J., Aguila, F., Hurtubia, R., 2009. The constrained multinomial logit: a semi–compensatory choice model. Transportation Research Part B 43, 365–377.

Martínez, F.J., Araya, C., 2000. A note on trip benefits in spatial interaction models. Journal of Regional Science 40 (4), 789–796.

Martínez, F.J., Henríquez, R., 2007. A random bidding and supply land-use equilibrium model. Transportation Research Part B 41, 632–651.

Rosen, S., 1974. Hedonic pricing and implicit markets: product differentiation in pure competition. Journal of Political Economy 82 (1), 34–55.

Shelling, T.C., 1978. Micromotives and Macrobehavior. W.W. Norton & Co., New York, NY.

Swait, J.D., 2001. A non-compensatory choice model incorporating attribute cutoffs. Transportation Research Part B 35 (7), 903–928.

Swait, J.D., Ben-Akiva, M.E., 1987. Incorporating random constraints in discrete models of choice set generation. Transportation Research Part B 21 (2), 91–102.

The Land-Use and Transportation System

6

6.1 Introduction

This chapter studies the interaction between land use and transportation, where we extend the land-use (LU) partial equilibrium discussed previously to an equilibrium model of the integrated land-use and transportation (LUT) system. The following chapters discuss the extensions to the production and labor markets (LUTE) and the system of cities.

First, let us very briefly overview the history of LUT modeling. It is a story of complementary and converging approaches. Computable models of the integrated LUT system were first proposed by Lowry (1964), with very limited data and lack of a sound theory. At the same time, Alonso's (1964) foundation theory of urban economics was published (although his doctoral thesis had been available since 1961).

Inspired by Lowry's work, a branch of LUT models of metropolitan areas following different paths were developed over time, initially loosely related to urban economic theories, but flexible enough to represent spatial interaction and increasing degrees of heterogeneity of consumers. However, after some time, all the models developed introduced economic concepts while allowing for heterogeneity and computability.

Lowry's first model is a type of gravity spatial interaction model, with population and jobs following a simple gravity spatial distribution. An interesting feature of this model is that it is initiated by an exogenous seed location of "basic activities," defined as those production activities that are independent of local demand, i.e., those for industrial exports. This seed allocation initiates a double process of residential allocation regarding job locations and services, (nonbasic) activities generated in proportion to population and its allocated according to the access of residents. Transportation costs are exogenous in this model. Lowry-type models were subsequently developed and applied.

An important innovation came with Wilson (1970, 1971), who reinterpreted and extended the gravity model as an entropy maximization approach. He generated the spatial interaction model, well supported by nonlinear optimization and statistical theories, and applied it to a wide spectrum of location problems with computable solutions. An example is the DRAM-EMPAL model (Putman, 1983), including innovations on the entities modeled (e.g., household and firm types) and on the specification of attraction factors, but these models did not have any economic support.

At the same time, Herbert and Stevens (1960) used linear programming to implement an economically consistent and solvable partial equilibrium model. They applied Alonso's bid rent theory in a discrete spatial (with zones) context with deterministic behavior of agents. Wilson bridged the entropy and linear programming model by showing that Herbert and Stevens' model can be formulated as a limited case of the

Microeconomic Modeling in Urban Science. https://doi.org/10.1016/B978-0-12-815296-6.00006-8

entropy model, i.e., the case in which the stochasticity is null and the entropy model becomes deterministic (see Wilson and Bennett, 1985, p. 264). Using this connection, the entropy model can be interpreted as an economic stochastic equilibrium model. Mills (1972) and followers, e.g., Hartwick and Hartwick (1974) and Kim (1979), used a general equilibrium model of urban structure along with linear programming with a fixed coefficient technology, extending the model to traffic congestion and endogenous capacity.

The difficulties of linear programming in representing heterogeneity and the lack of microeconomic interpretation were subsequently overcome by discrete choice modeling (Anas, 1982). This technology allows economic representation of consistent behavior of heterogeneous agents in a discrete and heterogeneous spatial context. This approach, called the stochastic user equilibrium, was also widely applied in transportation modeling, eventually emerging as an increasingly unified framework for modeling LUT under a discrete choice random utility framework. Eventually, the popular multinomial logit model was proven to be equivalent to the entropy model under some conditions (Anas, 1983), thus merging the two then most popular techniques applicable to spatial contexts.

Most of the advanced applied models use discrete choice modeling combining different modeling techniques (see Pagliara et al., 2010). For example, UrbanSim (Waddell, 2002) and DELTA (Simmonds, 1999) avoid complex equilibrium calculations by simulating the urban system as an interaction process of agents over time. This approach, however, lacks relevant mathematical properties, and its predictions are likely to be unstable, i.e., the model predicts different solutions of the LUT system at every run.

Closer to urban economics principles, RELU-TRANS (Anas and Liu, 2007), MUSSA (Martínez, 1999), and Elliasson and Mattsson's (2000) models solve the LU market for equilibrium, interacting with a transportation equilibrium model to attain convergence.

6.2 The Integrated Land-Use and Transportation Equilibrium

The LU partial equilibrium model described in Chapter 5 assumes that the transportation system interacts with the LU system. We emphasize the word *interaction* between LU and T, where the two subsystems attain equilibrium independently, followed by an iterative process, i.e., a heuristic that transfers the solution of one to the other, for example, as accessibility measures.

This interaction, however, does not lead to the *integrated* equilibrium on the urban system, understood as a state where LUT feedbacks stabilize. That is, a state where LUT choices induce impacts on the system—such as densities, congestion, and land prices—that feed back into choices leading to a steady-state equilibrium where such feedbacks stabilize. This state is called the LUT equilibrium. In some specific cases, the interaction heuristic can converge to the integrated equilibrium, but this depends on the specific formulation of the model and the solution algorithms.

Integrating the transportation and the LU system to a unified equilibrium is the subject of this chapter. This involves extending the LU demand side to a larger number of choices in the transportation system and modeling not only the static spatial location but also the complex movement of agents and vehicles in the transportation network.

The transportation model has been developed in recent decades with significant advances on both the supply and demand sides and on the resulting equilibrium. All these methods assume that the land-use system is exogenous, i.e., in our notation the matrix $\{H_{hi}\}$ is exogenous in the transportation model. The transportation model then calculates trips, travel times, and costs at equilibrium, which provide accessibility measures. The interaction occurs when these accessibility indices are used in the LU model as location attributes, representing the feedback between LU and transportation in a simple variable.

The Classical Four-Step Transportation Model

The classical urban transportation model was designed for passenger transportation as a sequence of four-step submodels: trip generation, trip destination, transportation mode choice, and route assignment models, as shown in Fig. 6.1. This model is described in Ortúzar and Willumsen (1994). First used in the 1950s for the Detroit Metropolitan Area Traffic Study and the Chicago Area Transportation Study (CATS), this conceptual model was influential in independently developing the submodels. In particular, the trip destination model was largely developed using the entropy model pioneered by A. Wilson in the 1960s and 1970s (1967, 1970, 1971;

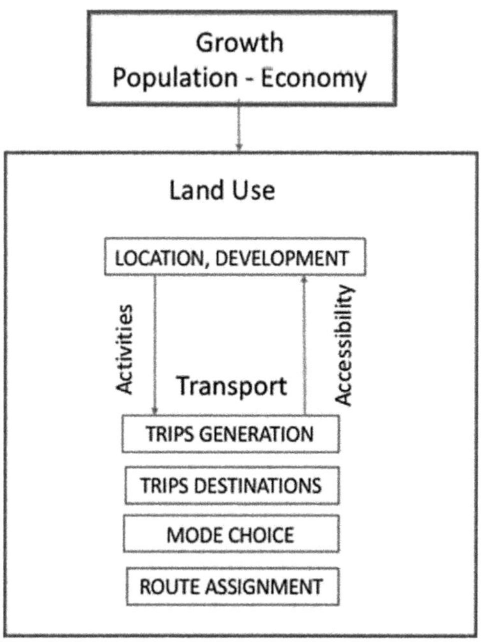

Figure 6.1 The land-use and transportation system.

see also Chapter 2). The transportation mode choice model was developed later using mainly the random utility theory following D. McFadden's approach (described in Ben-Akiva and Lerman, 1985).

Whereas the entropy model emerges from population statistical arguments and is interpreted by modeling aggregate trips, the random utility approach emerges from microbehavior of individuals. Despite this theoretical difference, both models share a stochastic setting and have been widely used in transportation demand models (Williams, 1976, 1977; Williams and Senior, 1978). Their equivalence was eventually rigorously established under specific conditions, particularly for the multinomial model (Anas, 1983).

Transportation assignment models predict the route that a traveler will take based on equilibrium conditions. The pioneering fundamental equilibrium conditions were formulated by Wardrop (1952) in a deterministic setting. The essential idea is that at the *transportation user equilibrium*, travelers cannot change routes and improve their decision rule; usually this rule is minimizing travel time, or a travel composite cost, or more generally, maximizing a utility measure. In the presence of a congested network, the travel time of a network link increases with its traffic, and the level of this traffic, or link flows of vehicles, depends on the route choices. Thus, travel time depends on demand for routes, and routes times depend on traffic on the links and routes; this interaction thus defines an equilibrium problem. The original equilibrium conditions were then formulated as Beckmann's *equivalent optimization transportation model* (Beckmann et al., 1956), which allowed the use of efficient optimization algorithms. Assuming the variability of travel times in the network, Dial (1971) and Daganzo and Sheffi (1977) used logit choice models to formulate the *stochastic user equilibrium*.

Although originally designed as a group of four interdependent submodels, the four-step model evolved to an integrated formulation of the transportation equilibrium, in which travel demand and assignment submodels simultaneously reach a steady state (De Cea and Fernández, 1993). For a review of transportation models, see Boyce (2007).

The Integrated Land-Use and Transportation Model

The idea of combining LUT modeling in a unified framework has been long pursued by LUT modelers (e.g., Boyce, 1986; Mattsson, 1987). The first attempts lacked a common framework, but the entropy model provided such a common approach for LUT demand. Later, logit models, integrated with the stochastic user equilibrium, provided a common and economically sound framework for the LUT model (Boyce and Mattsson, 1999; Elliasson and Mattsson, 2000).

The LUT model integrates the LU complex equilibrium discussed earlier with a network equilibrium. The solution of this double equilibrium problem can be characterized as complex and computationally demanding. However, under a common multinomial *logit* model for each choice problem in LUT systems, the integrated problem has been successfully solved, thereby establishing fundamental properties of the integrated equilibrium. Essentially, the *logit* model provides closed-form probabilities and computable equilibrium variables defined by the known *logsum* formula.

In Briceño et al. (2008) the existence of a unique equilibrium of the LUT model was proved, considering congestion but without location externalities. The approach followed by this work can be explained as an extension of Beckmann's equivalent transportation optimization model, which expands the network with fictitious location nodes to model the LU system, in what was called a hypernetwork. The merit of this approach is that the solution of this LUT optimization problem replicates simultaneously the stochastic transportation user equilibrium and the LU equilibrium, (i.e., the short- or long-term equilibrium, depending on the specification). The useful implication is that it allows us to use optimization theory and techniques to solve the LUT model; for example, to prove the existence and uniqueness of the LUT equilibrium without externalities. Conversely, in the case of equilibrium with externalities, e.g., location externalities and agglomeration economies, there does not exist an equivalent optimization problem for LUT. In this case, the problem was reformulated as a fixed-point problem to prove uniqueness on the integrated LUT equilibrium solution in Bravo et al. (2010).

The interpretation of the integrated LUT system as an extended hypernetwork is useful to explain the problem. In Fig. 6.2, an exogenous number of H_h consumer agents emerge in the LUT system (depicted as nodes h and g in the figure for the respective clusters), at the fictitious nodes away from the transportation network plane, one for each agent's cluster. These agents face net benefits, e.g., consumers' surplus $(w_{hi} - p_i)$, to cross the fictitious arcs from node h to a real node at location i. This benefit is attained if the agent chooses the real estate unit, i, which can be compared to benefits derived from other nodes and is measured as the difference between the willingness to pay, w_{hi}, and the location price, p_i.

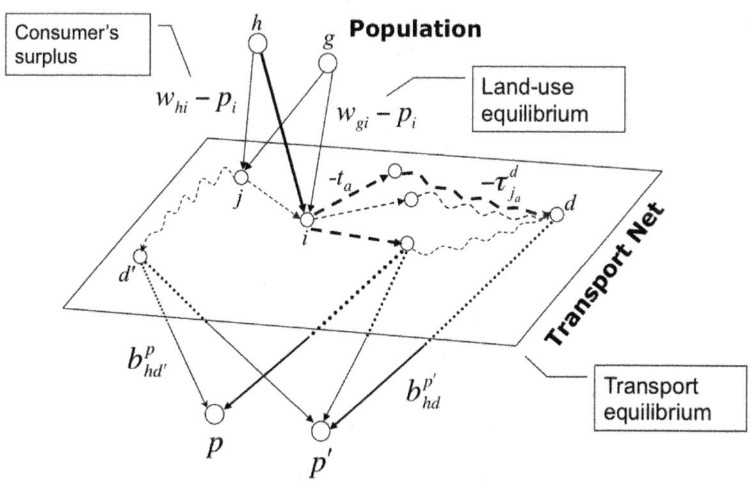

Figure 6.2 The integrated land-use and transportation system.

The benefit, w_{hi}, depends on the activities that the agent will perform at the residence location and at all other destinations. To "collect" benefits from the interaction with distant activities, the agent travels where the benefit, or utility, of performing the activity, net of travel costs, is maximal. The aggregate of interaction benefits represents the accessibility of the residential location. Thus, willingness to pay depends on the travel times in the network, $w_{hi}(t)$. After assessing the consumer surplus at every alternative location, the agent chooses the optimal location depending on the travel times.

Starting from a residential location at real node, i, the agent makes trips intending to engage in different activities (i.e., trips with some purpose) at different destination nodes, denoted by $d \in D$, traveling through the network of arcs (A) and nodes (N) described by the graph (A,N). Each trip between nodes (i,d) implies a travel time (or time plus monetary cost called composite cost), which is the accumulated travel time on arcs on the less costly route (i,d). At the destination, the agents traverse a final fictitious arc (d,p), which is a representation of the activity performed at that location. This final arc ends at the fictitious node, P, where all trips with the same purpose, P, conclude. The amount of benefit for traversing the final link arc (d,p) depends on the activities located at the destination, d, denoted by the matrix, $(\{H_d\})$, and on the activity duration time and its monetary cost, which together yield a net benefit, $b^p_{hd}(\{H_d\})$. Summing up the benefits and costs of all trip purposes and destinations generates an accessibility index for h at every potential residential location, allowing the agent to calculate the bid for each location.

The Transportation Equilibrium Problem

Let us first summarize the formulation of the transportation equilibrium problem as an equivalent optimization problem (Beckmann et al., 1956) using the following additional notation describing the transportation system. Consider the set of graphs (A,N) with $a \in A$ denoting arcs and $i \in N$ denoting nodes. Vectors $t = (t_a)$, $x = (x_a)$, and $v = (v^{dh}_a)$ denote, respectively, travel times on each arc t_a, total flow on arcs x_a, and the flow of trips on arcs by agents of socioeconomic cluster h with destination node d given arc a, v^{dh}_a. The trips' origin–destination matrix between nodes i and d is $g = (g^{dh}_i)$, and $O = (O_{hi})$ stands for the number of trips generated by agents of cluster h located at location node i. Additionally, the LU system is described by vector $\{H_{hi}\}$ with the number of agents by cluster located at each node.

The LUT model is built by embedding the Markovian traffic equilibrium (MTE) model (Baillon and Cominetti, 2006) in a logit choice setting and a private transportation network. The stochastic Markovian equilibrium defines a recursive process assuming that the traveler reaches any node $i \in N$ in the graph and makes an elemental decision as to which exit arc takes the minimum time to the destination, that is, what is the best route between nodes (i,d). To make this choice, the traveler considers the travel times for the (i,d) pair on all alternative routes, as shown in Fig. 6.3. The travel time for a given route is the travel time along the exit arc from node i, denoted by t_a, plus the expected travel time from the next node, j_a (the arc exit node), to the destination node d, denoted by $\tau^{dh}_{j_a}$. Then, the agent selects the exit arc with the minimum

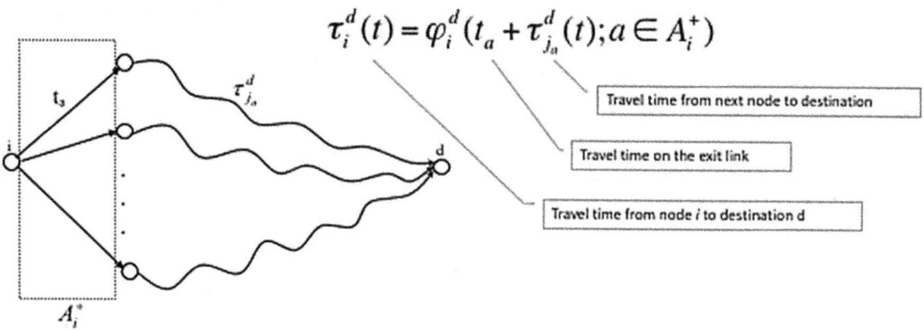

Figure 6.3 The Markovian traffic equilibrium process.

travel time, τ_i^{dh}, between (*i*,*d*). After this choice is made, travel times, $t = (t_a)$, are updated in all the arcs of the network.

Repeating this elemental choice and travel time update generates a recursive Markovian process. This process is highly intuitive because it assumes that minimum information is required to make the choice at each intermediate node, *i*, on the route to a destination, *d*, because the traveler simply concentrates on choosing the optimal exit arc at each node. Applying this choice process recursively, conditional on the set of travel times (t_a^n) at each iteration, *n*, the equilibrium travel times on each arc can be obtained as was proved by Baillon and Cominetti (2006).

The travel time equilibrium is the solution of the following problem:

$$\min_t \Phi(t) = \sum_{a \in A} \int_{t_a^0}^{t_a} s_a^{-1}(z)dz - \sum_{h \in C} \sum_{\substack{d \in D \\ d \neq i}} g_i^{dh} \tau_i^{dh}(t) \tag{6.1}$$

where $t_a = s_a(x_a)$ is the flow-dependent travel time in arc $a \in A$ as a function of the arc flow x_a. The expected travel time from node i to d for a type h user is $\tau_i^{dh}(t) = \varphi_i^{dh}\left(t_a + \tau_{j_a}^{dh}(t),\ a \in A_i^+\right)$, which calculates the expected value; A_i^+ denotes the set of arcs whose tail (entry) is node i, and j_a denotes the head (exit) node of arc a. Assuming that travel time is independent and identically distributed Gumbel variates, then φ_i^{dh} is the known logsum function defined as: $\varphi_i^{dh}(x) = -\frac{1}{\mu}\ln\left[\sum_{a \in A_i^+} e^{-\mu x_a}\right]$.

Baillon and Cominetti (2006) included the following conditions for the congestion function $s_a(x_a)$:

1. $s_a(\cdot)$ strictly increasing, unbound from above, and continuous;
2. $s_a(0) = t_a^0 \geq 0$, the free flow travel time is positive; and
3. $\varphi_i^{dh}(t^0) > 0, \quad \forall i \neq d$, the initial travel time is strictly positive.

This is to prove that Eq. (6.1) is convex and coercive and that the optimal conditions yield the transportation equilibrium conditions $s_a^{-1}(t_a) = \sum_{\substack{d\in D \\ h\in C}} v_a^{dh} = x_a$, with $v_a^{dh} = \sum_{i\in VI} g_i^{dh}\frac{\partial \tau_i^{dh}}{\partial t_a}$.

Eq. (6.1) is the transportation equivalent optimization problem with elastic demand on travel times if $g_i^{dh} = g^h\left(\tau_i^{dh}\right)$. The first term represents the Beckmann equivalent optimization problem whose solution reproduces Wardrop's traffic equilibrium. The second double sum term on the right-hand side represents the total expected travel time spent on the network to perform the trips defined by the origin–destination matrices, g_i^{dh}.

Fig. 6.4 aids in the understanding of this problem. It depicts the following cases: Fig. 6.4A and B consider inelastic demand; Fig. 6.4C and D consider an elastic demand, $g(t)$; and travel time is represented by a linear congestion function, $s(x)$.

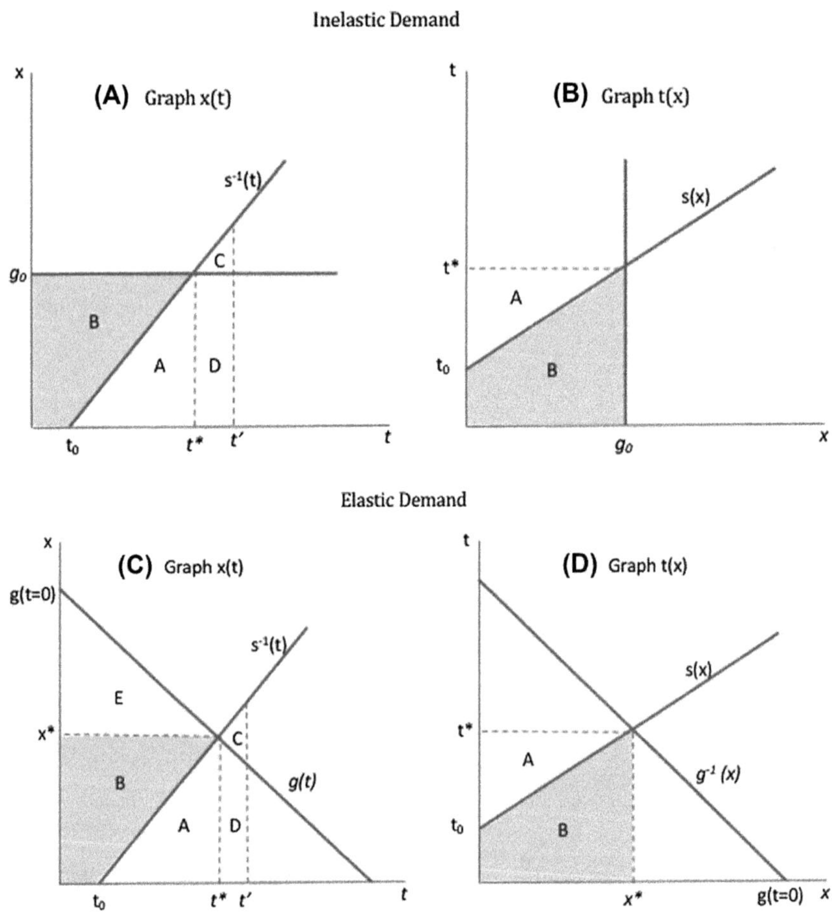

Figure 6.4 Beckmann's equivalent optimization problem.

They are drawn in two ways: in Fig. 6.4A and C, labeled Graph $x(t)$, the demand decreases with travel time, and in Fig. 6.4B and D, labeled Graph $t(x)$, the axes are inverted, showing increasing travel times with the traffic flow.

To analyze these figures, consider the point (x^*,t^*) where travel demand intercepts travel time, which defines the areas labeled A and B. The first term of Eq. (6.1) is represented by area A, and the second term is represented by the square $g(t^*)\cdot t^* = (A + B)$ (in the inelastic case, $g(t^*) = g_0$). The graphical representation thus shows that $\Phi(t^*) = A - (A + B) = -B$. Hence, the optimum is $\min_t \Phi(t^*) = \max_t B$. To represent the optimum graphically, Fig. 6.4A shows the incremental areas C and D when travel time increases from t^* to t', such that $\Phi(t') = A + C + D - (B + A + D) = C - B = \Phi(t^*) + C$, which is suboptimal. Similarly, in Fig. 6.4C we obtain $\Phi(t^*) = A - (A + B + E) = -B - E$ and $\Phi(t') = A + C + D - (A + B + E + D) = C - B - E = \Phi(t^*) + C$, which is also suboptimal.

We can analyze optimization problem Eq. (6.1) from an economic perspective. It is well known that Wardrop's first principle states that the individual's equilibrium does not yield a social optimum due to congestion externalities; i.e., *the individual's equilibrium yields a suboptimal use of the network*, which means that there is another distribution of flows in the network that minimizes total travelers time. Furthermore, Wardrop's second principle states that *if users consider the marginal travel instead of the average cost, the equilibrium attains a social optimum.*

To explain the difference between the individual's equilibrium and social optimum, consider the following definition of marginal travel time (tmg_a) as the change in total travel time in the arc with a marginal increment of the arc flow (x):

$$tmg_a(x) = \frac{\partial(t_a x_a)}{\partial x} = s_a(x) + x_a\frac{\partial s_a(x)}{\partial x} \tag{6.2}$$

which states that while travelers perceive a travel time, t_a, they engender additional travel time, $s'(x) = \frac{\partial s_a(x)}{\partial x}$, for all the other travelers in the arc due to incremental congestion. This incremental travel time is an externality not considered by the traveler who chooses the arc. Fig. 6.5 compares the individual's equilibrium depicted as (x^*,t^*) and the social optimum, (x^{**},t^{**}), with the shaded area showing the social loss at equilibrium.

In Fig. 6.5 we observe a similarity between the equilibrium and the optimal points. This similarity can be established mathematically if we consider the following Beckmann's optimization problem, which formulates the equivalent optimization problem, instead of the inverse function s_a^{-1} in terms of the travel times s_a. Then, the equilibrium traffic under inelastic demand is the following solution:

$$\min_t \Phi^1(x) = \sum_{a\in A}\int_0^{x_a} s_a(z)dz \tag{6.3}$$

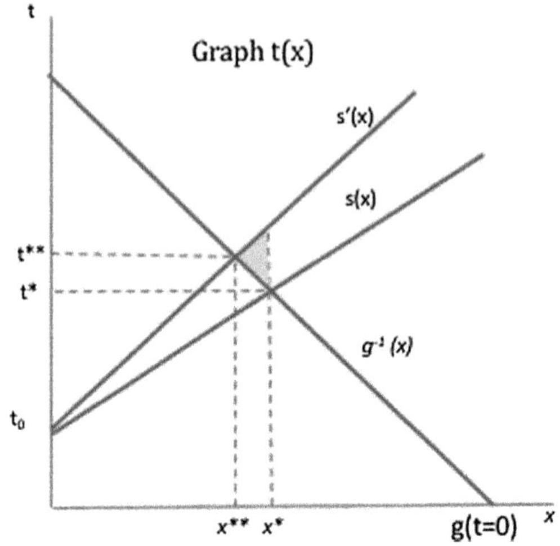

Figure 6.5 The individual versus optimal traffic.

and the optimal traffic is the following solution:

$$\min_t \Phi^2(x) = \sum_{a\in A} t_a x_a = \sum_{a\in A} \int_0^{x_a} tmg_a(z)dz \tag{6.4}$$

Thus, the social optimum is obtained by replacing the individual's perception of the travel time, $s_a(x_a)$, by the respective social cost given by $tmg_a(x_a)$. We can conclude that, to attain a social optimum traffic, travelers must consider the marginal travel time instead of the average travel time. This statement motivates road pricing schemes aimed at making the traveler consider a travel time plus a road price that in total is equivalent to the marginal time.

The economic analysis concludes that the individual's equilibrium derived from the optimization problem in Eq. (6.3) does not yield a social optimum, unless congestion is null, i.e., $\frac{\partial s_a(x)}{\partial x} = 0$, which implies that $tmg_a(x) = s_a(x)$ so that both the individual and the social optimization problems coincide.

The LUT Short-term Optimization Problem

The Logit Model

The transportation equilibrium model can be generalized to formulate the short-term LUT equivalent *logit* optimization problem (Briceño et al., 2008). Consider bids given by $w_{hi}(\overline{u}, t) = y_h - \overline{u}_h + z_{hi} - \sum_{d\in D} N_h^d \tau_i^{hd}(t)$, with z_{hi} denoting constant attributes of the location and $\sum_{d\in D} N_h^d \tau_i^{hd}(t)$ denoting the accessibility index, with the trip matrix N_h^d giving the number of trips per destination, d, for type h users, which is assumed to be exogenous.

The LUT equivalent optimization problem is as follows:

$$(D)\ \min_{t,\overline{u},p} \Phi(t,\overline{u},p) = \sum_{a\in A} \int_{t_a^0}^{t_a} s_a^{-1}(z)dz + \sum_{h\in C} H_h \overline{u}_h + \sum_{i\in VI} S_i p_i + \frac{1}{\beta}\left[\sum_{\substack{h\in C\\ i\in VI}} S_i H_h e^{\beta(w_{hi}(\overline{u},t)-p_i)}\right] \tag{6.5}$$

where S_i's are exogenous.[1]

Note that Eq. (6.5) extends the LU optimization problem discussed in Chapter 5; in fact, both problems are identical for constant travel times (t). Moreover, the last three terms represent the dual optimization problem (D) of the doubly constrained entropy problem shown in Chapter 5, which yields the maximum social benefit in the LU model as discussed in that chapter. Because the transportation component (first term) does not yield social optima, it follows that Eq. (6.5) does not yield the optimum LUT system.

In Technical Note 6.1 we prove that the problem in Eq. (6.5) yields the *LUT equilibrium simultaneously* for the aggregate bid-auction LU model and the MTE of the transportation systems (Baillon and Cominetti, 2006). Thus, the dual unconstrained optimization problem (D) combines the transportation network problem, represented by the first term and depending on travel times[2] (t), with the LU problem represented by the following two terms, depending on utilities (u) and location prices (p). The last term combines both problems through the bids, which depend on location attributes and travel times.

The solution of the optimization problem yields (see Technical Note 6.1):

$$H_{hi} = S_i H_h e^{\left[\beta\left(w_{hi}(\overline{u}^*,t^*)-p_i^*\right)\right]} = S_i Q_{h/i}(\overline{u}^*,t^*) = H_h P_{i/h}(\overline{u}^*,p^*,t^*) \tag{6.6}$$

with $Q_{h/i}$ and $P_{i/h}$ representing the bid-auction and choice probabilities, and defining $z_{hi}(t^*) = z_{hi} - \sum_{d\in D} N_h^d \tau_i^{hd}(t^*)$ we get:

$$\overline{u}_h^* = \frac{1}{\beta}\ln\left[\sum_{i\in VI} S_i e^{\beta\left(z_{hi}(t^*)-p_i^*\right)}\right],\quad \forall h\in C \tag{6.7}$$

$$p_i^* = \frac{1}{\beta}\ln\left(\sum_{h\in C} H_h e^{\beta w_{hi}\left(\overline{u}_h^*,t^*\right)}\right) \tag{6.8}$$

[1] The original formula of Briceño et al. (2008) has been modified in Eq. (6.2) to reproduce aggregate LUT models.

[2] To include time and fares, the transportation problem can be specified in travel costs instead of travel times.

$$s_a^{-1}\left(t_a^*\right) = \sum_{\substack{d \in D \\ i \in I}} g_i^d \cdot \frac{\partial \tau_i^d}{\partial t_a}(t^*) = \sum_{d \in D} v_a^d = x_a \tag{6.9}$$

which reproduce the LUT equilibrium conditions.

The importance of the equivalent optimization problem of Eq. (6.5) is that $\Phi(t, \overline{u}, p)$ is convex and coercive under the assumptions made for the transportation equilibrium problem, provided that the three following conditions hold: there are no location externalities (i.e., z_{hi} are constant), the trip matrix N_h^d is exogenous, and $\sum_{i \in VI} S_i = \sum_{h \in C} H_h$ (i.e., total real estate supply equals total demand). Additionally, as discussed in the LU equilibrium model, the solution is unique if utilities are normalized by a constant, $k \in \mathbb{R}$, such that $\overline{u}^* = \overline{u} + k$; with this condition $\Phi(t, \overline{u}, p)$ is strictly convex.

The optimal solution of Eq. (6.5) reproduces both the transportation equilibrium conditions with trip demands, $g_i^{dh} = N_h^d H_{hi}$, and the LU equilibrium, $\sum_{i \in VI} H_{hi} = H_h$, with $H_{hi} = S_i Q_{h/i}$ and $Q_{h/i}$ standing for the aggregate bid-auction location probability that maximized random bids at the auctions. Therefore, the LUT problem admits an optimization formulation that extends Beckmann's problem for the transportation system under the conditions established: no externalities and exogenous trip matrix N_h^d, plus the classical conditions for the transportation and LU equilibrium.

The Frechit Model

It is worth mentioning that an equivalent optimization problem for the *frechit* model, analogous to Eq. (6.5), has not yet been defined. Therefore, the properties of existence and uniqueness for the solution for the integrated *frechit* LUT equilibrium model cannot be analyzed using this method. However, the uniqueness of the solution in this model is studied below as an equilibrium fixed point (see the succeeding section on the long-term LUT model with externalities).

The Long-term LUT Optimization Problem (Without Externalities)

The LUT equilibrium problem of Eq. (6.5) is further extended to consider a long-term equilibrium with endogenous supply. Briceño et al. (2008) consider heterogeneous producers, indexed by $k \in K$, and the following problem:

$$\begin{aligned} \min_{t,\overline{u},p} \Phi(t) = & \sum_{a \in A} \int_{t_a^0}^{t_a} s_a^{-1}(z)dz + \sum_{h \in C} H_h \overline{u}_h + \sum_{k \in K} S_k \xi_k(p) \\ & + \frac{1}{\beta}\left[\sum_{\substack{h \in C \\ i \in VI}} S_i H_h e^{[\beta(w_{hi}(\overline{u},t) - p_i]}\right] \end{aligned} \tag{6.10}$$

where $\xi_k(p) = \frac{1}{\theta_k}\ln\left[\sum_{i\in VI} S_i e^{\theta_k(p_i - c_{ik})}\right]$ represents the expected profit yielded by real estate k. In this formulation, suppliers are differentiated by their real estate costs $\{c_{ik}\}$ and variances $\{\theta_k\}$.

This problem is strictly convex and coercive under the same conditions as the problem in Eq. (6.5) and that $\sum_{k\in K} S_k = \sum_{h\in C} H_h$, which guarantees unique global equilibrium with the supply defined endogenously. The solution again reproduces the transportation and LU equilibrium conditions and yields the *logit* supply probability:

$$P^s_{ki} = \frac{S_i e^{\theta_k(p_i - c_{ik})}}{\sum_{j\in VI} S_j e^{\theta_k(p_j - c_{jk})}} \tag{6.11}$$

Thus, the optimization problem in Eq. (6.5) yields the long-term LUT equilibrium.

Notice that the case of homogeneous suppliers is obtained directly by replacing $\sum_{k\in K} S_k\xi_k(p_i)$ by $S\xi(p_i)$, where $\xi(p_i) = \frac{1}{\theta}\ln\left[\sum_{i\in VI} S_i e^{\theta(p_i - c_i)}\right]$, which represents a single supplier and yields a solution that replicates the urban LU market equilibrium discussed in Chapter 5.

The LUT Equilibrium With Externalities

Externalities introduce a significant difficulty into the analysis of the LUT equilibrium problem because, with them, it is no longer possible to formulate the model as an optimization problem. It is worth recalling that externalities enter the LUT model when the agents' choices are mutually interdependent. In previous chapters, we have demonstrated that this interaction appears in the LU model, where they are called location externalities and agglomeration economies, leading to fixed-point problems. However, there is yet another externality linking LUT subsystems because the location of activities, i.e., densities, depends on the profile of accessibilities, and, vice versa, accessibilities depend on activities—densities available at trip destinations. This also defines a fixed-point problem. Mathematically, the difficulty arises when the willingness-to-pay attributes, z_{hi}, are not exogenous in the equilibrium problem because they are dependent on the allocation of agents, e.g., $z_{hi}(\{H_{hi}\})$.

The Logit Model

In Bravo et al. (2010) this equilibrium problem is formulated as a fixed-point problem on the location matrix, $M_H = (\{H_{hi}\},\ \forall h\in C,\ i\in I)$, i.e., $M_H = F^{LUT}(M_H)$, for the short-term equilibrium with externalities, i.e., exogenous supply, and

$\sum_{h \in C} H_h = \sum_{i \in I} S_i = H$, the LUT equilibrium. The fixed-point problem is defined by the following set of equations:

1. The short-term *logit* LU equilibrium:

$$H_{hi} = S_i \frac{e^{\beta w_{hi}(H)}}{\sum_{g \in C} e^{\beta w_{gi}(H)}}, \quad \forall i \in VI \tag{6.12}$$

$$\sum_{i \in VI} H_{hi} = H_h, \quad \forall h \in C \tag{6.13}$$

$$w_{hi} = z_{hi}(H, O, \alpha, t) - \overline{u}_h, \quad \forall h \in C, \quad i \in VI \tag{6.14}$$

with O the vector of trips generated and α the accessibility vector, both by cluster and location.

2. The transportation subproblem:

$$O_{hi}(H) = N_{hi} H_{hi} + \delta_{hi}, \quad \forall h \in C, \quad i \in VI \tag{6.15}$$

calculates the number of trips generated at each location as a function of the fixed number of trips generated by an agent N_{hi}, with $\delta_{hi} > 0$ (a constant ensuring that O_{hi} is strictly positive).

To simultaneously solve the joint trip destination and network assignment problems, Bravo et al. (2010) used the following optimization subproblem for the transportation system:

$$\min_{\alpha, t} \psi(\alpha, t) = \sum_{a \in A} \int_{t_a^0}^{t_a} s_a^{-1}(z) dz + \sum_{h \in C} O_{hi} \alpha_{hi} + \sum_{h \in C} \frac{1}{\mu_h} \left[\sum_{i \in VI} \sum_{d \in D} e^{\left[\mu_h \left(\alpha_{hi} - c_i^{dh}(t, H)\right)\right]} \right] \tag{6.16}$$

where $-c_i^{dh}(t, H) = \gamma_{dh}(H) - \tau_i^{dh}$ is the transportation benefit defined as the benefit associated with the interaction of activities at the destination, $\gamma_{dh}(H)$, minus the travel times, τ_i^{dh}. The optimality conditions, $\frac{\partial \psi}{\partial t_a}$, yield the following MTE conditions (Baillon and Cominetti, 2006):

a. The traffic flow per arc by destination and cluster is

$$v_a^{dh}(H, t) = \sum_{i \in VI} g_i^{dh} \frac{\partial \tau_i^{dh}}{\partial t_a}, \quad \forall a \in A, \quad d \in D, \quad h \in C \tag{6.17}$$

b. The total traffic at each arc is

$$x_a(H, t) = \sum_{\substack{d \in D \\ h \in C}} v_a^{dh}, \quad \forall a \in A \tag{6.18}$$

c. The travel time on each arc is

$$t_a(H) = s_a(x_a), \quad \forall a \in A \tag{6.19}$$

Additionally, the destination trip matrix is the *logit* model:

$$g_i^{dh}(H,t) = O_{hi}\frac{e^{\mu_h\left(\gamma_{dh}(H)-\tau_i^{dh}\right)}}{\sum\limits_{j\in D} e^{\mu_h\left(\gamma_{jh}(H)-\tau_i^{jh}\right)}} \tag{6.20}$$

which depends on the attraction or net benefit for agent, h, defined as the benefit obtained from interacting with the activities located at the destination, d, $\gamma_{dh}(H)$, minus the travel time from the trip origin, i, to destination, d: $\tau_i^{dh} = \varphi_i^{dh}\left(t_a + \tau_{ja}^{dh} : a\in A_i^+\right)$. This submodel yields the expected maximum benefit per trip:

$$\alpha_{hi} = \frac{1}{\mu_h}\ln\left[\frac{1}{O_i}\sum_{j\in D} e^{\mu_h\left(\gamma_{jh}(H)-\tau_i^{jh}\right)}\right] \tag{6.21}$$

representing an accessibility measure for agent h resident at i who integrates the expected benefits among all the alternative destinations considering the minimum travel times $\left(\tau_i^{jh}\right)$ for the set of available routes to each destination.

In summary, the problem in Eq. (6.16) integrates the *logit* transportation demand and the MTE model and yields accessibility measures given by the map, assigning the optimal solution for the transportation subproblem, i.e., $(\alpha,t) = \varphi(M_H,O)$ to each couple (M_H,O).

Thus, the LUT fixed-point equilibrium problem is

$$M_H^* = F^{LUT}\left(\{H_h\}, O\left(M_H^*\right), \varphi\left(M_H^*, O\right)\right) \tag{6.22}$$

Bravo et al. (2010) proved that a solution to this fixed-point problem exists and, if the bids (Eq. 6.12) have enough dispersion, i.e., β are sufficiently small, F^{LUT} is a contraction, and the solution is unique. The proof proceeds as shown in Fig. 6.6, connecting three steps sequentially starting with identifying an initial matrix $M_H = (\{H_{hi}\}, h \in C, i \in I)$, $M_H \in K$. Then, trip generation is computed by direct evaluation of $O(M_H)$; second, with (M_H,O) the vector of accessibility variables (α,t) is calculated through the accessibility map $\varphi(M_H,O)$, which implies solving the MTE. Finally, the triple $(M_H,O, (\alpha,t))$ determines unique optimal utilities and prices, $\left(u^*, p_i^*\right)$, through the equilibrium fixed point, F^u, having had uniqueness proven

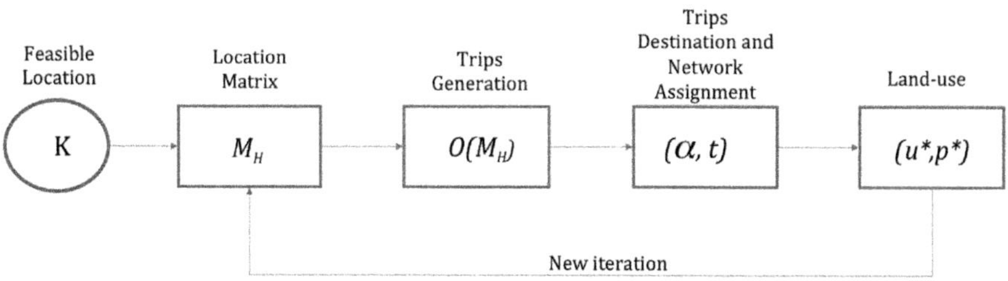

Figure 6.6 The LUT fixed-point iteration.

with and without externalities in Technical Notes 5. This sequential process gives a mapping of the solution matrix M_H^* from an initial matrix M_H. The integrated LUT equilibrium is defined as the solution of the fixed-point F^{LUT}:$M_H \rightarrow F^{LUT}(M_H)$.

The proof of existence and uniqueness follows because K is a nonempty compact polytope and the map $F^{LUT}(\cdot)$ is continuous (because it is composed by continuous maps), and by Banach's fixed-point theorem. Bravo et al. (2010) show the existence and uniqueness of a solution to the LUT equilibrium problem as follows: the map is of class C1 and because K is compact, it is Lipschitz so there is at least one LUT equilibrium. In Technical Note 6.2 we prove that for $\beta \in (0,\beta_c)$ in Eq. (6.12), the map $\varphi(M_H,O)$ is a contraction and that the upper bound β_c is computable. In this case, we conclude that the LUT equilibrium problem has a unique solution.

It is worth commenting that the condition for uniqueness, $\beta \in (0,\beta_c)$, implies that the willingness-to-pay variates must have a minimum variance, i.e., the agents have a minimum idiosyncratic heterogeneity in the aggregate model or each agent's behavior has a minimum variance (nondeterministic) in the disaggregate model. Conversely, if the behavior is sufficiently deterministic, this result implies that the equilibrium is not unique.

The Frechit Model

We now analyze the integrated LUT system modeled by a *frechit* LU model, replacing Eqs. (6.12) and (6.14) by the corresponding *frechit* equations:

$$H_{hi} = S_i \frac{w_{hi}(H)^{\beta}}{\sum\limits_{g\in C} w_{gi}(H)^{\beta}}, \quad \forall i \in VI \tag{6.23}$$

$$w_{hi} = z_h(H, O, \alpha, t)e^{-\overline{u}_h}, \quad \forall h \in C, \quad i \in VI \tag{6.24}$$

and consider the same *logit* transportation demand and network assignment problem in Eq. (6.11) that yields the equilibria in Eqs. (6.12)–(6.15).

Let us analyze whether the property of existence of a unique solution holds in the *frechit* LU model. The existence of a unique solution follows directly from the *logit* model, where the mapping is as follows:

$$M_H = F^{LUT}(\{H_h\}, O(M_H), \varphi(M_H, O)) \tag{6.25}$$

with an identical sequence of *logit* models: $O(M_H)$, $\varphi(M_H,O)$. The difference is in the LU fixed-point problem, F^u, which has the same mathematical form but different parameters. Thus, this problem yields equilibrium utilities and prices (u^*,p^*) derived from the triple (M_H,O,α,t) through the *frechit* version of the equilibrium fixed point. Because F^u is identical in the *logit* and *frechit models*, uniqueness is also proved with and without externalities in Technical Note 5. Because the map is also of class C^1 and K is compact, it is Lipschitz. Again, if the shape parameter β in Eq. (6.23) is sufficiently small, the map $\varphi(M_H,O)$ is a contraction, with the upper bound β_c calculated in Technical Note 6.2.

Remarks and Comments

The mathematical properties of the integrated LUT equilibrium proven in this chapter, i.e., the existence of a unique solution and the convergence of the iteration algorithm, are powerful tools for modelers. These results hold for the aggregate LU condition $\sum_{i \in VI} S_i = \sum_{h \in C} H_h = H$.

To summarize, these properties guarantee that if the modeler formulates a LUT system with *logit* models for the transportation MTE, and with *logit* or *frechit* models for the bid-auction LU equilibrium, then the iteration process described in Fig. 6.6 converges to the unique equilibrium. This statement holds for the case with and without externalities.

However, it is worth bearing in mind that these properties do not necessarily hold if the agents' bids are close to being deterministic (low variance) or if the location probabilities are subject to constraints that are not included in our analysis, which may also reduce the behavior variability of the agents. The extension of the mathematical properties to these cases depends on the specific formulation of the penalizations used to represent constraints.

The LUT models analyzed here consider the classical four-step trip-based transportation equilibrium model. Other approaches, such as activity-based models and tour-based models, simulate a more complex decision process that considers trip chains.

It is also important to note that the transportation system modeled is limited to the private transportation mode because the MTE model does not consider public transportation. Moreover, the extension to public transportation is not trivial because it involves a multiple service choice process with the delays caused by stops and congestion of vehicles. This yields a public transportation equilibrium problem that is different from the private transportation case.

6.3 Summary

In this chapter, we have analyzed the LUT model, which integrates LU and T equilibrium submodels. This approach has the merit of providing very important properties for the modeler because despite the complexity of the LUT system, it yields unique equilibria under certain plausible conditions. Indeed, the minimum heterogeneity required for the equilibrium to be unique is likely to be reached in applied models because of the heterogeneity of consumers' idiosyncratic behavior and the variety of real estate options, which induce a variety of stochastic sources in the location process.

From a different perspective, the likelihood of the existence of a unique equilibrium gives rise to interesting thoughts if we assume that the model represents the city reasonably well. Indeed, it tells us that cities have a *natural attractor*. If we think about a sequence of the city's unique equilibria as population grows, it defines a unique path for the city's dynamics, which implies that cities are pulled toward an attractor. If that were the case, one should try to identify the drivers of this attractor. In the following chapters, we shall further explore the notion of natural attractors, but it is worth stressing here that the LUT equilibrium model provides a strong basic argument for this notion. Of special relevance is the fact that the LUT equilibrium attractor includes not only agents' location externalities, i.e., interactions between neighboring households and firms, but also interactions with distant activities, which involve travel. Then, the attractor defines a unique solution imposed on the complex LUT system under the common law of rational behavior.

Technical Note 6.1: The LUT Equivalent Optimization Problem

The Short-term Logit Model (Without Location Externalities)

Let us reproduce the result of Briceño et al. (2008) that proved that for the short-term case without externalities, the LUT *logit* equilibrium has the following equivalent optimization problem (Eq. 6.5):

$$\min_{t,\overline{u},p} \Phi(\overline{u},p,t) = \sum_{a\in A}\int_{t_a^0}^{t_a} s_a^{-1}(z)dz + \sum_{h\in C} H_h\overline{u}_h + \sum_{i\in VI} S_i p_i + \frac{1}{\beta}\left[\sum_{\substack{h\in C\\ i\in VI}} S_i H_h e^{\left[\beta(w_{hi}(\overline{u},t)-p_i\right]}\right] \tag{T6.1}$$

with $w_{hi}(\overline{u},t) = z_{hi}(t) - \overline{u}_h$; $z_{hi}(t) = y_h + \frac{f_h(z_i(t))}{\lambda_h}$; and $f_h(z_i(t))$ the utility yield by location attributes including the transportation accessibility index $z_i(t)$.

Denoting $(\overline{u}^*, p^*, t^*)$, we obtain the following solution of the problem in Eq. (T6.1):

$$\frac{\partial\Phi(\overline{u},p,t)}{\partial\overline{u}_h} = 0 \Rightarrow H_h = \sum_{i\in VI} S_i H_h e^{\left[\beta\left(w_{hi}(\overline{u}^*,t)-p_i^*\right)\right]} \tag{T6.2}$$

Defining $H_{hi} := S_i H_h e^{\left[\beta\left(w_{hi}(\overline{u}^*,t^*)-p_i^*\right)\right]}$, we observe that the consumers' equilibrium condition, $H_h = \sum_{i\in VI} H_{hi}$, holds. Solving Eq. (T6.2) for $\overline{u}^*$ reproduces the equilibrium utilities obtained in Chapter 5:

$$\overline{u}_h^* = \frac{1}{\beta}\ln\left[\sum_{i\in VI} S_i e^{\beta\left(z_{hi}(t)-p_i^*\right)}\right], \quad \forall h\in C \tag{T6.3}$$

Additionally,

$$\frac{\partial\Phi(\overline{u},p,t)}{\partial p_i} = 0 \Rightarrow S_i = \sum_{h\in C} S_i H_h e^{\left[\beta\left(w_{hi}(\overline{u}^*,t)-p_i^*\right)\right]} \tag{T6.4}$$

which reproduces the supply constraints, and solving for p_i^* yields the equilibrium prices:

$$p_i^* = \frac{1}{\beta}\ln\left(\sum_{h\in C} H_h e^{\beta w_{hi}\left(\overline{u}_h^*, t\right)}\right), \quad \forall i \in VI \tag{T6.5}$$

Substituting optimal utilities into the location definition, $H_{hi} := S_i H_h e^{\left[\beta\left(w_{hi}(\overline{u}^*, t^*) - p_i^*\right)\right]}$, yields the aggregate location choice model:

$$H_{hi} := H_h \frac{S_i e^{\left[\beta\left(z_{hi}(t) - p_i^*\right)\right]}}{\sum_{j\in VI} S_j e^{\left[\beta\left(z_{hj}(t) - p_j^*\right)\right]}} = H_h \frac{S_i e^{\left[\beta\left(w_{hi}\left(\overline{u}_h^*, t\right) - p_i^*\right)\right]}}{\sum_{j\in VI} S_j e^{\left[\beta\left(w_{hj}\left(\overline{u}_h^*, t\right) - p_j^*\right)\right]}} = H_h P_{i/h}(\overline{u}^*, p^*, t) \tag{T6.6}$$

where we have multiplied both the numerator and denominator by $e^{-\beta\overline{u}_h^*}$. Replacing optimal prices in the same definition yields the aggregate bid-auction model:

$$H_{hi} := S_i H_h e^{\beta\left(w_{hi}\left(\overline{u}_h^*, t\right) - p_i^*\right)} = S_i \frac{H_h e^{\beta w_{hi}\left(\overline{u}_h^*, t\right)}}{\sum_{g\in C} H_g e^{\beta w_{gi}\left(\overline{u}_g^*, t\right)}} = S_i Q_{h/i}(\overline{u}^*, t) \tag{T6.7}$$

These results show that the solution of the optimization problem, Eq. (T6.1), replicates simultaneously the bid-auction and the choice models defined in Chapter 4. Note that the optimization problem in Eq. (T6.1) is also consistent with the problem analyzed in Chapter 5, denoted by $\varphi(\overline{u})$ in Technical Note 5.1, because the latter is a subproblem that can be obtained by replacing the equilibrium price of Eq. (T6.5) in Eq. (T6.1), assuming that travel times are constants $\left(t = \tilde{t}\right)$; then: $\varphi(\overline{u}) = \Phi\left(\overline{u}, p^*, \tilde{t}\right)$.

Finally, the optimum travel times are given by:

$$\frac{\partial \Phi(\overline{u}, p, t)}{\partial t_a} = 0 \Rightarrow s_a^{-1}(t_a) = -\left[\sum_{\substack{h\in B\\ i\in VI}} S_i H_h e^{\left[\beta\left(w_{hi}(\overline{u}, t^*) - p_i\right]\right.} \frac{\partial z_{hi}(t^*)}{\partial t_a}\right]$$

$$= -\left[\sum_{\substack{h\in B\\ i\in VI}} H_{hi} \frac{\partial z_{hi}(t^*)}{\partial t_a}\right] \tag{T6.8}$$

The solution of this equation depends on the specific transportation demand model, but we know that congestion increases travel times and reduces accessibility; that is, $\frac{\partial z_{hi}(t^*)}{\partial t_a} < 0$. Consider, for example: $\frac{\partial z_{hi}(t^*)}{\partial t_a} = -\sum_{d\in D} N_i^{dh} \cdot \frac{\partial \tau_i^d}{\partial t_a}(t)$, with N_i^{dh} the number of trips between nodes i to d by agent h, and $\tau_i^{dh} = \varphi_i^{dh}\left(t_a + \tau_{j_a}^{dh},\ a\in A_i^+\right)$ the corresponding expected travel time. Define $g_i^d := \sum_{h\in C} H_{hi} N_i^{dh}$, with N_i^{dh} the total trips generated by household type between locations (zones) i and d, to write $s_a^{-1}(t_a) = \sum_{\substack{d\in D\\ i\in I}} g_i^d \cdot \frac{\partial \tau_i^d}{\partial t_a}(t)$. Then,

$$s_a^{-1}\left(t_a^*\right) = \sum_{\substack{d\in D\\ i\in VI}} g_i^d \cdot \frac{\partial \tau_i^d}{\partial t_a}(t^*) = \sum_{d\in D} v_a^d = x_a \tag{T6.9}$$

which reproduces the MTE (Baillon and Cominetti, 2006), i.e., $t_a^* = s_a\left(x_a^*\right)$ and x_a^* the total flow on link a at equilibrium.

Thus, we conclude that the optimization problem in Eq. (T6.1) yields a solution that replicates the *logit* model equilibrium of the integrated LUT system.

The Long-Term Logit Model (Without Location Externalities)

These conclusions can be extended for the long-term LUT optimization problem in Eq. (6.10):

$$\min_{t,\overline{u},p} \Phi(t) = \sum_{a\in A} \int_{t_a^0}^{t_a} s_a^{-1}(z)dz + \sum_{h\in C} H_h \overline{u}_h + \sum_{k\in K} S_k \xi_k(p) + \frac{1}{\beta}\left[\sum_{\substack{h\in C\\ i\in VI}} S_i H_h e^{\left[\beta(w_{hi}(\overline{u},t)-p_i\right]}\right]$$

with $\xi_k(p) = \frac{1}{\theta_k}\ln\left[\sum_{i\in VI} S_i e^{\theta_k(p_i - c_{ik})}\right]$ the expected maximum profit. S_k is the market share of firm k and c_{ik} stands for the firm's costs; both are exogenous.

We need only to prove that $\frac{\partial \Phi(\overline{u},p,t)}{\partial p_i} = 0$ yields the equilibrium condition because the other conditions hold as in the short-run case. Then,

$$0 = \sum_{k\in K} S_k \frac{\partial \xi_k(p^*)}{\partial p_i} - \left[\sum_{h\in C} S_i H_h e^{\left[\beta\left(w_{hi}(\overline{u},t) - p_i^*\right)\right]}\right] \tag{T6.10}$$

where $\frac{\partial \xi_k(p)}{\partial p_i} = \frac{S_i e^{\theta_k(p_i - c_{ik})}}{\sum_{j \in I} S_j e^{\theta_k(p_j - c_{jk})}} = P^S_{ki}(p)$ is the aggregate *logit* supply probability that supplier k offers for a real estate unit i. Then, $\sum_{k \in K} S_k \frac{\partial \xi_k(p^*)}{\partial p_i} = \sum_{k \in K} S_k P^S_{ki}$, and $H_{hi} := S_i H_h e^{[\beta(w_{hi}(\overline{u},t) - p^*_i]}$. Therefore,

$$\sum_{k \in K} S_k P^S_{ki}(p^*) = \sum_{h \in C} H_{hi} = S_i \tag{T6.11}$$

which proves that the equivalent optimization problem also yields the equilibrium conditions. This conclusion also holds for homogeneous suppliers, which is seen by replacing $\sum_{k \in K} S_k \xi_k(p)$ by $S \cdot \xi(p)$ in Eq. (6.10), with $\xi(p) = \frac{1}{\theta} \ln \left[\sum_{i \in VI} S_i e^{\theta(p_i - c_i)} \right]$ representing the expected maximum suppliers' profit in the city and $S = \sum_{i \in VI} S_i$.

Technical Note 6.2: Bounds for the Model With Externalities

Here, we summarize the result of Bravo et al. (2010) for $\beta \in (0, \beta_c)$ in Eq. (6.12): when β is sufficiently small, the location with externalities map $M_H = F^{LUT}(\{H_h\}, O(M_H), \varphi(M_H, O))$ is a contraction.

Consider the bid-auction probability in Eq. (6.12):

$$\Theta_{hi} = S_i Q_{h/i} = S_i \frac{e^{\beta w_{hi}(H)}}{\sum_{g \in C} e^{\beta w_{gi}(H)}} \tag{T6.12}$$

and compute the derivatives:

$$\begin{aligned} \frac{\partial \Theta_{hi}}{\partial H_{kj}} &= \beta S_i Q_{h/i} \left[\frac{\partial w_{hi}}{\partial H_{kj}} - \sum_{g \in C} Q_{g/i} \frac{\partial w_{gi}}{\partial H_{kj}} \right] \\ &= \beta S_i Q_{h/i} \left(1 - Q_{h/i} \right) \left[\frac{\partial w_{hi}}{\partial H_{kj}} - \sum_{\substack{g \in C \\ g \neq h}} \frac{Q_{g/i}}{1 - Q_{h/i}} \frac{\partial w_{gi}}{\partial H_{kj}} \right] \end{aligned} \tag{T6.13}$$

Take a uniform bound $\left| \frac{\partial w_{gi}}{\partial H_{kj}} \right| \leq B$ and observe that $\sum_{\substack{g \in C \\ g \neq h}} \frac{Q_{g/i}}{1 - Q_{h/i}} = 1$ and $\frac{\partial w_{hi}}{\partial H_{kj}} - \sum_{\substack{g \in C \\ g \neq h}} \frac{Q_{g/i}}{1 - Q_{h/i}} \frac{\partial w_{gi}}{\partial H_{kj}} \leq B + B \sum_{\substack{g \in C \\ g \neq h}} \frac{Q_{g/i}}{1 - Q_{h/i}} \leq 2B$ to write:

$$\left|\frac{\partial \Theta_{hi}}{\partial H_{kj}}\right| \leq 2B\beta S_i Q_{h/i}\left(1 - Q_{h/i}\right) \tag{T6.14}$$

Finally, using $\max_{x \in (0,1)} x(1 - x) = \frac{1}{4}$, we obtain the upper bound:

$$\left|\frac{\partial \Theta_{hi}}{\partial H_{kj}}\right| \leq \frac{1}{2}B\beta S_i \tag{T6.15}$$

Therefore, because the contraction holds for $\left|\frac{\partial \Theta_{hi}}{\partial H_{kj}}\right| < 1$, then $\beta_c < \frac{2}{BS_i}$ defines the upper bound if $B > 0$.

Let us now consider the *frechit* model:

$$\Theta_{hi} = S_i Q_{h/i} = S_i \frac{w_{hi}(H)^{\beta}}{\sum\limits_{g \in C} w_{gi}(H)^{\beta}} \tag{T6.16}$$

with $\frac{\partial \Theta_{hi}}{\partial H_{kj}} = \beta S_i Q_{h/i}\left[\frac{1}{w_{hi}}\frac{\partial w_{hi}}{\partial H_{kj}} - \sum\limits_{g \in C} Q_{g/i}\frac{1}{w_{gi}}\frac{\partial w_{gi}}{\partial H_{kj}}\right]$. Define $x_{hi} = \frac{1}{w_{hi}}\frac{\partial w_{hi}}{\partial H_{kj}}$ and write:

$$\frac{\partial \Theta_{hi}}{\partial H_{kj}} = \beta S_i Q_{h/i}\left(1 - Q_{h/i}\right)\left[x_{hi} - \sum_{\substack{g \in C \\ g \neq h}} \frac{Q_{g/i}}{1 - Q_{h/i}} x_{gi}\right] \tag{T6.17}$$

Take a uniform bound $|x_{hi}| \leq B'$, assume that $|w_{hi}| \geq \varepsilon, \ \forall h \in C, \ i \in VI$ to avoid dividing by zero, and follow the same analysis as above to get the upper bound for the *frechit* model:

$$\left|\frac{\partial \Theta_{hi}}{\partial H_{kj}}\right| \leq \frac{1}{2}B'\beta S_i \tag{T6.18}$$

References

Alonso, W., 1964. Location and Land-Use. Harvard University Press, Cambridge, MA.

Anas, A., 1982. Residential Location Markets and Urban Transportation. Academic Press, London.

Anas, A., 1983. Discrete choice theory, information theory and the multinomial logit and gravity models. Transportation Research B17 (B), 13–23.

Anas, A., Liu, Y., 2007. A regional economy, land-use, and transportation model (RELU-TRAN): formulation, algorithm, and testing. Journal of Regional Science 47 (3), 415–455.

Baillon, J.B., Cominetti, R., 2006. Markovian traffic equilibrium. Mathematical Programming Series B 111 (1–2), 35–36.

Beckmann, M., McGuire, C.B., Winstein, C.B., 1956. Studies in the Economics of Transportation. Yale University Press, New Haven, CT.

Ben-Akiva, M., Lerman, S.R., 1985. Discrete Choice Analysis: Theory and Application to Travel Demand. MIT Press, Cambridge, MA.

Boyce, D., 1986. Integration of supply and demand models in transportation and location: problem formulations and research questions. Environment and Planning A 18 (4), 485–489.

Boyce, D., 2007. Forecasting travel and congested urban transportation networks: review and prospects for network equilibrium models. Network and Spatial Economics 7, 99–128.

Boyce, D.E., Mattsson, L.-G., 1999. Modeling residential location in relation to housing location and road tolls on congested urban highway networks. Transportation Research Part B 33, 581–591.

Bravo, M., Briceño, L., Cominetti, R., Cortés, C., Martínez, F., 2010. An integrated behavioral model of the land-use and transportation systems with network congestion and location externalities. Transportation Research Part B 44, 584–596.

Briceño, L., Cominetti, R., Cortes, C., Martinez, F.J., 2008. An integrated behavioral model of land-use and transportation system: an extended network equilibrium approach. Networks and Spatial Economics 8 (2–3), 201–224.

Daganzo, C., Sheffi, Y., 1977. On stochastic models of traffic assignment. Transportation Science 11, 253–274.

De Cea, J., Fernández, E., 1993. Transit assignment for congested public transport systems: an equilibrium model. Transport Science 27 (2), 133–147.

Dial, R.B., 1971. A probabilistic multipath traffic assignment model which obviates path enumeration. Transportation Research 5, 83–111.

Elliasson, E.A., Mattsson, L.-G., 2000. A model for integrated analysis of household location and travel choices. Transportation Research Part A (34–35), 375–394.

Hartwick, P.G., Hartwick, J.M., 1974. Efficient resource allocation in a multinucleated city with intermediate goods. Quarterly Journal of Economics 88, 340–352.

Herbert, J.D., Stevens, B.H., 1960. A model for the distribution of residential activity in urban areas. Journal of Regional Science 2, 21–36.

Kim, T.J., 1979. Alternative transportation modes in a land use model: a general equilibrium approach. Journal of Urban Economics 6 (2), 197–215.

Lowry, I.S., 1964. A Model of Metropolis. Rand Corporation, Santa Monica, CA.

Martínez, F.J., 1999. MUSSA: a land-use model for Santiago City. Transportation Research Record 1552, 126–134.

Mattsson, L.-G., 1987. Urban welfare maximization and housing market equilibrium in a random utility setting. Environment Planning A 19, 247–261.

Mills, E.S., 1972. Markets and efficient resource allocation in urban areas. The Swedish Journal of Economics 74, 100–113.

Ortúzar, J.D., Willumsen, L.G., 1994. Modelling Transport, second ed. John Wiley & Sons, Chichester, UK.

Pagliara, F., Preston, J., Simmonds, D., 2010. Residential Location Choice: Models and Applications. Springer, New York, NY.

Putman, S.H., 1983. Integrated Urban Models. Pion Press, London.

Simmonds, D.C., 1999. The design of the DELTA land-use modelling package. Environment and Planning B 26, 665–684.

Waddell, P., 2002. UrbanSim: modeling urban development for land-use, transportation and environmental planning. Journal of the American Planning Association 68 (3), 297–314.

Williams, H.C.W.L., 1976. Travel demand models, duality relations and user benefit analysis. Journal of Regional Science 16, 147–166.
Williams, H.C.W.L., 1977. On the formation of travel demand models and economic evaluation measures of user benefit. Environment and Planning A 9, 285–344.
Williams, H.C.W.L., Senior, M.L., 1978. Accessibility, spatial interaction and the evaluation of land-use transportation plans. In: Karlovist, A., Lundovist, L., Snickars, F., Weibull, J.W. (Eds.), Spatial Interaction Theory and Planning Models. North Holland, Amsterdam, pp. 253–287.
Wardrop, J., 1952. Some theoretical aspects of road traffic research. Proceedings Institute of Civil Engineering 1, 325–378.
Wilson, A.G., 1967. A statistical theory of spatial distribution models. Transportation Research 1, 253–269.
Wilson, A.G., 1970. Entropy in Urban and Regional Modeling. Pion, London.
Wilson, A.G., 1971. A family of spatial interaction models and associated developments. Environment and Planning 3 (1), 1–32.
Wilson, A.G., Bennett, R.J., 1985. Mathematical Methods in Human Geography and Planning. John Wiley & Sons, Hoboken, NJ.

The General Urban System

7

7.1 Introduction

A general equilibrium of the system is studied in this chapter, extending the land-use and transportation integrated model (LUT) discussed in Chapter 6 to include the general economy (LUTE), that is, by including the production and labor markets. Fig. 7.1 illustrates this model, in which the production submodel simulates the equilibrium of the goods, leisure, and labor production markets, whose interaction leads to an integrated equilibrium.

In the LUTE model, each goods market is modeled with a specific technology for production, and supply and demand are matched at every location by a set of equilibrium prices differentiated by location. Consumers buy goods and enjoy leisure activities at the most attractive locations, whereas producers optimize production profit by buying inputs from least-cost producers.

There are very few examples of a LUTE equilibrium model. The first LUTE model to be widely applied and successfully implemented was MEPLAN (Echeñique, 1994), which has been used in various cities since the 1980s. It was followed by two sister models, TRANUS (De la Barra, 1989) and PECAS (Abraham and Hunt, 1997). These models, embedded with the LUT systems, interact with an input−output approach (IO) used in regional economics. They thus integrate all the production sectors of the urban and regional economy. Later, with the RELU-TRANS model, Anas and Liu (2007) developed a general equilibrium model for a Cobb−Douglas technology with constant returns to scale.

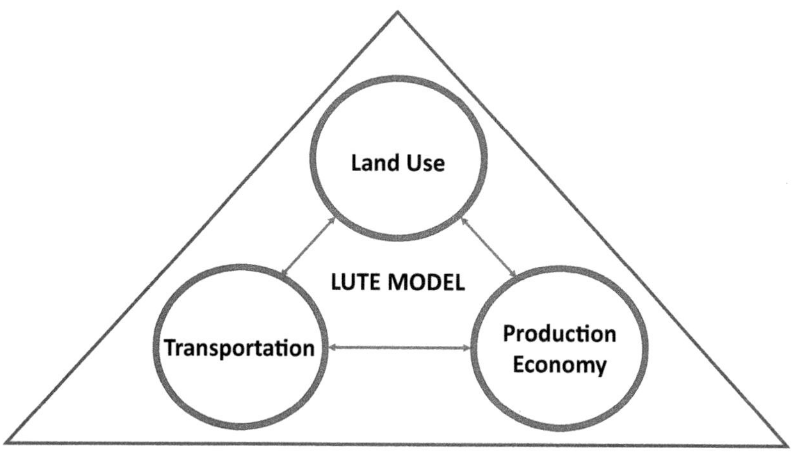

Figure 7.1 The land-use, transportation, and production model.

Microeconomic Modeling in Urban Science. https://doi.org/10.1016/B978-0-12-815296-6.00007-X

As we shall see in this chapter, these models have advanced in integrating all markets of the urban system in a consistent LUTE model, which is a highly demanding task. Moreover, these models have been applied to various large cities, proving their successful implementation with available data. To make this task feasible, the models share a common simplification: they ignore location externalities, agglomeration economies, and economies of scale. When these issues were included, they simplified the phenomena, assuming constant attractors incapable of incorporating the important dynamics of a nonlinear system. Although these constants help in fitting the model to observed data, they are only useful for a short-term analysis.

Incorporating externalities does, indeed, change the mathematical structure of the model, switching it from a linear to a complex nonlinear system. Urban economists have highlighted the importance of incorporating this phenomenon in urban studies (Krugman, 1991; Fujita and Thisse, 2002), but no applied model has yet been formulated with this nonlinear process. However, because the mathematical difficulty has been ameliorated with the increased capacity of computing, we explore a formulation of such a complex LUTE system in this chapter.

7.2 The Integrated LUTE Model

The extension of the LUT model to simulate the equilibrium of goods and labor markets, i.e., all production and services markets, is here called the land-use, transportation, and productive economy (LUTE) model. The LUTE model seeks to solve the spatialized equilibrium of the production and consumption of goods in conjunction with the allocation of activities in the urban area and the transportation of cargo and passengers.

The integration of the production economy into the LUTE model is a major task because the number of market equilibrium conditions expands with the number of goods and jobs. To illustrate this problem, we consider a set of goods, or sectors of goods, or industries, K, indexed by $k = (1, 2, \ldots, |K|)$, as well as a set, F, of job types characterized by skill requirements and indexed by $f = (1, 2, \ldots, |F|)$. Then, considering that production and consumption are spatially distributed in $|I|$ zones, our task is to model $(|K| + |F|) \cdot |I|$ related markets to obtain the corresponding equilibrium prices of goods $p = \{p_{kj}\}$ and salaries $\omega = \{\omega_{fj}\}$, $\forall k \in K, f \in F, j \in I$.

Modeling approaches can be differentiated by their different technical aspects, e.g., the aggregation level of goods, the agents and the space, and by the way the interactions occur among land-use (LU) transportation (T) and markets for goods (E), if they are formulated. They can also be differentiated by their economic complexity, which fundamentally defines the outcome of predictions. Models whose variables are physical objects subject to market totals, e.g., goods, land, and trips, which in their simplest version are multisector IO models with fixed coefficients, can be grouped into a class. Their output reflects a linear distribution with exogenous parameters of the flow of goods. The second class includes price signals that equate supply and demand at equilibrium, leading to a multimarket and spatialized application of the well-known Walras equilibrium. A third class leads to Nash's equilibrium because the behavior rules of agents are sensitive to nonlinear dependencies: LU externalities, production agglomeration economies, and production economies of scale and scope. Nash's LUTE model describes a complex nonlinear system.

7.3 The Input–Output Model

IO technology (Leontief, 1986) is an accounting method that considers not only all sectors of the economy ($k \in K$), including manufacturing and services, but also residential land and real estate. As shown in Fig. 7.2, these sectors are row entries in this table of the total supply of all goods and services. They are also entries in columns, representing the "intermediate demand" of resources used for production. The table also shows the final demand for investment, consumption, government expenditure, and exports. The basic idea of the table is that the totals in each row, k, X_k, are distributed into intermediate production and final consumption.

Intermediate transactions, representing inputs from sector k for the production process of sectors k', denoted $x_{kk'}$, are calculated as $x_{kk'} = a_{kk'} X_{k'}$, i.e., the amount of input, k, required by sector output, k', with $A = (\{a_{kk'}\};\ \ k, k' \in K \times K)$, called the matrix of *technical coefficients*. This model represents production with a linear technology that ignores the economies of scale and of agglomeration.

The equilibrium condition is that the total supply by sector equals the total demand, i.e., $X_i = \sum_{k \in K} x_{ik} + Y$ and $Y = x_{iI} + x_{iC} + x_{iG} + x_{iE}$, thus clearing all sectors' markets. The equilibrium is calculated as the production amounts that comply with: $X = (I - A)^{-1} Y$, with I being the unit matrix. This is a linear problem that requires inverting the matrix $I - A$.

The IO model, originally conceived for a single location market, evolved to more sophisticated models accounting for the spatial locations of consumers and producers from each sector, which defines the Spatial IO Table. De la Barra (1989) explains an implementation of this extension by expanding the production sectors from X_k to origin–destination flows by commodity sectors, defining the matrix of commodity

DEMAND		INTERMEDIATE DEMAND					FINAL DEMAND				TOTAL
		Production Sectors					Investment	Consumption	Government	Export	$X_i = \sum_{j \in J} x_{ij}$
		S_1	...	S_j	...	S_K					
SUPPLY Production Sectors	S_1	x_{11}	...	x_{1j}	...	x_{1K}	x_{1I}	x_{1c}	x_{1G}	x_{1E}	X_1
	...	...	...	...	...	...	....	....	....	....	...
	S_i	x_{i1}	...	x_{ij}		x_{iK}	x_{iI}	x_{ic}	x_{iG}	x_{iE}	X_i
	...	...	...	...	...	...	....	....	....	....	...
	S_K	x_{K1}	...	x_{Kj}	...	x_{KK}	x_{KI}	x_{Kc}	x_{KG}	x_{KE}	X_K

Figure 7.2 The input–output table.

flows of products, k, produced at zone i and shipped to zone j, $\{X_{kij}\}$, $k, i, j \in K \times I \times I$. The matrix expansion is modeled as a spatial distribution model: $X_{kij} = X_k P_{ij/k}(p,c)$, where the distribution probability, $P_{ij/k}(p,c)$, is usually based on an entropy or a *logit* model, with spatial distribution rules that include differentials in the prices of goods, $p = \{p_{ki}\}$, and transport costs, $c = \{c_{kij}\}$. The land market is modeled as an immobile commodity sector in which exogenous land is demanded by the real estate sector to produce floor space, which is a final product demanded by consumers. The equilibrium conditions are extended to all spatialized markets, generating $|K| \cdot |I|^2$ equilibrium equations with the same number of unknown flows, X_{kij}.

The model can be formulated by considering price elastic demands, i.e., the technical coefficients matrix is dependent on prices, $A = A(p)$. In this case, the model yields a Walras equilibrium, with prices adjusting to clear all markets simultaneously. Moreover, if transport costs are endogenous, the model leads to a LUTE equilibrium, where transport costs are also adjusted for congestion in the transportation mode.

The implementation of a spatialized IO method requires the estimation of many parameters, which is a difficult task even if good data are available, but it also overparameterizes the model. It assumes linear production technology, ignoring nonlinear relationships in the system, such as externalities or economies of scale and scope, which would lead to a Nash equilibrium. This simplicity permits simple calculations of amounts and prices of goods produced and consumed at every location and the spatial distribution of cargo and passengers, but it can also oversimplify the nonlinear dynamics of the system.

The IO approach has generated various implementations in applied software that interact with transport models that provide the travel costs for (k, i, j) tuples and accessibility indices, e.g., MEPLAN (Echeñique, 1994), TRANUS (De la Barra, 1989), and PECAS (Abraham and Hunt, 1997). These models have been applied in several cities and for different purposes, mostly for transport policy analysis. Implementations may differ in the number of sectors that are price elastic, reducing the number of parameters to estimate and saving on computing resources.

7.4 The Mixed Discrete-Continuous Model

In contrast to the IO approach based on aggregate flows, this approach is based on microeconomics principles, focused on the interaction between agents at a microscopic level. Here, agents can be characterized by behavioral rules that lead to a Walras equilibrium if externalities are excluded or, otherwise, to a Nash equilibrium.

Fig. 7.3 illustrates the interactions between agents and the markets involved (except with the transportation market). On the left-hand side, households demand real estate units at different locations in the LU market; then job locations in the labor market, depending on the locations of their residences; and, finally, goods and leisure at different spatialized markets of products. In the process of product supply, shown on the left-hand side, total supply is allocated to zones in the LU market, which then offers jobs because labor is an input of production and demands other

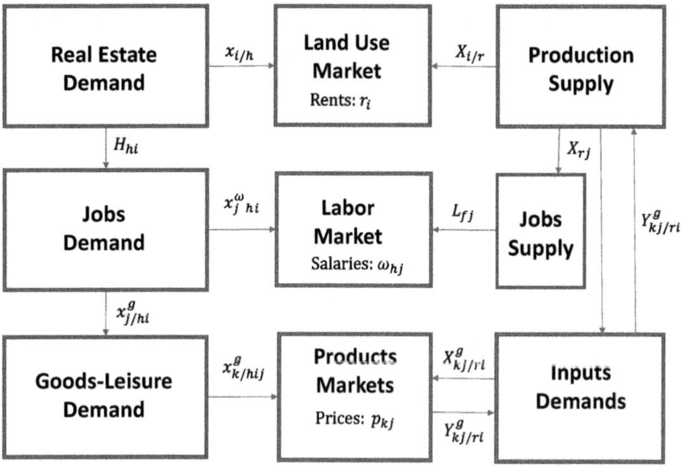

Figure 7.3 The land use, transportation, and economic system.

intermediate products from suppliers. The markets clear the demand and supply by defining land rents, salaries, and product prices at each location, represented by the middle column.

In this section, we discuss and then modify the demand model developed by Anas and Liu (2007), hereafter denoted A-L. In this model, prices are obtained from the *Walras* price equilibrium—without externalities—approach, implemented in the RELU-TRANS model.

The A-L Demand Model

Consumers are divided into clusters characterized by working skills (here indexed by $h \in C$), each one with an exogenous number of consumers. The behavior of an agent is modeled in the A-L model using a mix of random-discrete choice and deterministic-continuous frameworks. In this mixed approach, the discrete entities are locations, represented by zones, transportation modes and routes. Discrete choices are residences—real estate types—including their locations and relation to job locations (v, i, j). The continuous choices are consumption of a bundle of retail goods at each location $x = \{x_k, k \in K\}$, with $|K| = |I|$, and residential floor space $b = \{b_{hi}, h \in C, i \in VI\}$.

A brief description of this model follows. Household utilities are described by a Cobb–Douglas utility function between housing and consumption and by a constant elasticity of substitution (CES) subutility function with the Dixit–Stiglitz form for consumption, which in our notation reads:

$$U_{ijv/h} = \alpha_h \ln\left(\sum_{k \in K} \beta_{k/hij} x_k^{\theta_h}\right)^{\frac{1}{\theta_h}} + \gamma_h \ln(b) + \rho_{ijv/h} + e_{ijv/h} \tag{7.1}$$

where the utility of each household, h, conditional on discrete residence and job location choices (i, j, v) depends on the following continuous variables: the aggregated consumption bundle of retail goods, x, and the floor space, b, in the chosen dwelling type, $v \in V$. The authors also add an idiosyncratic constant, $\rho_{vij/h}$, and the random variables, $e_{vij/h}$. $\beta_{k/hij}$ are constants representing an inherent attractiveness to retail at location k in the (h, i, j) case. The exogenous parameters are $\alpha_h, \gamma_h > 0$ with $\alpha_h + \gamma_h = 1$, which impose constant returns to scale, and $0 < \theta_h < 1$ with $\frac{1}{1-\theta_h}$ defining the constant elasticity of substitution between retail locations. Thus, the subutility of retail $\left(\sum_{k \in K} \beta_{k/hij} x_k^{\theta_h}\right)$ has a Dixit–Stiglitz form, which is embeded in a Cobb–Douglas utility.

The consumer is constrained by time and monetary budgets, which have the endogenous working hours in common. These constraints are combined to obtain a single monetary constraint, which after simplifying for some factors for our exposition, including taxes, reads:

$$\sum_{k \in K} (p_k + c_{ik}) d_k x_k + b\, r_{vi} + dc_{ij} = \omega_{hj} \left(T - dt_{ij} - \sum_{k \in K} t_{ik} d_k x_k \right) \tag{7.2}$$

with $T - dt_{ij} - \sum_{k \in K} t_{ik} d_k x_k > 0$.

This budget constraint equals the household's total expenditure (left term) with the income (right term) over the period (e.g., 1 year). The exogenous parameters are the following: the total time endowment, T; the number of commutes to work, d; the number of trips per unit of goods bundle, d_k; and all units of time. The endogenous variables are the following: consumption of goods and floor space, (x, b); the unit price of retail goods at zone k, p_k; the land rent per unit of floor space type v at location i, r_{vi}; and travel times and expected monetary costs, including all transport modes and purposes, (t_{ij}, c_{ij}) in the pair (i, j); ω_{hj}, which is the hourly wage at zone j for household type h (with type h defined by the workers' skills).

The authors obtain the *Marshallian* demands for the continuous variables analytically by maximizing the utility in Eq. (7.1) subject to the constraint of Eq. (7.2), which yields:

$$b_{vi/hj} = \gamma_h \frac{\psi_{hij}}{r_{vi}}; \quad x_{k/hij} = \beta_{k/hij} \frac{p_{k/hij}}{r_{vi}} \tag{7.3}$$

with ψ_{hij} the net income given by the right-hand side of Eq. (7.2) and $p_{k/hij} = p_k + c_{ik} + \omega_{hj} t_{ik}$ the delivered price of retail goods from the production location, k, to consumer h residing at i and working at j (i.e., with income ω_{hj}).

The demand model follows two steps: the set of continuous choices (x, b) is price elastic and is calculated analytically conditional on discrete choices, i.e., resident type, its location and job location (v, i, j). These are then used to derive indirect utilities for the discrete choices. In the second step, a random indirect utility yields choice probabilities using a logit model. The model solves the market-clearing *Walrasian* price equilibrium on the prices of goods, land rents, and labor salaries (p, r, ω), yielding the consumption of retail goods and land (x, b). The solution attains a LU and economic production equilibrium conditional on transport costs and times, which is called the RELU model. This model iterates with the transport model, TRANS, in a heuristic process.

It is worth commenting on the A-L's approach to explain potential improvements. The authors do not explain the logic of defining the subutility of continuous choices—retail shopping and residential land—as deterministic, while the utility of discrete–location choices is assumed to be random. This asymmetric assumption is intriguing theoretically because random utilities in discrete choices are justified as representing an "idiosyncratic utility" capturing "the horizontal taste differentiation among consumers." But this argument is also valid for continuous choices, i.e., the continuous or discontinuous characteristic of consumption is dependent only on the variability of tastes across the population in a cluster. This issue has a practical implication because the assumption of continuous and deterministic consumption of floor space requires that real estate supply is also continuous in floor space, which implicitly ignores the use and redevelopment of old stock in the real estate market. This assumption is valid for modeling a city that emerges from empty land, ignoring the fact that real estate units are durables.

The second comment is that the consumers' behavior regarding the interaction with working and shopping activities is merely economic, i.e., it is based on minimizing prices, transportation costs, and time. This assumption ignores that shopping is not solely utilitarian but that it also combines entertainment, socializing, and gathering information about varieties of goods. Modeling this more complex behavior requires that the interaction between consumers and suppliers is extended from the prices of goods to include a quality attribute of both goods and the environment. However, quality is an attribute that is not only difficult to describe but that also introduces mathematical complexity if it is dependent on the concentration of opportunities and the size of shops, i.e., density attributes. This is because the equilibrium problem is no longer a *Walrasian* price equilibrium problem but a nonlinear *Nash* equilibrium caused by location externalities and economies of scale.

Third, the model recognizes differentiated attraction factors, $\rho_{vij/h}$, for options (v, i, j), but it assumes that they are exogenous, thus avoiding modeling location externalities that appear if attractiveness is assumed to depend on location choices. This assumption also avoids formulating a nonlinear Nash equilibrium.

Finally, the model assumes a simultaneous choice of residence and job location (v, i, j), thus conveniently avoiding defining any sequence between them. Whether residence–job choice is a simultaneous or sequential process and, if it is sequential, which choice is based on the other, is debatable.

Despite these issues, the A-L model is consistent with microeconomic and urban economic theories, making it theoretically sound, comparable with microeconomic models of other markets and computable. In the following, we will formulate a model that offers innovations regarding the comments mentioned above.

7.5 The Random Discrete-Continuous Goods Demand Model

The discrete-continuous model can be reformulated as a fully random choice model in all consumption variables. In this section, we formulate such a model, applying the extreme value distribution for consumption of goods variables, which yields the multiple discrete-continuous extreme value (MDCEV) model proposed by Bhat (2008), and then use it to define the equilibrium conditions.

The subproblem we address here is how consumers decide where and how much to consume retail goods, based on retail and job locations. The MDCEV model uses a CES random subutility function, defined as:

$$U(x) = \sum_{k \in K} \frac{\gamma_k}{\alpha_k} \left(e^{\delta' z_k + \varepsilon_k} \right) \left\{ \left(\frac{x_k}{\gamma_k} + 1 \right)^{\alpha_k} - 1 \right\} \tag{7.4}$$

where $U(x)$ is quasiconcave, increasing, and has a continuously differentiable function on the goods vector $x = (\{x_k\};\ x_k \in \mathbb{R}^+,\ k \in K)$; γ_k and α_k are parameters associated with each of the goods; vector z_k describes the set of attributes that differentiates goods by their locations; δ is the vector of taste parameters of attributes, where $\delta' z_k = \sum_m \delta_m z_{km}$; and ε_k's are the random terms.

As in the A-L model, we assume that the subutility in Eq. (7.4) is conditional on the consumers' residential and job locations (h, i, j), and we interpret Bhat's variety of goods, indexed by $k \in K$, as the variety of locations. Thus, we simplify behavior assuming that the consumer purchases the same bundle of retail goods despite the location, although this simplification is for the benefit of the exposition rather than a modeling recommendation. To consider different sets of goods consumed at each location, the modeler can expand the set of goods, adding an index, such that goods are indexed by $(k, l) \in K \times L$, with $l \in L$ being the index for the varieties of goods. For simplicity in this chapter, we shall consider a common bundle consumption set here, i.e., $|K| = |I|$.

We define a good's composite price, or cost, $\overline{p}_{k/hij} = p_k + c_{ik} + \omega_{hj} t_{ik}$. This considers the full delivery cost of consuming at location k and residing at location i, including the price of the goods, p_k, the transport cost, c_{ik}, and the travel time cost, $\omega_{hj} t_{ik}$. The perceived travel time disutility of purchasing retail goods at zone k based on residence location i, t_{ik}, should also be included in the attributes vector, z_k, if time is considered a variable in the direct utility function.

It is important to represent the quality of goods in the set of attributes, z_k. These attributes are difficult to identify and select because the set of quality aspects of goods may be very large. However, some of these attraction factors are associated with aggregate market structures of the retail and services sectors, such as the density of commercial and service activities. The quality factor is modeled here by defining $z_k(\rho_k)$, with ρ_k the density of retail and services activities at location k. We can anticipate that ρ_k

emerges from the location choice of firms, i.e., $\rho_k(H)$, affecting the equilibrium of the LU model with the phenomenon of location externalities.

The MDCEV model, summarized in Technical Note 7.1, assumes an extreme value distribution for the random terms ε_k, $\forall k \in K$, with ε_k being independent of z_k and ε_k's being independently distributed across alternative zones with shape parameter σ. The disposable income budget, E_{hij}, is a constraint, with $\sum_{k \in K} e_{k/hij} = E_{hij}$, where $e_{k/hij} = \overline{p}_{k/hij} x_k$ is the expenditure at each location. Bhat obtains indirect utilities from the Kuhn–Tucker conditions of the maximum utility problem based on consumers' budgets. He then estimates the consumption probability for $M \subseteq I$ goods options, which we interpret as consumption at M alternative locations where a common bundle of retail goods can be purchased, differentiated by a set of attributes, or qualities, z_k. This probability is denoted as $P\left(x_1^*, \ldots, x_M^*, 0, \ldots 0\right)$, which we use to calculate the expected household demand for the retail goods at all locations, i.e., $M = I$, as:

$$x_{k/hij} = \left\{ \left[\int_{x_k=0}^{E_k/\overline{p}_k} P_{hij}(x_1, \ldots, x_{k-1}, y, x_{k+1}, \ldots, x_I) y dy \right] \right\}_{hij} \quad \forall k \in K \tag{7.5}$$

where we consider the consumption of an item of outside goods with the unit to be an exogenous price defined as the *numeraire price*. The analysis in Technical Note 7.1 yields the following result for Eq. (7.5):

$$x_{k/hij}(\overline{p}, E_k) = C(\overline{p}) \left(a_k \frac{E_k^2}{\overline{p}_k} + b_k(p-k) \left(\left(\frac{E_k}{\overline{p}_k} - \gamma_k ln \left(\frac{E_k}{\overline{p}_k} + \gamma_k \right) + c_k \right) \right) \right) \tag{7.6}$$

with $a_{k/hij}(x_{m \neq k}),\ b_{k/hij}(x_{m \neq k},\ p_{m \neq k}) \in \mathbb{R}^+,\ c_{k/hij}(V(z)) \in \mathbb{R}\ \overline{p}$ are defined in Technical Note 7.1.

The optimal consumption of Eq. (7.6) represents a system of equations at each location, one for each tuple (h, i, j), and it defines a fixed-point problem on demands: $x = F^C(x; p,\ t,\ c,\ z)$. The solution distributes demand optimally subject to the consumers' budgets (E_{hij}), which depends on the job market, which in turn defines salaries. Then, we write:

$$x_{k/hij}^* = F_h^C\left(x_{m \neq k/hij};\ p_m,\ t_{im},\ c_{im},\ z_m,\ E_{hij}\right); \quad m \in K; \ \forall k \in K \tag{7.7}$$

which yields the optimal consumption depending on market prices and residential and job locations. The demand for goods model is continuous with the amounts of the consumption of goods. It is discrete for each of the locations for consumption alternatives, and, in contrast with A-L's model, it is stochastic in both variables.

From Eq. (7.7), the total demand at each location is $x_k = \sum_{hij} P_{hij} x^*_{k/hij}, \forall k \in K$, with P_{hij} the residential and job location probability discussed below. From Eq. (7.6), we deduce that $\frac{\partial x_{k/hij}}{\partial p_k} < 0$ and $x_{k/hij} \in (0, E_{hij}/p_k)$, with E_{hij} being consumer h's expected income depending on the residential and job choice model. This monotonic behavior is sufficient for a nonnull solution in the demand–supply equilibrium if the following holds: the supply of goods functions is increasing in prices and is positive for prices where demand is nonnull, i.e., $0 < p_k < \max_{hij} E_{hij}$.

Obtaining market prices requires solving the equilibrium of goods and leisure markets, conditional on the households' and firms' location problem, i.e., conditional on the LUT equilibrium. We discuss this equilibrium below.

7.6 The Household Stochastic Demand Model for Location and Consumption

In this section, we propose an advanced demand model for the LUTE system built on the contributions presented above. We assume a time-hierarchical decision process in which consumer behavior combines consumption of goods and leisure as a short-term process (days to weeks) and residence and job location as a long-term process (years). Then, the hierarchy is ordered on the period chosen, or how long the decision will last. This criterion is justified in that long-term choices are few and involve large amounts of resources, whereas short-term choices are many and involve fewer resources. Here, the resources considered are money and time. Moreover, all choices are based on a stochastic utility maximization context in which goods and leisure are continuous quantities that are consumed by the consumer in the space in different quantities, while residence and job locations are discrete choices.

Fig. 7.4 describes the hierarchical choice process for two locations, i.e., $|I| = 2$. In a long-term period, the household chooses a residential location, $i \in I$, and then, depending on the residence location, a job location $j \in I$. Residence implies rents and job income, which yields a limited money surplus for expenditure on goods and leisure. The goods and leisure consumption choices are defined with two dimensions, the good type and its location, $K \times I$. However, for the exposition of the model, we consider a bundle of goods and leisure, with the consumer deciding where to consume them, i.e., index $k \in K$ is the location of the representative good.

Additionally, we assume that residential and job location choices are made sequentially, and we deliberately define floor space and land consumption as a discrete variable, in contrast to the simultaneous residence and job choice and the continuous floor space and land consumption considered by the A-L model.

We start defining the consumer's problem in the LUTE model context as:

$$\max_i \left[\max_{j/i} \left[\max_{x/ij} U_{ij/h} = U_h\left(z_i^r, z_j^\omega, T_{hi}, x_{ij}(z^g)\right) \right] \right] \tag{7.8}$$

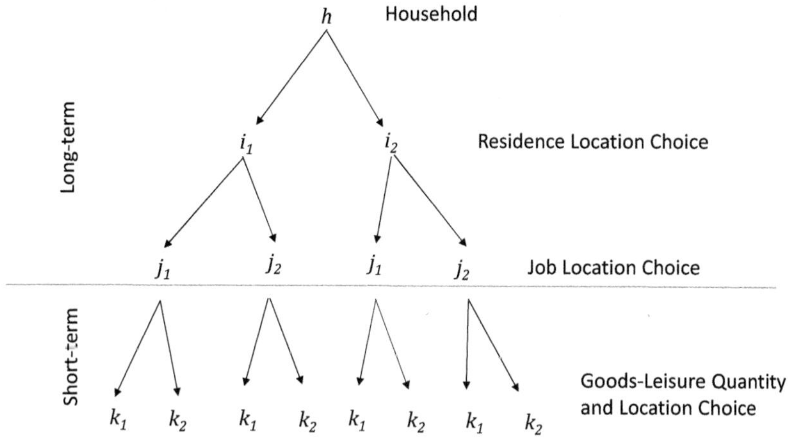

Figure 7.4 The time-hierarchical demand process.

where $U(\cdot)$ is a stochastic utility and z_i^r, z_j^ω, z_j^g are the residence, work, and goods/leisure attraction attribute vectors. If these attractors are then defined as dependent on densities, they represent location externalities affecting the equilibrium, i.e., $z_k^m = z(\rho_k^m)$, with ρ_k^m the density of activities relevant for the type $m = (r, \omega, g)$ interactions at location k. T_{hi} is the total leisure time, including time at home and elsewhere; and x_{ij} is the goods/leisure consumption. We define the consumption of leisure as a bundle of events that include social and entertainment activities.

The optimization problem of Eq. (7.8) is divided into subproblems that represent different time windows realistically: the long-term residence and job choices last from years to decades, and the short-term goods/leisure choices last from weeks to months. The long-term subproblem combines residence and job choices, assumed to be sequential in a hierarchical process. Which location choice is higher in this hierarchy—residence or job—has been debated for a long time. We may consider the following criteria: if residence involves several members of the household, potentially with several workers, then jobs are likely to be dependent on the entire household's agreement on the residence location and the coordination of its members' activities, thus making jobs location conditional on the residence location. This does not apply for single-person households where the residence and job choices may be simultaneous.

Additionally, if social factors are strong enough to cause the choice of residential location to be dominated by social ties, then the residence is also higher in the choice hierarchy. We shall present the long-term model as job location choice depending on the residential choice. Ultimately, however, the construction of the actual hierarchy may be left to empirical evidence obtained from estimating location models.

In this context, we define the income budget constraint as:

$$\sum_{k \in K} (p_k + d_k c_{ik}) x_k + r_i + d c_{ij} = \omega_{hj} t_j \tag{7.9}$$

where we use the notation of the A-L model (see above). The time budget is:

$$T = t_i + t_j + dt_{ij} + \sum_{k \in K} (t_k + d_k t_{ik}) x_k \tag{7.10}$$

where the exogenous time endowment (per period), T, is fully spent on activities: at home t_i, at work t_j, commuting dt_{ij}, and consuming goods and leisure $\sum_{k \in K} (t_k + d_k t_{ik}) x_k$.

From Eq. (7.10), we obtain $t_j = T - \left(t_i + dt_{ij} + \sum_{k \in K} (t_k + d_k t_{ik}) x_k \right)$, which can be replaced in Eq. (7.9), unifying the limited resources of time into a single constraint:

$$\sum_{k \in K} p_k + d_k c_{ik}) x_k + r_i + dc_{ij} = \omega_{hj} \left(T - t_i - dt_{ij} - \sum_{k \in K} (t_k + d_k t_{ik}) x_k \right) \tag{7.11}$$

Therefore, consumer demand in the LUTE model is studied further in three submodels: the consumption of goods/leisure, job choice, and residential location.

The Goods/Leisure Consumption Model

We use the MDCEV model to solve the most internal maximization problem on consumption x variables in Eq. (7.8) conditional on location choices (i, j), assuming, for example, the CES utility in Eq. (7.4), which yields the optimal shopping distribution, $x^g_{k/hij}$, and leisure consumption, $x^l_{k/hij}$. For this purpose, leisure is seen as an activity similar to the consumption of goods: both require travel time and costs, duration time, and have prices or costs. However, leisure has a nontrivial quantity definition. Thus, we define the quantity of leisure $x^l = \left(\{x^l_k\},\ k \in K \right)$, where x^l_k is the time spent in leisure activity at location k, and p_l is the cost per unit of leisure time.

Thus, the optimal consumption of goods and leisure at each location can be modeled with the MDCEV model by redefining the goods vector as $x^*_k = \left(\{x^{g*}_k, x^{l*}_k\},\ k \in K \right)$, with x^{g*}_k and x^{l*}_k denoting the optimal quantities of goods and leisure bundles consumed at each location. As mentioned above, these vectors can be modeled by disaggregating x_k by types of goods and leisure activities. For simplicity in the exposition, we consider here bundles of goods and leisure, and we apply the MDCEV model for two types of goods, i.e., $x_k = \left(\{x^g_k, x^l_k\},\ k \in K \right)$.

We proceed by calculating the expected optimal consumption for each consumer, denoted by $x^*_{hij} = \sum_{k \in K} x^*_{k/hij}$, as the solution of Eq. (7.7) conditional on location choices (h, i, j). Then, the expected price of the optimal goods/leisure bundle is defined as $p^*_{hij} = \frac{\sum_{k \in K} p^*_k x^*_{k/hij}}{\sum_{k \in K} x^*_{k/hij}}$ and the optimal expenditure as $e^*_{hij} = \sum_{k \in K} p^*_k x^*_{k/hij} = p^*_{hij} x^*_{hij}$, both conditional on (h, i, j). Finally, the expected maximum utility of goods consumption is calculated as $V_{hij}^{g*} = \sum_{k \in I} P_{k/hij}^{g*} U\left(x_{k/hij}^{g*}\right)$ and that of leisure consumption as $V_{hij}^{l*} = \sum_{k \in K} P_{k/hij}^{l*} U\left(x_{k/hij}^{l*}\right)$, with $U(\cdot)$ given in Eq. (7.4), and the consumption probabilities $P_{k/hij}^{g*}$ and $P_{k/hij}^{l*}$ follow from Technical Note 7.1.

Observe that V_{hij}^{g*} and V_{hij}^{l*} represent accessibility measures for the consumption of goods and leisure. They are calculated as the expected optimal, or rational, interaction of an individual, given (h, i, j), with the large set of goods/leisure consumption activities available in the city.

The Job Location Choice Model

The job choice is assumed to affect the individual's transportation time and cost, while the job itself is differentiated by the salary, ω_{hj}, and its quality at each location, denoted by z_j^{ω}.

We define $\widetilde{p}_{hij} := \left(x_{hij}^*\right)^{-1} \sum_{k \in K} (p_k + d_k c_{ik}) x_{k/hij}^*$ and $\widetilde{t}_{hij} = \left(x_{hij}^*\right)^{-1} \sum_{k \in K} (t_k + d_k t_{ik}) x_{k/hij}^*$, the expected monetary and time expenditures in goods/leisure consumption activities, including travel costs and time. Then, the job location problem in Eq. (7.8) is

$$\begin{aligned} &\max_{j/i} U_{hij} - U_h\left(z_i^r, z_j^{\omega}, T_{hi}, x_{hij}^*(z^g)\right) \\ &\text{subject to:} \quad x_{hij}^* \widetilde{p}_{hij} + r_i + dc_{ij} = \omega_{hj}\left(T - t_i - dt_{ij} - x_{hij}^* \widetilde{t}_{hij}\right) = E_{hij} \end{aligned} \tag{7.12}$$

where $t_{j/hi}^{\omega} = \left(T - t_i - dt_{ij} - x_{hij}^* \widetilde{t}_{hij}\right)$ is the working time. Then, the optimization is conditional on the residential location and $y_{j/hi} = \omega_{hj} t_{j/hi}^{\omega}$ is the corresponding income from the salary.

We replace $x_{hij}^*(z^g)$ in the utility of the optimal yield by the constraint, which can be rewritten as: $x_{hij}^*\left(\widetilde{p}_{hij} + \omega_{hj} \widetilde{t}_{hij}\right) = \omega_{hj}(T - t_i - dt_{ij}) - r_i - dc_{ij}$. Then, solving for x_{hij}^* and replacing it in the utility in Eq. (7.12) yields the following job location problem:

$$\max_j V_{j/hi} = U\left(z_j^{\omega}, \frac{\omega_{hj}(T - t_i - dt_{ij}) - r_i - dc_{ij}}{\widetilde{p}_{hij} + \omega_{hj} \widetilde{t}_{hij}}; z_i^r, r_i, T_i, t_i\right) \tag{7.13}$$

where $V_{j/hi} = V_{hij}\left(\left\{z^{\omega}, \omega_{h\cdot}, t_{i\cdot}, c_{i\cdot}, \widetilde{p}_{hi\cdot}, \widetilde{t}_{hi\cdot}\right\}_{j \in I}\right)$ is the indirect utility conditional on the residential location. In this problem, z_j^{ω} is the set of job attraction factors at zone j, e.g., natural and constructed environmental amenities, and job opportunities, which define location externalities on the job demand function associated with the densities, i.e., $z_j^{\omega}|\{H_{hj}\}|, \{H_{hj}\}, \quad \forall h \in C, \ j \in I$.

We assume $V_{j/hi}$, a random variate, such that $V_{j/hi} = v_{j/hi} + \varepsilon_{hj}$. Here, ε_{hj} is assumed identical and independent Gumbel, with shape parameter θ_h. Therefore, considering one worker per household, the demand for jobs is $x_{hj}^{\omega} = \sum_{i \in I} H_h P_{j/hi}$, with H_h the population in cluster h and $P_{j/hi}$ the *logit* probability. Then:

$$x_{j/hi}^{\omega} = H_h \frac{L_{hj} e^{\theta_h v_{j/hi}}}{\sum_{m \in I} L_{hm} e^{\theta_h v_{m/hi}}}, \quad \forall j \in I \tag{7.14}$$

is the number of jobs demanded from the type h household at location j. L_{hj} is the total employment at zone j for individuals of cluster h, which is exogenous for the consumers and is calculated from the production model for market equilibrium salaries (see below). The total demand for jobs of a specific skill, f, at zone j is $x_{fj}^{\omega} = \sum_{hi} x_{j/hi}^{\omega} \varphi_{hf}$, with φ_{hf} the proportion of workers with type f skills per unit type h household.

The expected maximum benefit from goods and leisure consumption and from job choice, conditional on the residential choice, is $V_{hi}^{*} = \frac{1}{\theta_h} \ln \sum_{j \in I} e^{\theta_h v_{j/hi}}$, which measures accessibility to jobs and consumption opportunities from location i for consumer h.

The Residential Location Model

For the residential location, we consider the bid-auction location model. The consumer's problem is

$$\begin{aligned} &\max_{i \in VI} U_{hi} = U_h\left(z_i^r, T_{hi}, \ x_{hi}^{*}(z^g)\right) \\ &\text{subject to :} \quad r_i = g_{hi} \end{aligned} \tag{7.15}$$

The expected disposable income for a residential location is defined as:

$$\begin{aligned} g_{hi} &:= \sum_{j \in I} P_{j/hi} \left[\omega_{hj}\left(T - t_i - dt_{ij} - x_{hij}^{*} \widetilde{t}_{pij}\right) - \left(x_{hij}^{*} \widetilde{p}_{hij} + dc_{ij}\right) \right] \\ &= \sum_{j \in I} P_{j/hi} \left[\omega_{hj}(T - t_i - dt_{ij}) - dc_{ij} \right] - \sum_{j \in I} P_{j/hi} \left[x_{hij}^{*} \left(\widetilde{p}_{ij} + \omega_{hj} \widetilde{t}_{ij} \right) \right]. \end{aligned}$$

The expected consumer income net cost of commuting is defined as $y_{hi} = \sum_{j \in I} P_{j/hi} \left[\omega_{hj}(T - t_i - dt_{ij}) - dc_{ij} \right]$ and the expected expenditure in goods/leisure consumption and transportation is $e_{hi}^{*} = \sum_{j \in I} P_{j/hi} \left[x_{hij}^{*} \left(\widetilde{p}_{hij} + \omega_{hj} \widetilde{t}_{hij} \right) \right] = \widetilde{p}_{hi}^{*} x_{hi}^{*}$, with

$x_{hi}^* = \sum_{j \in I} P_{j/hi} x_{hij}^*$ and $\widetilde{p}_{hi}^* := \left(x_{hi}^*\right)^{-1} \left(\sum_{j \in I} P_{j/hi} \left[x_{hij}^* \left(\widetilde{p}_{hij} + \omega_{hj} \widetilde{t}_{hij} \right) \right] \right)$. Then, we write $x_{hi}^* = \frac{(y_h - r_i)}{\widetilde{p}_{hi}^*}$. Additionally, the expected leisure time is $T_{hi} = t_i + x_{hi}^{l*}$, with $x_{hi}^{l*} = \sum_{j \in I} P_{j/hi} x_{hi}^{l*}\left(z_j^l\right)$ the time expenditure on leisure; vector $z_j^l(\{H_{hi}\})$ the set of leisure attraction attributes that define a location externality; and t_i the exogenous amount of leisure time spent at home.

Replacing $x_{hi}^* = \frac{(y_h - r_i)}{\widetilde{p}_{hi}^*}$ and T_{hi} in Eq. (7.15) yields the following indirect utility for residential location:

$$V_{hi} = U_h\left(z_i^r, t_i + x_{hi}^{l*}, \frac{y_h - r_i}{\widetilde{p}_{hi}^*} \right), \quad \forall h \in C, \ i \in I \tag{7.16}$$

To obtain the willingness-to-pay function for a residential option, we invert V_{hi} on r_i for a given utility reservation, u_h, i.e. common to all locations, yielding:

$$w_{hl} = y_{hi} - \widetilde{p}_{hl}^* V_h^{-1}\left(z_i^r, t_i + x_{hi}^{l*}, u_h \right), \quad \forall h \in C, \ i \in I \tag{7.17}$$

where z_i^r, $\widetilde{p}_{hi}^*\left(x_{hi}^{g*}(z^g), z^\omega\right)$, and $x_{hi}^{l*}\left(\left\{z_j^l\right\}, \ \forall j \in I\right)$ are assumed to be dependent on densities. Then, we denote $z = (\{z^m\}, m = \{r,g,\omega,l\})$ with $z^m(\{H_{hi}\}, \forall h,m)$ to group all attributes inducing location externalities.

It is worth recalling that $\widetilde{p}_{hi}^* = \phi(\varrho)$, with $\varrho = \left(\{p_j\}, \{\omega_{hj}\}, \left\{z_j^g\right\}, \left\{z_j^\omega\right\}, \{c_{ij}\}, \{t_{ij}\}; \ \forall h \in C; \ i, \ j \in I\right)$. This represents the marginal utility of income, which depends on goods, labor choice, market prices, transportation choices, and costs. Then, we write: $w_{hi} = w_h(y, z^r, \varrho, u)$.

Finally, using the bid-auction model and assuming the willingness to pay to be a random variable with an extreme value that is independent and has an identical distribution with shape parameter β, we can define the location auction probability $Q_{h/i}(w_{hi}, \beta)$ and the location choice probability $P_{i/h}(w_{hi} - r_i, \beta)$, defined as a *logit* or *frechit* model (see Chapter 4). Therefore, the total consumer demand for a piece of real estate indexed by $(v,i) \in VI$ is $D_{vi} = \sum_{h \in C} H_h P_{i/h}(y, z^r, \varrho; u)$, the demand for urban land is $D_i = \sum_{v \in V} q_v D_{vi}(y, z^r, \varrho; u)$, and the allocation of agents is $H_{hi} = \sum_{h \in C} H_h P_{i/h}(y, z^r, \varrho; u)$, conditional on the reservation utilities u.

In this model, accessibility measures consumption of goods and leisure time, and jobs are implicit in the consumer's willingness to pay w_{hi}. We can also calculate the consumer's expected utility conditional on location rents $V_h^* = \sum_{i \in I} Q_{i/h} U_h\left(z_i, t_i + x_{hi}^{l*}, \frac{y_h - r_i}{\tilde{p}_{hi}^*}\right)$.

7.7 The Production Model

The following model of production calculates the amount of production of goods and leisure activities supplied at each location in the city, assuming that producers are rational agents facing deterministic profits.

The Production of Goods and Leisure Activities

As discussed in Chapter 3, a firm's behavior emerges from the economic opportunities the city offers to entrepreneurs. From the perspective of the firm's decision makers, the deterministic behavior assumed in the A-L model in the production process may be considered a better representation of their behavior than in the case of consumers. This is because, compared with households, the decisions of firms regarding production are more strictly quantitative and economic, i.e., profit-based. Moreover, firms have better information about the input and output markets because of their higher specialization with some goods and leisure activities. Here, we shall assume deterministic profits in production, although an alternative stochastic model, similar to the consumers' demand model, can be formulated using the MDCEV approach.

Furthermore, A-L assumptions of a Cobb–Douglas technology underlying markets of competitive goods, e.g., zero profit, are standard in microeconomics for calculating the optimal mixture of capital, labor, and land inputs. By including delivery transport costs, the model yields different equilibrium prices for the same goods and different salaries at each location, which recognizes the production advantages associated with delivery transport costs.

However, delivery transport cost differentials, although relevant, are not a sufficient explanation for the behavior of firms in their location strategies, particularly in the urban context where such differences are limited. A second important factor is economies of scale in production because they define the degree of concentration of the city's production in one or more firms and in one, few, or many zones. A third source of location differential on profits is the location of immobile inputs that induce agglomeration economies.

Indeed, immobile inputs are recognized as highly important push and pull factors for knowledge-based industries, such as technology research and finance, because they cause the emergence of city structures, such as subcenters, as was discussed in Chapter 3. Moreover, they are concentrated in large or in highly specialized cities, as has been highlighted by economic geography (Krugman, 1991). Immobile inputs can be classified into two main groups for our purpose: permanently immobile, such as natural resources, and long-term immobile, such as city structures. While the former are relevant inputs for the emergence of towns and cities, the latter are dominant factors in city dynamics.

In the following, we extend the A-L producer's model, introducing nonconstant returns to scale, and immobile attraction factors, the latter a source of agglomeration economies. Additionally, the A-L model assumes floor space as a continuous variable, which we consider to be more plausible than in the case of households, because in many cases, firms demand very specific buildings and land lots. However, most of the floor space supply in the urban context is recycled from old stock real estate, which is provided in a discrete form. In the following, we also assume that firms demand specific discrete real estate units in some industries, e.g., large retail and manufacturing companies or a very specific type of building, but in other industries they integrate with the residential supply, e.g., offices.

The Firm Location Model

To formulate the production model, we consider the Cobb–Douglas production function. Define $j, m \in I$ as the location zones for jobs and inputs, respectively, and $r, k \in K$ the production sectors (of the input and output products, respectively), including goods, services, and leisure. We consider that firms in each industry are homogenous and are described by the following Cobb–Douglas production function regarding inputs, with Dixit–Stiglitz differentiation of varieties of an input (as in the A-L model). The production function, by industry at each zone, is

$$X_{r/vj} = A_r K^{\upsilon_r} q_v^{\mu_r} Z_{rj}^{\theta_r} \left(\sum_{f \in F} L_f^{\widetilde{\delta_r}} \right)^{\frac{\delta_r}{\tilde{\delta}_r}} \prod_{k \in K} \left(\sum_{m=0}^{|I|} Y_{km}^{\widetilde{\gamma_{kr}}} \right)^{\frac{\gamma_{kr}}{\tilde{\gamma}_{kr}}}, \quad \forall r \in K; \ v, \ j \in VI \quad (7.18)$$

where $X_{r/vj}$[1] is the production of industry r (measured in physical units per unit of time) conditional on real estate v and location j. Observe that this formulation defines the different behaviors of firms in the same industry depending not only on their location but also on their real estate choice. This intraindustry differentiation in production will be carried out on input demands and production costs.

The production inputs are as follows: K is capital; q_v is the floor space or land size of real estate type v; Z_{rj} is an immobile attraction factor specific to industry r; L_f are labor inputs by variety of skill type f; and Y_{km} are the intermediate inputs of products from different industries, $k \in K$ (excluding their own industry, r, as input for their own production) brought from a variety of zones ($m \in I$, with $m = 0$ denoting foreign regions). The input constant elasticities are $\upsilon_r, \mu_r, \theta_r, \delta_r, \sum_{k \in K} \gamma_{kr}$, and their sum is the degree of returns to scale, denoted by η.[2]

[1] Notation: capital X denotes product supply, and lower case x denotes product demand.

[2] Eq. (7.18) may also include linear parameters for each input, as in the A-L model, which are useful for ruling out some inputs exogenously by setting the corresponding parameters to zero. We have ignored such parameters to simplify the model and to avoid the risk of overparameterization.

Labor is differentiated by skill types $f \in F$, which are mapped to household socio-economic clusters, $h \in C$. Labor and intermediate inputs transported from different zones are assumed to be perfectly substitutable, i.e., the constant elasticity of substitution among labor skills is $\frac{1}{1-\tilde{\delta}_r} > 1\tilde{\delta}_r$ and among inputs is $\frac{1}{1-\tilde{\gamma}_{kr}} > 1, \quad \forall k \in K$. Finally, A_r is a Hicksian neutral scaling factor per sector.[3]

A fundamental issue in the urban context is that economies of scale and agglomeration economies interact, affecting the classical solution of the production problem. To illustrate this interaction, observe that the production function in Eq. (7.18) has the form $X(Z, f(Y))$, combining agglomeration economies represented by the location of immobile attractors (Z) with the subproduction function on inputs, $f(Y)$, representing economies of scale. Then, while $f(Y)$ is a common production technology, $X(Z, f(Y))$ is differentiated by location, i.e., firms have different technologies at each location, denoted above as $X_{rj}(Z_j, f(Y))$, which we can call the *urban production technology*. In this context, the production model can be interpreted in terms of the standard economics as a system where goods are differentiated by location. A direct implication of this observation is that the production function is different at each location; therefore, standard conclusions are not necessarily valid.

We describe the behavior of producers in two steps: first, in the short-term, they produce choosing inputs to maximize profit, conditional on the building location choice (v, i), and second, in the long-term, they optimize the location in the LU market. We assume that these steps are sequential because of the different timescales.

The complete problem is expressed by:

$$\max_{v,j \in VI} \left[\max \pi_{rj} = p_{rj} X_{r/vj} - C_{rj}\left(X_{r/vj}\right) \right] \tag{7.19}$$

with π_{rj} the business profit, given by the income minus the production cost.

The optimization problem is solved in the steps described by:

$$\max_{v,j \in VI} \left[p_{rj} X_{r/vj} - r_{vj} - \min_{\psi} C_{rvj}\left(\psi_{X_{rvj}}\right) \right] \tag{7.20}$$

with $\psi_{Xrj} = (\mathrm{K}, \{L_{f/rvj}\}, \{Y_{kr/rvj}\})$ the set of input factors, p_{rj} the output equilibrium price, and r_{vj} the real estate rental price. The problem is defined per period, e.g., 1 year, and then immobile assets are represented by their rental price per period instead of by their selling prices.

[3] We note that the A-L model considers exogenous Hicksian neutral "scaling factors," i.e., it does not affect the balance between factors. Because they are different for each zone, these factors might be interpreted as representing immobile inputs, but they are exogenous in their model.

The first step is the following cost minimizing problem, conditional on the output, $X_{r/vj}$:

$$\min_{\psi} C_{rvj}(\psi) = \rho K_{rvj} + \sum_{f \in F} \omega_{fj} L_{f/rvj} + \sum_{k \in K} \sum_{m} (p_{km} + c_{kmj}) Y_{km/rvj} \tag{7.21}$$

where ρ is the exogenous capital cost or interest rate of capital; ω_{fj} is the labor salary for a worker with a type f skill at the firm's location, j; p_{km} is the price of input factor, k, at location m; and c_{kmj} is the transportation cost of a unit of input, k, from the origin, m, to destination j, which yields a total input cost at the output location, $\widehat{p}_{kmj} = p_{km} + c_{mj}$.[4] Observe that prices are differentiated by location due to intermediate input transportation costs.

The analysis of producers' behavior, i.e., how much to produce, in how many firms, and how much of each input, crucially depends on the degree of returns to scale (η). It is well known that if $\eta \leq 1$, the maximization of the firm's profit is concave; then, there is an optimum production size. Conversely, if $\eta > 1$, the profit function is convex and there is no optimal solution for this problem; then, industry produces to serve all demand in one firm. Despite this important difference, the mathematical analysis is similar. To avoid duplication, therefore, we shall study the more general case $\eta > 1$ and consider the case $\eta \leq 1$ as special. For details of the mathematical analysis, see Technical Note 7.2.

The Case of Nonincreasing Returns to Scale

In this case, the firms' behavior is to produce following the rule of maximizing profit, which yields the condition that $\omega_i = p\frac{\partial X}{\partial y_i}$, with ω_i representing the cost of input y_i and p the output price. The solution for optimal input demand functions, conditional on the output locations, are

$$K^*_{rvj} = p_{rj} X_{r/vj} \upsilon_r \rho^{-1} \tag{7.22}$$

$$L^*_{f/rvj} = p_{rj} X_{r/vj} \delta_r \omega_{fj}^{\frac{-1}{1-\tilde{\delta}_r}} \overline{\omega}_{rj}^{-1}, \quad \text{with} \quad \overline{\omega}_{rj} := \sum_{g \in F} \omega_{gj}^{\frac{-\tilde{\delta}_r}{1-\tilde{\delta}_r}} \tag{7.23}$$

$$Y^*_{km/rvj} = p_{rj} X_{r/vj} \Upsilon_{kr} \widehat{p}_{kmj}^{\frac{-1}{1-\tilde{\gamma}_{kr}}} \overline{p}_{krj}^{-1}, \quad \text{with} \quad \overline{p}_{krj} := \sum_{n \in K} \widehat{p}_{knj}^{\frac{-\tilde{\gamma}_{kr}}{1-\tilde{\gamma}_{kr}}} \tag{7.24}$$

We observe that in this case, optimal input factors under the Cobb–Douglas/Dixit–Stiglitz technology are linearly dependent on output, $X_{r/vj}$, and on its price, p_{rj}.

[4] The total cost $\widehat{p}_{kmj} = p_{km} + c_{mj}$ at the output location is called the CIF (cost, insurance, and freight) cost.

Therefore, dividing optimal intermediate inputs by $X_{r/vj}$ yields the physical interindustry input/output coefficients:

$$\widehat{a}_{km/rvj} = \frac{Y^*_{km/rvj}}{X_{r/vj}} = \widehat{p}_{kmj}^{\overline{\frac{-1}{1-\tilde{\gamma}_{kr}}}} \overline{p}_{krj}^{-1}, \gamma_{kr} p_{rj} \tag{7.25}$$

and the corresponding value-based coefficients are

$$a_{km/rvj} = \frac{\overline{p}_{krj} Y^*_{km/rvj}}{p_{rj} X_{r/vj}} = \widehat{p}_{kmj}^{\overline{\frac{-1}{1-\tilde{\gamma}_{kr}}}} \gamma_{kr} < 1 \tag{7.26}$$

In contrast with Leontief's IO model, the $a_{km/rvj}$ constant coefficients here (as noted by Anas and Liu (2007)) are endogenous factors based on Cobb–Douglas technology that depend on the vector of market prices. An important merit of defining endogenous coefficients rather than IO fixed coefficients is that the latter requires the estimation of a larger number of parameters, which overparameterize the model and remain fixed when the model makes predictions.

A special case of this model is the assumption of constant returns to scale,[5] which implies: $\eta = v_r + \mu_r + \theta_r + \delta_r + \sum_{k \in K} \gamma_{kr} = 1$. In this case, a larger production in Eq. (7.18) renders the same average profit per unit. This implies that each industry in a competitive market, and each firm in this sector, makes zero profit independent of the output level, X_{rvj}, and that prices equal marginal costs. Thus, the output price can be calculated depending on the firm's location by:

$$p^*_{rj}(p, \omega) = \left(\frac{\rho}{v_r}\right)^{v_r} \tau_r^{-1} \overline{\omega}_{rj}^{\hat{\delta}_r} \prod_{k \in K} \overline{p}_{krj}^{\hat{\gamma}_r}, \quad \forall r \in K, \ j \in I \tag{7.27}$$

where we have denoted $\widehat{\delta}_r := \frac{\delta_r(\tilde{\delta}_r - 1)}{\tilde{\delta}_r}$, $\widehat{\gamma}_r := \frac{\gamma_r(\tilde{\gamma}_r - 1)}{\tilde{\gamma}_r}$, and $\tau_r := \frac{1}{A_r \delta_r^{\delta_r} \sum_{k \in K} \gamma_{kr}^{\gamma_{kr}}}$.

The constant returns assumption guarantees that prices given by Eq. (7.27) are equilibrium prices, independent of the output level. Computing these prices using Eq. (7.27) requires solving a linear system of equations, one for each industry and location, with a dimension, $|K| \cdot |I|$. This dimension is usually large in real cities because $|I|$ lies within the range of hundreds to thousand zones, and therefore, the fact that constant returns yield a linear problem is important in terms of making this model easily computable.

[5] Constant returns to scale holds if the production technology is homogeneous at degree one, i.e., $X(\lambda Y) = \lambda X(Y)$ for any scalar $\lambda > 0$. For example, if the Cobb–Douglas technology is $X(Y_1, Y_2) = Y_1^\alpha Y_2^\beta$, then $X(\lambda Y_1, \lambda Y_2) = \lambda^{\alpha+\beta} Y_1^\alpha Y_2^\beta = \lambda^{\alpha+\beta} X(Y_1, Y_2)$. Thus, $\alpha + \beta = 1$ corresponds to constant returns to scale, $\alpha + \beta < 1$ corresponds to decreasing returns to scale, and $\alpha + \beta > 1$ corresponds to increasing returns to scale (Mas-Colell et al., 1995, pp. 133, 142).

Despite its convenience of computation, from here on we consider the general case with returns to scale, with constant returns used only for specific industries for which the evidence supports that assumption.

The optimal production, depending on location choice, is obtained by replacing optimal input demands (Eqs (7.22)–(7.27)) in Eq. (7.18) to obtain the optimal production level, X_{rj}:

$$X_{r/vj} = A_r q_v^{\mu_r} Z_{rj}^{\theta_r} \left(p_{rj} X_{r/vj} \rho^{-1} \upsilon_r\right)^{\upsilon_r} \left(p_{rj} X_{r/vj} \delta_r\right)^{\delta_r} \left(\sum_{f\in F}\left(\frac{\omega_{fj}^{\frac{1}{\tilde{\delta}_r - 1}}}{\overline{\omega}_{rj}}\right)^{\tilde{\delta}_r}\right)^{\frac{\delta_r}{\tilde{\delta}_r}}$$

$$\prod_{k\varepsilon K}\left(p_{rj} X_{r/vj} \gamma_{kr}\right)^{\gamma_{kr}} \left(\sum_{m=0}^{|I|+1}\left(\frac{\widehat{p}_{kmj}^{\frac{1}{\tilde{\gamma}_{kr}-1}}}{\overline{p}_{krj}}\right)^{\tilde{\gamma}_{kr}}\right)^{\frac{\gamma_{kr}}{\tilde{\gamma}_{kr}}} \quad \forall r \in K;\ v,\ j \in VI \tag{7.28}$$

To simplify the notation, we denote $\upsilon_r + \delta_r + \sum_{k\in K} \gamma_{kr} = \eta_r \leq 1$ and define:

$$A_{rvj} := A_r q_v^{\mu_r} Z_{rj}^{\theta_r} (\upsilon_r)^{\upsilon_r} (\delta_r)^{\delta_r} \prod_{k\in K} (\gamma_{kr})^{\gamma_{kr}}$$

and

$$\Phi_{rj}(\sigma) := \rho^{-\upsilon_r} \overline{\omega}_{rj}^{\delta_r\left(\frac{1-\tilde{\delta}_r}{\tilde{\delta}_r}\right)} \prod_{k\in K} \overline{p}_{krj}^{\gamma_{kr}\left(\frac{1-\tilde{\gamma}_{kr}}{\tilde{\gamma}_{kr}}\right)} > 0,$$

where $\sigma := \left(\rho, \{\omega\}, \{\widehat{p}\}\right)$ is the set of input prices; and $\overline{\omega}_{rj} := \sum_{f\in F} \omega_{fj}^{\frac{-\tilde{\delta}_r}{1-\tilde{\delta}_r}} > 0$ and $\overline{p}_{krj} := \sum_{n\in K} \widehat{p}_{knj}^{\frac{-\tilde{\gamma}_{kr}}{1-\tilde{\gamma}_{kr}}} > 0$ are functions of the set of prices, salaries, and input elasticity parameters.[6]

Then,

$$X_{r/vj}(q, Z, p, \omega) = \left(X_{r/vj} p_{rj}\right)^{\eta_r} A_{rvj} \Phi_{rj}, \quad \forall r \in K,\ v,\ j \in VI \tag{7.29}$$

[6] See Eq. (T7.19) in Technical Note 7.2, where A represents A_{rvj}.

Observe that $\overline{\omega}_{rj}^{\delta_r\left(\frac{1-\tilde{\delta}_r}{\tilde{\delta}_r}\right)}$ has the dimension of $\omega^{-\delta_r}$ and $\overline{p}_{krj}^{\gamma_{kr}\left(\frac{1-\tilde{\gamma}_{kr}}{\tilde{\gamma}_{kr}}\right)}$ of $\widehat{p}^{-\gamma_{kr}}$. Then, Φ has the dimension of $p^{-\eta}$, and therefore, $p^{\eta}\Phi^{-1}(\sigma)$ is dimensionless.

We rule out the use of inputs $Y_{rj/rj}$ to produce the same product $X_{r/vj}$, then, p_{rj} is not included in $\widehat{p}$, which is highlighted denoting $\widehat{p}_{-rj}$. Then, solving for $X_{r/vj}$ yields:

$$X_{r/vj}(q,Z,p,\omega) = \left[p_{rj}^{\eta}A_{rvj}\Phi_{rj}\right]^{\frac{1}{1-\eta_r}} \quad \forall r \in K;\ v,\ j \in VI \tag{7.30}$$

which defines the optimal production size, i.e., the optimal firm size, at each location for $\eta_r < 1$. If $\eta_r = 1$, the optimal firm size is undefined, i.e., all sizes yield equal profit, which in a competitive market is zero.

Additionally, replacing optimal inputs in the cost function, i.e., $C_{rj} = \rho K^* + \sum_{f \in F} \omega_{fj} L_f^* + \sum_{k \in K} \sum_m \widehat{p}_{kmj} Y_{km}^*$, yields the minimum production cost:

$$C_{rvj}\left(\sigma, X_{r/vj}\right) = \eta_r p_{rj} X_{r/vj} \tag{7.31}$$

Then, the average production costs are constant. Using the optimal firm size, $X_{r/vj}^*$of Eq. (7.30), we obtain the firms' minimum cost:

$$C_{rvj}^*(\sigma) = \eta_r \left[p_{rj}A_{rvj}\Phi_{rj}\right]^{\frac{1}{1-\eta_r}} \tag{7.32}$$

It is worth noting that the minimum C_{rvj}^* represents the accessibility of type r industrial production to inputs from all the other industries, which in the Cobb–Douglas technology is linear in both the output quantity and its value.

The firm location problem is the second step of the optimization problem in Eq. (7.20). In this step, the firm optimizes the location in the city considering the minimum production cost for a given output level, $X_{r/vj}$, the real estate price, and the size and agglomeration economies.

This problem is rewritten as:

$$\max_{v,j \in VI} \pi_{r/vj}(p,X) = p_{rj}X_{r/vj} - C_{rvj}^*\left(p,\omega,X_{r/vj}\right) - r_{vj} = p_{rj}X_{r/vj}[1-\eta] - r_{vj} \tag{7.33}$$

For the optimum firm size given in Eq. (7.30), the problem is

$$\max_{v,j \in VI} \pi_{r/vj}(p,\omega) = \left[p_{rj}A_{rvj}\Phi_{rj}\right]^{\frac{1}{1-\eta_r}}(1-\eta) - r_{vj} \tag{7.34}$$

In the case of constant returns to scale, i.e., $\eta_r = 1$, the exponent in Eq. (7.32) is undefined because there is no optimum production, or no level of production yields a profit independent of the location.

The profit in Eq. (7.33) defines the break-even condition for each firm at vj: $p_{rj}X_{r/vj}(1-\eta) \geq r_{vj}$. Then, the minimum production size should be: $X_{r/vj}^{\min} = \frac{r_{vj}}{p_{rj}(1-\eta)}$. Otherwise, the business is not economically feasible, i.e., some locations and some types of real estate might not support feasible production.

Finally, if:

- $\eta_r = 1$, the optimal firm size is undefined, or any size is optimum;
- $\eta_r < 1$, then $X_{r/vj}^{\min}$ defines the minimum firm size, and the number of firms, denoted as F_{rvj}, is defined at equilibrium by dividing total demand at each location by the firms' optimal size, subject to $F_{rvj} \geq 1$.

In Eq. (7.34), the profit function is conditional on the location choice represented by the location attributes in $A_{rvj}(q_v, Z_j)$ and on the set of prices in $\Phi(\sigma)$ and rents r_{vj}. Additionally, recall that Z_{rj} is the vector of the immobile attractors that may include natural and LU attributes, which represent agglomeration economies in the industry, r, described by $Z_{rj}(\{H_{kj}\}), \forall k \in K, j \in I$.

Let us now analyze the firms' willingness to pay. We define the reservation profit, $\pi_{r/vj} = \pi_r \geq 0, \ \forall vj \in VI$, as equal for all firms in industry r, which makes firms indifferent to the location zone and the type of real estate. Inverting the profit Eq. (7.34) on land rents defines the following firms' willingness-to-pay functions:

$$w_{rvj}(\eta < 1, p) = p_{rj}\left[p_{rj}A_{rvj}\Phi_{rj}\right]^{\frac{1}{1-\eta_r}}(1-\eta) - \pi_r, \quad \forall r \in K; \ v, \ j \in VI \tag{7.35}$$

which is defined for firms with the optimal production, $X^*_{r/vj}$.

These results yield a firm's willingness to pay for each real estate alternative (v,j) under the Cobb–Douglas technology with nonincreasing scale economies in a competitive market (i.e., we assume that there are many firms that are price takers; no single firm is able to influence prices). Observe that $Z_j = Z_j(\{H_{kj}\}), \forall k \in K$, $j \in I$, in A_{rvj}, defines agglomeration economies associated with immobile attractors in the production sector, which is mathematically equivalent to the location externalities in the residence location problem, and therefore, the results of uniqueness of the solution and the convergence of the succession prevail.

The Case of Increasing Returns to Scale

We now analyze the case in which the industry has the same Cobb–Douglas/Dixit–Stiglitz technology, but unlike the previous case, it has increasing returns to scale, i.e., $\eta_r > 1$. In this case, the classical model concludes that it is not possible to compute an optimum firm size. The technical reason is that the profit function is concave and yields an unbounded optimum size. That is, in a closed market, the standard solution concentrates total production on only one firm, leading to imperfect competition, and the production model becomes more difficult to analyze.

In the urban context, increasing returns to scale is extremely important for the system analysis because it concentrates some industries in a few locations (or even one), which in turn induces highly relevant agglomeration effects—push and pull forces—on other agents' location choices, which impact the city's dynamics fundamentally. Consider, for example, the financial industry, where we observe several firms (banks), but they are highly concentrated in only a few zones, normally in the central business district. Because they can centralize operations, they can serve a large number of clients with high economies of scale on labor, infrastructure, and technology, especially when such operations are increasingly automated. The urban impact of this example is that there is, on the one hand, the classical monopolistic power of the firm in that industry, but on the other hand, there is the impact of their location in creating subcenters, e.g., financial subcenters. Another good example is the high-technology industry, whose economies of scale and (temporal) monopoly of innovation yield concentration of the industry at a global scale, such as Silicon Valley, in the United States.

In this context, and recalling that goods are differentiated by location, we expect that the standard conclusion of the concentration of production in only one firm is restated as follows: in each zone, there is only one firm. Additionally, the number of zones with production, which is equal to the number of firms, depends on the balance between the degree of economies of scale and the density profile in the city. An interesting case to observe is the small city where agglomeration economies are weak, leading us to expect that economies of scale dominate and production is concentrated in one firm. This dominance is expected to be diluted as cities increase in size and agglomeration economies have increasing relevance. Another case is an industry whose scale economies dominate agglomeration economies, inducing the unique location of only one firm in the city.

In the context of urban production technology, it is also plausible that despite increasing returns to scale, the firms behave as price takers. This conclusion follows from the product differentiation and the expectation of multiple firms in the city. Therefore, it is relevant to discuss a model of the industry with increasing returns to scale in production in a competitive market, i.e., behaving as a price taker, where the firm can neither define the price, as in the pure monopolistic case, nor influence the price, as in the oligopolistic case.

The urban production technology model in Eq. (7.18) allows us to simulate the double effect because economies of scale are represented by parameters, $\eta_r > 1$, and agglomeration by immobile factors, Z (including push and pull forces). These two different sources of endogeneity in the location problem lead to a complex dynamic problem and, in general, to multiple equilibria.

Let us analyze the optimal production problem. The firms' behavior is assumed to be described by the minimization of the production cost subject to the production size, which yields the optimum input levels of capital, $K^*(\rho, X)$; labor, $L^*(\omega, X)$; and intermediate goods, $Y^*(p,X)$. Using the production function in Eq. (7.18), the minimum cost optimization problem yields (see Technical Note 7.2):

$$K^*_{rvj}(\sigma, X) = X_{rvj}^{\frac{1}{\eta_r}}(A_{rvj}\Phi_{rj})^{\frac{-1}{\eta_r}}\upsilon_r\rho^{-1} \tag{7.36}$$

$$L^*_{f/rvj}(\sigma, X) = X_{rvj}^{\frac{1}{\eta_r}}(A_{rvj}\Phi_{rj})^{\frac{-1}{\eta_r}} \cdot \delta_r\overline{\omega}_{rj}^{-1}\omega_{fj}^{\frac{-1}{1-\tilde{\delta}_r}} \tag{7.37}$$

$$Y^*_{km/rvj}(\sigma, X) = X_{rvj}^{\frac{1}{\eta_r}}(A_{rvj}\Phi_{rj})^{\frac{-1}{\eta_r}} \cdot \gamma_{kr}\overline{p}_k^{-1}\widehat{p}_{km}^{\frac{-1}{1-\tilde{\gamma}_{kr}}} \tag{7.38}$$

Then, the minimum cost function is

$$C^*_{rvj}(\sigma, X) = \eta_r X_{rvj}^{\frac{1}{\eta_r}}(A_{rvj}\Phi_{rj})^{\frac{-1}{\eta_r}} \tag{7.39}$$

with an average cost function (see Eq. T7.26 in Technical Note 7.2):

$$\overline{C}^*_{rvj}(\sigma, X) = \eta_r X_{rvj}^{\frac{1-\eta_r}{\eta_r}}(A_{rvj}\Phi_{rj})^{\frac{-1}{\eta_r}} \tag{7.40}$$

which decreases with the production's size, as expected. In Technical Note 7.2, we prove that this result is consistent with the case of nonincreasing returns to scale.

The firm's willingness to pay in now derived from its profit:

$$\pi_{r/vj}(p, X) - p_{rj}X_{r/vj} - C^*_{rvj}\left(\upsilon, X_{r/vj}\right) - r_{vj} = p_{rj}X_{r/vj} - \eta_r X_{rvj}^{\frac{1}{\eta_r}}(A_{rvj}\Phi_{rj})^{\frac{-1}{\eta_r}} - r_{vj} \tag{7.41}$$

Then, the industry's profit increases with the firm size, inducing concentration (caused by the exponent $\frac{1}{\eta_r} < 1$), although the differentiation by agglomeration economies, captured in A_{rvj}, and by prices in Φ_{rj}, may yield production in several locations. Therefore, the industry with increasing returns to scale will have production in one or more locations and, at most, one firm at each location at the most profitable real estate option $v_j^* = \text{argmax}\,\pi_{rvj}$; this location is not necessarily the lowest real estate price because $A_{rvj}(q_v)$ values several real estate amenities. Additionally, some zones will have no firm if the profit is nonpositive. Figure 7.5 shows the polynomial profit function of Eq. (7.41), which is positive if:

$$X > X_{rvj}^{\min} = \left(\frac{p_{rj}}{\eta_r}\right)^{\frac{\eta_r}{1-\eta_r}}(A_{rvj}\Phi_{rj})^{\frac{1}{1-\eta_r}} + \frac{r_{vj}}{p_{rj}} \tag{7.42}$$

where the first term of the right-hand side makes profit null if the rent is null, and the second term covers the real estate cost. The figure shows that the minimum production

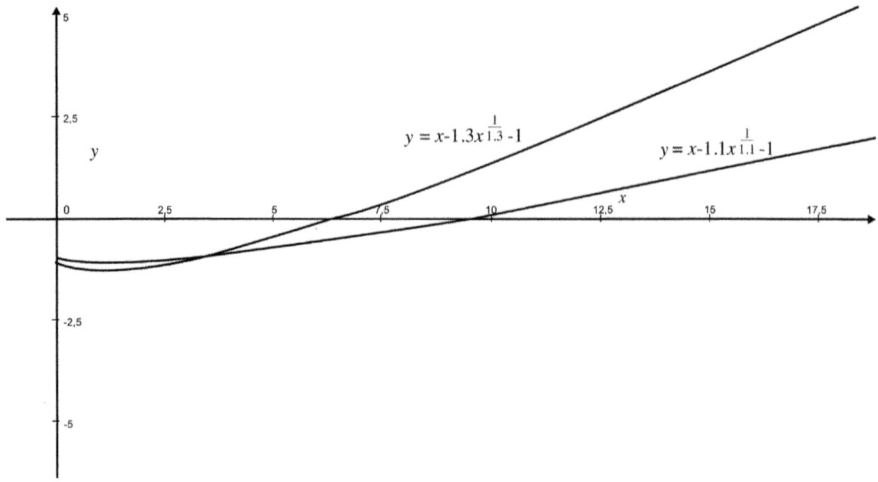

Figure 7.5 The profit function for increasing returns to scale.[7]

$\left(X_{rvj}^{\min}\right)$ increases with the economies of scale, inducing a higher concentration of production in fewer firms.

Then, if η is small, i.e., has weak scale economies, the zones that satisfy the condition $\pi_{rj} \geq 0$, so that $F_{rj} = 1$, will be those that exhibit large enough agglomeration economies, which permits some dispersion. Conversely, if $\eta \gg 1$, i.e., has strong scale economies, they will be concentrated in one or very few locations in the city. If transportation costs are not large enough, economies of scale will induce lower costs and prices in zones with larger production. These zones attract more demand, inducing a concentration cycle that stops once agglomeration and scale economies equal transportation costs, i.e., once profits are equal across zones.

Let us now introduce the firms' willingness to pay, with a reservation profit $\pi_{r/vj} = \pi_r \geq 0, \forall v, j \in VI$ that makes firms of an industry indifferent regarding site location. Inverting the profit in Eq. (7.41) on land rents defines the following firm's willingness to pay:

$$w_{rvj}(\eta, p) = p_{rj} X_{r/vi} - \eta_r X_{rvj}^{\frac{1}{\eta_r}} (A_{rvj} \Phi_{rj})^{\frac{-1}{\eta_r}} - \pi_r \tag{7.43}$$

where $w_{rvj} = w_{rvj}(\eta_r, p, X, A(Z); \pi_r)$, X is the demand at equilibrium, and $Z_j = Z_j(\{X_{kj}\}, k \in K)$ defines the agglomeration economies defined in terms of total production at each location rather than the number of firms.

This result yields the firm's willingness to pay for each real estate alternative (v, j) under the Cobb–Douglas technology with increasing returns to scale economies in a competitive market. Our model implies that despite the increasing returns to scale and in contrast to the classical solution for this case, production is not necessarily

[7] Fig. 7.5 depicts the profit for $\eta_r = 1.1$ and 1.3, with $p_{rj} = 1$, $(A_{rvj} \Phi_{rj})^{\frac{-1}{\eta_r}} = 1$ and $r_{rj} = 1$.

concentrated in one firm or one location. Moreover, in contrast to the previous case with nonincreasing returns to scale, the willingness to pay of firms with increasing returns to scale ($\eta > 1$) depends on the production at each location, which induces the following potential *hyperconcentration:* the stronger the scale economies, the higher the concentration of production in one location and on one firm, and the higher the willingness to pay for the location with the highest agglomeration economies. Thus, the likelihood of outbidding other agents at that location is also high.

We can conclude that a firm's willingness to pay for a location is differentiated by the scale economies of the industry's technology. Within the industry, the space is differentiated by agglomeration economies and the real estate by the land input; these differences are dependent on the transportation system. Thus, synthetically, we can write: $w(Z(\{H_{hi}\}, \{X_{ri}\}), \eta; T)$, with $\{H_{hi}\}, \{X_{ri}\}$ the allocation location profile of households and firms, η the scale economies, and T the transportation system.

In this book, we skip the classical case reported in the literature: the industry in a market with imperfect competition, where producers have enough monopoly power to influence prices. This case requires in-depth analysis of the producers' behavior on setting prices, which depends on the number of firms in the oligopoly, and the analysis of optimal strategies, which leads to different and interesting types of spatial Nash equilibria.

7.8 The LUTE System Equilibrium

We now formulate the general system equilibrium (LUTE), which implies the simultaneous equilibrium in LU, transportation (T), and the production economy (E) markets.

The LU equilibrium implies finding the set of household utilities, $u^* = \left(\{u_h^*\}, h \in C\right)$, and set of profits, $\pi^* = \left(\{\pi_r^*\}, r \in K\right)$, that allocate all the households and production in the city, considering the following externalities: agglomeration economies, $Z_j(\{X_{kj}\})$, in the industries' bid functions, and residential location attractors, $Z_i\{H_{hi}\}$, in the households' bid functions. The equilibrium in the transportation market implies finding travel times, $t_i^* = \left(\left\{t_{ij}^*\right\}\right)$, and costs, $c_i^* = (\{c_{ij}\})$, that comply with Beckman's equilibrium, as was discussed in Chapter 6. The equilibrium in the production economy implies finding a price vector, $p^* = \left(\left\{p_{rj}^*\right\}, r \in K, j \in I\right)$, that clears all goods and leisure markets, and a set of salaries, $\omega^* = \left(\left\{\omega_{hj}^*\right\}, h \in C, j \in I\right)$, that clear the labor market.

The following market-clearing conditions must hold simultaneously at the LUTE equilibrium.

The Goods/Leisure Equilibrium Prices

The equilibrium condition for each industry is to clear the market for each good and location, which recognizes that goods are differentiated by locations:

$$X_{rj}\left(p^*\right) = x_{rj}\left(p^*\right) + \sum_{km} Y_{rj/km}\left(p^*\right) + E\left(p\right) \tag{7.44}$$

i.e., equilibrium prices, p^*, are such that supply at each location equals total demand, composed of consumption, $\left(x_{rj}\left(p^*\right)\right)$, and intermediate demand, $\left(Y_{rj/km}\left(p^*\right)\right)$, plus the external demand $E\left(p\right)$ from other cities and international regions.

The product demand includes final consumption and demand for production inputs. The consumers' expected demand is $x_{rj}(p) = \sum_{hvim} H_h Q_{vi/h} P_{m/hvi} x_{rj/hvim}(p)$, with H_h the number of households in cluster h; $Q_{vi/h}$ consumer h's bid-auction probability of being located at zone i; $P_{m/hi}$ the probability of consumer h at location vi of having a job at zone m; and $x_{rj/hvim}$ the household's demand for goods/leisure at destination zone j.[8]

The expected production of product r at each zone j is $X_{rj} = \sum_{v \in V} Q_{r/vj} X_{r/vj}(p^*) \delta_{rvj}(F_{rvj})$, with $Q_{r/vj}$ the bid-auction probability of the industry, r, of being allocated at the real estate unit, vj. In the case of nonincreasing returns to scale ($\eta \leq 1$), the optimal production is given by Eq. (7.30), and we define $\delta_{rvj}(F_{rvj}) := 1$ if $X_{r/vj}(p^*)$ is feasible, i.e., $F_{rvj} \geq 1$ and $\delta_{rvj}(F_{rvj}) := 0$, otherwise.

In the case of increasing returns to scale ($\eta > 1$), there is no optimal production size, and the producer's decision is to maximize production and use optimal inputs. This means that if the demand at a given location, calculated using Eq. (7.44), fulfills the minimum size condition $X\left(p^*\right) > X^{\min}$ given in Eq. (7.42), then $\delta_{rvj}(F_{rvj}) = 1$ and $F_{rvj} = 1$; otherwise, $\delta_{rvj}(F_{rvj}) = 0$.

The equilibrium problem in Eq. (7.44) is solved by: $p^* = \left(\left\{p^*_{rj}\right\},\ k \in K,\ j \in I\right)$, which defines a fixed-point problem denoted as $p^* = F^p$. In the simpler case of constant returns to scale, the solution of this problem is given directly by Eq. (7.27), which defines a linear equations system conditional on the demand profile that defines the production size at each location. The solution allows calculating the production at each location. In Technical Note 7.3, we prove that Eq. (7.44) has an equilibrium price under two conditions: the parameter γ in Eq. (7.17) complies with its upper bound and, in some cases, elasticities comply with the condition defined in the Note.

[8] Notation $x_{rj/him}$ in Eq. (7.6) and thereafter is written here as $x_{rj/hvim}$, expanding i to vi.

The Labor Market Equilibrium

Labor equilibrium salaries, $\omega^* = \left(\left\{\omega^*_{fj}\right\},\ \forall f\in F,\ j\in I\right)$, are obtained by solving the equilibrium that clears the labor market for job demand, given by $x_{fj} = \sum_{h\in C} x^{\omega}_{hj}(\omega)\varphi_{hj}$, where φ_{hf} is the exogenous ratio of the average number of workers per household in cluster h and per type f skills. The demand by cluster is $x^{\omega}_{hj} = \sum_{i\in I} H_h P_{j/hi}$. The expected salary per household is $\omega_{hj} = \sum_{f\in F} \omega_{fj}\varphi_{hf}$.[9] The total supply of jobs for workers with type f skills at zone j is $L_{fj} = \sum_{r\in K} L_{f/rj}\left(X_{r/vj},\ p,\ \omega_j\right)$. Thus, the labor market equilibrium condition is

$$\sum_{r\in K} L_{f/rj}\left(\omega^*_{fj}\right) = \sum_{hi} H_h P_{j/hi}\left(\omega^*_{fj}\right)\varphi_{hf} \tag{7.45}$$

which defines the fixed-point problem of salaries denoted by $\omega^*_j = F^{\omega}$. We note that the solution in salaries induces full employment because $\sum_{fj}\sum_{r\in K} L_{f/rj}\left(\omega^*_{fj}\right) = L = \sum_{fj}\sum_{hi} H_h P_{j/hi}\left(\omega^*_{fj}\right)\varphi_{hf} = H$. See Technical Note 7.3 for the existence of equilibrium salaries in Eq. (7.45).

The Land-Use Clearing Condition

The LU model yields the equilibrium utilities, u^*, and profits, π^*, by solving the location bid-auction problem for the case with externalities. Indeed, Eqs (7.17), (7.35), and (7.43) represent the bid functions of households and firms, respectively, both with location externalities $Z_i(\{H_{hi}\},\{X_{ri}\})$.

Recall that households' bids in Eq. (7.17) are $w_{hi} = w_h(\{p_{ri}\},\{\omega_{hi}\},Z_i,\{c_{ij}\},\{t_{ij}\};u)$, with $Z_i = \left(\{z^r_i\},\ \{z^g_i\},\ \{z^{\omega}_i\}\right)$ the location externalities on residence, shopping, and job locations, respectively. Firms' bids in Eqs (7.35) and (7.41) are $w_{rvi}(p_{ri},\omega_i,q_v,Z_i,\{c_{ij}\},\{t_{ij}\};\eta_r,\pi_r)$, with Z_i the agglomeration attractors. Hence, because the bids of households and firms are functions of the same set of variables, we can consider them as agents with different random bids and solve the LU equilibrium for all agents, conditional on the following vectors: $\{p_{rj}\},\{\omega_{hi}\},\{c_{ij}\},\{t_{ij}\}$.

We now analyze how to implement the LU location model assuming w_{rvj} to be an extreme value variate. To apply the LU model for the spatial allocation of production industries, we need to realize that the bid-auction model distributes an exogenous number of agents, which in the residential model, for example, is the exogenous number of households by cluster $\{H_h\}$. In the case of production, we must assign production of industries to locations $\{X_{ri}\}$, depending on a feasible number of firms at each location,

[9] As in the A-L model, a simplified model would define the household cluster by the worker's skills type and one worker per household, i.e. h=f.

($F_{rvj} \geq 1$). To implement these feasibility conditions, we can apply a constrained probability, as was discussed in Chapter 5, where the cutoff is $\phi(\cdot) \in (0, 1)$, with $\phi_{rvj}(F_{rvj}) \rightarrow 0$ if $F_{rvj} < 1$. This cutoff concentration production eliminates infeasible small production and concentrates the production in fewer firms, which is particularly effective in industries with increasing returns to scale.

With the constrained bid-action model for production allocation, the fixed-point problem for the LU equilibrium in the integrated LUT model (called F^{LUT} in Chapter 6) can be specified explicitly for households and firms, denoted by $M_{HF}^{LUT} = (\{H_{hvi}, X_{rvi}\}, \forall h, r, v, i)$, which solves the simultaneous LU equilibrium. This extension requires a transportation model that simulates cargo transport and passenger transportation simultaneously to obtain travel times and costs on congested urban roads. The solution yields the number of households (by cluster) and production (by industry) in each location zone and the equilibrium utilities, u^*, and profits, π^*, which allows the calculation of real estate prices, r^*, and densities, $\rho^* = (\{\rho_i^*\})$, at equilibrium.

7.9 Summary of the LUTE System Equilibrium

The LUTE system equilibrium integrates the LU, transportation, and production markets. The set of equilibrium variables is $x = (\{u_{hi}\}\{\pi_{ri}\},\{p_{ri}\},\{\omega_{fi}\},\{c_{ij}\},\{t_{ij}\})$. The solution to this problem is given by the set of fixed-point problems:

$$\Xi^c(x) = ((u^*, \pi^*) = M_{HP}, p^* = F^p, \omega = F^\omega, S^* = F^s, VI^*) \tag{7.46}$$

with the allocation of households and production to real estate units; the development and redevelopment of real estate; the city limits; real estate rents; population and floor space densities; production quantities, prices, and salaries by zone; travel times, costs to consumers for goods and leisure trip purposes and by travel destination; delivery times; and costs of products. Technical Note 7.3 shows that a solution of the fixed-point problems F^p and F^ω exists and is unique under certain conditions.

The model allows the evaluation of the effects of location externalities and agglomeration economies on location and building patterns; the impact on the population and the economy with regard to LU zoning plans; pricing and subsidies in LUT subsystems; and infrastructure development programs.

The main characteristics of the LUTE model are the following:

1. It depends on the exogenous scenario defining the household population by cluster $(\{H_h\}, h \in C)$, the transport infrastructure, T, and agricultural rents, R_A.
2. The set of parameters are those of the agents' behavior: the utility function of consumers and the production function of producers, including real estate developers.
3. The equilibrium approach is static.
4. The city is assumed to be isolated from other cities, although an external zone, m, represents the aggregated external world.

These topics are analyzed in the succeeding chapters of this book.

Technical Note 7.1: The Discrete-Continuous Extreme Value Demand Model

This model was presented by Bhat (2008) to estimate the demand for multiple alternative goods that are imperfect substitutes. We use it here to derive the demand for retail goods at each location, assuming a stochastic subutility for the consumption of goods.

This model uses the CES random utility function, defined as:

$$U(x) = \sum_{k \in K} \frac{\gamma_k}{\alpha_k} \left(e^{\delta' z_k + \varepsilon_k} \right) \left\{ \left(\frac{x_k}{\gamma_k} + 1 \right)^{\alpha_k} - 1 \right\} \tag{T7.1}$$

where $U(x)$ is a quasiconcave, increasing, and continuously differentiable function on the goods vector $x \in \mathbb{R}^+$; and γ_k and α_k are parameters associated with each product. For this function to be a valid utility function, it is required that $0 < \alpha_k \leq 1$ and $\gamma_k > 0$ for all k. Vector z_k describes the set of attributes that differentiates each product by location, δ is the vector of taste parameters of attributes, $\varepsilon_k' s$ are the random terms, and $\delta' z_k = \sum_m \delta_m z_{km}$. For more details on this function, see Bhat (2008) and its references.

The model assumes extreme value distribution for the random terms, ε_k, $\forall k \in K$, which are independent of z_k and are independently distributed across alternative zones with shape parameter σ. It is convenient to assume an external zone for retail purchases with a unit price equal to one, denoted by $k = 1$, with strictly positive consumption, which is used as the *numeraire* to normalize prices. We define the expenditure budget as $\sum_{k \in K} e_{k/hij} = E_{hij}$, where $e_{k/hij} = \overline{p}_{k/hij} x_k$ is the expenditure at each location, with $\overline{p}_{k/hij} = p_k + c_{ik} + \omega_{hj} t_{ik}$ the composite price, including the price of goods, and the transportation cost and time. Here time represents the opportunity cost of time valued at the wage rate.

Applying Kuhn–Tucker's conditions, Bhat (see Bhat, 2008, Eq. 34) obtains the following three optional indirect utilities for $k \geq 2$:

$$V_{k/hij}(\alpha_k) = \delta' z_k - (\alpha_k - 1) \ln \left(\frac{e^*_{k/hij}}{\overline{p}_{k/hij}} - 1 \right) - \ln \left(\overline{p}_{k/hij} \right);$$

$$V_{k/hij}(\gamma_k) = \delta' z_k + \ln \left(\frac{e^*_{k/hij}}{\gamma_k \overline{p}_{k/hij}} - 1 \right) - \ln \left(\overline{p}_{k/hij} \right); \tag{T7.2}$$

$$V_{k/hij}(\gamma_k, \alpha_k) = \delta' z_k - (\alpha_k - 1) \ln \left(\frac{e^*_{k/hij}}{\gamma_k \overline{p}_{k/hij}} - 1 \right) - \ln \left(\overline{p}_{k/hij} \right);$$

and $V_1 = (\alpha - 1) \ln \left(x_1^* \right)$, where α is a constant.

These are three alternative indirect utilities because both α_k and γ_k represent the same satiation of consumption in Eq. (T7.1), and only one of them can be identified.

Therefore, Bhat proposes these alternative utility functions as optional specifications with identifiable parameters.

In this case, the probability that an individual allocates expenditure to the first M of the $|K|$ zones is the following closed expression in which we omit the conditional indices (hij):

$$P\left(e_1^*, \ldots, e_M^*, 0, \ldots 0\right) = \frac{(M-1)!}{\sigma^{M-1}} \left(\prod_{m=1}^{M} c_m \right) \left(\sum_{m=1}^{M} c_m^{-1} \right) \left[\prod_{m=1}^{M} \frac{e^{\frac{V_m}{\sigma}}}{\left(\sum_{n=1}^{M} e^{\frac{V_n}{\sigma}} \right)^M} \right] \quad \text{(T7.3)}$$

and the corresponding probability of consumption is

$$P\left(x_1^*, \ldots, x_M^*, 0, \ldots 0\right) = \frac{(M-1)!}{\sigma^{M-1}} \left(\prod_{m=1}^{M} f_m \right) \left(\sum_{m=1}^{M} \frac{\overline{p}_m}{f_m} \right) \left[\prod_{n=1}^{M} \frac{e^{\frac{V_m}{\sigma}}}{\left(\sum_{n=1}^{M} e^{\frac{V_n}{\sigma}} \right)^M} \right] \quad \text{(T7.4)}$$

where $c_m := \left(\frac{1-\alpha_m}{e_m^* + \gamma_m \overline{p}_m} \right) > 0$ and $f_m := \left(\frac{1-\alpha_m}{x_m^* + \gamma_m} \right) = \overline{p}_m c_m > 0; f_m,\ c_m \in \mathbb{R}^+$.

Let us examine these probabilities. Note that: $\prod_{m=1}^{M} \frac{e^{\frac{V_m}{\sigma}}}{\left(\sum_{n=1}^{M} e^{\frac{V_n}{\sigma}} \right)^M} = \prod_{m=1}^{M} P_m^M$, with P_m^M the multinomial logit probability of choosing to purchase in zone k if purchases are performed in M locations. If we replace $\delta' z_k$ by $\delta' \ln(z_k)$ in Eq. (T7.2), we obtain the *frechit* probabilities $P_m^M = \frac{v_m^\sigma}{\sum_{n=1}^{M} v_n^\sigma}$ in Eq. (T7.4).

We note that these consumption probabilities allow the estimation of retail purchases across the alternative locations, including zones with null consumption (corner solutions), with the consumption subutility in Eq. (T7.1) assumed to be a random variable.

Now, we use the MDCEV model to calculate the household demand for the bundle of goods at each location, k, conditional on residential and job locations (i,j,k), denoted $x_{k/hij}$. We consider the instance in which consumers purchase at all locations, i.e., $M = I$. Then:

$$x_{k/hij} = \left\{ \left[\int_{x_k=0}^{E_k/\overline{p}_k} P_{hij}(x_1, \ldots, x_{k-1}, y, x_{k+1}, \ldots, x_I) y \ dy \right] \right\}_{hij}, \quad \forall k \in K \quad \text{(T7.5)}$$

where $E_k = \sum_{\substack{l \in K \\ l \neq k}} \overline{p}_l x_l$ is the disposable income, and the maximum that can be spent in zone k, which is conditional on hij. To calculate the integral in Eq. (T7.5), we recognize that only f_k depends on x_k, and we define the following constants for the integral: $A_k := \prod_{m \neq k}^{I} f_m(x_m)$; $B_k := \sum_{m \neq k}^{I} \frac{\overline{p}_m}{f_m(x_m)}$; $C(y) = \frac{(I-1)!}{\sigma^{I-1}} \left[\prod_{m=1}^{I} \frac{e^{\frac{V_m}{\sigma}}}{\left(\sum_{n=1}^{I} e^{\frac{V_n}{\sigma}} \right)^I} \right]$ $(I-1)$, with $A,\ B,\ C \in \mathbb{R}^+$, to write:

$$y_{k/hij} = \left\{ \int_{y_k=0}^{\frac{E_k}{\overline{p}_k}} \left[(A_k f_y) \cdot \left(B_k + \frac{\overline{p}_k}{f_y} \right) \cdot C \right] y \ dy \right\}_{hij}$$

$$= \left\{ \left[\frac{1}{2} A_k C \overline{p}_k (x_k)^2 \right]_0^{\frac{E_k}{\overline{p}_k}} + (A_k B_k C)(1 - \alpha_k) \left[\int_{x_k=0}^{\frac{E_k}{\overline{p}_k}} \left(\frac{y}{y + \gamma_k} \right) dy \right] \right\}_{hij}$$

Considering that $y/y + \gamma k = d/dy(y - \gamma k \ln(y + \gamma k))$, then we obtain:

$$x_{k/hij} = \left\{ \left[\frac{1}{2} A_k C\, \overline{p}_k (y_k)^2 \right]_0^{\frac{E_k}{\overline{p}_k}} + (A_k B_k C)(1 - \alpha_k) [y_k - \gamma_k \ln(y_k + \gamma_k)]_0^{\frac{E_k}{\overline{p}_k}} \right\}_{hij}$$

$$= \left\{ \frac{1}{2\overline{p}k} A_k C \ E_k^2 + (A_k B_k C)(1 - \alpha_k) \left(\frac{E_k}{\overline{p}_k} - \gamma_k ln \left(\frac{E_k}{\overline{p}_k} + \gamma_k \right) + \gamma_k ln(\gamma_k) \right) \right\}_{hij} \tag{T7.6}$$

To make the conditionality on hij explicit, we recall that:

$A_k = A(\{x_{m/hij}\}, m \neq k)$, with $x_{m/hij}$ the consumption in zone m;

$B_k = B\left(\left\{ x_{m/hij}, \overline{p}_{m/hij} \right\},\ m \neq k \in I \right)$, with $\overline{p}_{m/hij} = p_m + c_{im} + \omega_{hj} t_{im}$; and

$C = C(\{V_{m/hij}\}, m \in I)$, with $V_{m/hij} = V_m\left(z_{mhij}, \overline{p}_{m/hij} \right)$, with $C = \varphi \left[\prod_{m=1}^{I} P_m \right] > 0$ and P_m the *logit* choice probability of good m. Note that z_{mhij} may include shopping travel time t_{im} to model the disutility of travel, as has been proposed in the value of time literature (Jara-Díaz, 2007).

It is important to analyze this demand function with respect to prices and to the expenditure constraint; we first analyze the demand on its own price $x_{k/hij}(\overline{p}_k, E_k)$.

For this purpose, observe that A_k is constant on all prices and B_k is constant on price $\overline{p}_k$. Additionally, $C(\overline{p}) = \varphi\prod_m P_m(\overline{p}) > 0$, with $\varphi := \frac{(I-1)!}{\sigma^{I-1}} > 0$ and P the logit probability function: $P_m(\overline{p}) = \frac{e^{\frac{V_k(\overline{p}_m)}{\sigma}}}{\sum_{n=1}^{I} e^{\frac{V_n(\overline{p}_n)}{\sigma}}}$. Then:

$$C' = \frac{dC}{d\overline{p}_j} = \varphi\sum_k\left[\left(\prod_{m\neq k} P_m\right)(P_k(\delta_{kj} - P_j))\right]\frac{\partial V_j}{\partial p_j} = \varphi\left(\prod_m P_m\right)V'\sum_k[(\delta_{kj} - P_j)] =$$

$CV'(1 - |K|P_j)$. Then, $C' < 0$ if $\delta_{kj} = 1$ because from Eqs (T7.2) we get $\frac{\partial V_j}{\partial p_j} < 0, \forall j$. Then, rewrite Eq. (T7.6) as:

$$x_{k/hij}(\overline{p}, E_k) = C(\overline{p})\left(a_k\frac{E_k^2}{\overline{p}_k} + b_k(p_{-k})\left(\left(\frac{E_k}{\overline{p}_k} - \gamma_k ln\left(\frac{E_k}{\overline{p}_k} + \gamma_k\right) + c_k\right)\right)\right) \tag{T7.7}$$

where, denoting $x_{-k} = \{x_{m\neq k}\}$ and $\overline{p}_{-k} = \{\overline{p}_{m\neq k}\}$, we define: $a_k = a_k(x_{-k}) := \frac{1}{2}A_k$; $b_k = b_k(x_{-k}, \overline{p}_{-k}) := (A_kB_k)(1 - \alpha_k)$ and $c_k := \gamma_k \ln(\gamma_k)$; with $a_k, b_k \in \mathbb{R}^+$ and $c_k \in \mathbb{R}$.

Figure T7.1a depicts the demand function conditional in partial budgets E_k, showing that demand is strictly positive and monotonically decreasing on its own price ($x'_k < 0$). As expected, it also increases with the budget, $E_k = E - \overline{p}_k x_k$, which changes as: $E'_k = -x_k - \overline{p}_k x'_k$, i.e., if the own-price elasticity is $e_{p_k} = x^{-1}\overline{p}_k x'_k > -1$, then E'_k decreases; for this case, as price increases, the partial budget decreases and the demand curve shifts to the left in Fig. T7.1a. Regarding the factor $C(\overline{p})$, it also shifts the curve to the left as price increases. Therefore, we conclude that $\frac{\partial x_k}{\partial \overline{p}_k} < 0$ if the own-price elasticity is $e_{p_k} > -1$. Figure T7.1.b depicts increasing demand function regarding prices of other goods $\left(\overline{p}_{j\neq k}\right)$, showing that it is linear for a constant budget and increases with this budget; this linear relationship in Eq. (T7.7) comes from $b_k(p_{j\neq k}) = \sum_{m\neq k,j}\frac{p_m}{f_m} + \frac{p_j}{f_j}$.

Then, the consumer demand function in Eq. (T7.7) represents a system of equations that defines an optimal consumption fixed-point problem, $x = F^C(x,p,t,c)$.

$$x_{k/hij} = F_h^C\left(x_{m\neq k/hij}, p_m, t_{im}, c_{im}\right); \quad m \in I; \quad \forall k \in K. \tag{T7.8}$$

Technical Note 7.2: Optimal Production

The theoretical model of production, spatially distributed and for different technologies, is discussed in this Note. Let us start revising the concept of returns to scale. A function is defined as homogeneous regarding degree η if $X(\lambda y) = \lambda^\eta X(y)$, $\lambda > 0$, that is, if all inputs are equally scaled by a positive scalar, λ, and the production scales by λ^η.

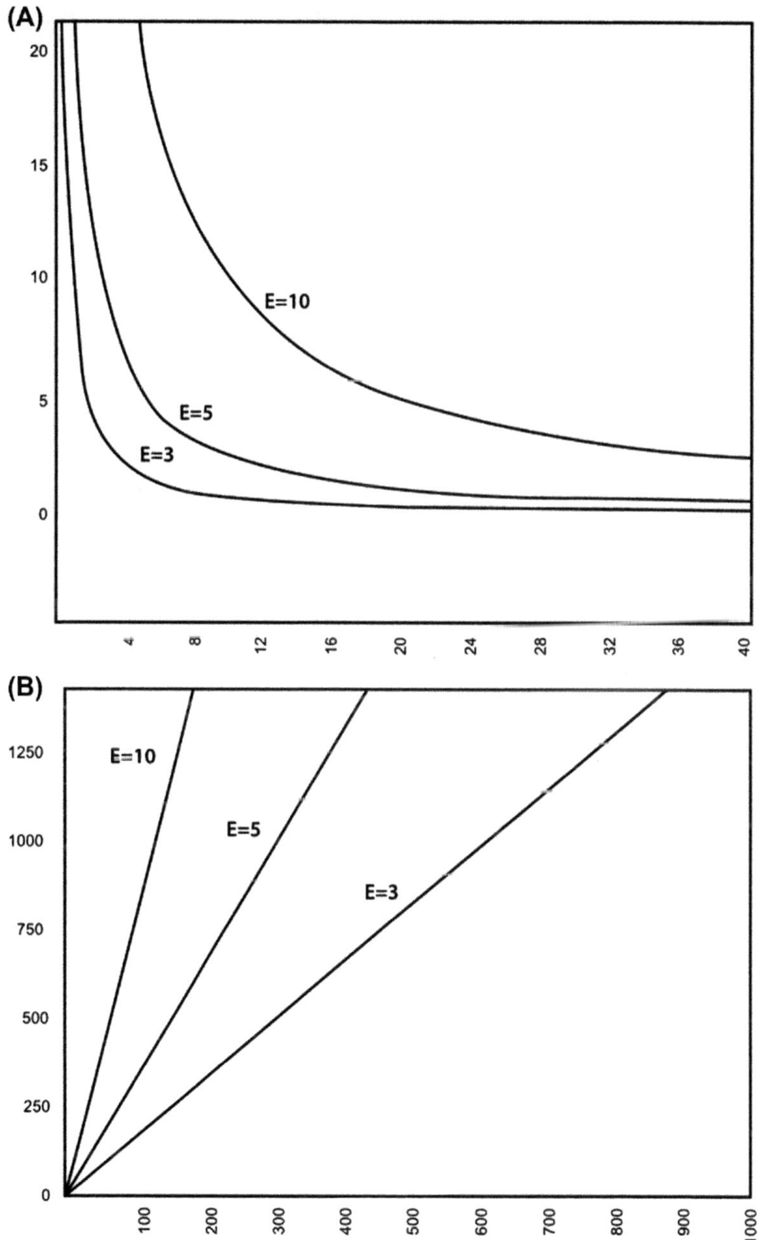

Figure T7.1 The Demand Function (Eq. T7.7) for Parameters *a*, *b* and *c*.

In the case of a Cobb–Douglas/Dixit–Stiglitz production function, given by:

$$X = K\prod_{k\in K}\left(\sum_{i\in I} y_{ki}^{\alpha_k}\right)^{\frac{\beta_k}{\alpha_k}}$$

the following property holds:

$$\begin{aligned} X(\lambda y) &= K\prod_{k\in K}\left(\sum_{i\in I}(\lambda y_{ki})^{\alpha_k}\right)^{\frac{\beta_k}{\alpha_k}} = K\prod_{k\in K}\left(\sum_{i\in I}(\lambda y_{ki})^{\alpha_k}\right)^{\frac{\beta_k}{\alpha_k}} \\ &= \lambda^{\Sigma_k\beta_k}\cdot K\prod_{k\in K}\left(\sum_{i\in I} y_{ki}^{\alpha k}\right)^{\frac{\beta_k}{\alpha_k}} = \lambda^{\eta}X \end{aligned}$$

with $\eta = \sum_{k\in K}\beta_k$ the degree of returns to scale: $\eta < 1$ decreasing returns, $\eta = 1$ constant returns, and $\eta > 1$ increasing returns.

To derive the optimum production, we proceed by finding the set of inputs that minimize the production cost, given the output level. The production function is:

$$X(y) = Ky_0^{\upsilon}\prod_{k\in K}\left(\sum_{i\in I} y_{ki}^{\alpha_k}\right)^{\frac{\beta_k}{\alpha_k}} \tag{T7.9}$$

The cost optimization problem is:

$$\begin{aligned} &\min_y C(y) = \rho y_0 + \sum_{ki\in K\times I}\omega_{ki}y_{ki}, \\ &\text{s.t.} \quad X = X(y) \end{aligned} \tag{T7.10}$$

where ρ is the per unit cost of a non-spatial input y_0, e.g. capital, and ω is the vector of input prices. The Lagrange function is:

$$\mathcal{L} = \rho y_0 + \sum_{ki\in K\times I}\omega_{ki}y_{ki} + \lambda(X - X(y)) \tag{T7.11}$$

where $\lambda \in \mathbb{R}$. It is important to mention that the optimal condition, $\frac{\partial\mathcal{L}}{\partial y_{ki}} = 0$, yields $\omega_{ki} = \lambda\frac{\partial X(y)}{\partial y_{ki}}$. Consider the profit $\pi = pX - C(y) = pX - \left(\rho y_0 + \sum_{ki\in K\times I}\omega_{ki}y_{ki}\right)$ to observe that the maximum profit condition can be applied only if the profit function is concave, which holds for $\eta \leq 1$; in this case, we obtain $\omega_{ki} = p\frac{\partial X(y)}{\partial y_{ki}}$. Therefore, the solution of the problem in Eq. (T7.10) is equivalent to the solution of the profit maximization for $\eta \leq 1$, taking $\lambda = p$. We now consider the solution for the general problem of Eq. (T7.10).

The optimal input is obtained from:

$$\frac{\partial \mathcal{L}}{\partial y_{ki}} = 0 \Rightarrow \omega_{ki} = \lambda \frac{\partial X(y)}{\partial y_{ki}}$$

$$= \lambda \beta_k K Y_k^{\frac{\beta_k}{\alpha_k} - 1} y_{ki}^{\alpha_k - 1} \prod_{\substack{g \in K \\ g \neq k}} \left(\sum_{i \in I} y_{gi}^{\alpha_g} \right)^{\frac{\beta_g}{\alpha_g}} \tag{T7.12}$$

$$- \lambda \beta_k X Y_k^{-1} y_{ki}^{\alpha_k - 1}$$

where $Y_k = \sum_{i \in I} y_{ki}^{\alpha_k}$. Then, we can write:

$$y_{ki} = \lambda X \beta_k \omega_{ki}^{-1} Y_k^{-1} y_{ki}^{\alpha_k} \tag{T7.13}$$

Calculating $Y_k^{-1} y_{ki}^{\alpha_k}$:

$$\frac{y_{ki}}{y_{kj}} = \frac{\omega_{kj} y_{ki}^{\alpha_k}}{\omega_{ki} y_{kj}^{\alpha_k}} \Rightarrow y_{ki}^{\alpha_k} = y_{kj}^{\alpha_k} \left(\frac{\omega_{kj}}{\omega_{ki}} \right)^{\frac{\alpha_k}{1-\alpha_k}} \tag{T7.14}$$

and

$$Y = \sum_{i \in I} y_{ki}^{\alpha_k} = y_{kj}^{\alpha_k} \omega_{kj}^{\frac{\alpha_k}{1-\alpha_k}} \sum_{i \subset I} \omega_{ki}^{\frac{-\alpha_k}{1-\alpha_k}} \tag{T7.15}$$

Defining $\overline{\omega}_k := \sum_{i \in I} (\omega_{ki})^{\frac{-\alpha_k}{1-\alpha_k}}$ yields:

$$Y_k^{-1} y_{kj}^{\alpha_k} = \omega_{kj}^{\frac{-\alpha_k}{1-\alpha_k}} \overline{\omega}_k^{-1} \tag{T7.16}$$

Then, we obtain input as:

$$y_{ki}(\lambda, X, \omega) = \lambda \beta_k X \omega_{ki}^{\frac{-1}{1-\alpha_k}} \overline{\omega}_k^{-1} \tag{T7.17}$$

Similarly, we obtain the optimal y_0 from $\frac{\partial \mathcal{L}}{\partial y_0} = 0$, obtaining

$$y_0(\lambda, X, \rho) = \lambda X \upsilon \rho^{-1} \tag{T7.18}$$

where we recall that for the case $\eta \leq 1$, $y_{ki}(p, X, \omega) = p \beta_k X \omega_{ki}^{\frac{-1}{1-\alpha_k}} \overline{\omega}_k^{-1}$ and $y_0(p, X, \rho) = p X \upsilon \rho^{-1}$.

Now, we calculate λ from $\frac{\partial \mathcal{L}}{\partial \lambda} = 0$, which replicates the constraint $X = X(y)$, where Eq. (T7.9) is used:

$$X(X,\lambda,\rho,\omega) = Ky_0^{\upsilon}\prod_{k\in K}\left(\sum\nolimits_{i\in I} y_{ki}^{\alpha_k}\right)^{\frac{\beta_k}{\alpha_k}}$$

$$= K\left(\lambda X\upsilon\rho^{-1}\right)^{\upsilon}\prod_{k\in K}\left(\sum\nolimits_{i\in I}\left[\lambda\beta_k X\omega_{ki}^{\frac{-1}{1-\alpha_k}}\overline{\omega}_k^{-1}\right]^{\alpha_k}\right)^{\frac{\beta_k}{\alpha_k}}$$

$$= K\lambda^{\eta}X^{\eta}\left(\upsilon\rho^{-1}\right)^{\upsilon}\prod_{k\in K}\beta_k^{\beta_k}\overline{\omega}_k^{-\beta_k}\left(\sum\nolimits_{i\in I}\left[\omega_{ki}^{\frac{-1}{1-\alpha_k}}\right]^{\alpha_k}\right)^{\frac{\beta_k}{\alpha_k}} \quad \text{(T7.19)}$$

$$= K\lambda^{\eta}X^{\eta}\left(\nu p^{-1}\right)^{\nu}\prod_{k\in K}\beta_k^{\beta_k}\overline{\omega}_k^{\beta_k}\left(\frac{1-\alpha_k}{\alpha_k}\right) = A\lambda^{\eta}X^{\eta}\Phi(\rho,\omega)$$

with $\Phi(\rho,\omega) = \rho^{-\upsilon}\prod_{k\in K}\overline{\omega}_k^{\beta_k\left(\frac{1-\alpha_k}{\alpha_k}\right)}$, $A = K\upsilon^{\upsilon}\prod_{k\in K}\beta_k^{\beta_k}$ and $\eta = \upsilon + \sum_{k\in K}\beta_k$. Again, we recall that for the case $\eta \le 1$, we obtain $X(p) = Ap^{\eta}X^{\eta}\Phi$.

For the case $\eta > 1$, we solve Eq. (T7.19) for λ:

$$\lambda(X,\omega,\rho) = X^{\frac{1-\eta}{\eta}}(A\Phi)^{\frac{-1}{\eta}} \quad \text{(T7.20)}$$

and replace this result in Eqs (T7.17) and (T7.18) to obtain the optimum inputs:

$$y_{ki}(X,\omega,\rho) = X^{\frac{1}{\eta}}(A\Phi)^{\frac{-1}{\eta}}\cdot\beta_k\omega_{ki}^{\frac{-1}{1-\alpha_k}}\overline{\omega}_k^{-1}$$

$$y_0(X,\omega,\rho) = X^{\frac{1}{\eta}}(A\Phi)^{\frac{-1}{\eta}}\upsilon\rho^{-1} \quad \text{(T7.21)}$$

We can now calculate the minimum cost functions. In the case of $\eta \le 1$, we have:

$$C(p,X) = \rho y_0 + \sum_{ki\in K\times I}\omega_{ki}y_{ki}$$

$$= pX\upsilon + pX\sum_{k\in K}\left(\beta_k\,\overline{\omega}_k^{-1}\sum_{i\in I}\omega_{ki}\omega_{ki}^{\frac{-1}{1-\alpha_k}}\right)$$

$$= pX\upsilon + pX\sum_{k\in K}\left(\beta_k\overline{\omega}_k^{-1}\sum_{i\in I}\omega_{ki}^{\frac{-\alpha_k}{1-\alpha_k}}\right) \quad \text{(T7.22)}$$

$$= pX\left(\upsilon + \sum_{k\in K}\beta_k\right) = \eta pX$$

and the average cost is $\overline{C} = \frac{C}{X} = \eta p$. Then, the profit is

$$\pi(p, X) = pX - \eta pX = pX(1-\eta) \tag{T7.23}$$

which implies that for $\eta = 1$, the profit is null, and if $\eta < 1$, the profit is positive.

In the case of $\eta > 1$, we use Eq. (T7.21) to write:

$$\begin{aligned}
C(X, \omega, \rho) &= \rho y_0 + \sum_{ki \in K \times I} \omega_{ki} y_{ki} \\
&= \upsilon X^{\frac{1}{\eta}} (A\Phi)^{\frac{-1}{\eta}} + \sum_{ki \subset K \times I} \omega_{ki} X^{\frac{1}{\eta}} (A\Phi)^{\frac{-1}{\eta}} \cdot \beta_k \, \omega_{ki}^{\frac{-1}{1-\alpha_k}} \overline{\omega}_k^{-1} \\
&= X^{\frac{1}{\eta}} (A\Phi)^{\frac{-1}{\eta}} \left(\upsilon + \sum_{k \in K} \beta_k \overline{\omega}_k^{-1} \sum_{i \in I} \omega_{ki}^{\frac{-\alpha_k}{1-\alpha_k}} \right) \\
&= X^{\frac{1}{\eta}} (A\Phi)^{\frac{-1}{\eta}} \left(\upsilon + \sum_{k \in K} \beta_k \right) = \eta X^{\frac{1}{\eta}} (A\Phi)^{\frac{-1}{\eta}}
\end{aligned} \tag{T7.24}$$

Observe that this result implies that the average cost is:

$$\overline{C}(X, \omega, \rho) = \frac{C}{X} = \eta X^{\frac{1-\eta}{\eta}} (A\Phi)^{\frac{-1}{\eta}} \tag{T7.25}$$

and

$$\frac{\partial \overline{C}(X, \omega, \rho)}{\partial X} = (1-\eta) X^{\frac{1-2\eta}{\eta}} (A\Phi)^{\frac{-1}{\eta}} \tag{T7.26}$$

In this case, the average production cost decreases with the production size because $(1\text{-}\eta)<1$. It follows that for $\eta > 1$, it is convenient to increase production size up to the feasible maximum, then it is expected that production is concentrated in only one firm.

Let us now prove that Eq. (T7.24) is valid for $\eta \leq 1$. The profit maximization criterion implies that:

$$p = \frac{\partial C(X, \omega, \rho)}{\partial X} = X^{\frac{1-\eta}{\eta}} (A\Phi)^{\frac{-1}{\eta}} \tag{T7.27}$$

and solving for the optimum production yields:

$$X(p, \rho, \omega) = (p^{\eta} A\Phi)^{\frac{1}{1-\eta}} \tag{T7.28}$$

Now, replacing $X(p,\omega,\rho)$ in the cost function Eq. (T7.24), we can calculate the cost conditional on the price:

$$C(X,p) = \eta(A\Phi)^{\frac{-1}{\eta}}(p^{\eta}A\Phi)^{\frac{1}{(1-\eta)\eta}} = \eta(pA\Phi)^{\frac{1}{1-\eta}} = \eta pX \tag{T7.29}$$

Technical Note 7.3: Analysis of the LUTE Equilibrium

To analyze the properties of the equilibrium in LUTE, we study the derivatives of demand and production functions with respect to prices and salaries.

Analysis of demand

Let us first analyze the demand model, following the decisions by steps.

1. The goods−leisure demand model is given in Eqs (7.5) and (T7.7) as:

$$x_{k/hij}(\overline{p},E_k) = C(\overline{p})\left(a_k\frac{E_k^2}{\overline{p}_k} + b_k(p_{-k})\left(\left(\frac{E_k}{\overline{p}_k} - \gamma_k ln\left(\frac{E_k}{\overline{p}_k}+\gamma_k\right)+c_k\right)\right)\right) \tag{T7.30}$$

where we drop conditional indices for (h,i,j). Then, recalling that $a_k = a_k(x_{-k}) := \frac{1}{2}A_k$; $b_k = b_k(x_{-k},\overline{p}_{-k}) := (A_kB_k)(1-\alpha_k)$; $c_k := \gamma_k \ln(\gamma_k)$; $A_k = \prod_{m\neq k}^{I} f_m(x_m) > 0$; $B_k = \sum_{m\neq k}^{I}\frac{\overline{p}_m}{f_m(x_m)} > 0$; $E_k = \sum_{l\in K, l\neq k}\overline{p}_l x_l = E - p_k x_k > 0$; $C = \theta\left[\prod_{m=1}^{I}P_m(\overline{p})\right] > 0$; we differentiate the demand function with respect to any price $\overline{p}_j \in \overline{p}$:

$$\begin{aligned}
x'_{kj} = \frac{\partial x_k}{\partial \overline{p}_j} = C(\overline{p})\Bigg[&\frac{a'_{kj}E_k^2}{\overline{p}_k} - \delta_{kj}\frac{a_k E_k^2}{\overline{p}_k^2} + \frac{2a_k E'_{kj}}{\overline{p}_k} \\
&+ (1-\delta_{kj})b'_{kj}\left(\left(\frac{E_k}{\overline{p}_k} - \gamma_k \ln\left(\frac{E_k}{\overline{p}_k}+\gamma_k\right)+c_k\right)\right) \\
&+ \delta_{kj}b_k\left(\overline{p}_k^{-1}E'_{kk} - E_k\overline{p}_k^{-2}\right)\left(1-\gamma_k\left(\frac{\overline{p}_k}{E_k+\overline{p}_k\gamma_k}\right)\right)\Bigg] \\
&+ C'(\overline{p})\left(a_k\frac{E_k^2}{\overline{p}_k} + b_k\left(\left(\frac{E_k}{\overline{p}_k} - \gamma_k \ln\left(\frac{E_k}{\overline{p}_k}+\gamma_k\right)+c_k\right)\right)\right)
\end{aligned} \tag{T7.31}$$

with $\delta_{kj}=0$ if $j\neq k$ and $\delta_{kj}=1$ if $j=k$. Note that: $a_k>0;\ b_k>0;\ a'_{kj}=0;\ b'_{kj}=\frac{1}{f_j}>0;$ $E_k\geq 0; E'_{kk}=-x_k<0;\ E'_{kj\neq k}=x_j>0; C>0; C'=CV'(1-|K|P_j)$, with $|K|$ the number of locations.

Then the own-price derivative is

$$x'_{kk}=C(\overline{p})\left[-\delta_{kj}\frac{a_kE_k^2}{\overline{p}_k^2}-\frac{2a_kx_k}{\overline{p}_k}+\ \delta_{kj}b_k\left(-\overline{p}_k^{-1}x_k\ -E_k\overline{p}_k^{-2}\right)\left(1-\gamma_k\left(\frac{\overline{p}_k}{E_k+\overline{p}_k\gamma_k}\right)\right)\right]$$
$$+C'(\overline{p})\left(a_k\frac{E_k^2}{\overline{p}_k}+b_k\left(\left(\frac{E_k}{\overline{p}_k}-\gamma_k\ln\left(\frac{E_k}{\overline{p}_k}+\gamma_k\right)+c_k\right)\right)\right) \tag{T7.32}$$

Note that $1>\gamma_k\left(\frac{\overline{p}_k}{E_k+\overline{p}_k\gamma_k}\right);\frac{E_k}{\overline{p}_k}>\gamma_k\ln\left(\frac{E_k}{\overline{p}_k}+\gamma_k\right)$ for $\frac{E_k}{\overline{p}_k}$ large enough for the γ_k or $\gamma_k<1;\ C'>0$ if $P_j<\frac{1}{|K|}$. These are sufficient conditions $x'_{kk}<0$ to hold. Nevertheless, simulations in Technical Note T7.1 show that conditional $x'_{kk}<0$ holds, indicating that the negative term in square brackets is larger than the last term.

The cross-price derivatives are

$$x'_{kj\neq k}=C(\overline{p})\left[\frac{2a_kx_j}{\overline{p}_k}+\frac{1}{f_j}\left(\frac{E_k}{\overline{p}_k}-\gamma_k\ln\left(\frac{E_k}{\overline{p}_k}+\gamma_k\right)+c_k\right)\right]$$
$$+C'(\overline{p})\left(a_k\frac{E_k^2}{\overline{p}_k}+b_k\left(\frac{E_k}{\overline{p}_k}-\gamma_k\ln\left(\frac{E_k}{\overline{p}_k}+\gamma_k\right)+c_k\right)\right) \tag{T7.33}$$

In this case, the tem in squared bracket is positive under the previous condition for γ_k, then the sign of $x'_{kj\neq k}$ depends on the sign $C'(\overline{p})$, unless the first term is always larger than the second one, as indicted by simulations in Technical Note T7.1.

Therefore, we conclude that the mathematical analysis is not conclusive, but with the support of simulation, the result is that $x'_{kk}<0$ and $x'_{kj\neq k}>0$.

2. The jobs demand model is given in Eq. (7.13) as:

$$x^{\omega}_{j/hi}=H_hP_{j/hi}=H_h\frac{L_{hj}\ e^{\theta v_{j/hi}}}{\sum_{m\epsilon I}L_{hm}\ e^{\theta v_{m/hi}}}\ ,\ \forall j\in I \tag{T7.34}$$

with $v_{j/hi}=U\left(z^{\omega}_j,\frac{\omega_{hj}(T-t_i-dt_{ij})-r_i-dc_{ij}}{\tilde{p}_{hij}+\omega_{hj}\tilde{t}_{hij}}\right)$ and $\tilde{p}_{hij}=\frac{\sum_{k\in K}(p_k+dc_{ik})x^*_{hij}}{\sum_{k\in K}x^*_{hij}}$, which implies that $\frac{\partial x^{\omega}_{j/hi}}{\partial p_k}=H_h\frac{\partial P^{\omega}_{j/hi}}{\partial\tilde{p}_{hij}}\frac{\partial\tilde{p}_{hij}}{\partial p_k}<0$ because $\frac{\partial P^{\omega}_{j/hi}}{\partial\tilde{p}_{hij}}<0$.

Additionally, the derivative on salaries is $\frac{\partial x^{\omega}_{j/hi}}{\partial \omega_{hk}} = H_h \frac{\partial P^{\omega}_{j/hi}}{\partial \omega_{hk}}$. Let us first analyze the derivative on the own salary:

$$\frac{\partial P^{\omega}_{j/hi}}{\partial \omega_{hj}} = \frac{\partial P^{\omega}_{j/hi}}{\partial v_{j/hi}} \frac{\partial v_{j/hi}}{\partial \omega_{hj}} = \theta P^{\omega}_{j/hi}\left(1 - P^{\omega}_{j/hi}\right) \frac{\partial v_{j/hi}}{\partial \omega_{hj}} > 0 \text{ if } \frac{\partial v_{j/hi}}{\partial \omega_{hj}} > 0.$$

To verify this condition, recall that: $x^{*}_{hij}\widetilde{t}_{hij} := \sum_{k \in K} (t_k + d_k t_{ik}) x^{*}_{k/hij}$; from Eq. (7.9): $t_j = T - t_i - dt_{ij} - x^{*}_{hij}\widetilde{t}_{hij}$; from Eq. (7.11): $x^{*}_{hij}\left(\widetilde{p}_{hij} + \omega_{hj}\widetilde{t}_{hij}\right) = \omega_{hj}(T - t_i - dt_{ij}) - r_i - dc_{ij}$. Define $\sigma_{hij} := \left(\widetilde{p}_{hij} + \omega_{hj}\widetilde{t}_{hij}\right) > \omega_{hj}$ and $\tau_{ij} := (T - t_i - dt_{ij})$ to obtain:

$$\frac{\partial v_{j/hi}}{\partial \omega_{hj}} = \frac{\tau_{ij}}{\sigma_{hij}} - \frac{\omega_{hj}\tau_{ij} - r_i - dc_{ij}}{\sigma_{hij}{}^2} \widetilde{t}_{hij} = \frac{1}{\sigma_{hij}}\left(\tau_{ij} - x^{*}_{hij}\widetilde{t}_{hij}\right) = \frac{t_j}{\sigma_{hij}} \geq 0$$

with $\frac{t_j}{\sigma_{hij}} = 0$ only if the working time $t_j = 0$.

For the cross-derivative:

$$\frac{\partial P^{\omega}_{j/hi}}{\partial \omega_{hm}} = \frac{\partial P^{\omega}_{j/hi}}{\partial v_{m/hi}} \frac{\partial v_{m/hi}}{\partial \omega_{hm}} = P^{\omega}_{j/hi}\left(\sum_{j' \in I} P^{\omega}_{j'/hi} \frac{\partial v_{j'/hi}}{\partial \omega_{hm}}\right) = -\theta P^{\omega}_{j/hi} P^{\omega}_{m/hi} \frac{\partial v_{m/hi}}{\partial \omega_{hm}}$$
$$< 0 \text{ because } \frac{\partial v_{m/hi}}{\partial \omega_{hm}} > 0.$$

Therefore, $\frac{\partial x^{\omega}_{j/hi}}{\partial \omega_{hk}} > 0$ if $k = j$ and $\frac{\partial x^{\omega}_{j/hi}}{\partial \omega_{hk}} < 0$ if $k \neq j$.

3. The residential location model is represented by the bid-auction probabilities $Q_{h/i}(w_{\cdot i}, \beta)$ and the willingness to pay given by Eq. (7.16):

$$w_{hi} = y_{hi} - \widetilde{p}^{*}_{hi}\, V_h^{-1}\left(z^r_i, t_i + x^{l*}_{hi},\ u_h\right)\ ,\ \forall h \in C, i \in I \tag{T7.35}$$

with $y_{hi} = \sum_{j \in I} P_{j/hi}\left[\omega_{hj}(T - t_i - dt_{ij}) - dc_{ij}\right]$.

In this model, we prove that $\frac{\partial Q_{h/i}}{\partial p_k} < 0$. We have that $\frac{\partial Q_{h/i}}{\partial p_k} = \frac{\partial Q_{h/i}}{\partial w_{hi}} \frac{\partial w_{hi}}{\partial \widetilde{p}_{hi}} \frac{\partial \widetilde{p}_{hi}}{\partial \widetilde{p}_{hij}} \frac{\partial \widetilde{p}_{hij}}{\partial p_k}$, where $\frac{\partial Q_{h/i}}{\partial w_{hi}} = \beta Q_{h/i} > 0$ if $Q_{h/i}$ is *logit* and $\frac{\partial Q_{h/i}}{\partial w_{hi}} = \frac{\beta}{w_{hi}} Q_{h/i} > 0$ if $Q_{h/i}$ is *frechit*, with β the scale parameter of $Q_{h/i}$; $\frac{\partial w_{hi}}{\partial \widetilde{p}_{hi}} < 0$ from Eq. (7.17) because $\widetilde{p}^{*}_{hi} V_h^{-1}(\cdot) > 0$ is consumption; $\frac{\partial \widetilde{p}_{hi}}{\partial \widetilde{p}_{hij}} > 0$ because $\widetilde{p}^{*}_{hi} := \left(x^{*}_{hi}\right)^{-1}\left(\sum_{j \in I} P_{j/hi}\left[x^{*}_{hij}\left(\widetilde{p}_{hij} + \omega_{hj}\widetilde{t}_{hij}\right)\right]\right)$; and $\frac{\partial \widetilde{p}_{hij}}{\partial p_k} > 0$ because $\widetilde{p}_{hij} := \left(x^{*}_{hij}\right)^{-1} \sum_{k \in K} (p_k + d_k c_{ik}) x^{*}_{k/hij}$.

Additionally, we prove that $\frac{\partial Q_{h/i}}{\partial \omega_{hj}} > 0$. This is $\frac{\partial Q_{h/i}}{\partial \omega_{hj}} = \frac{\partial Q_{h/i}}{\partial w_{hi}} \left(\frac{\partial w_{hi}}{\partial \omega_{hj}} + \frac{\partial w_{hi}}{\partial \tilde{p}_{hi}} \frac{\partial \tilde{p}_{hi}}{\partial \tilde{p}_{hij}} \frac{\partial \tilde{p}_{hij}}{\partial \omega_{hj}} \right) > 0$ because $\frac{\partial w_{hi}}{\partial \omega_{hj}}, \frac{\partial \tilde{p}_{hij}}{\partial \omega_{hj}} > 0$.

Thus, from the analysis of the demand model, we conclude that, as expected:

- $\frac{\partial x^{\omega}_{j/hi}}{\partial p_j} < 0$ if $k = j$ and $\frac{\partial x^{\omega}_{j/hi}}{\partial p_j} > 0$ if $k \neq j$ subject to the upper bound on γ parameters;
- $\frac{\partial x^{\omega}_{j/hi}}{\partial \omega_{hk}} > 0$ if $k = j$ and $\frac{\partial x^{\omega}_{j/hi}}{\partial \omega_{hk}} < 0$ if $k \neq j$; and
- $\frac{\partial Q_{h/i}}{\partial p_k} < 0$, and $\frac{\partial Q_{h/i}}{\partial \omega_{hj}} > 0 \ \forall k, j$.

References

Abraham, J.E., Hunt, J.D., 1997. Specification and estimation of nested logit model of home, workplaces, and commuter mode choice by multiple-worker households. Transportation Research Record 1606, 17–24.

Anas, A., Liu, Y., 2007. A regional economy, land-use, and transportation model (RELU-TRAN): formulation, algorithm, and testing. Journal of Regional Science 47 (3), 415–455.

Bhat, C.R., 2008. The multiple discrete-continuous extreme value (MDCEV) model: role of utility function parameters, identification considerations and model extensions. Transportation Research Part B 42, 274–303.

De la Barra, T., 1989. Integrated Land-use and Transport Modelling: Decisions Chains and Hierarchies. Cambridge University Press.

Echeñique, M.H., 1994. Urban and regional studies at the Martine Centre: its origin, its present, its future. Environment and Planning B 21, 157–533.

Fujita, M., Thisse, J.-F., 2002. Economies of Agglomeration: Cities, Industrial Location and Regional Growth. Cambridge University Press.

Jara-Díaz, S.R., 2007. Transport Economic Theory. Emerald Group Publishing.

Krugman, P., 1991. Geography and Trade. MIT Press.

Leontief, W., 1986. Input-output Economics, second ed. Oxford University Press, New York.

Mas-Colell, A., Whinston, M.D., Green, J.R., 1995. Microeconomic Theory. Oxford University Press.

Systems of Cities

8

8.1 Introduction

Any observer will first describe a city by its macroscale features and describe a country by its cities. In previous chapters, we have developed a bottom-up learning process that spans from individual activities to land-use (LU), transportation, and production markets. In this chapter, we complete this bottom-up study by analyzing a city's macroscale features—focusing on its dynamic—and the development of a system of cities in a country.

We use the LUTE model of the city discussed in Chapter 7, which is illustrated at an agent level in Fig. 8.1, depicting the agents' complex behavior as a rational beings. The model assumes a partition of the land into a set of zones I, a partition of the population into a set of clusters C, and a partition of goods, leisure, and other industries into a set K. LUTE is formulated as a hierarchical choice process that is described by the stochastic models presented in Chapters 4, 5, 6, and 7. In this structure, each choice is made conditional on the previous one (i.e., the higher level in the figure).

In the case of households, the agent's choices, from top to bottom, are as follows: residential location in the city ($i \in I$), job location ($j \in I$), set of goods and leisure consumed ($k \in K$), and locations for performing these activities ($m \in I$). A similar structure represents firms' behaviors, with location choice ($i \in I$); a combination of

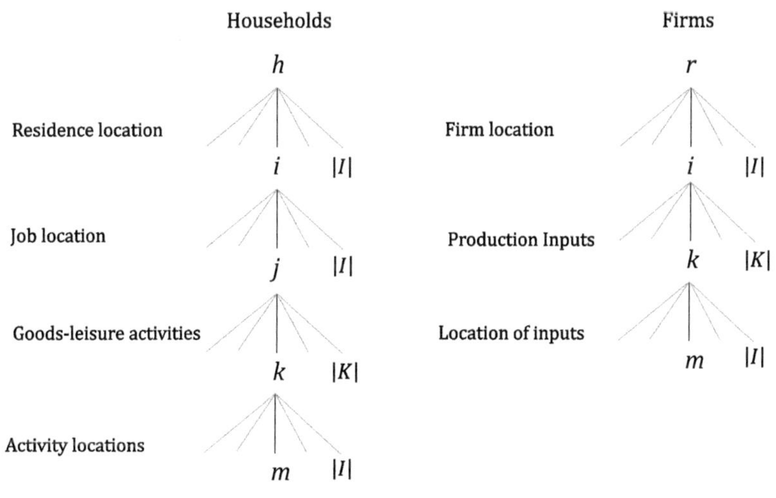

Figure 8.1 The agent's choice process in land use, transportation, and economic (LUTE) model.

Microeconomic Modeling in Urban Science. https://doi.org/10.1016/B978-0-12-815296-6.00008-1

inputs for production, including labor ($k \in K$); and the choice of locations from which to obtain inputs ($m \in I$).

Note that this hierarchical structure is not arbitrary but rather follows the order of resource consumption and considers a limited cognitive capacity. At the upper level, we find long-term decisions, which involve a larger amount of household resources (i.e., residential and job locations), followed by short-term choices, such as consumption, leisure, and social interactions. The main resources are income and time, which constrain the feasible set of choices and make them interdependent. Therefore, the hierarchical order follows a time-resource structure, wherein longer-term choices condition the resources available for shorter-term activities. The hierarchy also represents cognitive constraints because agents are assumed to think in a hierarchical structure when facing a choice-making process with a large set of alternatives, such as the set of all possible locations in a city or country. To reduce the cognitive burden, the agent assigns time and income to the search process for each set of alternatives proportionally to the amount of resources associated with the hierarchy; this strategy also spreads decisions and cognitive costs over time. Finally, the spatial search is also hierarchical, such that a macrozone is represented by a set of macroattributes that describe the zone, and the agent chooses a city, or an area within a city, based on these macroattributes.

The LUTE model yields the following joint probabilities:

$$P_{hijkm} = Q_{h/i} P_{j/hi} P_{k/hij} P_{m/hijk}, \quad \forall h \in C; \; i,j,m \in I; \; k \in K \tag{8.1}$$

which measure the odds that household h has a location and activity profile $ijkm$, which includes, respectively, residential and job locations and the consumption of goods and leisure at different locations. This model estimates demand for goods/leisure and labor at each location by household cluster and residence $\left(x_{hikj}, x^{\omega}_{hij}\right)$, Eqs (7.5) and (7.6). It also yields the travel profile for work and shopping/leisure activities, which identifies the traveler's origin–destination profile and the use of the road network. Using standard transportation modeling techniques, travel demand can be described by time of day.

Similarly, for firms, production is allocated regarding inputs locations:

$$X_{ri} = F_r(Y), \quad \forall r \in K; \; i \in I \tag{8.2}$$

which yields the production of industry r allocated at i and demanding good inputs (Y). The LUTE model yields the number of agents and total production of each industry by location (F_{ri},X_{ri}) according to the industry's technology—scale economies (η). It also yields the jobs profile (L_{ri}), shipments of cargo between industries and zones of the city ($Y_{kj/ri}$), and exports of goods from each industry and zone.

The LUTE model imposes a multiple market-clearing equilibrium condition: households' demand and firms' supply clear the good/leisure markets at each location, which yields prices in all markets and locations (p_{ri}). Additionally, the labor market yields salaries by household and residence location and by skill type (ω_{hi},ω_{fi}). Individuals traveling for shopping, leisure, and other activities and cargo trip profiles are equilibrated in the network, yielding travel times and costs (t_{ij}, c_{ij}), which allows us to compute households' and firms' activity profiles.

In the LU market, suppliers provide a variety of real estate units that clear the LU market at equilibrium rents (r_i). Households and firms—i.e., agents—define their willingness to pay for the variety of real estate units (w_{hi}, w_{ri}), and an absentee auctioneer assigns locations to households and firms such that only one agent is allocated to each location and all agents are allocated. At the location equilibrium, each household obtains a utility level and each industry obtains a profit (u_{hi}, π_{ri}).

The LUTE model yields a static equilibrium solution that is conditional on the city population of households (H) broken down into socioeconomic clusters ($\{H_h\}$); the transportation infrastructure (T); and agricultural land rents (R_A). In Chapter 5, we show an important property of the LU market equilibrium model, namely, it is socially optimal if the social objective is defined by the known utilitarian or Benthamite social welfare function: $W = \sum_{h \in C} u_h + \sum_{i \in I} r_i$. However, we observe that this property does not necessarily apply to other social welfare objectives, such as those seeking social equity.

In this chapter, we extend the modeling approach for a city (i.e., the LUTE model) to a system of cities to develop a model of the country's urban system. This model is called CLUTE, for country land-use, transportation, and economic equilibrium. This country (or regional) model seeks to simulate how cities interact in the wider market for goods production and LU on a national scale. The regional model introduces the interdependence between cities, which defines cities' demographic and firmographic profiles.

We shall discuss the idea that cities in a region, or country, share a common macroscale order and growth dynamics, i.e., common laws of dynamics, called the *scaling laws* of cities. This order can be empirically observed by plotting macroscale variables of the city (e.g., the number of gas stations, the length of the city network, city size, etc.) against its population. This is also the case for aggregated economic variables, such as rents and production. We argue that this common regularity allows us to confidently think in terms of the emergence of an *urban science*, as proposed by Batty (2013a), based on microeconomics.

We shall analyze whether the LUTE model is consistent with this observed order, thereby providing a microeconomic explanation (i.e., a bottom-up process) of the emergence of scaling laws and, conversely, the contribution of scaling laws to the consistency of LU, production, and transportation submodels with this macroscale order.

8.2 The Equilibrium of a System of Cities

Introduction

The structure of cities in a country and the distribution of activities in a city must be consistent in an economic sense, i.e., they should follow socioeconomic forces for the allocation and growth of activities under the common economic system defined at the country level. We postulat that the driving forces for such allocation are the following:

- Migration,
- Transportation costs,
- Agglomeration externalities, and
- Immobile attractors.

Immobile attractors in a system of cities may explain why cities emerged in specific locations (for example, the location of natural resources and amenities, such as minerals, water, mountains, etc.). These resources might later have been complemented by a constructed environment (i.e., transportation networks, including crossings) that agglomerated activities and induced the emergence of new towns. Thus, the original location of ancient towns and cities may have resulted largely from the rational behavior of individuals who responded to these driving forces in the past with a given spatial distribution of immobile basic resources, high transportation costs, and negligible agglomeration, which was followed by a human-built environment that added new towns and cities, increasing the attraction through agglomeration.

Migration is a balancing process that tends to eliminate spatial differentials in agent benefits, both between cities and between zones in a city. Thus, our underlying argument is that the same rational agent criteria is applicable to cities at any developmental stage and thus can describe their dynamics.

Basic Assumptions

We consider an exogenous total population of a given nation to analyze how the population is distributed across multiple existing cities, i.e., we focus on the dynamics of a system of cities and towns already established and ignore the problem of the emergence of new cities.

Then consider an exogenous taxonomy for the system, including the partition of households into a set C of socioeconomic clusters, the partition of production into a set K of industries with common technology, and the partition of geography into sets of microzones $I_i \in I^C$ and macrozones I^C. Note that in this partition, the definition of a city border becomes highly relevant when we analyze a system of cities and towns because it is not always evident whether a nearby town belongs to the city or is an independent urban unit. In our model, cities' borders are defined by the land competition between urban and rural activities, i.e., they are endogenous. In practical modeling, it is essential that the partition of space provides a microscale zoning that is fine enough to model the city's internal differentials in density and transportation costs and a macroscale aggregation that provides the location of cities and their respective transportation costs.

For each household socioeconomic group, the LUTE model of a city yields the *internal microutility*. We also consider a *city macroutility*. The macrolevel utility is constant within the city and represents the city's economic footprint. Thus, macroutility differentiates cities in terms of accessibility to the rest of the system and to the world (e.g., international trade and tourism), to other immobile amenities provided by the natural environment and to agglomeration economies.

The equilibrium of a system of cities comprises three subproblems. First, there is a demographic problem, i.e., how the population is distributed across the country by socioeconomic cluster. People are assumed to be born in a city and in a socioeconomic cluster, i.e., to be born with a geographical and social identity, and then decide whether to stay or to move to another city and/or to transfer to another cluster, both of which entail transition costs. Our fundamental assumption is that agents move freely between cities and clusters to maximize utility; however, there are system capacities defined by labor vacancies in each city and the total population in the country is exogenous.

The second problem is firmography, i.e., how production and firms enter and exit the system. In contrast to the demographic model, production emerges endogenously in each city and is calculated with the city's LUTE model. However, in CLUTE, we recognize that industry profits are not independent in each city and that certain industries concentrate in a few cities or even a single city in the country. Therefore, the CLUTE model yields an endogenous production in each city that is consistent with a country-wide equilibrium criterion for profits.

The third problem refers to the consistency of utilities and prices across the country. Because the LUTE model yields relative equilibrium utilities and prices, which are then normalized to agriculture land rents at the city border, the problem is ensuring a consistent set of agricultural rents across cities, i.e., these rents must represent equilibrium values in the country, meaning that all prices and rents are consistent across the country.

The Demography Model

This model estimates population distribution in the city system based on its distribution in a previous period by cluster and city. The model describes three processes: population growth, mobility between socioeconomic clusters, and migration between cities. We assume that household and job profiles at any point in time for each zone are described by the tuple $(\{H_{hi}\},\{L_{hi}\}, \forall h \in C, i \in I^C)$, with I^C denoting the set of cities in the country. For the model specification, we assume that job profiles are as endogenously estimated by the LUTE model.

Population growth models usually assume a constant per capita growth rate, denoted by θ, whereby the population follows a geometric process, i.e., $H^t = \theta H^{t-1}$. This model was used by Gibrat (1930) for the growth of firms assuming an additive random growth rate $(\theta + \varepsilon)H^{t-1}$. This model approximates to a log-normal growth assuming $\varepsilon \gg \theta$ (Batty, 2013a) or to a power law with a heavy or fat tail if the growth rate is bounded from below, i.e., cities cannot become too small (Gabaix, 1999). We note that the formulation of the growth model has a relevant effect on the dynamics of the city and the city system, i.e., on the emergence of scaling laws, as discussed later.

In contrast to previous models, we consider growth rates that are differentiated by household cluster. Moreover, we recognize that people are born with a sociospatial identity, i.e., with a specific city and cluster identification (h,i), and may later move, both socially (to another socioeconomic cluster) and spatially (to another city). To model this process, we assume that population growth is a geometric process with a random rate at the microscale, i.e., a microgrowth model:

$$H_{hi} = (\theta_h + \varepsilon)H^0_{hi} \tag{8.3}$$

where H^0_{hi} is the demography at the initiation of the modeling period and ε is a random term that is assumed to be common to all agents and cities (i.e., it is a noise caused by purely random incidents) and is limited to $\varepsilon \ll \theta_h$. We assume an independent and identical normal distribution with parameter (0,σ); thus, the expected value is $H_{hi} = \theta_h H^0_{hi}$.

The model considers socioeconomic mobility and spatial migration. Such a model of spatial migration was proposed by Barthelemy (2016), following Bouchaud and Mézard (2000), as a diffusion noise model that offered an alternative to the regularization method of Gabaix (1999) for Gibrat's model and avoided the minimum population size assumption. In our model, we add the socioeconomic dimension of migration, which assumes that agents are born and die with differentiated rates and move between clusters; this social dimension of growth and mobility is seldom considered in the urban modeling literature. Our model also considers international migration, including entry and exit, by defining a macrozone in the set I^C that represents the rest of the world; in this case, growth rates are assumed to be defined exogenously by immigration policies and the international economic environment.

The model is complemented by equilibrium conditions that apply to the system. At any time, the equilibrium criterion is that the final distribution of workers matches the distribution of employment in each city. Therefore, the problem is distributing an initial population profile H^0_{hi} into a final profile $\{H_{hi}\}$, matching the labor vacancies $\{L_{hi}\}$ by allowing for sociospatial mobility. If labor vacancies are estimated by the LUTE model, then adding the demography model to the LUTE model makes population distribution endogenous in the CLUTE model of city systems.

The social mobility submodel calculates the probability $P_{g/h}$ of a household born in cluster h transitioning to cluster g, which is assumed to be independent of the city of birth. The spatial migration submodel calculates the probability of migrating between cities $i \rightarrow j$, $\forall i, j \in I^C$, conditional on the cluster, denoted $P_{j/hi}$. Assuming that these decisions are independent, the joint probability is $P_{hi,gj} = P_{g/h} \cdot P_{ij/h}$. These models follow the microeconomic rational rule, i.e., agents move socially and spatially to maximize utility. We consider transition costs and the risks of changing one's identity. The social migration costs, denoted as c_{hg}, represent the monetary, time, and social disutility of transitioning between clusters, which can describe an *aspirational* mobility structure. That is to say, $c_{hg} > 0$ if $h < g$ and $c_{hg} = 0$ if $h \geq g$, with $h < g$ meaning that cluster g is richer or more skilled than h, i.e., there are costs associated with the acquisition of skills (for the sake of convenience, a higher index h represents higher skills, income, and salary). Spatial migration costs, denoted as c_{ij}, represent distance-related difficulties, including networking and family ties, which are assumed here to be independent of the cluster.

Consider the following stochastic transition utilities from cluster h to g:

$$V_{g/h} = v_{g/h} + \varepsilon_h = v_g - v_h - c_{hg} + \varepsilon_h \quad (8.4)$$

and between cities i and j:

$$V_{ij/h} = U_{ij/h} + \varepsilon_i = U_{hj} + u_{hj} - U_{hi} - u_{hi} - c_{ij} + \varepsilon_{hi} \quad (8.5)$$

with $c_{hh} = 0$, $c_{ii} = 0$, and $c_{ij} = c_{ji}$; these costs are measured in utility units. Recall that u_{hi} is the internal equilibrium utility of cluster h in city i, which is calculated by LUTE and is exogenous in the demographic model; U_{hj} are city equilibrium utilities.

We assume the stochastic terms ε_h and ε_{hi} are i.i.d. Gumbel variables, with shape parameters μ_h and δ_h, respectively, which yields the following choice probabilities:

$$P_{g/h} = \frac{e^{\mu_h(v_g - c_{hg})}}{\sum_{g' \in C} e^{\mu\left(v_{g'} - c_{hg'}\right)}} = e^{\mu_h\left(v_g - c_{hg} - \hat{v}_h\right)} \quad (8.6)$$

where the utility at the initial cluster (v_h) cancels out and

$$P_{ij/h} = \frac{e^{\delta_h(U_{hj} + u_{hj} - c_{ij})}}{\sum_{j' \in I} e^{\delta_h\left(U_{hj'} + u_{hj'} - c_{ij'}\right)}} = e^{\delta_h\left(U_{hj} - c_{ij} - \hat{U}_{hi}\right)} \quad (8.7)$$

where the utilities at the origin city ($U_{hi} + u_{hi}$) also cancel out.

The population distribution after mobility and migrations is as follows:

$$H_{hi} = \sum_{\substack{g \in C \\ j \in I}} \theta_g H^0_{gj} P_{g/h} P_{ji/h} = \sum_{\substack{g \in C \\ j \in I}} \theta_g H^0_{gj} e^{\mu_g\left(v_g - c_{gh} - \hat{v}_g\right)} e^{\delta_h\left(U_{hi} + u_{hi} - c_{ji} - \hat{U}_{hj}\right)} \quad (8.8)$$

The equilibrium condition for this distribution is that the number of workers and jobs match at each location and cluster, i.e., $H_{hi} = \tau_h L_{hi}$, with τ_h denoting the exogenous number of workers per household. This implies that:

$$\tau_h L_{hi} = \sum_{\substack{g \in C \\ j \in I}} \theta_g H^0_{gj} e^{\mu_g\left(v_g - c_{gh} - \hat{v}_g\right)} e^{\delta_h\left(U_{hi} + u_{hi} - c_{ji} - \hat{U}_{hj}\right)} \quad (8.9)$$

Then, solving for U_{hi} yields utility levels that comply with and compensate for job constraints:

$$U_{hi} = -u_{hi} - \frac{1}{\delta_h}\left[\ln\frac{1}{(\tau_h L_{hi})}\sum_{\substack{g\in C\\ j\in I}}\theta_g H_{gj}^0 e^{\mu_g\left(v_g - c_{gh} - \hat{v}_g\right)} e^{\delta_h\left(-c_{ji} - \hat{U}_{hj}\right)}\right] \tag{8.10}$$

where $\widehat{U}_{hj}(U_{hi})$, which implies that Eq. (8.10) is a fixed-point problem in U_{hi}, whose solution $U^* = \left(\left\{U_{hi}^*\right\},\ \forall i \in I^c\right)$ is unique. The interpretation of the solution U^* is the compensating utility in each city that makes households in each cluster indifferent across cities, which accounts for employment differentials between cities. These compensation factors emerge as willingness-to-pay differentials across cities for the same cluster (ceteris paribus), and because they are constant for a city, they affect the average rent of the city and rents in every microzone of the city. In other words, if rents do not include these utility differentials, there are incentives for further migration. Thus, these utilities represent constant reservation utilities in the bid-auction process that consumers are willing to pay for a job in the city.

Observe that the CLUTE model defines a system equilibrium because, as we showed in Chapter 7, the LUTE model yields job vacancies that comply with full employment at internal equilibrium (i.e., at internal utilities u_{hi}) and the demographic equilibrium model yields population profiles that match with jobs for system equilibrium utilities U_{hi}. Therefore, denoting the population profile yielded by CLUTE as $M_i = (\{H_{hi}\},\ \forall h \in C)$; $M = (\{M_i\},\ \forall i \in I^c)$ and the jobs profile as $L_i = (\{L_{hi}\},\ \forall h \in C)$, with $L = (\{L_i\},\ \forall i \in I^c)$, we conclude that the pair (M, L) should attain equilibrium for the set of utilities $U + u$ in every city's LUTE model, which implies solving a system fixed-point problem F^C.

The Firmography Model

This model calculates the production and number of firms per industry in each city, such that the city system attains a general equilibrium at the country level. Recall that in the LUTE model, the emergence of production and firms in cities is endogenously generated, resulting from the population's and producers' demands for intermediate goods and exports. However, at the country level, concentration of production in one city or a few cities is an issue not considered by the LUTE model, which is independent for each city.

Nonetheless, observe that pull (centripetal) and push (centrifugal) forces that operate within the city and define the internal concentration of production among the city's microzones also affect the distribution of production at the country level. We refer to pull forces that induce concentration (e.g., economies of scale, high fixed costs, and agglomeration economies) and push forces that induce the dispersion of production among several cities (e.g., transportation costs and immobile inputs such as natural resources).

The model of the city system, CLUTE, considers an equilibrium condition for each industry in the country, i.e., *industry profits are equal in all cities where production is nonzero*. This condition implies that small cities may not have enough demand to satisfy certain industries' equilibrium profit levels, which means that the industry does not emerge and the demand for its product is transferred to larger cities. This mechanism generates hierarchies of cities and industries, wherein certain products are produced in every city, e.g., food retail products, for which returns to scale are constant, whereas other products, e.g., those with production economies of scale, concentrate in a few cities or even in only one city.

Denote by π_{ri} the internal equilibrium profit of industry $r \in K$ attained by producers in city $i \in I^c$, with K representing the set of industries, which is calculated by the city's LUTE model. Additionally, the industry benefits from the city-specific attributes, denoted by vector Z_i, which include, for example, immobile factors, agglomeration economies, and transportation advantages for imports and exports. Then, the total profit in the city is $\Pi_{ri} = \pi_{ri} + \Pi_r(Z_i)$ and the equilibrium profit for the city system is:

$$\Pi_r = \pi_{ri} + \Pi_r(Z_i), \quad \forall i \in I^c; \ \forall r \in K \tag{8.11}$$

This profit equilibrium is imposed in each city's LUTE model, such that production and labor emerges only in cities with enough demand to yield this profit level. Because π_{ri} is calculated by the LUTE model and Π_r is calculated by the CLUTE model, Eq. (8.11) implies that the set of profits by the industry attain equilibrium in the fixed-point problem denoted by F^{Π}.

Agricultural Land Rents Equilibrium

Let us analyze the equilibrium condition for agricultural land rents in the country. The issue is that the profile of agricultural land rents in the country, which is denoted as $R = (\{R_{Ai}\}, \forall i \in I^c)$, is assumed to be exogenous in each LUTE model but should emerge from a market process such that all prices, utilities, and profits are economically consistent and comparable across the country, which eliminates fictitious incentives for population and goods mobility between cities caused by the lack of normalized economic variables.

The equilibrium criteria in the agricultural land market are that rural activities attain the same profit per land unit at all locations in the country, particularly at city borders. Then,

$$\pi_A = \pi_{Ai}, \quad \forall i \in I^c. \tag{8.12}$$

Define the rural land profit as $\pi_{Ai} = \tau_i - c_i - R_{Ai}$, where τ measures the value of rural production per land unit at macrozone i and c_i is the transportation cost of products and inputs. Note that Eq. (8.12) considers a representative rural industry, but this rural industry may be disaggregated into a set of rural industries indexed by $k \in K^R$. In this case, $\pi_{Ai}(\tau_i, c_i)$ represents the maximum profit at each macrozone location considering all types of rural production. Maximum profit is defined by the rural land auction market, which may also be modeled as a stochastic bid-auction process.

Then, the equilibrium condition yields

$$R_{Ai}^* = \tau_i - c_i - \pi_A, \quad \forall i \in I^c \tag{8.13}$$

which defines equilibrium rents for rural land everywhere in the country, particularly at city borders. It follows that the use of equilibrium rural land, R_{Ai}^*, in each city's LUTE model yields consistent absolute values for utilities and profits, land, and product prices in urban and rural areas across the country; all of these values depend on the profits from the international trade of products.

Therefore, the common rural profit π_A is a country parameter assumed to be exogenous and defined by the international trade of rural products, i.e., it represents the country's *price numeraire* that normalizes economic values with the global economy. Note that this parameter is the unique numeraire value for all prices in the country because the price of goods in each city is dependent on each industry's internal profit, which is normalized to the country profit per industry in Eq. (8.11). Additionally, the industry profit depends on consumers' demand for goods, which depends on their income and land rents; in turn, income depends on production salaries, i.e., on profits, and rents depend on agriculture land rents. Therefore, this chain of dependencies is ultimately contingent on agriculture rent values, which according to Eq. (8.13) depend on the country's numeraire parameter π_A. Thus, this parameter closes the CLUTE model. Moreover, observe that migration equilibrium yields households' utility differentials between cities, U_{hi}, which are dependent on the city border agricultural rent; therefore, such differential are endogenous and adjust at the CLUTE equilibrium.

System Equilibrium

We define the city system's equilibrium Ξ^{CLUTE} as a set of fixed-point problems:

$$\Xi^{\text{CLUTE}}(x;\varphi) = \left(u_i^* = F^{u_i},\ \pi_i^* = F^{\pi},\ S_i^* = F^{S_i}, VI_i^*,\ (Q_i, r_i) = F^{Q_i}, M^* = F^C,\ (X,L)^* = F^{\Pi}\right) \tag{8.14}$$

The LUTE model defines for each city $i \in I^c$ the tuple $\left(u_i^*,\ \pi_i^*,\ p_i^*\right)$, i.e., each city's profile of the relative values of utilities by cluster and profits by industry. It also yields real estate development (S_i), location profiles (Q_i), and rents (r_i). These values yield a complete location profile for each city that is conditional on the city's population profile (M_i). Then, CLUTE defines the equilibrium population profile (M*) and production and employment profiles (L)* in the system of cities, and the equilibrium for agricultural land rents defines absolutes values for utilities and prices across the country.

Thus, the system's equilibrium is conditional on the following set of exogenous parameters $\varphi = (H,\ \eta,\ \pi_A,\ T)$: the country's population (H), the set of production technologies (η), international trade (π_A), and transport infrastructure (T). It also depends on immobile natural resources and amenities.

The spatial dimensions of the microzones of each city $|VI_i|$ totalize at the country level $|VI^c| = \sum_i |VI_i|$. Because the partition of the population into cities and clusters has a dimension size $|C| \cdot |I^C|$, the CLUTE model has a dimension size $|C| \cdot |I^c| \cdot |VI^c|$.

8.3 Cities' Scaling Laws

In recent years, better access to city data has allowed scientists to study the hypothesis of macroscale regularities across a system of cities, i.e., a country. The general hypothesis asserts that city populations explain most of the macroscale features of cities, regardless of their geographical location, culture and history, or their economic steering policies. The main feature of such regularity is that *cities follow universal scaling laws*; this feature affects how our societies are organized and prompts fundamental questions about what generates the common structure of socioeconomic systems. For a motivating reading with detail explanations see West (2017).

Evidence of Scaling Laws

The existence of universal laws has been recognized for a long time. We know that cities follow Zipf's rank-size law (Zipf, 1949), which is common across many human and natural objects, e.g., it is observed in the frequency of the appearance of words in texts and in eroded rocks. This law is named after George Kingsley Zipf (1902–50), who found that the nth most frequent word in any text appears r^{-a} times, with a being close to one; hence, if words are ranked from most to least frequent, $r = 1,2,3\ldots$, then, the second most frequent word appears one-half of the number of times that the first most frequent word appears, and the third most frequent word appears 1/3 of the number of times, and so on. The usual example of the most frequent word in the English language is the word "the."

To explain this law in cities, we rank cities (r) in decreasing order based on population; i.e., the ranking of the largest city is $r = 1$. Then, we plot the logarithm of the cities' ranks against their populations ($N(r)$) to obtain a linear plot, which appears to fit for all countries and for global data on cities, with a slope very close to one. This result seems to be highly robust and invariant to the microdynamics associated with the evolution of the urban system.

Zipf's law has the form of a power law between rank and population:

$$N(r) = \frac{N(1)}{r^{\upsilon}} \tag{8.15}$$

where $N(1)$ is the population of the largest city. This law follows Pareto-type distribution for the number of cities (r) that are larger than $N(r)$: $r = \frac{A}{N(r)^a}$, with $a = \frac{1}{r}$ as the Pareto distribution parameter[1]. According to Pumain (2004), the fit of data to the Pareto distribution is "rather good," but one to eight of the largest cities per state exceed the expected values, i.e., $N(1)/N(2)$ is usually larger than the value predicted by the model.

This law is equivalent to saying that the population is distributed according to the power law (Barthelemy, 2016):

$$\rho(N) = \frac{1}{N^{1+\mu}} \tag{8.16}$$

with $\mu = \frac{1}{v}$ close to one. The number of cities in country (n) is proportional to its population (N):

$$n \sim N^{\zeta} \tag{8.17}$$

with ζ also very close to one. The number of cities with populations larger than P is

$$n(P) \simeq \frac{n}{P^{\mu}} \tag{8.18}$$

There are several models that attempt to provide a theoretical explanation for Zipf's law for cities, including those of Gibrat (1930) and Gabaix (1999), which assume that population growth is proportionate to population and has a random growth rate. Nonetheless, there is no clear explanation for this problem yet (Barthelemy, 2016).

Several studies have presented global empirical evidence that the relationship between the macromagnitudes of a city (y) and its population (N) follows a power law:

$$y = y_0 N^{\gamma} \tag{8.19}$$

where γ is the *scale parameter* and y_0 is a constant. Empirical evidence has been obtained from cross-sectional data regarding American, European, and Chinese cities (Bettencourt et al., 2007, 2008). The main conclusions are as follows: the scale parameter is statistically constant for the set of cities; for attributes of material infrastructure, $\gamma < 1$, i.e., it is sublinear, indicating economies of scale based on city size; for economic quantities, $\gamma > 1$, i.e., it is superlinear, indicating returns to scale. Therefore, we can say that cities are very efficient factories of welfare with economies of scale on input factors (decreasing per capita costs) and returns to scale on outputs (increasing per capita output); together, these conclusions imply a per capita output/cost ratio that increases with city size. This finding can explain why humans build cities: because the agglomeration of population makes cities an efficient factory in the production of wealth, using sublinear inputs to get superlinear socioeconomic benefits.

[1] The Pareto distribution, which is named after Vilfredo Pareto, is defined as a continuous function; its discrete equivalent is normally called the zeta distribution or Zipf's law, although the term Zipf's law usually refers to a Pareto distribution with an exponent equal to one.

However, scaled outputs are not limited to positive impacts on society, e.g., income and intellectual production; crime also scales superlinearly.

The power law is observed in biology, where the enigmatic scale parameter of organisms is empirically determined as a multiple of ¼ in nearly all forms of life West (1999), defining metabolic rate (energy consumption), timescales (life span and heart rate), and size (aorta lengths and tree heights). West et al. (1999, 2001) offer a theoretical explanation for this regularity based on fractal geometry, and the fact that on a microscale, different fractal structures exhibit a common dimension: the size of the organism's cells; however, Banavar et al. (2010) demonstrate that the fractal may not be needed to explain metabolic scaling. We observe that cities also have common discrete dimensions of space and time: the minimal space for human life or the minimum residence size; the daily schedule, e.g., the commuting cycle; and the minimum intellectually productive unit: the human. Thus, the metaphor of cities as human or social organisms is appealing (Samaniego and Moses, 2008).

The scale relationship defines cities as fractal objects (Batty, 2005). To explain this notion, we deem the frequency of city attribute y and its size N to be related by $y \sim N^{\gamma}$. The rate of change $\frac{\partial y}{\partial N} = \gamma \frac{y}{N}$ yields the following elasticity: $\frac{\partial y}{\partial N}\frac{N}{y} = \gamma$. Then, the power law reflects constant elasticity to population, i.e., if the population changes from N to $N' = cN$, then the scaled attribute is $y' = (cN)^{\gamma} = c^{\gamma}y$. This attribute-size relation defines a *fractal city*, i.e., the city is an object that scales with respect to its attributes and thus exhibits self-similar patterns at different scales. A good example is the transportation system, which tends to evolve from macroscale highways to microscale roads, providing accessibility at different scales. Batty (2005) provides examples of the fractal geometries of cities in time and space dimensions and remarks that the various models suggesting fractal geometry employ a physical rather than economic approach.

One theory that explains the emergence of cities' power law was proposed by Bettencourt (2013). This theory is based on the following four fundamental assumptions:

1. A mixing population: the city can be explored fully with urbanite resources, i.e., the minimum resources accessible to an urbanite match the cost of reaching any location in the city. This restrains the growth of city area (A) and output (Y).
2. Incremental network growth: the network develops as the population grows or the average distance between individuals equals the average infrastructure network length per capita.
3. Human effort is bounded: the level of social interactions is independent of city size.
4. Socioeconomic outputs are proportional to local social interactions.

Based on these assumptions, the author predicts scale parameter γ in Eq. (8.19) for a variety of social and infrastructure indicators. The model combines the physics notion that citizens fully explore the city with economic concepts, such as the minimum resources required and bounded human effort. The incremental network is aligned with transportation infrastructure, responding to congestion in a hierarchical or fractal structure; this notion is supported by empirical evidence in the United States. Moreover, the proportionality between socioeconomic outputs and social interactions is based on empirical evidence from telecommunications data (Schläpfer et al., 2014).

Batty (2013b) extends Bettencourt's model for a city system by analyzing accessibility measures. For a simplified physical model linking population, roads, and socioeconomic interactions, see Li et al. (2017).

These modeling efforts are an important contribution to our understanding of the microscopic interactions that explain scaling phenomena, albeit the assumptions are substantial. Although physics provides several models that explain the empirical evidence of cities' power laws, these models offer no explanation for why humans follows the rules observed by physicists in nature. For example, the links between potential interactions and economic processes and the scaling of the socioeconomic indices of cities are missing. As suggested by Batty (2013a), to obtain a more convincing explanation, we must integrate urban economists' models, particularly those that analyze urban complexity, e.g., the model of Fujita et al. (1999) that measures agglomeration economies in cities, which is the subject of this section.

A known difficulty in the analysis of cities is defining the city or, more precisely, defining the city's borders. This question is relevant because all city statistics depend on and vary significantly with city definition. This issue can be illustrated as follows: if the border is defined as a minimum density threshold, then cities' areas increase inversely with this threshold and city statistics are increasingly affected by semirural areas that diminish the effect of high density on aggregated city variables. Based on this difficulty, Arcaute et al. (2014) question the existence of a scaling phenomenon in cities because they obtained ambiguous results using UK data, although they also relied on a particular definition of city borders (a minimum of 14 persons per hectare and 30% of daily commuting). Another criticism relates to the influence of heteroscedastic data and modeling errors on the reported evidence of scaling laws in cities. Specifically, according to Leitão et al. (2016), these factors call into question the evidence on nonlinear scaling in cities. Depersin and Barthelemy (2017) analyze longitudinal data (1982–2014) of 101 US cities on annual congestion delays, observing that the power law of delays with population has different exponents for each city, and in some cases one city shows two regimes with different exponents. For these cities, they observe superlinear increase of delays with population (with high exponents) followed by a linear regime; remarkably, these data show that the change of regime occurs in all cities around the same number of 200,000 commuters (a proxy of the population) and at a congestion delay of approximately 40 h per year and per commuter. They conclude that congestion delays and potentially other magnitudes of the city depend not only on the population but also on time, i.e., the city's evolution is path dependent and the cross-section analysis is inappropriate.

The critical views have the scientific value of calling for better methodologies and understanding of the scaling phenomena, although they do no reject the existence of scaling laws in cities. Indeed, the ambiguity on the city definition (Arcaute et al., 2014) implies that we need to have a consensus on the geographical definition of cities because the lower the density threshold considered, the larger the rural area involved, and the less clear the scaling model is; nevertheless, the scaling effect remains observed above some threshold that it is a matter of further study. The observation of Depersin and Barthelemy (2017) that congestion delays follow two regimes is unexpected if we assume the monocentric city, but it is less surprising in a multicentric city, as proposed by Samaniego and Moses (2008). The critical values of 200,000 commuters and 40 h may signal the average magnitudes where multicentricity appears in US cities. Overall, the critics do not reject evidence of the scaling phenomena but highlight important topics worth a more in-depth study.

Physics models provide an attractive theoretical corpus for analyzing the macroscopic performance of cities but fall short in explaining why and how interactions actually occur and what interactions do not contribute to the scaling phenomena. In these models, the underlying dynamic that explains the existence of cities is a gravitational force that represents people's tendency to interact. Homogenous individuals, who are undifferentiated from particles, blindly respond to this force, i.e., each particle interacts with the entire city. This approach is clearly useful for extracting certain essential macroscale characteristics from the urban system and is very enlightening in this regard. Difficulties arise when we want to establish verifiable relationships and not merely conceptual links between the macroscale features of cities and the microbehavior of real individuals and markets, e.g., the links between scaling parameters and individuals' utilities, firms' profits, and prices.

To study the system in more detail, Batty makes a controversial assertion (see Batty, 2005, p. 457) that is likely shared by many scholars: *"It is unlikely…that there can ever be an all-embracing theory, for cities are composed of a multiplicity of actors who perceive the world in many different ways."* However, this statement motivates the following argument: humans are characterized as rational beings, which essentially implies a common behavioral rule, i.e., there is a fundamental and universal driver in social organizations, such as cities. This argument, combined with the evidence regarding cities' power laws, gives rise to the following hypothesis: *there are common and fundamental forces that dominate human behavior everywhere, which explains why social organizations tend follow a universal scaling law*. This is our research hypothesis in this chapter, which we develop using economics instead of physics.

The CLUTE model attempts to embrace such complexity using microeconomic principles, i.e., it follows human behavior theory and the human institution of the market. Thus, we can use this model of cities and city systems to analyze the emergence of a scaling law from microeconomics. Therefore, the aim of this chapter is to assess whether the city scaling law emerges as the natural consequence of the most basic rule common to all humans, namely, that they are rational beings. In other words, we shall analyze whether economists' view of human behavior is sufficient to generate common attractors of a complex city system and whether these attractors follow a scaling law.

Scaling Rents

The scaling of total rents was proved in Martínez (2016), who considered the *frechit* bid-auction approach of the LU model presented in Chapter 5. To reproduce this result, recall that rents are obtained from auctions in which agents' willingness to pay is assumed to be i.i.d. Fréchet variates, which are derived as the inverse of the agents' utility. Then, within the city, the willingness-to-pay variate is

$\theta_{hi} = w_{hi} \cdot \xi_{hi} = y_h e^{\lambda_h^{-1}(-u_h + f_h(z_i))} \cdot e^{\left(\lambda_h^{-1} \varepsilon_{hi}\right)}, \forall h \in C, i \in I_i$, where λ_h is the marginal utility of income, ε_{hi} is the utility i.i.d. Gumbel variates (0, μ_h), and $\xi_{hi} = e^{\left(\lambda_h^{-1} \varepsilon_{hi}\right)}$ is the agent's bid i.i.d. Fréchet variates (1,β_h). The variance of utilities and bids are thus related by $\beta_h = \lambda_h \mu_h$ (see Technical Note 8.1).

Rents are stochastic variates defined as the maximum of agents' willingness to pay for location i, which is denoted by $\theta_i = r_i \xi_i$, where ξ_i is also an i.i.d. Fréchet variate with parameters (1, β), assuming $\beta = \beta_h$, $\forall h \in C$. The maximum expected value of rent yielded by i.i.d. Fréchet willingness-to-pay variates is defined for $\beta > 1$ as:

$$r_i = K' \left[\sum_{h \in C} H_h w_{hi}^{\beta} \right]^{\frac{1}{\beta}} \tag{8.20}$$

where C is the set of agents in the city, including households and firms, and $K' = \Gamma\left(1 - \frac{1}{\beta}\right) > 1$ is a constant.[2] We define $w_i^{\beta} = \frac{K'}{H} \sum_{h \in C} H_h w_{hi}^{\beta}$, an instrumental variable without a simple economic interpretation, to represent the average of w_{hi}^{β}'s values and write:

$$r_i = w_i H^{\frac{1}{\beta}} \tag{8.21}$$

where $H = \sum_{h \in C} H_h = |C|$ is the number of agents in the city. Note that Eq. (8.21) shows that real estate and land rents scale with population at the spatial level of a microzone. This result is depicted in Fig. 8.2 as a log−log graph, with log(r/w) versus

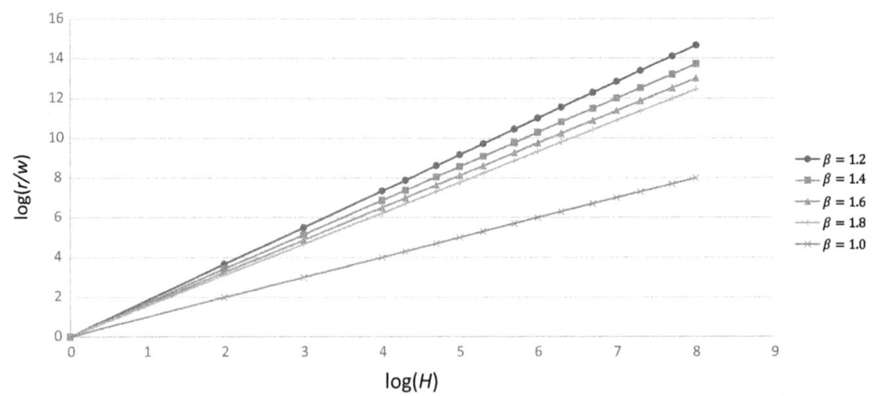

Figure 8.2 The scaling law of microzone rents.

[2] The Γ distribution has a domain $\mathbb{R}^{++}$and is defined as: $\Gamma(x) = \int_0^{\infty} t^{x-1} e^{-t} dt > 0$. Note that $0 < 1 - \frac{1}{\beta} < 1$ and Γ decreases in this range; for example, $\Gamma(\beta = 1) = \infty$, $\Gamma(\beta = 2) = \sqrt{\pi} \approx 1.77$ and $\Gamma(\beta = \infty) = 1$. Then, $K' > 1$ and $\frac{\partial K'}{\partial \beta} < 0$.

$\log(H)$. The graph shows a superlinear scaling of the rents with population dependent on the shape parameter of the distribution, i.e., the larger the variance (the smaller the β), the closer to linear the relationship is.

Let us analyze the rent scaling law in Eq. (8.21). If hypothetically all agents where homogeneous in their preferences and income, then w_i would represent their uniform willingness to pay in the microzone $i \in I$. If this hypothetical population lives in a city of size $H = 1$, then $r_i = w_i$. However, if there are two clone bidders, then rents increase to $r_i = w_i \cdot 2^{\frac{1}{\beta}}$, which implies an amplification of rents by a factor of 1.88 if $\beta = 1.1$ and by 1.6 if $\beta = 1.4$. The explanation for this phenomenon is as follows: in the model, the agent's willingness to pay is assumed to be an extreme value stochastic variate. In this case, the auction selects the highest values of the stochastic terms, inducing a systematic selection toward winning bids higher than the average, i.e., a *selection bias toward maximum values*.

The scaling of rents at the microzone is reflected at the city level as the total land rent value of the city. Consider an average number of people per agent in the city, denoted by a, such that the population is $N = aH$, with $a \geq 1$. Then, the total land rent of the city is

$$R = \left(a^{-1}N\right)^{\frac{1}{\beta}} \sum_{i=1}^{|VI_c|} w_i \tag{8.22}$$

Denote by $w = \frac{1}{|VI_c|} \sum_{i=1}^{|VI_c|} w_i$ the average of w_i and notice that the number of locations matches the number of agents at equilibrium. Then, $|VI_c| = H = a^{-1}N$ to obtain:

$$R = AwN^{\gamma} \tag{8.23}$$

where $\gamma = 1 + \frac{1}{\beta}$ and $A = a^{-\gamma}$. This result verifies that the total land value in a city scales with population. Additionally, because $\beta > 1$ in the Fréchet distribution, it follows that the scale parameter $\gamma = 1 + \frac{1}{\beta} \in (1, 2)$, i.e., the rents–population law is superlinear. This result is consistent with empirical studies and theoretical work that explain the scaling phenomena using physical models.

Analysis of the Rents Power Law

- *The speed of growth.* Let us analyze how fast rents change with a city's population. The average rent per capita increases with the population as $r = \frac{R}{N} = wN^{\frac{1}{\beta}}$. If $N' = \rho N$, then $r' = \rho^{\frac{1}{\beta}} r$ yields the amplifying factor (ρ) shown in Table 8.1. This result illustrates that if the population doubles, i.e., *(N′/N)=2*, then average rents amplify in the range of 60% ($\beta = 1.4$) to nearly double (90% for $\beta = 1.1$).
- *Attraction to larger size.* The marginal increment on rents induced by a new citizen is $\frac{\partial R}{\partial N} = \frac{1+\beta}{\beta} AwN^{\frac{1}{\beta}}$, which increases with N, indicating that the potential additional wealth created by an extra citizen is larger in larger cities. That is, if a foreigner migrates to a particular country, the expected impact on average rents depends on the city in which

Table 8.1 **Amplifying Factor of Rents**

Population Change	Scale Parameter Beta			
N'/N	1.1	1.2	1.3	1.4
2	1.9	1.8	1.7	1.6
5	4.3	3.8	3.4	3.2
10	8.1	6.8	5.9	5.2

the foreigner resides. This argument, however, must be consistent with the condition that population must match employment in each city; otherwise, there is unemployment and the results do not hold.

- *Equity*. The scaling rule means that society concentrates wealth in larger cities in amounts per capita that favor inhabitants in those cities. Larger cities also concentrate crime, pollution, and congestion. These potential benefits and costs are compensated by scaling rents, which yield egalitarian utilities for all citizens in the same socioeconomic cluster in all cities.

It is important to note the origin of the scaling result in rents. The power law for rents emerges from the Fréchet distribution of agents' willingness to pay in an auction market. Because the variance is proportional to $1/\beta$, a larger variance strengthens the superlinear law. Looking farther down in the LU choice structure, the variance of bids emerges from Gumbel utilities of performing activities because $\beta = \mu\lambda$, i.e., the scaling exponent emerges from the microinteractions between agents. Thus, the scaling phenomena described for rents is an expression not only of the accumulation of diversity of human interactions in the hierarchical choice process of the complex urban system but also of the selection process biased by the human rational behavior rule: *utility maximization*. One can describe this process as agents searching in the space of urban opportunities and squeezing the urban "juice of opportunities" to distill the opportunities with the best value. It is worth recalling that this process of biased selection is precisely what is represented by the extreme value models, i.e., the *logit* and *frechit* models.

However, the model might exaggerate the scaling effect because the assumptions regarding independent and identical utilities and willingness-to-pay variates are somehow more extreme than in a real city, i.e., they exaggerate diversity by ignoring the correlated behavior. Indeed, the *logit* and *frechit* models of probability and expected values of economic variates (utilities, profits, prices, and rents) are asymptotic, i.e., they apply to an extremely large number of draws on random terms. Under these conditions, the *selection bias* induced by the i.i.d. extreme value distribution may exaggerate the rate of rent increases with population that is represented by Eq. (8.23), which may be understood as an upper limit.

An observation regarding the choice of modeling approach follows. Following similar calculations, the reader may find that if we assume a *logit* bid-auction model in the LU model instead of the *frechit* model, then total rents also scale superlinear with population. However, instead of a power law, it yields an entropy law, i.e., $R = \beta N \ln N$. It is thus worth asking which law is more realistic, and the evidence

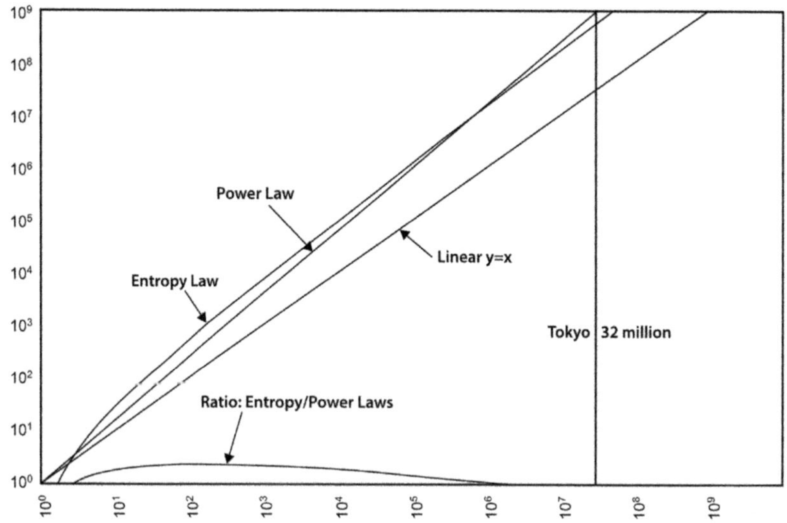

Figure 8.3 Comparison between entropy and power laws.

is not conclusive. The numerical comparison between these optional models is shown in Fig. 8.3 for $\beta = 1.2$, which illustrates that the entropy and power models are very similar in the range of current cities, i.e., $N \approx 3 \times 10^7$ for Tokyo and Shanghai; hence, this analysis is inconclusive. The argument in favor of the power law is theoretical, i.e., the assumption that willingness to pay is a *frechit* variate with the support of nonnegative values is more realistic than the *logit* assumption of nonbounded bids.

Scaling in Production

Let us now analyze whether the scaling phenomenon is replicated for other economic variables. From the LUTE in Chapter 7, we can aggregate the expected profit of industry r to obtain the total profit level in each city m, and we use the equilibrium criteria that profits are equal for an industry across cities.

Recall that at equilibrium, the internal profit is constant in the mth city, i.e., $\pi_{r/i \in Im} = \pi_{rm}$, and from the migration model, the industry profit is constant in the country, i.e., $\Pi r = \Pi_{rm}(Z_m) + \pi_{rm}$, where $\Pi_{rm}(Z_m)$ is the additional profit yielded by agglomeration economies of immobile factors Z_m. To simplify the analysis, we assume agglomeration economies proportional to production and to its value, i.e., $\Pi_{rm}(Z_m) = \tau p_r X_{rm}$.

1. In the case of nonincreasing returns to scale ($\eta \leq 1$), consider the aggregate profit in the city using Eq. (7.32), where the optimal production is $p_r X_{rm} = \sum_{vj \in I_m} p_{rj} X_{r/vj}[1 - \eta]$ to write: $\Pi_{rm} = p_r X_{rm}[1 - \eta + \tau] - R_m = \Pi_r, \ \forall m$, with $R_m = \sum_{vj \in I_m} r_{vj}$. Recall Eq. (7.28) where $pX \propto X^{1/\eta}$ and using Eq. (8.23) we obtain:

$$X_r \propto N^{\gamma\eta}, \quad \forall r \in K \tag{8.24}$$

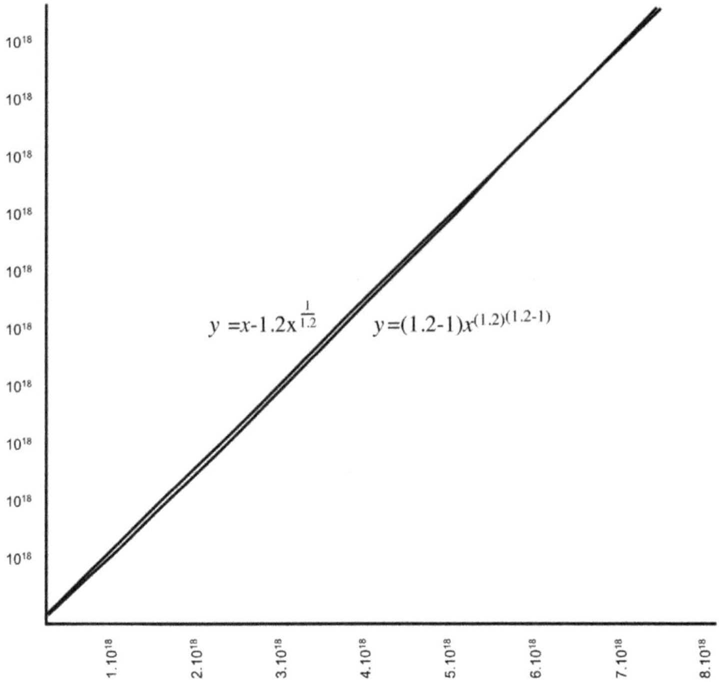

Figure 8.4 The Break-Even Function if and the lower bound for $\eta = 1.2$.

This result shows that the production of a city scales with population with parameter $\gamma\eta > 0$, which can be superlinear if $\eta > \gamma^{-1}$.

2. In the case of increasing returns to scale ($\eta > 1$), the profit in Eq. (7.41) is $\pi_{r/vi}(\eta, p, X) = \tau p_r X_{rm} + p_{rj} X_{r/vi} - \eta_r X_{rvj}^{\frac{1}{\eta_r}} (A_{rvj}\Phi_{rj})^{\frac{-1}{\eta_r}} - r_{vj}$ and the null profit condition defines $\varphi(X,\eta) = p_{rj} X_{r/vj}(1+\tau) - \eta_r X_{rvj}^{\frac{1}{\eta_r}} (A_{rvj}\Phi_{rj})^{\frac{-1}{\eta_r}} = r_{vj}$.

   To analyze $\varphi(X,\eta)$, consider the following lower bound function of φ in the relevant domain: $\psi(X,\eta) = (\eta - 1)X^{\eta^{\eta-1}}$, which has the feature that $\varphi(X,\eta) > \psi(X,\eta)$ for scale economies $\eta \in [1.0, 1.2]$ and for large values of production (larger than 10^{18}) as shown in Fig. 8.4 (for larger values of η, the approximation is valid for lower values of production). Using $\psi(X,\eta)$ as a lower bound approximation of $\varphi(X,\eta)$, we obtain that for the aggregate profit to be constant across cities, the following holds: $\varphi(X,\eta) = p_r X_{rm}[1+\tau] - \eta X^{\frac{1}{\eta}} (A_{rvj}\Phi_{rj})^{\frac{-1}{\eta_r}} \leq (\eta - 1)X^{\eta^{\eta-1}} \propto R_m$. Then, solving for production and using Eq. (8.23), we obtain:

$$X_r \propto N^{\frac{\gamma}{\eta^{\eta-1}}} \tag{8.25}$$

   where the exponent $\gamma/\eta^{\eta-1}$ is close but lower that γ: $1/\eta^{\eta-1}$ is 0.9905 for $\eta = 1.1$; 0.9642 for $\eta = 1.2$; 0.9243 if $\eta = 1.3$. Hence, it is plausible to conclude that approximately $X_r \propto N^{\gamma}$.

3. The case of the labor market deserves special analysis because it defines migration constraints, city sizes, and wages. From Chapter 7, we consider the input demand for the two

Table 8.2 Scale Parameters for Production, Prices, and Labor

	Nonincreasing Returns to Scale $0 < \eta \leq 1$		Increasing Returns to Scale $\eta > 1$	
Production Variable	**Scale Parameter**	**Super-linear if**	**Scale Parameter**	**Super-linear if**
Total production	$X \propto N^{\gamma\eta}$	if $\eta > \frac{1}{\gamma}$	$X \propto N^{\frac{\gamma}{\eta^{\eta-1}}} \approx N^{\gamma}$	Always
Wages	$\omega \propto N^{\gamma-1}$	Always	$\omega \propto N^{\frac{\gamma}{\eta}-1}$	$\eta < \gamma$

technologies for each labor type *f*. Recall the labor Cobb–Douglas parameter for labor input $0 < \widetilde{\delta}_r < 1$ and consider *p* an average price for total city production (*X*).

For $\eta \leq 1$, consider Eq. (7.22) to write:

$$L_f = \sum_{rvj} L^*_{f/rvj} = \sum_{rvj} \omega_{fj}^{\frac{1}{\widetilde{\delta}_r - 1}} \overline{\omega}_{rj}^{-1} \delta_r p_{rj} X_{r/vj} \propto p_r X_r \propto N^{\gamma}, \tag{8.26}$$

because $\omega_{fj}^{\frac{1}{\widetilde{\delta}_r - 1}} \overline{\omega}_{rj}^{-1}$ has dimension of ω_f^{-1}. Using $pX \propto X^{1/\eta}$ in Eq. (8.26) we obtain $\omega_f^{-1} p_r X_r \propto \omega_f^{-1} X^{\frac{1}{\eta}}$; using Eq. (8.24) we obtain $L_f \propto \omega_f^{-1} X^{\frac{1}{\eta}} \propto \omega_f^{-1} (N^{\gamma\eta})^{\frac{1}{\eta}}$. Because L_f is the proportion of the population with skills type *f*, then we conclude that: $\omega_f^{-1} N^{\gamma} \propto N$ or that $\omega \propto N^{\gamma-1}$. In this case, total wages $\Omega \propto N^{\gamma}$ scale superlinearly with population following a power law with the same exponent of rents.

For $\eta > 1$, consider Eq. (7.36) to write:

$$L_f = \sum_{rvj} L^*_{f/rvj} = \sum_{rvj} X_{rvj}^{\frac{1}{\eta_r}} A_{vrj}^{\frac{-1}{\eta_r}} \cdot \delta_r \omega_{fj}^{\frac{1}{\widetilde{\delta}_r - 1}} \overline{\omega}_{rj}^{-1} \propto \omega_f^{-1} X_r^{\frac{1}{\eta}}, \tag{8.27}$$

With this result and using Eq. (8.25) approximated by $X \propto N^{\gamma}$, yields: $L_f \propto \omega_f^{-1} X_r^{\frac{1}{\eta}} \propto \omega_f^{-1} (N^{\gamma})^{\frac{1}{\eta}}$. Because labor is proportional to population, then $N \propto \omega_f^{-1} N^{\frac{\gamma}{\eta}}$; thus, we conclude that $\omega_f \propto N^{\frac{\gamma}{\eta}-1}$ and total labor scales with population as $\Omega \propto N^{\frac{\gamma}{\eta}}$.

Consumer Surplus

Let us analyze if consumers' surplus scale with population. Recall that in Chapter 5, we defined consumer surplus at the LU equilibrium as:

$$\overline{u}_h = \frac{1}{\beta} \ln\left(\sum_{i \in VI} S_i \left[K' \frac{z_{hi}}{r_i} \right]^{\beta} \right) \tag{8.28}$$

with $z_{hi} = y_h e^{\lambda_h^{-1} f_h(z_i)}$. Replace r_i by Eq. (8.21),

$$\overline{u}_h = \frac{1}{\beta} \ln\left(\sum_{i \in VI} S_i \left[\frac{z_{hi}}{w_i H^{\frac{1}{\beta}}} \right]^{\beta} \right) = \frac{1}{\beta} \ln\left(H^{-1} \sum_{i \in VI} S_i \left[\frac{z_{hi}}{w_i} \right]^{\beta} \right) \tag{8.29}$$

and define $w^{\beta} = \frac{1}{H} \sum_{i \in VI} S_i \left[\frac{z_{hi}}{w_i}\right]^{\beta}$ to obtain:

$$\overline{u}_h = \frac{1}{\beta} \ln\left(w^{\beta}\right) \tag{8.30}$$

The main conclusion is that utilities are constant per cluster and are independent of the city's population because rents in the denominator of Eq. (8.28) cancel the scaling effect of the number of bidders, i.e., rents extract the increase in wealth from bidders, which is transferred to land owners as capital gains. This result is consistent with the invariance of utilities across cities in the mobility model for the population in each cluster. It can also be interpreted as the economic explanation for the *bounded human effort* assumption proposed by Bettencourt (2013) because, despite the large differences in interaction opportunities between cities, there are no differences in expected utilities across intracity microzones or across cities.

The importance of the scaling results in production and wages, is that they complete our understanding of the process that generates super-linear socioeconomic outputs in cities, i.e., the link between the main causes: economies of scale and agglomeration, with their impact on the capitalization of profits into super-linear rents. In this process super-linear wages transfer resources from production to residents' income, which in turn transfer income into real estate and land rents.

8.4 City Dynamics

An important assumption thus far is that the model is static, which implies that consumers' income and firms' profits are spent in the present and resources are not saved for the future, i.e., there is no capital investment. This assumption has been helpful in setting a static model but is unrealistic in the analysis of urban dynamics. We should reinterpret rents as societal wealth or available resources, i.e., the sum of land rents plus capital savings. In this case, it is reasonable to presume that land rents do not scale at the speed of the theoretical exponent γ and that production variables do not scale according to the exponents shown in Table 8.1. In this section, we consider that resources are invested in the country for future development to see in a dynamic process how cities evolve on time.

The power law of rents or resources described was used to analyze cities' growth by Bettencourt et al. (2007, 2008). They consider a simple dynamic process for the use of resources: certain resources are used to maintain the current population, and the remaining resources are invested to support the population increase. Let E_0 denote the per capita cost of population maintenance, E denote the per capita investment for population growth, and $N(t)$ denote the population of the city in time t. Then, total resources are split into maintenance and investment by:

$$R(t) = E_0 N(t)^{\rho} + E \frac{\partial N}{\partial t} \tag{8.31}$$

where ρ allows for nonlinear maintenance costs with the population. The evidence shows that $0 < \rho \leq 1$ and most likely that $\rho \in [0.8,1.0]$ for a variety of items necessary in modern life (see Bettencourt et al., 2007, 2008; Ribeiro et al., 2017).

Considering the interpretation that Eq. (8.31) represents wealth or resources produced by the city inhabited by population N at time t, then resources are given by $R(t) = KwN(t)^{1+\frac{1}{\beta}} = AN(t)^{\gamma}$, with$\gamma = 1 + \frac{1}{\beta} > 1$ because $\beta > 1$. Then, solving for $\frac{\partial N}{\partial t}$ yields the urban system dynamic equation:

$$\frac{\partial N}{\partial t} = \frac{A}{E}N(t)^{\gamma} - \frac{E_0}{E}N(t)^{\rho} \tag{8.32}$$

This equation is illustrated in Fig. 8.5, which shows the speed of increase of $\frac{\partial N}{\partial t}$ for different γ and ρ parameters. It shows that the speed increases with γ and decreases with ρ (observe the constant $\gamma = 1.1$ with variable $\rho = (0.7,0.9)$). In our model, these parameters have the following characteristics: γ scales the city's resource yield (outputs) and ρ scales the city's expenditures (inputs). These exponents are related to the socioeconomic and infrastructure exponents of the physics model (Li et al., 2017; Ribeiro et al., 2017), which link the three basic components of cities' growth: population, socioeconomic interactions, and infrastructure.

The solution for the differential Eq. (8.32) depends on its parameters. We consider $\rho = 1$ as an upper bound for the maintenance cost dynamic with population. This assumption is supported by evidence that infrastructure and services scale either

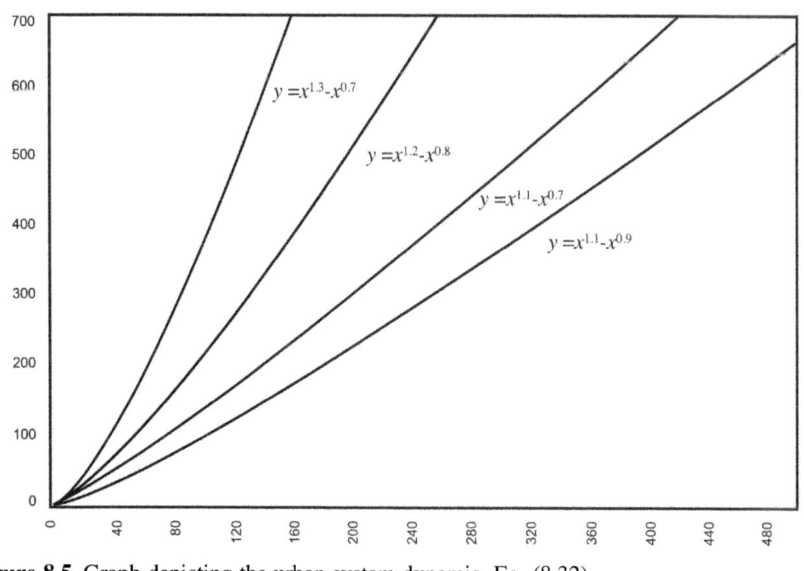

Figure 8.5 Graph depicting the urban system dynamic, Eq. (8.32).

linearly or sublinearly with population, i.e., city inputs for human life are nonincreasing; thus, constant returns to scale represent an upper bound on maintenance costs.

Bettencourt et al. (2007) analyzed the dynamic model of this case (ρ=1) as follows. It has a unique solution given by:

$$N(t) = \left[\frac{A}{E_0} + \left(N_0^{1-\gamma} - \frac{A}{E_0}\right)e^{-\frac{E_0}{E}(1-\gamma)t}\right]^{\frac{1}{1-\gamma}} \tag{8.33}$$

where $N_0 = N(t = 0)$ is interpreted below. The authors studied this equation for three interesting values of the scale parameter γ:<1, =1,>1. The case of $\gamma = 1$ simplifies to an exponential growth, $N(t) = N_0 e^{\frac{(A-E_0)t}{E}}$, and the case of $\gamma < 1$ leads to a sigmoidal curve with an upper population limit in the very long run, $N_\infty = \left(\frac{A}{E_0}\right)^{\frac{1}{1-\gamma}}$, which is the characteristic dynamic of biological systems.

According to our model, however, a more realistic case is $\beta > 1$ and$\gamma = 1 + \frac{1}{\beta} > 1$. For this parameter, the city dynamic changes dramatically, leading the authors to an interesting interpretation of the evolution of cities. Specifically, they interpreted the case of $\gamma > 1$ as representing a society where growth is driven by innovation and wealth creation. In our model, it represents the natural emergence of wealth from a simple universal rule, namely, utility maximization under stochastic choice processes.

If $\gamma > 1$ and $N_0 < \left(\frac{A}{E_0}\right)^{\frac{1}{1-\gamma}}$, then Eq. (8.33) describes unbounded growth, with population increasing faster than exponentially and reaching a mathematical singularity where population becomes infinite (N_∞) in a *finite time window* t_c, as shown in Fig. 8.6 for different values of γ. The authors derived the expression for this critical time window as:

$$t_c = -\frac{E}{(\gamma - 1)E_0}\ln\left[1 - \frac{E_0}{A}N_0^{1-\gamma}\right] \approx \frac{E}{(\gamma - 1)E_0}\frac{1}{N_0^{\gamma-1}} \tag{8.34}$$

This growth limit is theoretical because resources eventually become insufficient and the singularity is never reached because the system becomes unsustainable, i.e., the system cannot produce at the speed required to sustain the extremely rapidly growing population. At this point, the system enters a transition phase that leads to a collapse, as represented by the mathematical solution after this limit, where population decreases steadily.[3]

The existence of a critical time window implies that cities have a predictable fatal destiny: the collapse occurring at time t_c. However, history reports very few instances

[3] In Fig. 8.6, the collapsing phase after time window t_c is only shown for $\gamma = 1.5$ because the exponent $\frac{1}{1-\gamma} = -2$ is an integer for which $N(t)$ can be calculated.

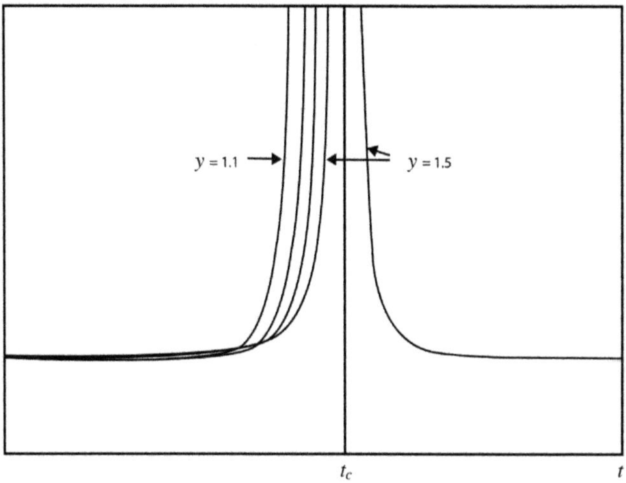

Figure 8.6 System dynamics with $\gamma > 1$ and $\rho = 1$.

of the collapse of cities; when collapse has occurred, it was in cities with populations far smaller than our current megacities. Nevertheless, there is evidence of temporal decline in the rate of population growth, e.g., Bettencourt et al. (2008) cited the example of New York City in the 1970s. They estimated t_c for $\gamma = 1.1$ as $t_c \approx 50\left(\frac{T}{n^{0.1}}\right)$ years, where T is a number of the order of unity and $N_0 = n(10^6)$ is the population measured in millions of inhabitants. This equation implies that compared with a city of 1 million inhabitants, a city with 10 million inhabitants has a 20% shorter window and a city of 100 million inhabitants has a 36% shorter window. For example, Shanghai, China (24 million), has a time window 12% shorter than Santiago, Chile (7 million). This feature is an important and highly surprising characteristic of the critical time window: it shrinks over time, i.e., the next cycle will be shorter than the current cycle.

To understand this apparent paradox between the mathematical prediction of collapse and the historical evidence, we observe that Eqs (8.33) and (8.34) are dependent on a clock initialized by N_0, which is only required to be strictly positive ($N_0 > 0$). What does this mean for the population? Bettencourt et al. (2008) explained that "major adaptations must take place to initiate a new cycle of innovations, in the process of which growth is reset at a new population level N_0." This idea is represented in Fig. 8.7, which shows new cycles of development after an innovation shock takes place, which resets the initial population clock, ends a critic time window, and opens a new and shorter time window.

This process implies that resetting the system requires a major innovation. However, blindly hit a system shock is not really necessary; rather, it may be a smooth process of adaptation. Indeed, the urban system is a complex interaction of many subsystems, e.g., social, economic, legal, political, technological, educational, etc., each of which has some population capacity available before it becomes critical. At a certain

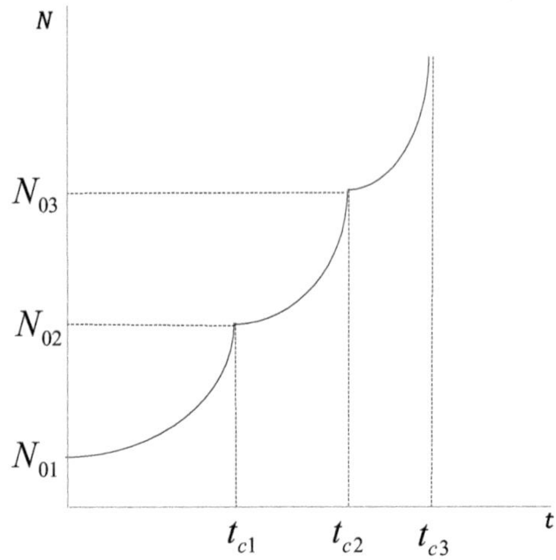

Figure 8.7 The cyclical evolution.

population level, the capacity of one or more subsystems of the city approaches zero and the entire resource production system becomes less efficient. A timely innovation in these critical subsystems will expand the growth potential of the urban system, allowing it to recover its development track; however, such timely innovation requires the political wisdom to anticipate which subsystem is running out of capacity.

In the long run, the critical time window becomes too short for humans to innovate, and the collapse of a very large city is unavoidable. This collapse is "fatal" for the city but not necessarily for the inhabitants, who can migrate to smaller cities with available system capacities. In smaller cities, innovation and adaptation processes are more likely to be smooth because lessons are learned from larger cities that previously confronted innovation demands and because innovation is usually exportable. Consequently, the largest cities may stop growing or shrink, whereas smaller cities continue to grow, such that the country's population continues to grow. Therefore, the fatal time is perhaps less dramatic for inhabitants than it may first appear to be, despite its impact on the city.

Nonetheless, the shrinkage of time windows over time seems less avoidable. This phenomenon means that *urban systems accelerate* over time as populations increase and that all subsystems may deliver their services at a faster pace. We can all perceive that life moves faster in larger cities than it does in smaller cities in the same country, a phenomenon that is observed in biological systems with similar scaling rules.

8.5 Comments on Urban Scaling

This chapter completes the bottom-up presentation of a model, from the microzone to the city and then to the system of cities, through the integration of its macroscale features.

The macroscale model CLUTE is not a trivial spatial extension of the isolated urban equilibrium model LUTE. The integration of several cities in a system of cities is based on individuals' or households' choice of residence city in the migration model. However, their choices are interdependent because they cannot overcrowd cities; rather, they can only migrate to areas where there are job vacancies. Hence, population distribution is driven by birth/death rates and migration processes, both of which are proportional to city size, i.e., larger cities become larger, creating more jobs, which attract migrants.

This condition introduces a country-wide equilibrium for migration flows between birth city and final residence. This criterion is not used for firms, which emerge and disappear according to the demand for products and are located in cities where they can optimize production. This optimization behavior is differentiated by technology according to their respective economies of scale. The economically based distribution of population and firms in the country links all cities in a way that maximizes the country's welfare (in the sense of Benthamite's social welfare).

Thus, we analyzed a macroscale economic feature of cities, namely, the scaling law of rents to population and the correlated scaling of production and labor markets. Our model provides a microeconomic explanation of global evidence of a universal law regarding macroscale indices of cities that provides a different and more microscopic interpretation of the scaling phenomenon compared with previous models based on physics and geography. The microeconomic justification is based on a single and clearly universal law of agents' behavior: humans are rational beings. This law is represented in microeconomics as a utility-maximizing behavior. It is important to note that the model does not specify what is meant by utility, its components, or how they interact. Therefore, it can be considered a very plausible and universal assumption: humans choose what they think is best for them.

In addition, we assumed that human behavior is stochastic because humans make choices with uncertain information, i.e., the consumer's stochastic approach. This assumption fundamentally differs from that used in demand modeling, where the stochastic choice is justified by the lack of information on the part of the modeler, i.e., the modelers' stochastic approach. This is a critical assumption in the emergence of scaling phenomena because if it is a modeling error, then the scaling effect would emerge as an accumulated error. By contrast, in our model, the scaling rule emerges from the random behavior of each individual in the entire system of cities interacting in a complex system.

A lesson of our model worthy of further exploration is that the macroscaling parameter is unique for the system of cities. As noted previously, this uniqueness implies that the behavioral parameters of all agents, including households and firms in a particular country, are mutually dependent. Therefore, the lesson is that methods of estimating behavioral parameters should introduce such a dependency. Furthermore, because international evidence shows that the macroscaling parameters are similar across countries and cultures (given some normalization), there is theoretical and empirical support for research on internationally consistent methods of estimating human behavior. In forecasting the future of existing cities, universal scaling parameters provide a scientific methodology for predicting the expected evolution of macroscale indices of cities, whereas our theory allows modelers to estimate evolution at the microscale level.

Utilities identify individuals' preferences, which are subject to context-specific factors, such as cultural and socioeconomic characteristics, and thus reflect peoples' freedom to choose their fate. However, the universal scaling law tells us that at the scale of the social organization, our system follows a common order and evolutionary track; this proposition is supported by evidence and explained by theory. These two concepts seem to present a paradox: freedom of choice leads to very similar outcomes. Our model explains this paradox as follows: humans follow a common universal rule, i.e., rational behavior, which implies that we have a selection bias that maximizes utility in spite of our preferences. This behavior leads societies to follow a common rule even if preferences differ between cultures. Nevertheless, freedom of choice remains, because the utility maximization paradigm is subject to individuals' preferences, which remains free in the model. Then, the clarification of the apparent paradox is as follows: *while humans enjoy free will leading to differentiated preferences, their choices are constrained by technology available and governed by their rational behavior in the market, leading to equilibrium outcomes that fall in universal attractor, the power law.*

The biologic organism metaphor remains attractive after the analysis performed in this chapter. We are similar in that we minimize production costs, leading to economies of scale, but we are different in that our intellectual capacity allows humans to innovate, avoid collapse, and create wealth in superlinear evolution. In both systems, we observe fractal geometry, which is a feature of complex systems.

All of these factors lead us to consider the idea of an emerging urban science, where universal rules describe our social systems.

8.6 Toward a Unified Theory of Organic Systems

Research on the evidence of the universal scaling of urban systems' indicators show sublinear scaling for inputs and superlinear scaling for outputs. Moreover, West (2017) summarizes these findings, concluding that the universal observed trend is 15% in inputs economies of scale; i.e., the power law has a parameter $\gamma = 1 - 0.15$ and $+15\%$ in outputs returns to scale ($\gamma = 1 + 0.15$). More striking, West postulates a unified theory for all organic systems. In this chapter, we have explained theoretically the origin of the positive returns to scale based on the microeconomic interactions of human activities in the city. In this section, we aim at contributing to the study of West's arguments in favor of a universal macroscale order in all organic systems.

West explains such economies by three *physical properties* common to complex systems: space filling, invariance of terminal units, and optimization in the system processes. These properties have a clear expression in cities because accessibility to products and services covers the whole city area by the—space filling—transportation network that reaches every spatial location of real estate and agents—invariant unit terminals—who interact as rational optimizers. These properties allow us to conceive a unified explanation for all organic complex systems including human organizations. However, the case of human systems is exceptional in producing socioeconomic superlinear outputs, arguably associated with the innovation capacity allowed by higher intelligence, unlike other organisms who apply simple optimizing rules on energy production and consumption without further creativity, i.e., the alleged human superiority in evolution.

Nevertheless, the highly inspiring unified theory of scaling systems in nature falls short in explaining the surprising number of $\pm 15\%$; i.e., why this number is the same for inputs and outputs and what explains this value? This apparent coincidence calls for a scientific explanation. The cost reductions or economies of scale in -15% can be explained by a physical property: the increasing density of cities with population implies that each point in supply networks (water, petrol, electricity, transportation, services, etc.) provides services to a larger population; therefore, larger cities require less per capita infrastructure but remains to be explained why the figure is 15%.

Regarding the more surprising superlinear outputs, let us look back in our model for a potential explanation using the economic analysis. Recall that the outputs' returns to scale emerge from two sources: economies of scale in production, which includes transportation savings, and location—agglomerations economies (i.e., increase in interaction opportunities). It is straightforward to see in our microeconomic model that production economies of scale embed the per capita lower costs associated with sublinear scaling in inputs. Therefore, the physical property that explains the -15% in infrastructure costs is captured in our microeconomic model as economies of scale that explains superlinear socioeconomic outputs. The second source, namely agglomeration economies, is much more difficult to analyze because it has no direct expression on physical terms and considers the concentration of industries with higher economies of scales in larger cities. In the model, household and firm agents value these economies in their willingness to pay and on final rents. This implies that *higher rents must be feasible and consistent with market equilibrium principles*; i.e., they must be generated from production profits and wages. This means that location—agglomerations—yield opportunities that must have an economic expression on productions; i.e., such opportunities must be captured as additional production, either as scale economies on current production or on new industries. In Chapter 7, we showed that our model explains why industries with positive returns to scale concentrate in space, particularly in larger cities. This argument is supported by evidence in West (2017), which shows that in the United States diversity of production scales increases with city size or that larger cities have higher diversity of business. Therefore, we argue that household's location and firms'—agglomeration economies—must have an economic result in the production function of business, which transforms location advantages into production and economic values; otherwise, they remain as potential benefits which have no expression in the outputs' superlinear scaling.

This analysis led us to conclude that the microeconomic model yields an explanation for the $\pm 15\%$ scaling parameters: the -15% on inputs is the economic mirror expression of the physical property, and the $+15\%$ must be the mirror expression of the same phenomenon. This explains the enigmatic coincidence of the same amount in the scaling on costs savings and on socioeconomic production. Still, it remains to explain why the figure is around 15%; i.e., how we explain that the ³⁄₄ (or 25%) parameter in energy savings observed in other organic systems and explained by fractal network principles by West, which naturally follows the persistent multiple of the ¹⁄₄ fraction associated with a four-dimensions system, is converted by the urban economy in a much smaller parameter close to 5/6 or 6/7, not a multiple of the ¹⁄₄ fraction and approximately 2/3 of the physical potential. We can make the conjecture that the 15% economic transformation of ³⁄₄ potential must be explained, at least partially, as the resulting parameter from two factors: i) the economic translation into actual production of the 25% of physical savings in all cities, that is, the baseline for savings under small economies of scale in production and ii) the hierarchy of industries that emerges with different population sizes where industries with larger economies of scale concentrate only in the largest cities; this means that the baseline economic transformation of physical potential savings yields an output scaling less that 15%, which, combined by agglomeration of industries with higher economies of scale in larger cities, increases the economic output up to the 15% figure. Moreover, the economic transformation of the physical potential should consider carefully the urban analogue of the "space filling" principle, or how we humans explore the large amount of city opportunities, in contrast with the space filling process in the distribution of basic goods. Because, unlike particles in physics, human behavior faces additional constraints, introduced in the model in previous chapters, on the following resources: daily time cycle (or commuting costs), income (money for exploration), and cognitive capacity, which are arguably constant across city sizes. That is, the urban space filling principle must be less efficient than its analogue in physics.

Technical Note 8.1: The Link Between Bids and Utility Parameters[4]

Consider the random variates u and z. $u = v + \varepsilon$, with ε i.i.d. Gumbel $(0,\mu)$, i.e., its $F_\varepsilon(x) = e^{-e^{-\mu x}}$. $z = y + \xi$, with ξ i.i.d. Fréchet $(1, \beta)$, i.e., its $F_\xi(x) = e^{-\left(\frac{1}{x}\right)^\beta}$. If $\xi = e^{\frac{\varepsilon}{\lambda}}$, then we prove that $\beta = \lambda\mu$.

Thus

$$F_\xi(x) = e^{-\left(\frac{1}{x}\right)^\beta} = \Pr(\xi \le x) = \Pr\left(e^{\frac{\varepsilon}{\lambda}} \le x\right) = \Pr\left(\frac{\varepsilon}{\lambda} \le \ln(x)\right)$$

$$= \Pr(\varepsilon \le \lambda \ln(x)) = e^{-e^{-\lambda\mu \ln(x)}} = e^{-\left(\frac{1}{x}\right)^{\lambda\mu}}$$

proves that $\beta = \lambda\mu$.

[4] Thanks to L-G. Mattsson for his contribution to this proof.

References

Arcaute, E., Hatna, E., Ferguson, P., Youn, H., Johansson, A., Batty, M., 2014. Constructing cities, deconstructing scaling laws. Journal of the Royal Society Interfaces 12 (20140745). https://doi.org/10.1098/rsif.2014.0745.

Banavar, J.R., Moses, M., Brown, J.H., Damuth, J., Reinaldo, A., Sibly, R.M., Maritan, A., 2010. Proceedings of the National Academy of Sciences 107 (36), 15816–15820.

Barthelemy, M., 2016. The Structure and Dynamics of Cities. Cambridge University Press, Cambridge.

Batty, M., 2013a. The New Science of Cities. MIT Press.

Batty, M., 2013b. A theory of cities. Science 340, 1418–1419.

Batty, M., 2005. Cities and Complexity. MIT Press.

Bettencourt, L.M.A., Lobo, J., Helbing, D., Kühnert, C., West, G.B., 2007. Growth, innovation, scaling, and the pace of life in cities. Proceedings of the National Academy of Sciences 104, 7301–7306.

Bettencourt, L.M.A., Lobo, J., West, G.B., 2008. Why are large cities faster? Universal scaling and self-similarity in urban organization and dynamics. The European Physical Journal B 63, 285–293.

Bettencourt, L.M.A., 2013. The origins of scaling in cities. Science 340, 1438–1441.

Bouchaud, J.-P., Mézard, M., 2000. Wealth condensation in a simple model of economy. Physica A: Statistical Mechanics and Its Applications 282 (3), 535–545.

Depersin, J., Barthelemy, M., 2017. From Global Scaling to the Dynamics of Individual Cities arXiv:1710.09559. physics.soc-ph.

Fujita, M., Krugman, P., Venables, A.J., 1999. The Spatial Economy: Cities, Regions and the International Trade. The MIT Press, Cambridge, Mass.

Gabaix, X., 1999. Zipf's law for cities: an explanation. Quarterly Journal of Economics 114, 739–767.

Gibrat, R., 1930. Une loi des réparations économiques: l'effet proportionnel. Bull. Statist. gén Fr 19, 469.

Leitão, J.C., Miotto, J.M., Gerlach, M., Altman, E.G., 2016. Is this scaling nonlinear? Royal Society Open Science 3 (159649). https://doi.org/10.1098/rsos.150649.

Li, R., Dong, L., Zhang, J., Wang, X., Wang, W.-X., Di, Z., Stanley, H.E., 2017. Simple spatial scaling rules behind complex cities. Nature Communications 8, 1841. https://doi.org/10.1038/s41467-017-01882.

Martínez, F., 2016. Cities' power law: the stochastic scaling factor. Environment and Planning B: Planning and Design 43 (2), 257–275.

Pumain, D., 2004. Scaling laws and urban systems. Santa Fe Institute Working Papers 2004–02–002.

Ribeiro, F.L., Meirelles, J., Ferreira, F., Neto, C.R., 2017. A model of urban scaling laws based on distance-dependent interactions. Royal Society Open Science 4, 160926.

Samaniego, H., Moses, M.E., 2008. Cities as organisms: allometric scaling of urban road networks. Journal of Transport and Land Use 1 (1), 21–39.

Schläpfer, M., Betterncourt, M.A., Grauwin, S., Raschke, M., Claxon, R., Smoreda, Z., West, G.B., Ratti, C., 2014. The scaling oh human interactions with city size. Journal of the Royal Society Interface 11, 20130789. https://doi.org/10.1098/rsif.2013.0789.

West, G.B., 1999. The origin of universal scaling law in biology. Physica A 263, 104–113.

West, G.B., Brown, J.H., Enquist, B.J., 1999. The fourth dimension of life: fractal geometry and allometric scaling of organism. Science 284, 1667–1679.

West, G.B., Brown, J.H., Enquist, B.J., 2001. A general model of ontogenetic growth. Nature 413, 628–631.
West, G.B., 2017. Scales. Pinguin Press.
Zipf, G.K., 1949. Human Behavior and the Principle of Least Effort. Addison Wesley Press.

Model Application and Planning

9

9.1 Introduction

Here, the theoretical model presented in previous chapters is considered as an application tool for modelers. The experience applying an operational land-use (LU) model —based on the bid-auction theory— in cities around the world, is used to analyze two topics. We first discuss implementation topics and the methodology used to estimate the model parameters. Then, the next section is dedicated to a discussion of planning issues, i.e., what is understood by an optimal city, how to formulate and solve this question mathematically as an optimization problem, and how to implement the optimal city using policy instruments, e.g., subsidies and regulations.

The set of submodels discussed in previous chapters, the LU model, with endogenous transportation (LUT) and the economy (LUTE), and a system of cities (CLUTE), are increasingly difficult to implement. The application of these submodels as "stand-alone programs" assumes that other subsystems are exogenous and they are externally predicted or remain static, which limits the scope of the predictions and results. Despite this strong assumption, they are commonly used in the absence of more complex integrated models or are used with other models instead of integrated with them; a common example is the interaction of LUT models using accessibility measures.

In this chapter, we focus on a simplified approach. We consider the application of the LU model, assuming the internal growth and migration of the city's population as exogenously represented in the modeling scenario. The transportation system is simulated using a model that interacts with the LU model by adjusting accessibility to the changing LU, as shown in Fig. 9.1. The goods and services economy is represented in the LU model by the allocation of firms, whereas market prices, production, and the number of firms are exogenous.

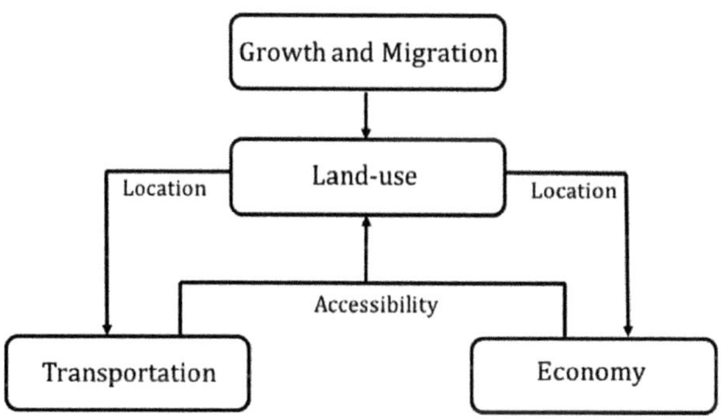

Figure 9.1 The model structure.

Microeconomic Modeling in Urban Science. https://doi.org/10.1016/B978-0-12-815296-6.00009-3

9.2 Implementation of the Land-Use Model

The bid-auction model was implemented as software[1] and has been applied in several cities worldwide; this software is described here as an example of the implementation of the theory.

The model has the feature of solving the MNL *logit* equilibrium in the short and long terms, i.e., with exogenous or endogenous supply of real estate units. The equilibrium considers households' location externalities that describe neighbors' qualities and firms' agglomeration economies. The experience shows that for this basic setting and with different pull and push forces between agents, the model converges to a unique solution, empirically proving the theory in Chapters 4 and 5.

The Input Scenario

The usual taxonomy of models considers space, agents, and real estate supply dimensions, which define the dimensions of the model. The city is spatially partitioned into zones, typically 500 to 1000, defined by administrative and traffic zoning; this is usually determined by available data because the software and hardware can handle larger sizes. In current applications, the city border is exogenously defined by the set of zones.

The population is divided into socioeconomic clusters whose members are assumed to be homogeneous, i.e., they are represented by a common bid function. Clusters are usually defined by the household's income range, ethnic group, and life cycle. Firms are clustered by industry, including commercial and social institutions, and by their dependency on the access to consumers and input suppliers and on the type of building and land lot they need, e.g., services, manufacturing, offices, education, or government. The number of agents, i.e., number of households and firms, per cluster is exogenously defined in the imputed scenario and denoted by H_h, $\forall h \in C$. The exogenous growth estimates the change of each cluster size in the forecasting period.

Real estate units are usually clustered by housing and land lot type, e.g., detached, semidetached, back-to-back houses, or differentiated by building height. In a short-term application, real estate units are exogenously defined as a portfolio of projects, which must expand the total supply to match the total population for an equilibrium to exist; this condition is verified by the model. In the case of modeling the long-term application, the real estate supply is endogenously calculated by the model.

Planning regulations are defined in the forecasting scenario, which constrains the set of feasible supply units in each zone or the allocation of some types of agents. These regulations may represent existing conditions or a set of planned regulations

[1] The original software was called MUSSA, after the Spanish name for Santiago-Chile's land-use model, was developed by the team at the University of Chile for the Chilean government, then it was renamed as Land and integrated to the commercial package CUBE.

that the policy maker desires to assess. The forecasting scenario also includes the set of projects that the policy maker desires to evaluate, which usually includes housing affordability programs, changes in LU policy and new transportation plans, or combinations of these.

The model calculates the LU market equilibrium in the forecasting year and for the input scenario. The output yields the expected allocation of households and firms by cluster and zone, the consumers' benefits, and real estate rents. These outputs data allow the calculation of the profiles of several indices, which allows for the modeler to assess the city's performance for different scenarios, e.g., density profiles, sociospatial segregation (Gini), the gap between regulations and LU, or emergence of subcenters, spatial equity, etc. However, this model is positive (instead of normative), i.e., it simulates the expected changes after a policy or a set of projects but does not provide information about the "best city," a normative topic called optimal planning that is discussed later.

The Bid Function

Households and firms are modeled by cluster and a generic bid function for cluster h for real estate type v in zone i:

$$W_{hvi} = a_h + b_{hvi}(z_{vi}) + c_{vi} + d, \quad h \in C, \; v \in V, \; i \in I \tag{9.1}$$

Compared with the theoretical bids functions, these functions are amplified by the Gumbel shape parameter β, which remains implicit in the model, i.e., $W_{hvi} = \beta w_{hvi}$; thus, all terms in Eq. (9.1) are amplified by β. Note that because the shape parameter is implicit, then it is also implicit that this parameter is the same for all clusters, i.e., bids are i.i.d. Gumbel.

The term $a_h = \beta\left(y_h - \lambda_h^{-1} u_h\right)$ represents the bid component that is independent of the location so it is specific to the cluster only; $b_{hvi} = \beta\lambda_h^{-1} f(z_{vi})$ is the value of the location defined by the specific set of attributes $z_{vi} = (\{z_{kvi}\}, k \in K)$, where K is the set of real estate and zone attributes. In most applications, $b_{hvi}(z_{vi})$ is linear or polynomial in parameters. The term c_{vi} is constant for all agents and is specific to each location; it is intended to represent those variables with very similar values for all agents, which do not affect their relative preferences among consumers but do affect rents. d is constant across the LU market, adjusting all economic values (rents, utilities, and profits) to an absolute level; this value is adjusted ex post after the equilibrium is attained to match an exogenous rural land value.

The market equilibrium calculates the set $\left(\{a_h^*\}, \; h \in C\right)$ that clears the market, i.e., all consumer agents are allocated, and provides estimates of the relative utilities attained by each cluster. To obtain a unique solution, the modeler must set one term, e.g., $a_{h=1}^* = 0$. The equilibrium also solves the location externalities represented in the term b_{hvi}, attaining a stable solution for $z_{vi} = (\{z_{kvi}\}, k \in K)$. In the long-term application, the model also yields the real estate supply. Estimates of the economic impact of consumers' constraints and regulations are also estimated in the model outputs (see below).

Attributes

The set of attributes z_{vi} can be composed by exogenous and endogenous attributes. The definition of these attributes is contingent to the definition of the zoning system because larger zones define larger neighborhoods. However, this condition may be relaxed if required when zones are too small by defining neighborhoods as an aggregate of zones.

Exogenous attributes are independent of the allocation performed by the software, such as indices of access to the transportation system (distance to public transportation and to highways, availability of parking spaces, etc.), or to natural amenities (parks, rivers, coast front). For this subset of exogenous attributes, the term $b_{hvi}(z_{vi})$ is constant in the equilibrium algorithm.

Endogenous attributes are those that change at every iteration of the equilibrium algorithm because the agents' allocation change, such as average residents' income and density of specific firms in the neighborhood, which describe the set of pull and push forces that generate the cities dynamics. These forces are crucial in determining city structures as spatial segregation of socioeconomic clusters, hot spots or subcenters, and spatial clusters of specific industries. The functional form of $b_{hvi}(z_{vi})$ and the set of attributes z_{vi} is defined by the modeler, and they are specific for each cluster. These functions should be continuous and differentiable for the equilibrium to converge. This restriction permits specifying dummy variables in bid functions, which are frequently used in behavior models, if they are specific for clusters and real estate types, i.e., they are constants in the equilibrium algorithm, but they exclude conditions that generate step functions on endogenous variables, i.e., the bid value discontinuously jumps between two different values at threshold value of the attribute.

The transportation accessibility variables are exogenous attributes in this *LU* model, and the modeler can update these variables after the equilibrium using an external transportation model (T), inputting the predicted allocation of activities yielded by the *LU* model into T. Once the T model recalculates the number of trips and travel times on the network and updates the accessibility and attractiveness measures, these updated attributes are input in the *LU* model and the equilibrium is recalculated. This *LU-T* interactive procedure occurs through an automated transference of data files between models. The theory discussed in Chapter 6, particularly the results in Bravo et al. (2010), and experience with this iterative procedure shows that, if both models are based on MNL logit-choice functions, the sequence converges to a good approximation of steady-state equilibrium in few iterations and can be implemented using standard personal computers; this is not necessarily the case if other models are used in T, e.g., if the traffic assignment model is deterministic.

The Location Submodel

Bid-auction allocations are calculated using the *logit* model as:

$$H_{hvi} = H_h \frac{e^{W_{hvi}}}{\sum_{g \in B_{vi}} H_g e^{W_{gvi}}}$$
$$= H_h \frac{e^{a_h + b_{hvi}(z_{vi})}}{\sum_{g \in B_{vi}} H_g e^{a_g + b_{gvi}(z_{vi})}}, \quad h \in C, \; v \in V, \; i \in I \tag{9.2}$$

where B_{vi} is the set of agents that can be allocated in the real estate vi; this set is exogenously defined but can also be modeled as shown below. This set is defined by the modeler to exclude unfeasible allocations, e.g., manufacturing industry in small spaces or regulations that prohibit the location of some agents in specific areas. Note that Eq. (9.2) is invariant to the terms c and d of the bid function (Eq. 9.1), they cancel out. The matrix of spatial distribution of agents is defined as $M = (\{H_{hvi}\}, \; \forall h \in C, \; v \in V, \; i \in I)$. Note that endogenous attributes are functions of the bid-auction allocation, i.e., these attributes are expressed as $z_{vi} = f(\{H_{hvi}\}, \; \forall h \in C)$, so the model performs an iterative algorithm to solve the fixed-point problem $M = f(M)$ defined by Eq. (9.2).

The market equilibrium calculates the set of equilibrium values for parameters a_h, denoted by $\left(\{a_h^*\}, \; h \in C\right)$, that clears the market, i.e., all consumer agents are allocated, and provides the estimates of the relative utilities attained by each cluster. To obtain a unique solution, the modeler must set one term, e.g., $a_{h=1}^* = 0$, which defines the reference for all relative bids and rents. The equilibrium also solves the location externalities represented in the term b_{hvi} attaining a stable solution for $z_{vi} = (\{z_{kvi}\}, \; k \in K)$. In the long-term application, the model also yields the real estate supply. Estimates of the economic impact of consumers' constraints and regulations are also estimated in the model outputs (see below).

The condition established in Chapter 6 states that the shape parameter β must comply with the sufficient condition of being small enough for the model's equilibrium algorithm to converge to the unique solution (Bravo et al., 2010). This in not controlled ex ante by the user of the software because this parameter is embedded in the set of bids parameters estimated econometrically and imputed in the LU software. Therefore, the software's algorithm tests this condition to avoid lack of convergence. However, the experience shows that in real cities this condition holds, i.e., there is enough variance in agents' choices.

Consumers' decisions can be constrained by their exogenous incomes, denoted by y_h. The software applies the constrained multinomial logit (CMNL) technique

(Martínez et al., 2009; Castro et al., 2013) by introducing a cutoff factor or penalizing factor. In this case, the location model is modified as follows:

$$H_{hvi} = \frac{H_h \phi_{hvi}(y_h) e^{W_{hvi}}}{\sum\limits_{g \in B_{vi}} H_g \phi_{gvi}(y_g) e^{W_{gvi}}} = \frac{H_h e^{W_{hvi} + \ln\, \phi_{hvi}(y_h)}}{\sum\limits_{g \in B_{vi}} H_g e^{W_{gvi} + \ln\, \phi_{gvi}(y_g)}}, \quad h \in C, \ v \in V, \ i \in I \tag{9.3}$$

where the cutoff factor $\phi(y)$ penalizes the violation of constraints although it does not fully avoid choosing unfeasible choices; i.e., constraints are "softly complied" (see Chapter 4). Such a cutoff technique may be applied to implement other constraints on the consumer's behavior, such as imposing thresholds on attributes. Moreover, the modeler may define a set of constraints that are combined in a joint cutoff. An advantage of using the multinomial *logit* (MNL) cutoff, where $\phi(y)$ is a binomial *logit* function, is that Eq. (9.3) performs "appropriately" in the equilibrium; i.e., the equilibrium properties of existence, uniqueness, and convergence prevail in this formulation.

Rents

The profile of rents is calculated using the following *logsum* function of bids:

$$r_{vi} = \frac{1}{\beta} \ln \left(\frac{1}{S_{vi}} \sum_{h \in B_{vi}} H_h \, e^{(W_{hvi} + \ln\, \phi_{hvi}(y_h))} \right) = \frac{1}{\beta} \ln \left(\frac{1}{S_{vi}} \sum_{h \in B_{vi}} H_h e^{a_h + b_{hvi}(z_{vi}) + \ln\, \phi_{hvi}(y_h)} \right) + \frac{1}{\beta}(c_{vi} + d), \quad v \in V, \ i \in I \tag{9.4}$$

This equation uses estimates of the shape parameter β and the terms c and d of the bid functions, as discussed below.

Note that at equilibrium, the sum $a_h + b_{hvi}(z_{vi})$ is calculated for each modeled scenario, which has relevant impacts on predicted rents. This makes the rents consistent with the allocation of agents at equilibrium, including the effects of location externalities and agglomeration economies.

The set of income and other constraints and regulation affects rents. The former affects them directly by defining their upper bound values according to the profile of the population income and other thresholds; the latter affects them indirectly through the allocation and real estate development processes. Thus, rent adjustments incorporate the solution of the complex equilibrium of the city. This process makes the aggregate of rents in the city to scale with parameter β. Because this model is *logit*, the total rent follows the entropy scaling law: $R = \beta \ln N$, which can be verified from the model's outputs.

Real Estate Supply Submodel

While in the short-run application of the LU software, the modeled scenario is defined by policy options, demography, and real estate developments, in the long-run, the latter is calculated endogenously using the *logit* model:

$$S_{vi} = H\frac{e^{\mu\pi_{vi}}}{\sum\limits_{v'i' \in VI_i} e^{\mu\pi_{v'i'}}} = H\frac{e^{\mu(r_{vi}-C_{vi})}}{\sum\limits_{v'i' \in VI_i} e^{\mu(r_{v'i'}-C_{v'i'})}}, \quad v \in V, \ i \in I \tag{9.5}$$

where rent values are calculated using Eq. (9.4), and H is the population of agents in the modeled scenario, which assures that total supply equals total population.

The cost of a real estate indexed by vi, denoted by c_{vi}, is econometrically estimated exogenously as a function of the building characteristics and the input land value. Economies of scale may be considered in this model by embedding in this function the production size, i.e., $C_{vi} = C(S_{vi})$. Thus, the equilibrium algorithm includes Eq. (9.5) because it depends on endogenous rents and real estate development.

Regulations

This is an important matter in LU modeling because cities are usually subject to many regulations that limit the development of buildings and their use. In the model, regulations can be easily represented by cutoff factors in the supply Eq. (9.5), as follows:

$$\begin{aligned} S_{vi}(R_i) &= H\frac{\phi(R_{vi})e^{\mu\pi_{vi}}}{\sum\limits_{v'i' \in VI_i} \phi(R_{v'i'})e^{\mu\pi_{v'i'}}} \\ &= H\frac{e^{\mu(r_{vi}-C_{vi})+\ln \phi(R_{vi})}}{\sum\limits_{v'i' \in VI_i} e^{\mu(r_{v'i'}-C_{v'i'})+\ln \phi(R_{v'i'})}} \end{aligned} \tag{9.6}$$

where R_{vi} represents the constraint or bound imposed by the regulation on real estate vi.

Many of the usual regulations can be represented with this method but not all of them. As an example of those that can be feasibly represented, consider the most frequent regulation that constrains densities, which can be mathematically written as the following linear constraint:

$$\sum_{v \in V} q_v \rho_{vi} \le \rho_i \tag{9.7}$$

where q_v is a set of exogenous weighting factors of the density variable ρ_{vi} and ρ_i is the upper bound of the density. Because ρ_{vi} is a function of the supply, i.e., $\rho_{vi} = \rho(S_{vi})$, the cutoff is endogenous and the fixed-point Eq. (9.6) is solved by the software. An example of regulations that are not feasibly modeled are architectural regulations regarding building shapes.

The modeler may compose a set of cutoffs into a composite cutoff given by $\varphi(R_i) = \prod_{n \in R_i} \varphi(R_i^n)$, representing the set $R_i = (\{R_i^n\})$ of regulations in each zone i. Composing elemental cutoffs allows for the modeler to represent constraints on different subsets of agents and real estate types. For example, in some applications of the software, the cutoff technique has been used to implement multiple constraints on the development of building type, such as all or nothing dummies, and partial constraints such as a percentage of the land used by some building types.

Note that the CMNL's cutoffs make modeled supply comply only *softly* with the set of regulations at each zone; i.e., Eq. (9.6) does not guarantee that the regulation is fully complied with; it only induces the behavior of producers by adding the equivalent of an extra cost (or penalty) that increases as the regulation is violated.

The modeler may prefer to use an alternative method to impose *hard* compliance of regulations, such as capacity. In this case, the recommended algorithm is the entropy specification of the supply model given by:

$$S_{vi}(R_i) = S \frac{e^{\mu(r_{vi} - C_{vi}) - \gamma_i(R_i)}}{\sum\limits_{v'i' \in VI_i} e^{\mu(r_{v'i'} - C_{v'i'}) - \gamma_{i'}(R_{i'})}} \tag{9.8}$$

where the $\gamma_i(R_i) \geq 0$ parameters are the entropy *balancing factors* calculated following the method of Martínez and Henríquez (2007). Although this approach has the merit of imposing hard constraints, in contrast to the cutoff method, its impact on the LU equilibrium algorithm has only been studied empirically, without theoretical support for the uniqueness of the solution and convergence of the algorithm; this caveat may be problematic in more complex systems such as LUTE. However, the investigation with this heuristic showed that convergence to a stable solution is attained.

It is important to realize the role of regulations in the economic performance of the city. As discussed in Martínez et al. (2009), the value of the penalty (either a cutoff or a balancing factor) at equilibrium represents a measure of the economic value of the regulation. This implies that the modeler can simulate several scenarios describing different sets of planning regulations, including current regulations, to evaluate them against the economic and social impacts on the city. Because we proved that the unregulated system maximizes the utilitarian or Benthamite social welfare function, which adds agents' benefits $W = \sum_{h \in C} u_h + \sum_{i \in I} r_i$, then regulations can only reduce such welfare measures. Therefore, it is important to evaluate if the economic loss yield due to a regulation is compensated by other benefits that are not well represented by individual agents' behavior.

9.3 Parameter Estimation

The estimation of parameters in MNL models is well known in the econometric literature; recommended reading is Ben-Akiva and Lerman (1985) and Train (2009). In Chapters 4 and 5, we discussed the theoretical background of the bid-choice LU model, and in this section, we discuss the following specifics of the estimation of this model:

1. In contrast to most cases in the literature in which the MNL model is estimated to represent the demand under exogenous prices, in the LU model, prices or rents are endogenous and defined by the same set of willingness-to-pay functions estimated for the demand model. This implies that prices are endogenous in the utility and consumers' surplus functions, which requires specific methods for estimation of the choice models.
2. The set of real estate units, i.e., the set of goods demanded, is very large because it includes the spatial locations and real estate types, i.e., $|VI|$, which theoretically represent differentiated goods. This implies that goods attributes and the prices sets are both large. In addition to the difficulties in computation, data collection, and preparation, the econometric side is complex because the differentiation between real estates is relative, which implies correlation between attributes and prices, i.e., among locations in the same or neighbor zones. This topic has been termed Spatial Econometrics (Anselin, 2013).
3. The trade system is the auction. In Chapters 4 and 5, we discussed the equivalence between the choice and the bid-auction models, which provides two sets of equations to estimate willingness-to-pay parameters; in addition, the rent equation also depends on bids. Based on the theoretical equivalence, the modeler can use this set of equations to estimate the common set of willingness to pay such that the richness of the data is better captured by the estimated parameters.

The Set of Land-Use Equations

The bid-auction model described in Chapters 4 and 5 yields the following set of equations, in which we consider cutoff factors:

1. *The choice model* maximizes the consumer surplus, defined as the willingness to pay minus rent; its MNL model is:

$$H_{hvi} = \frac{S_{vi}e^{a_h+b_{hvi}(z_{vi})+c_{vi}+d+\ln\,\phi_{hvi}(y_h)-e_h r_{vi}}}{\sum\limits_{v'i'\in VI} S_{v'i'}e^{a_h+b_{hv'i'}(z_{v'i'})+c_{v'i'}+d+\ln\,\phi_{hvi}(y_h)-e_h r_{v'i'}}}$$

$$= \frac{S_{vi}e^{b_{hvi}(z_{vi})+c_{vi}-e_h r_{vi}}}{\sum\limits_{v'i'\in VI} S_{v'i'}e^{b_{hv'i'}(z_{v'i'})+c_{v'i'}-e_h r_{v'i'}}},\quad h\in C,\ v\in V,\ i\in I \tag{9.9}$$

where e_h is a parameter. In this equation, the agent's specific terms and constants, a_h, d, and $\ln\,\phi(y)$, cancel out and cannot be identified using this model. As mentioned previously, in this model the correlation problem between rents r_{vi} and the bid function terms $b_{hvi}(z_{vi})$ and c_{vi} is expected, which may cause biased estimated parameters.

The observed data used to estimate this model are (M, S, z, r): the agents' allocation data $M = (\{H_{hvi}\},\ \forall \in C, \forall vi \in VI)$; the supply pattern $S = (\{S_{vi}\},\ \forall vi \in VI)$; the set of attributes $z = (\{z_{vi}\},\ \forall vi \in VI)$; and the set of rents $r = (\{r_{vi}\},\ \forall vi \in VI)$. The maximum likelihood (ML) method is the standard to estimate the set of parameters of $b_{hvi}(z_{vi})$ and c_{vi} functions.

Notably, the choice model is particularly suitable to estimate parameters of variables that differentiate bids by location such as accessibility or densities because the denominator in Eq. (9.9) is defined for the space of locations; hence, its variability helps identify better estimates of these parameters.

The economic interpretation of this model is ambiguous. The terms in the exponents may represent utilities' or consumers' surplus, with different economic interpretations of its parameters. If they are interpreted as a utility function, then $e_h = \beta\lambda_h$, with λ_h the marginal utility of income, whereas if they are interpreted as a consumers' surplus, then $e_h = \beta$ because willingness-to-pay functions have no parameter for prices or rents. The ambiguity prevails unless β or λ_h is estimated independently of Eq. (9.9). This ambiguity does not affect the model calculations or parameter estimates but complicates the interpretation of parameters accompanying the rents.

Finally, we note that Eq. (9.9) assumes that rents are exogenous to the consumer, i.e., they behave as price takers, and considered deterministic; their value can be estimated by the expected value of rents. This assumption is necessary for the theoretical consistency of considering the consumers' surplus to be i.i.d. Gumbel and the choice mode to be MNL (see Chapter 4).

2. *The bid-auction model* maximizes bids and its MNL model is:

$$
\begin{aligned}
H_{hvi} &= \frac{H_h \delta_{hvi} e^{a_h + b_{hvi}(z_{vi}) + c_{vi} + d + \ln\,\phi_{hvi}(y_h)}}{\sum\limits_{g \in B_{vi}} H_g \delta_{gvi} e^{a_g + b_{gvi}(z_{vi}) + c_{vi} + d + \ln\,\phi_{gvi}(y_g)}} \\
&= \frac{H_h \delta_{hvi} e^{a_h + b_{hvi}(z_{vi}) + \ln\,\phi_{hvi}(y_h)}}{\sum\limits_{g \in C} H_g \delta_{gvi} e^{a_g + b_{gvi}(z_{vi}) + \ln\,\phi_{gvi}(y_g)}}, \quad h \in C,\ v \in V,\ i \in I
\end{aligned}
\tag{9.10}
$$

where the location-specific term c_{vi} and the constant d cancel out and cannot be identified in this model. This model allows estimation of the parameters of terms a_h and $b_{hvi}(z_{vi})$ and the cutoff factor $\ln\,\phi(y)$. The input data in this model are the same as in the choice model, although rents play no role in this model. In addition, the modeler defines the set of feasible locations for each cluster δ_{hvi}.

The standard method to estimate this model is the ML, which is particularly applicable here because the absence of rent variables eliminates the correlation problem in the choice model. Notably, the estimated parameters are affected by the cutoffs. This helps to avoid biased estimates caused by the problem of excluded variables, which occurs when H_{hvi} is very low or zero because in the absence of cutoffs, the ML model would wrongly attach the explanation of this observation to the attributes in $b(z_{vi})$ instead to the binding constraint ϕ_{gvi}.

3. *The rents model* in Eq. (9.4) allows estimation of all the parameters of bid functions. It is the only equation that allows for identifying the shape parameter β and constant d. Again, binding constraints aid in estimating unbiased parameters.

An advanced estimation methodology should consider the scaling law of rents and other indices. This additional information about the city performance at the aggregate level provides an estimate of the scale parameter by regressing $R = f(N)$, with $R = \beta \ln N$ if the model is *logit*. In terms of the contributions to the estimation, rents and population add no additional independent data, but this equation provides a very powerful condition for the estimate of the β-parameter, which is the same parameter for rents at the micro and macro spatial scales.

We conclude that the complete set of bid functions parameters of bid functions and the Gumbel shape parameter can be estimated using the set of equations (Eqs (9.4), (9.9), and (9.10)) and the scaling law. Lerman and Kern (1983) recognized this fact and developed an estimation method that combines the bid-auction model (Eq. 9.10) and rents (Eq. 9.4), defining the likelihood of the combined event: the agent's cluster and location and rents are both observed for each resident and firm. They defined the joint probability: $P_{hvi} = \text{Prob}\left(w_{hvi} + \varepsilon_{hvi} < w_{gvi} + \varepsilon_{gvi} \text{ and } r_{vi} = \max_{h \in B_{vi}} (w_{hvi} + \varepsilon_{vi}) \right)$ and applied this probability in the ML method. The use of the whole set of equations has not been reported, and its application eliminates the abovementioned ambiguity in the choice model regarding the interpretation of the rent parameter because β is also identified by the rent equations.

Experience Insights

Our experience applying the LU model in several cities, interacting with different transportation models, is worth being summarized.

The ready available data on cities are usually sufficient to estimate a simple model, but rent values may not be available or its quality may be questionable; in these cases, the modeler should judge the quality of data and apply an ad hoc estimation method. For example, if the quality of rent data is doubtful, a recommended methodology is to proceed in two steps: first, estimate the parameter using the ML method with bid-choice probabilities; second, use the estimated parameters to calculate a_h, $b_{hvi}(z_{vi})$, and the cutoff $\ln \phi(y_h)$; finally, use rents to estimate the remaining parameters. This two steps method is deliberately biased to reproduce the most trustful data, in this case the observed allocation of agents.

The available data may comprise a large variety of variables, which can allow for the modeler to capture agents' perceptions of real estate and location attributes. A diversity of parameters provides rich and direct estimates of the consumers' value of each attribute. However, many of these variables are highly correlated, and their independent contributions to explaining the location distribution and rents data may be negligible. In this common case, the modeler must choose the set of attributes that is most significant for the model application to reduce or eliminate biased estimates of parameters.

Finally, a list of some useful tips gathered from experience in estimating the model is as follows:

- The estimation samples should be statistically representative. They must provide a spatially undistorted distribution of location, rents, and supply in the study area.
- The real estate clusters and agent types must be properly observed with enough observations in the sample to allow the estimation of the bids parameters.
- Disaggregated samples usually are preferable than aggregated ones because their larger variability improves statistical significance of parameters and detection of wrong data is more evident.
- It is preferably to observe data where rent and location are simultaneously collected, which makes the theoretical relationship valid for the sample. If this is feasible, it is preferable to estimate location and rent models simultaneously (Lerman and Kern, 1983); if not, which is usually the case when location and rent are independent sources of data, then the modeler may consider a separate estimation procedure.
- Considering multiple access measures, regarding index definition and spatial scope, may improve the location model, e.g., time to access public transport and distance to the closest highway for the short distance accessibility, and opportunities within a distance and transport user's benefit measures for long distance.
- Large samples to have enough variability are important given the large number of parameters needing estimation.

9.4 Optimal Planning and Subsidies

Planning cities is an old, complex task that has critical impacts on human lives. The planning field is rich in interesting and diverse topics, such as crime, transportation quality, housing, public amenities, agglomeration economies, built environment, and accessibility, which reveal the diversity of matters in urbanites' lives and the complexity of city management for planners. However, there is a lack of scientific support of methodologies for planners to assist them in their work. In most cities, planning is performed by expert judgment and consists of setting many planning regulations, typically called zoning regulations because they are applied to regulate zones. Less common is the use of alternative methods of setting subsidies or taxes as economic incentives for agents to adjust their preferences in favor of a social goal.

Megacities (larger than 10 million inhabitants) face chronic problems such as congestion, social segregation, urban sprawl, high land values, crime, and environmental impacts. These are typically noted as problems of big cities, with a consequence of population reaction that claims to limit the size of cities. As we discussed in Chapter 8, cities are efficient factories of wealth and innovation, which justifies their existence and explains why bucolic towns eventually become megacities. Citizens may be uncomfortable with the costs of a city but certainly benefit from its opportunities.

In this section, we focus on how the *LU* model can contribute to urban planning by analyzing the data and informing planners about specific policy measures. LU and transport models have been used as tools to predict the impacts of planning policies by analyzing different planning scenarios (Hunt et al., 2005; Pagliara et al., 2010; Timmermans and Zhang, 2009; Wegener, 1994, 1998). These tools have contributed to the planners' work, providing a platform of scientific methods to analyze data and predict the expected impacts of planning scenarios. However, these tools assist in but do not solve the more complex problems of planners, leaving them unarmed to define optimal scenarios and identify good policy measures to implement them. These two tasks are called scenario definition, which is highly complex because of the large number of alternative scenarios and the difficulty of identification of optimal policies. To avoid defining and simulating scenarios, optimization models have been proposed for the utilitarian or Benthamite's social objective: maximize the aggregate of agents' benefits, which essentially internalizes traffic congestion such that the resulting equilibrium is optimum (Ma and Lo, 2012; Ying, 2015). Additionally, with the recent increasing availability of large urban databases, more sophisticated technology is required to exploit its richness in planning cities.

Building a more advanced mathematical tool to assist in planning cities in a wider set of social objectives implies tackling three basic problems: developing a methodology to define the optimal city plan in terms of the optimal allocation of residents and businesses in the city; identifying a methodology to define policy instruments to implement the plan, i.e., the set of regulations and incentives that lead the city to the optimum; and implementing these policies in an urban system model, such as LU, LUT, LUTE, or CLUTE, to simulate the system reaction to a set of policy instruments. Given that the last topic was discussed in previous chapters, we concentrate on the first two here, considering that the LU model is a bid-auction *logit* model. In this context, we follow the method of Briceño-Arias and Martínez (2018), which considers the following two problems: the planning problem, or the problem of identifying the optimal allocation, and the problem of calculating optimal subsidies.

The Planning Problem

The first problem we face is the definition of an "optimal city." From the residents' perspective, the city is full of difficulties and there are countless improvements to make; it is full of opportunities for developers, who desire relaxing of regulations and freeing of the market; for planners, there are many potential improvements, but resources are limited, and every plan is likely to yield winners and losers. Finding a consensus of what is the "optimal city" is a major difficulty. The scientific community has limited answers to this problem. For example, the standard answer for economists is to identify the city that maximizes welfare. This relies on a definition of welfare, which is usually assumed to be the utilitarian or Benthamite social welfare function because it simply adds the utilities and profits of all agents. In the LU system, this rule is attractive because, as discussed in Chapters 6 and 8, the utilitarian optimum is attained by the free auction market, although congestion externalities must be properly charged to transportation users. Thus, the market itself delivers the optimal city under the utilitarian goal. This social objective can be criticized by sociologists, as the utilitarian city disregards social effects such as inequality in the distribution of opportunities, and by ecologists, as it disregards environmental effects such as energy consumption and pollution. Although these effects may be considered externalities of the market and assessed in a more holistic welfare function, in this case, the market does not deliver the optimum city and policy measures must be implemented.

Some cities define the desired or optimum city using a participation process in which stakeholders share their views of an improved or optimal city, disregarding normative views. With that information, optimal city scenarios can be simulated with LU-T models to obtain several indices that participants can use to make informed choices. This approach has been welcomed when the community is concerned about ecological impacts.

The mathematical approach for the planning problem, proposed by Briceño-Arias and Martínez (2018), is useful to design optimal planning tools if the social objective can be described by a mathematical function $\psi(z,\cdot)$, where $z = (\{z_{hi}\},\ \forall h \in C,\ i \in VI)$ is the agents' value of location and real estate attributes. Although the existence of such a function is not guaranteed for every social objective, it is realistic in many cases and can be approximated in many others, providing interesting conceptual insights to the planning problem.

Consider a general class of objective functions whose optimal allocation, denoted by x^*, can be obtained by the algorithm provided in the cited paper. Denoted by $\mathcal{C}$, this class is defined as $\psi : \mathbb{R} \times [0, +\infty) \rightarrow (-\infty, +\infty)$ such that:

$$(\forall z \in \mathbb{R}) \begin{cases} \psi(z,\cdot) \text{is stricly convex} \\ \lim\limits_{x \rightarrow +\infty} \psi(z,x) = +\infty \end{cases} \tag{9.11}$$

where $x = (\{H_{hi}\},\ \forall h \in C, i \in VI)$ denotes the allocation pattern.

The primal problem is to

$$\underset{x \in \Xi}{\text{minimize}} \sum_{\substack{h \in C \\ i \in VI}} \psi_{hi}(z_{hi}, H_{hi}) \tag{9.12}$$

where Ξ denotes the equilibrium set discussed in Chapter 4, where:

$$\Xi = \left\{ \begin{array}{l} H_{hi} \in \mathbb{R}^{|C| \times |VI|},\ \ (\forall i \in VI), \sum\limits_{h \in C} H_{hi} \\ S_i,\ \ (\forall h \in C) \sum\limits_{i \in VI} H_{hi} = H_h \end{array} \right\} \tag{9.13}$$

and the objective function belongs to class $\mathcal{C}$, i.e., it is strictly convex and coercive.

The unconstrained *dual problem* is

$$\underset{(\overline{u}_h,r)\in\mathbb{R}^{|C|\times|VI|}}{\text{minimize}}\ \Phi(\overline{u},r):=\sum_{h\in C}H_h\overline{u}_h+\sum_{i\in VI}S_ir_i+\sum_{\substack{h\in C\\ i\in VI}}\varphi_{hi}(z_{hi},-\overline{u}_h-r_i)\quad(9.14)$$

where the function φ_{hi} is known as the Fenchel conjugate of ψ_{hi} and is also convex.[2] In Eq. (9.14), $(\overline{u},r)$ are the dual optimization variables, which can be interpreted as the utility and land rents in the bid-auction model. Note that it is invariant to the additive constant, i.e., $\Phi(\overline{u},r)=\Phi(\overline{u}+\alpha,\ r-\alpha)$. For the solution to be unique, the problem must be normalized, e.g., set $\overline{u}_{h=1}=0$; the same normalization was considered in the implementation of the abovementioned model.

For the variety of objective functions in class $\mathcal{C}$, the authors provide a general solution algorithm whose convergence is proven. The utilitarian or Benthamite social objective is a good example to analyze because it can be represented as a specific case of a function in class $\mathcal{C}$, defined by: $\psi_{hi}(z,x)=-xz+x(\ln x-1)/\beta$, for some $\beta\ \varepsilon\ (0,+\infty)$. Hence,

$$\underset{x\in\Xi}{\text{minimize}}\sum_{\substack{h\in C\\ i\in VI}}-H_{hi}z_{hi}+\frac{1}{\beta}H_{hi}(\ln H_{hi}-1)\quad(9.15)$$

which is the well-known entropy maximization problem that reproduces the bid-auction equilibrium problem in the *logit* model. The dual problem in this case is obtained by taking $\varphi_{hi}(z_{hi},y)\mapsto\psi_{hi}(z_{hi},\cdot)*(y):=e^{\beta(z+y)}$, which yields:

$$\underset{(\overline{u}_h,r)\in\mathbb{R}^{|C|\times|VI|}}{\text{minimize}}\sum_{h\in C}H_h\overline{u}_h+\sum_{i\in VI}S_ir_i+\sum_{\substack{h\in C\\ i\in VI}}e^{\beta(z_{hi}-\overline{u}_h-r_i)}\quad(9.16)$$

The first-order optimality conditions of this problem yield the following equilibrium conditions, previously formulated in Chapter 4, for the *logit* model:

$$\begin{aligned}\sum_{i\in VI}H_{hi}&=\sum_{i\in VI}e^{\beta(z_{hi}-\overline{u}_h-r_i)}=H_h\\ \sum_{h\in C}H_{hi}&=\sum_{h\in C}e^{\beta(z_{hi}-\overline{u}_h-r_i)}=S_i\end{aligned}\quad(9.17)$$

where $H_{hi}=e^{\beta(z_{hi}-\overline{u}_h-r_i)}$ and $\overline{u}_h$ and r_i are the unique solutions of the Lagrange multipliers of the equilibrium conditions in Eq. (9.13) and represent the willingness to

[2] See the proof in the appendix of Briceño-Arias and Martínez (2018).

pay and real estate price or rents of the bid-auction model, respectively, and are calculated from Eq. (9.17) as:

$$\bar{u}_h(z) = \frac{1}{\beta}\ln\left(\frac{1}{H_h}\sum_{i\in VI} e^{\beta(z_{hi}-r_i)}\right)$$
$$r_i(z) = \frac{1}{\beta}\ln\left(\frac{1}{S_i}\sum_{h\in C} e^{\beta(z_{hi}-\bar{u}_h)}\right) \tag{9.18}$$

where β represents the shape parameters of the Gumbel distribution of bids and explains the scaling law of rents. The reader may check that this are the same equations of the LUT equilibrium model.

Hence, this mathematical approach provides a methodology to calculate the optimal allocation of agents in the city, $x^* = (\{H^*_{hi}\}, \ \forall h\in C, \ i\in VI)$, for a large class of social objectives that can be expressed as a function of the location and real estate attributes. This social objective may be constructed from a combination of specific goals, allowing optimization of a multipurpose objective function.

Note that Eq. (9.17) assumes that transportation attributes are constant in the market equilibrium problem, i.e., the transportation system (T) is assumed to be exogenous, implying that congestion externalities are relevant in the planning problem. I the case that externalities are considered, e.g., in a total transportation cost minimization objective, then the methodology needs to be extended.

Optimal Subsidies

This problem seeks to identify a set of subsidies that leads to the optimal allocation defined in the planning problem, i.e., policy instruments that, once introduced, affect agents' location choices, inducing the optimal allocation through the market. Here, subsidies generically refer to positive or negative (taxes) transfers from the government to the agent or viseversa. We analyze two sets of subsidies: the feasible sets include all sets of subsidies that yield the optimal allocation and the optimal set is a feasible set that complies with an additional criterion defined by the planner to select from the feasible set.

A feasible subsidy set, denoted by $s = (\{s_{hi}\}, \ h\in C, \ i\in VI)$, is a positive or negative money quantity given to the agents such that the market equilibrium is attained at the optimal allocation. That is, subsidies allow for the planner to decentralize the optimal allocation of agents.

The following result asserts that for any desired optimal allocation of agents in the city, (x^*), and for $\alpha = (\{\alpha_h\}, h\in C)$, with $\alpha_{h=1} = 0$ and $\rho = (\{\rho_i\}, i\in VI)$ as arbitrary vectors, the set of feasible subsidies complies with:

$$s_{hi}(\alpha_h, \rho_i) = \frac{1}{\beta}\ln H^*_{hi} + \alpha_h + \rho_i - z_{hi} \tag{9.19}$$

Moreover, the unique solution of the market equilibrium with subsidies, with $\overline{u}_{h=1} = 0$, is: $\overline{u}_h(z + s(\alpha, \rho)) = \beta_h$ and $r_i(z + s(\alpha, \rho)) = \rho_i$. This result implies the following:

1. Every desired allocation can be obtained through market auctions by implementing a feasible set of subsidies that comply with Eq. (9.19);
2. Because α and ρ are arbitrary vectors, the set of feasible subsidies is large, which leaves the planner with the task of selecting the most convenient policy;
3. At the market equilibrium with subsidies, utilities and rents depend on the subsidy policy, which means that each policy yields a different distribution of benefits across the agents and, by choosing the policy, the planner can define who gains and who loses as a result of the policy.

The subsidized market equilibrium can be interpreted as the standard solution of the bid-auction equilibrium, in which agents' perceptions of attributes are modified by the planner to $z' = z + s(\alpha,\rho)$ such that the agents modify their bids to attain the desired optimal allocation.

Notably, optimal allocation is attained by feasible subsidies both with and without location externalities and agglomeration economies; i.e., it is attained when $z' = z(x^*) + s(\alpha, \rho)$. Despite the complexity of the externalities in the equilibrium problem, this statement is straightforward because the feasible subsidies are calculated in Eq. (9.19) for an optimal allocation x^*, which is exogenous to the equilibrium problem, i.e., $z(x^*)$ is constant when setting the optimal subsidies. Therefore, the problem of defining the set of feasible subsidies, whose solution is given in Eq. (9.19), is valid in the more complex case of location externalities and agglomeration economies.

The large set of feasible subsidies leaves the planner with the task of selecting a criterion to choose which vector of subsidies is optimal to implement as the policy instrument. Because this choice has relevant impacts on equity issues, i.e., it defines who is subsidized and who is taxed, this criterion is critical. It is also realistic to consider that the planner's flexibility is limited by external political constraints on the implementation of subsidy policies. Briceño-Arias and Martínez (2018) analyze this topic by studying and simulating the following policy criteria:

1. Zero impact. Set subsidies such that utilities and rents remain unchanged compared with the unsubsidized equilibrium, i.e., no winners and no losers. The optimal subsidies in this case are:

$$s_{hi}(\alpha_h, \rho_i) = \frac{1}{\beta} \ln H^*_{hi} + \overline{u}_h(z) + r_i(z) - z_{hi} \tag{9.20}$$

   with overlined u as in the equation: with $u_h(z)$ utilities and $r_i(z)$ rents at equilibrium, respectively, ex ante the subsidies.
2. Minimize transfers. Set subsidies that minimize the total subsidies plus taxes by solving the following optimization problem:

$$\begin{aligned} &\underset{\alpha,\rho}{minimize} \sum_{\substack{h \in C \\ i \in VI}} s^2_{hi}(\alpha_h, \rho_i) \\ &s.t. \quad SD(\alpha_h, \rho_i) \leq \varepsilon \end{aligned} \tag{9.21}$$

where $SD(\alpha_h, \rho_i) = \sum_{h \in C} (\alpha_h - \bar{u}_h)^2 + \sum_{i \in VI} (\rho_i - r_i)^2$ measures the social disturbance induced by the subsidy policy, which is constrained by an upper political tolerance ε. Note that this problem is feasible because there is a pair of vectors (α,ρ) such that $s_{hi}(\alpha_h,\rho_i) = 0$, $\forall h \in C, i \in VI$, which complies with the tolerance. The solution of this problem yields (α_h^*, ρ_i^*), which allows computing optimal subsidies as:

$$s_{hi}(\alpha_h, \rho_i) = \frac{1}{\beta} \ln H_{hi}^* + \alpha_h^* + \rho_i^* - z_{hi} \tag{9.22}$$

3. Minimum disturbance with budget constraints. Set subsidies by solving:

$$\begin{aligned} & \underset{\alpha,\rho}{minimize}\, SD(\alpha_h, \rho_i) \\ & s.t. \sum_{i \in VI} s_{hi}(\alpha_h, \rho_i) \le B_h, \quad \forall h \in C \\ & \sum_{\substack{h \in C \\ i \in VI}} s_{hi}(\alpha_h, \rho_i) \le B \end{aligned} \tag{9.23}$$

where B_h is the budget for each agent cluster, i.e., the cluster cannot be overtaxed, and B is the planners' budget; this problem is also feasible.

4. Constrained subsidies. The following cases are studied, where the planner applies policies that comply with exogenous political or other constraints (here the condition $\alpha_{h=1} = 0$ is relaxed):

a. One cluster should not be affected. Define this cluster as $h = 1$, and the policy is formulated defining its utility as $\alpha_1 = \bar{u}_h(z)$ and subsidies at $s_{1i}(\alpha_1,\rho_i) = 0$, $\forall i \in VI$, yields:

$$\rho_i = z_{1i} - \frac{1}{\mu} \ln H_{1i}^* - \bar{u}_h(z), \quad \forall i \in VI \tag{9.24}$$

The planner retains the flexibility to choose the subvector $\{\alpha_h\}_{h \neq 1}$.

b. One zone should not be affected. Define this zone as $i = 1$, and the policy is formulated defining its rents at $\rho_1 = r_i(z)$ and subsidies $s_{h1}(\alpha_h, \rho_1) = 0$, $\forall h \in C$, which yields:

$$\alpha_h = z_{h1} - \frac{1}{\mu} \ln H_{h1}^* - r_i(z), \quad \forall h \in C \tag{9.25}$$

The planner retains the flexibility to choose the subvector $\{\rho_i\}_{i \neq 1}$.

c. Self-funded policy by cluster, or zero clusters' cross-subsidies. i.e., total subsidies equal total taxes in each cluster. This condition is attained if: $\sum_{i \in VI} s_{hi}(\alpha_h, \rho_i) = 0$, $\forall h \in C$, which holds by setting $(\{\rho_i\}, \forall i \in VI)$ such that $\frac{1}{|VI|} \sum_{i \in VI} \rho_i = \theta$ and:

$$\alpha_h = \frac{1}{|VI|} \sum_{i \in VI} \left(z_{hi} - \frac{1}{\mu} \ln H_{hi}^* \right) - \theta, \quad \forall h \in C \tag{9.26}$$

The planner has the flexibility to choose a reference level of utilities by setting $\theta \in \mathbb{R}$.

d. Self-funded policy by zone, or zero spatial cross-subsidies, i.e., total subsidies equal total taxes in each zone. This condition is attained if: $\sum_{h \in C} s_{hi}(\alpha_h, \rho_i) = 0, \quad \forall i \in VI$, which holds setting $(\{\alpha_h\}, \forall h \in C)$ such that $\frac{1}{|C|} \sum_{h \in C} \alpha_h = \theta$ and:

$$\rho_i = \frac{1}{|C|} \sum_{h \in C} \left(z_{hi} - \frac{1}{\mu} \ln H_{hi}^* \right) - \theta, \quad \forall i \in VI \tag{9.27}$$

The planner has the flexibility to choose a reference level of rents by setting $\theta \in \mathbb{R}$.

Planning to Reduce Social Exclusion

Reducing social exclusion (SE), or maximizing inclusion, is a common objective of planners, particularly in less developed countries, and is one of the most difficult to address in urban planning. The difficulty arises because the real estate market mechanism naturally spatially segregates clusters because it is the natural outcome of individuals' preferences to reside among peers, a pull force for peers and push force for unequals, particularly in contexts with significant socioeconomic differences. The effect of this behavior is an increase in land rents in wealthy areas, which makes it unaffordable for the poor; this phenomenon occurs without the intervention of anybody, it is the natural outcome of economic forces in the spatial context. The social goal of reducing exclusion can be pursued by implementing optimal subsidies, which provides a good example of a case of the optimal planning problem.

Let us define an index of SE as:

$$SE = \sum_{i \in VI} \left(\frac{1}{S_i} \sum_{h \in C} H_{hi} I_h - I \right)^2 \tag{9.28}$$

which is null if the average socioeconomic index at each zone, defined by $\frac{1}{S_i} \sum_{h \in C} H_{hi} I_h$, is homogenous and equal to the average income in the city, given by $\left(I = \frac{1}{|C|} \sum_{h \in C} H_h I_h \right)$. The planner can select any socioeconomic index, I_h, for example, the cluster's income.

Note that *SE* increases with income segregation but it is not separable, i.e., it cannot be written as the separable and convex function in Eq. (9.12). To manage this technical issue, the authors define an auxiliary index, called the segregation level by zone $SL_i(x)$ and for the city $SL(x)$, defined as:

$$SL_i(x) = \sum_{h \in C} I_h \left(\frac{H_{hi}}{S_i} - \frac{H_h}{|C|} \right)^2 \text{ and } SL(x) = \sum_{i \in VI} SL_i(x) \tag{9.29}$$

which is a useful property because the unique minimizer of *SL* is also a minimizer of *SE*.

The social objective is defined as twofold, combining the social goal of minimizing SE with the agents' objective of maximizing utility. Because these objectives may be in conflict, it is necessary to define a parameter that weights the relative social value of these objectives, denoted as η. Then, the social objective function is defined as:

$$\underset{x \in \Xi}{\text{minimize}} - \sum_{\substack{h \in C \\ i \in VI}} H_{hi} z_{hi} + \frac{1}{\eta} \sum_{\substack{h \in C \\ i \in VI}} I_h \left(\frac{H_{hi}}{S_i} - \frac{H_h}{|C|} \right)^2 \tag{9.30}$$

where Ξ is the set of market-clearing conditions. Note that the problem in Eq. (9.30) is a case of the planning problem (Eqs 9.11 and 9.12) where $\psi(x) = -xz_{hi} + I_h \left(\frac{x}{S_i} - \frac{H_h}{|C|} \right)^2$, where the function $\psi(x)$ is in class $\mathcal{C}$. Therefore, it follows that the problem in Eq. (9.30) has a unique solution x^*_η called the *inclusion optimum* and a unique pair of utilities and rents $\left(\alpha^*_\eta, \rho^*_\eta \right)$, under the additional condition that $\alpha^*_{1,\eta} = 0$.

Because the segregation level at the optimum is expected to increase with η, the authors analyze this relationship and conclude that the increase of segregation with η is quadratic.

This is a good example of how the planning problem may be intuitively straightforward, as it is minimizing SE, but technically difficult to implement, as in cases in which it is necessary to formulate an auxiliary optimization problem.

Regulations

An alternative policy instrument to attain social goals in cities is to regulate the market, forcing the solution to comply with rules associated with the objective. The typical example is limiting the building density in a zone, i.e., a maximum floor space per land unit. In practice, the implementation of this policy is ad hoc, i.e., a specific regulation is implemented for each purpose based on expert judgment. Although this simple approach is easy to understand, its consequences are very difficult to assess and evaluation typically ignored.

Because the city is a complex system, any single regulation affects the area regulated by it and also has an impact in the rest of the city because it changes the equilibrium conditions. For example, consider a regulation that limits the building density in the city center. The direct effect is that the area tends to be developed up to the regulated density, leading to higher rents on the old and new real estate units as a consequence of scarce supply relative to its demand. This impact has further indirect and unintended consequences in the rest of the city, where demand increases compared with the unregulated situation inducing higher densities and rents. There are also impacts on traffic because the population resides further from the city center, and on the relocation of businesses, i.e., there is a new equilibrium in the LUTE systems that is complex to assess. This difficulty does not mean that regulations should not be recommended. Although they are easy to understand and politically simple to implement (mainly because they are common practice), their full impacts are very difficult to predict.

Theoretically, we can analyze regulation policies as equivalent to subsidies, although less flexible. The equivalence can be explained by recalling the regulation topic in Section 9.2 in this chapter. Regulations are represented in the *LU* equilibrium by introducing penalizing factors in bid functions when they regulate consumers' choices and in profit functions when the regulation constrains real estate developments. Thus, we conclude that every regulation can be fulfilled by an adequate set of subsidies and taxes. Regulations differ from subsidies in that administrative rules are less flexible in their definition: subsidies can easily be defined for each tuple (h,v,i), whereas regulations are more aggregate policies. The amount of subsidies can be easily adjusted over time, whereas regulations are more stable policies. Subsidies can be accommodated to accomplish equity goals, whereas regulations are difficult to differentiate among clusters.

Every regulation has an equivalent set of penalizing factors, which represents the economic value for agents of the regulation at equilibrium. For example, in Eq. (9.8), $\gamma_i(R_i)$ is the balancing factor representing the Lagrange multiplier of regulation R_i, and its value at equilibrium represents the shadow price of this regulation; i.e., it measures the impact on social welfare caused by the regulation; the same conclusion applies when regulations are represented by cutoffs using the CMNL, as proposed by Martínez et al. (2009).

We conclude that zoning regulations can be modeled in the *LU* model to estimate their impact on the agents' allocation profile to evaluate their contribution to specific social goals and to assess the market economic value of each regulation. If regulations have been defined without the proper analysis of their economic impact, as is typical, it is plausible that some of them may be imposing nonintended costs to society that have been ignored. Optimal regulations can be designed using the same methodology described for optimal subsidies.

Planning Policies and the Scale Law

Because regulations and subsidies imply welfare losses if measured using the standard utilitarian definition, i.e., the Benthamite measure, it raises the question about the impact of these policies on the scaling of rents and other socioeconomic indices.

Notably, this is an important advanced topic for research. It is straightforward to analyze the direct impact of these policies on rents using equation (Eq. 9.4):

$$r_{vi} = \frac{1}{\beta}\ln\left(\frac{1}{S_{vi}(R_i)}\sum_{h\,\in\,B_{vi}} H_h\, e^{a_h+b_{hvi}(z_{vi})+\ln\,\phi_{hvi}(\tau)+c_{vi}+d}\right),\quad v\in V,\ i\in I \qquad (9.31)$$

where R_i are supply regulations and τ represents the set of constraints affecting consumers' behavior and $\ln \phi_{hvi}(\tau)$ is the associated composite penalty. Consider $\frac{\partial r_{vi}}{\partial R_i} = \frac{\partial r_{vi}}{\partial S_{vi}} \frac{\partial S_{vi}}{\partial R_i} \geq 0$, because $\frac{\partial r_{vi}}{\partial S_{vi}} < 0$ and $\frac{\partial S_{vi}}{\partial R_i} \leq 0$, where ∂R_i implies making the regulation more constraining; then, we conclude that binding development regulations induce an increase in prices. Additionally, taking $\frac{\partial \varphi}{\partial \tau} < 0$, i.e., the penalty increases as the consumer's constraint is binding, then $\frac{\partial r_{vi}}{\partial \tau} = \frac{\partial r_{vi}}{\partial \phi} \frac{\partial \phi}{\partial \tau} < 0$ because $\frac{\partial r_{vi}}{\partial \phi} > 0$; i.e., LU regulations induce a reduction on demand and thus on prices. However, in this last case, reduced demand on some regulated locations implies relocation of demand to locations with spare capacity where prices increase; thus, the aggregate effect is ambiguous and may not be in the direction of reducing aggregate rents.

At the microlevel, the impact of planning policies is difficult to access without simulating the urban equilibrium. At the aggregate city level, the scaling law of rents with population prevails, although its parameters may be affected by the optimizing policy; i.e., the speed of the development is a matter of further analysis comparing the impacts of different policies.

Remarks

The planning problem can be defined as an open problem in the sense that there is no consensus on the social objective that societies should pursue. The utilitarian approach is typically followed by economists and has the merit of easy implementation by allowing for the free market to operate, but the planner must implement policies to internalize congestion externalities in travelers' choices, i.e., implement optimal transportation charges.

However, the utilitarian solution falls short of a shared perception of the best city, which is obvious from the number of regulations that operate in cities. However, if regulations are not properly assessed using an economically sound model of the LU market, the benefits of regulations cannot be taken for granted.

The complexity of the urban system makes planning difficult. This chapter describes a methodology to solve this problem for a set of social objectives that can be formulated as a function that belongs to a defined class, which is applicable for a variety of social objectives. For any feasible optimal allocation, there is a set of optimal subsidies that leads the market to attain the optimal allocation solution, i.e., there are policy instruments to implement the optimal planned city.

However, these tools face implementation constraints. The optimal city may require redeveloping a large part of the city, which implies a high investment and cultural and political costs that must be balanced by the benefits of the plan and should be financially feasible. To avoid excessive costs, the planning problem may be designed to optimize future developments or set limited impacts on the current allocation of agents, i.e., the optimal plan is conditional on the state of development of the city.

References

Anselin, L., 2013. Spatial Econometrics: Methods and Models. Springer Science & Business Media.

Ben-Akiva, M.E., Lerman, S.R., 1985. Discrete Choice Analysis: Theory and Application to Travel Demand, vol. 9. MIT press.

Bravo, M., Briceño, L., Cominetti, R., Cortés, C., Martínez, F., 2010. An integrated behavioral model of the land-use and transportation systems with network congestion and location externalities. Transportation Research Part B 44, 584–596.

Briceño-Arias, L.M., Martínez, F., 2018. Land Use Planning and Optimal Subsidies. Working Paper Available upon Request. https://200.27.27.49/fmartinez/bm_subsidies_2018.pdf.

Castro, M., Martínez, F., Munizaga, M., 2013. Estimation of a constrained multinomial logit model. Transportation 40, 563–581.

Hunt, J.D., Kriger, D.S., Miller, E.J., 2005. Current operational urban land-use-transport modelling frameworks: a review. Transport Reviews 25 (3), 329–376.

Lerman, S.R., Kern, C.R., 1983. Hedonic theory, bid rents, and willingness-to-pay: some extensions of Ellickson's results. Journal of Urban Economics 13 (3), 358–363.

Ma, X., Lo, H.K., 2012. Modeling transport management and land use over time. Transportation Research Part B 46, 687–709.

Martínez, F.J., Aguila, F., Hurtubia, R., 2009. The constrained multinomial logit: a semi–compensatory choice model. Transportation Research Part B 43, 365–377.

Martínez, F.J., Henríquez, R., 2007. A random bidding and supply land-use equilibrium model. Transportation Research Part B 41, 632–651.

Pagliara, F., Preston, J., Simmonds, D., 2010. Residential location choice: models and applications. Springer-Verlag, Berlin Heidelberg.

Timmermans, H.J.P., Zhang, J., 2009. Modeling household activity travel behavior: example of the state of the art modeling approaches and research agenda. Transportation Research Part B 43, 187–190.

Train, K.E., 2009. Discrete Choice Methods with Simulation. Cambridge University Press.

Wegener, M., 1994. Operational urban models: state of the art. Journal of the American Planning Association 60 (1), 17–29.

Wegener, M., 1998. Models of urban land use, transport and environment. In: Lundqvist, L., Mattsson, L.-G., Kim, T.J. (Eds.), Network Infrastructure and the Urban Environment. Advances in Spatial Science. Springer-Verlag, Berlin Heidelberg.

Ying, J.Q., 2015. Optimization for multiclass residential location models with congestible transportation networks. Transportation Science 49 (3), 452–471.

FAQs and Policy Analysis

10

10.1 Introduction

The complexity of urban systems described in previous chapters has generated many persistent questions regarding cities from several disciplines, such as geography, economy, sociology, urbanism, transportation, and, more recently, physics.

In this chapter, we provide direct and simple answers to a selection of these frequently asked questions to demonstrate how to employ the model described in this book as a conceptual, rather than mathematical, model. They are limited to the scope and validity of the CLUTE model, which is subject to further testing and research to expand its analysis potential.

10.2 How Cities Grow?

The objective of this book is answering this intriguing question. The answer can be obtained from the model, although it is dispersed across the chapters so it is worthy to explain here the growth mechanics of cities.

The first essential driver of cities' growth is demography, a permanent natural process that generates new humans so population increases; this is the essential energy of cities' growth. This process is multiplicative, although its rule is a simple rate of births and deaths, which implies that larger cities tend to grow faster. The rest of the mechanism explains how population generates cities of different sizes.

This mechanism is migration, which distributes population in a way that leads to highly uneven city sizes, a phenomenon difficult to understand with linear thinking because it is in fact a manifestation of complexity; I recommend reading West's book (2017). The migration mechanism is simple: agents migrate to the city that provides them the highest socioeconomic benefits to attain the following equilibrium condition: *households of the same socioeconomic level perceive the same utility anywhere in the country; firms of the same industry—same technology—obtain the same profit in all cities where production exists*. In other words, benefit differentials between cities induce migration until they disappear.

However, migration must match with job opportunities. The creation of jobs depends on production growth, the spatial distribution of natural resources, and technology innovation. Whereas production increases nonlinearly with population and industries that exhibit economies of scale concentrate in larger cities; such industries are not attracted to small cities where production of low or no economies of scale industries emerges, usually services to consumers and the exploitation of some natural resources. Additionally, socioeconomic location externalities and business agglomeration economies make

Microeconomic Modeling in Urban Science. https://doi.org/10.1016/B978-0-12-815296-6.00010-X

that richer households and larger firms benefit from a larger population. Then, there is circular mechanism: production and high-wage jobs increase faster in larger cities, inducing a higher migration, making larger cities grow faster.

Nevertheless, in large cities, there are also deterrent forces or costs, such as crime, diseases, congestion, and environmental impacts, that also increase superlinearly with population. Then, it is essential to understand that differential net benefits for urbanites across the country are captured in differential land rents if migration is free. That is, land rents and real estate prices increase superlinearly with population, such that households' net benefits (utilities) tend to be equalized across the country; business profits net of land rents are also equalized spatially, but in this case, some industries only develop in larger cities, defining a hierarchical or fractal structure of production in the space.

10.3 Why Cities Do not Collapse into a Single City or a City into a Single Building?

This question follows naturally from the scaling productivity and welfare with city size, which implies that higher densities are more efficient factories. A partial answer is because deterrent forces balance out superlinear production and creativity. In the case of a system of cities, there is also a second factor because natural resources and amenities are distributed unevenly across the country, which generates agricultural and other jobs in rural areas, attracting some population everywhere. This low-density rural population is served by small towns distributed in the country to minimize transportation costs of rural population, with production of consumers' services with no or very low economies of scale, which offer no significant agglomeration economies; these towns are served in turn by medium-size cities where industries with larger economies of scale and agglomeration economies emerge; finally, there is always a large city that concentrates production with higher economies of scale and offers larger agglomeration economies and salaries. These factors explain why total population does not collapse into one single city.

In the case of the city, we may naively think that one or very few giant buildings would maximize superlinear productivity by reducing transportation costs and increasing human interaction. However, high-density residence induces a higher concentration of waste and pollution, crowding and congestion on stairs and elevators, and the per capita perception of crime. Indeed, consider a system with two cities with the same population size but different in area and densities such that the push and pull forces are different and the system would not attain equilibrium.

In sum, coupling economies of scale and agglomeration economies makes the push—centripetal—superlinear force that creates large cities, whereas the superlinear negative factors, the dispersion of natural resources, and amenities coupled with transport cost build the push—centrifugal forces. Combined, they create a hierarchy of cities in size and limit their densities. These microeconomic forces explain the universality of fractal urban systems and their scaling power laws.

10.4 Are Universal Scaling Laws Paradoxical?

Although this question was briefly discussed in the previous chapter, it is of such importance that it is worth commenting further here.

We have shown that the dynamics of cities' macroscale indicators can be described by the power laws, but what is surprising is that the power law exponent is superlinear and its value belongs to a very narrow range. This universal law has increasing empirical and theoretical support. Such behavior of cities emerges *naturally* from human rational behavior, which we have shown is enough to demonstrate the socioeconomic origin of this law. We have remarked that this elemental rational force is universal because it defines humans, therefore it is coherent with a universal macroscale performance.

This statement seems to be somehow controversial regarding the commonly assumed condition that humans enjoy *freedom of choice* because one may expect that such freedom would naturally induce a plethora of different dynamics of humans' basic organization, the city. Then, apparently, freedom of choice and universal dynamics are paradoxical statements.

However, our microeconomic model embeds what seems to be a plausible coherent explanation: free choices are encapsulated in a market process that yields a universal dynamic; i.e. we are free to choose among a finite set of feasible choices. The word *free* in our model means that preferences and utilities are different and specific to each individual, i.e., without many constraints, whereas *feasible* is the key word for the explanation of the emergent universal law and it represents the word *market* in our economic model. Despite the freedom of choice, the feasible choice set is defined by the alternatives that the technology provides in the market, subject to the consumer's economic affordability, which is defined by equilibrium prices of goods and services and salaries. Then, the market imposes a homogenizing condition: agents' rational behavior leads to maximum utilities and profits, which are equal across alternative locations, both within the city and across cities. In Chapter 9 we proved that this market equilibrium condition explains why land rents and real estate prices, production, and wages must follow a superlinear power law. Because this explanation is valid independently of the specific preferences of residents and firms, the universal dynamic depends exclusively on the agents' rationality, i.e., the maximization of individuals' welfare and firms' profits, in a common and interdependent spatial system, despite the significant and rich diversity of the underpinning preferences in the populations and across cultures.

Individuals' preferences and culture, and their realization as free choice making, prevail at the microscale of cities. This is easy to observe in the diversity of building shapes and mixture of activities at a local level within a city, as well as in the diversity of cities' historical buildings. Think, for example, of New York, San Francisco, and Los Angeles; or London, Paris, and Rome; or Brasilia, Rio de Janeiro, and Sao Paulo; or Beijing, Seoul, and Tokyo. They are so very different that tourists enjoy visiting them, but they all follow the same scaling law.

Hence, the initially paradoxical statements have a rational explanation: individuals' differences are expressed as local differences, but their common rational interaction on the land market leads to a universal attractor on urban systems: the well-known power law in organic complex systems.

10.5 Are Megacities Too Large?

This question is usually rhetorical, implying the answer: yes, megacities are excessively large. This answer is usually intuitive or based on partial statistics of few indicators such as crime, congestion, and psychological stress. However, to provide a more scientific answer we first need to define what is an *optimal city* and analyze the impacts of city size on the system complexity; otherwise, the answer is dangerously biased. In Chapter 9, the discussion of this topic reveals that there is no unique definition of an optimal city, which implies that the answer to our question is contingent on the definition of the optimal city.

In Chapter 8, we conclude that cities are "magnificent factories" that can produce superlinear benefits to the society but also negative impacts such as crime. A large city is much more productive per capita than a small city, a universally valid conclusion. This is equivalent to a *gravitational social force* that explains and justifies why households freely decide to live in megacities instead of moving to less dense towns or rural areas, in spite of their negative impacts.

The metaphor of a gravitational social force is useful to understand why humans agglomerate in cities and we can also use it to analyze planning policies. For example, if the planners' objective were to develop only medium-sized cities with similar services and production, it would be equivalent to deciding that the planets and stars should be equally spaced in the universe, which requires spending a formidable amount of energy to neutralize the gravitational force. Beyond the validity of this metaphor, the relevant argument is that society would need to spend resources to fight against the social gravity force. Despite different regulatory regimes and economic setups, large and megacities develop in every country in the world.

The argument of a gravitational social force should be discussed before taking it for granted. First, it is derived from the acceptance of scaling laws, which are currently subject to the scrutiny of scholars; see Chapter 8. Second, even if the existence of a scaling law is agreed on, the following philosophical question arises: is the gravitational law the consequence of our social or economic rules? More specifically, would another economic system yield a similar result? This question is beyond the scope of this book; notably, the gravitational social force appears to operate within the current socioeconomic system and we have no evidence of other system to give a scientific answer. However, the theory of this book let us speculate that any economic system that respects rational behavior is likely to yield a similar universal law, although its parameters may be different.

Within this philosophical context, the planner must make decisions with awareness of the gravitational social force to avoid excessive costs. The recommendation is to generate a social process that provides answers regarding the optimal city and apply policy measures that lead to that goal. However, the planner should make this process politically sustainable and economically informed so that the costs and benefits are permanently monitored. Political sustainability is a matter for sociology experts, and the economic information should provide the population and decision-makers the best possible prediction of the positive impacts and associated costs of each definition of an optimal city, which can be obtained using analytical models such as CLUTE.

10.6 Is Urban Sprawl a Tragedy?

The general answer is similar to the previous answer: it depends on the definition of the best or optimal city. However, it is useful to examine this classical question in more detail.

The undesired impacts of urban sprawl are primarily the land taken from rural activities and the increased transport costs for citizens. In purely economic terms, the answer in both cases is straightforward: if land is freely traded, households and firms optimize their location, inducing an utilitarian or Benthamite's social optimum; this ignores some externalities, which can be exceptionally be made endogenous, as for traffic congestion if optimal road pricing policies are introduced, but other regulation policies are required to handle environmental impacts. If agricultural land is converted into urban land, there are economic justifications regarding the highest value of the land use (LU), but other ecological impacts are relevant to consider, such as the concentration of pollutants and lack of percolation of water into the land due to concrete coverage in cities.

The evidence regarding the alleged transportation costs is not clear. First, if transportation costs increase, they must be overcome by other benefits yielded by the city, otherwise migration begins to reduce the population and transportation costs; second, those residing in the periphery who pay larger transportation costs are compensated by lower rents and other amenities such as lower densities. Third, the cumulative impact of urban sprawl on social welfare is rarely studied in a comprehensive manner. For example, using a LUTE-type model, Anas and Xu (1999) found that the effect of urban sprawl is relatively small when considering the relocation of jobs as the city increases; i.e., there is a misconception of the potential transportation impacts of urban sprawl, which is associated with assuming cities as monocentric, where all workers and shoppers commute to the city center; these views may be different if a polycentric city is considered.

The economic analysis is only consistent for those that can choose between cities and locations in the city, which excludes the very poor. The economic model discussed in this book assumes that all consumers select their optimal choice, so the conclusions exclude those who cannot make independent choices. The decision-maker should consider this when implementing policies including the equity issues and to properly assess the impacts of the city sprawl.

Thus, the standard economic view is insufficient to analyze urban sprawl because it does not account for all impacts. The simple answer that the free market yields the optimal city size ignores the externalities that the market does not internalize into consumers' choices, e.g., pollution, accidents, crime, etc. The recommendation is to use the market wisely to implement optimal policies associated with a desired optimal city.

10.7 How to Handle Socioeconomic Exclusion?

In Chapter 9, we recognized that this is a difficult problem to manage because social exclusion is not a result of inappropriate policies, it is the outcome of the land market, which is caused by the underpinning force of individuals' preferences; i.e., it comes with the gravitational social force. This phenomenon occurs in all cities, although it is more evident and politically relevant in less-developed societies in which income inequalities become evident in the form of socially excluded groups. There are other forms of spatial segregation, such as racial and religion segregation, which may or may not imply a form of social exclusion depending on whether the residents have affordable location alternatives to move to.

The objective of improving integration levels is difficult because, to control the market effects, the planner needs to fight against the gravitational social force; this is a permanent fight until the inequality is reduced to a level at which other attributes of the locations are more relevant and the mixture generates a naturally integrated society.

The recommendation to attain this goal is to implement market-oriented policies such as optimal subsidies. Subsidies are preferred over regulations because the former is more flexibly adjusted over the urban space and time and regulations are more rigid policies with impacts that are more difficult to assess. The flexibility of subsidies is important because cities are complex systems, and a limited initial force inducing integration may be enough to reorganize the allocation profile to create sufficiently attractive neighborhoods to allow the market to continue with the integrating force. This bottom-up process has the advantage of producing more integrated cities with diversity, valuable attributes for equity, and creativity.

The advantage of a parsimonious process in which the policy is permanently adjusted to the changing conditions is that it is consistent with the complex nature of urban systems. Its complexity is high enough to be cautious with possible predictions, particularly when policies induce long-lasting infrastructure developments.

10.8 Does Accessibility Generate Development?

This is a classic chicken-and-egg type of dilemma in transportation: does transportation investment generate accessibility that induces economic development or it is the inverse? There are arguments for both causalities and policy makers use them conveniently and convincingly because there are good examples that appear to support either view. The model of the complex city discussed in this book provides a clear answer for this dilemma: it is inappropriate to attempt to identify causes and effects in complex systems, as they are unidentifiable in most cases because there is a circular causality.

Our model provides a clear analytical answer. Development will occur in places that agents are attracted to, and the attraction depends on several attributes: transportation costs, accessibility, business agglomeration economies, and residential location externalities, in addition to natural amenities and connections to other production systems. Hence, it is a multifactor attraction that circularly results in changes.

However, planners may use the theoretical discussion in this book to seek signals regarding where accessibility is restricting additional potential development, leading to effective improvement in the transportation system. This is difficult task even for experts; hence, the system should be analyzed using a well-defined and estimated model of the city, and optimization procedures should be performed to identify the best opportunities for development. This is the approach followed by Ma and Lo (2012), Ng and Lo (2015), and Yin (2015) who built integrated LUT-type models and developed optimizing methods to search for best policies in transportation and LU to maximize utilitarian social welfare; a different approach was followed by Briceño-Arias and Martínez (2018), whose method allows for a variety of social goals.

10.9 Who Captures the Benefits of Transportation Investments?

This is a typical question of policy makers who invest large amounts of public resources on transportation systems. For example, they wonder if investments in public transportation technology such as subways and buses benefit transportation users or landowners.

Considering our model, the theoretical answer is that every infrastructure investment in the city, either private or public, affects the attributes of the location where it is placed and is perceived by consumers who convert it to willingness to pay and, through the auction mechanism, percolate it into rents. Thus, in a frictionless system such as that described in urban economics, the answer is as follows: the final beneficiaries are the land and real estate owners. This is called the *capitalization* of benefits into land values, which explains why urban land is perceived as a lucrative investment asset.

Our stochastic behavioral model provides a slightly different answer because, in this model, the impact of a public investment is expected to be distributed probabilistically across agents in the market, including land users and owners, and across transport users and operators; nevertheless, our model concentrates much of the benefits in land values, where benefits tend to percolate in.

However, there is an upper limit for the capitalization phenomena: the consumers' income. For example, in very poor areas, residents' utilities cannot be converted into differential rents due to their income constraints, and in this case, the capitalization process is reduced or broken for the benefit of the residents who enjoy better access without equivalent rent increases. Hence, income constraints help control the capitalization of public policies into land rents.

10.10 How to Measure Transportation Project Benefits?

This question can be reformulated as follows. Because transport projects induce a new equilibrium in the transport system and a relocation of activities associated with the changes in the city's accessibility profile, how should the benefits be measured? For example, if transportation times are reduced with a project and land values increase, i.e., what we can deduct from the LUT model discussed in Chapter 6. We may extend the question to include the potential impacts on the economic system: prices and production in the goods and services markets and wages in the labor market, i.e., the LUTE model in Chapter 7.

This issue has been discussed in the field of transportation economics, where the focus has been to support the argument that transportation users' benefits measured in the transportation system properly capture the benefits of the transportation project, i.e., by assessing the benefits from the transportation demand and supply equilibrium (Jara-Díaz, 1986). Urbanists, on the other hand, focus on the impact on the expected development generated by the project, usually measured by the change in rents.

The LUT model integrates LU and T systems and provides an answer to our question. We begin by recognizing that a transportation project generates impacts on both systems and it is important to avoid duplication in accounting the same benefits, an issue called *double counting*. This is avoided by focusing on counting the benefits to individual agents rather than on specific systems because consumers or producers are the actual beneficiaries of the project. This approach implies analyzing three systems, i.e., using the LUTE, if there are no spillovers of impacts beyond the city. Consider a frictionless and perfectly competitive LUTE system to conclude that all transport users' benefits percolate into rent values through the consumers' valuation of the project benefits in the form of differential willingness-to-pay values. However, in a more realistic situation, with imperfect competition, we expect imperfect percolation of transportation users' benefits into rent values to conclude that the variation in expected rents before and after the project is a lower bound of total benefits. Transportation users' benefits are also a lower bound measure of the project benefits because it may ignore complex impacts on reallocation of agents. A proper accounting of all expected benefits requires an assessment using a LUTE model, which can measure impacts on the three subsystems.

The theoretical equivalence between transportation users' benefits and rents in the LU market can be applied to measure two lower bounds of benefits. Depending on the modeled system and assuming that the models properly replicate impacts, it is expected that land values capture the long-term benefits of transportation projects better than the users' benefits; this is true when rents are estimated considering agglomeration economies, location externalities, and impacts on the goods and labor markets, which directly impact land rents. Users' benefits measure the direct impact of a transportation project, whereas land rents measure the final impacts after accessibility changes have induced long-term LU developments.

10.11 Final Remarks

The set of questions discussed have a common origin: they emerge when we analyze a complex system but ignore the complexity and assume that plausible conclusions can be obtained by studying a subsystem. This linear thinking approach is very limited or simply wrong, depending on the question studied.

In this book, we consider a comprehensive approach to the complex urban system, which includes three subsystems with their own complexity. This high complexity is due to the large number of agents, each interacting with the others in the social system, organized in many production institutions that also interact among them and with the individual agents in the economic system.

Within such complexity, we find simple universal rules: all agents are rational households or firms and behave to maximize utility or profit, which makes them develop a system that is linked by interactions. This system can be viewed as comprised of particles, each with a specific rule that induces interactions, that all follow maximization rules. Despite the diversity of rules, this system at the aggregate of the city shows an attractor: the scaling law. This law is the outcome of the common rational rule governing all particles, representing the universality of human beings, and justifies the emergence of Urban Science, a field that brings together urban economics, transportation, human geography, sociology, ecology, and regional and global economics.

References

Anas, A., Xu, R., 1999. Congestion, land use, and job dispersion: a general equilibrium model. Journal of Urban Economics 45 (3), 451–473.

Briceño-Arias, L.M., Martínez, F., 2018. Land Use Planning and Optimal Subsidies. Working Paper Available upon Request. https://200.27.27.49/fmartinez/bm_subsidies_2018.pdf.

Jara-Díaz, S.R., 1986. On the relation between users' benefits and the economic effects on transportation activities. Journal of Regional Science 26, 379–391.

Ma, X., Lo, H.K., 2012. Modeling transport management and land use over time. Transportation Research Part B 46 (6), 687–709.

Ng, K.F., Lo, H.K., 2015. Optimal housing supply in a bid-rent equilibrium framework. Transportation Research Part B 74, 62–78.

Yin, J.Q., 2015. Optimization for multiclass residential location models with congestible transportation networks. Transportation Science 49 (3), 452–471.

Index

'*Note*: Page numbers followed by "f" indicate figures and "t" indicate tables.'

$160.00

13

CPI Antony Rowe
Chippenham, UK
2018-10-11 20:07